WESTERN CIVILIZATION
IN A GLOBAL CONTEXT:
THE MODERN AGE

WESTERN CIVILIZATION IN A GLOBAL CONTEXT: THE MODERN AGE

SOURCES AND DOCUMENTS

Kenneth L. Campbell

Bloomsbury Academic
An imprint of Bloomsbury Publishing Plc

B L O O M S B U R Y
LONDON · NEW DELHI · NEW YORK · SYDNEY

Bloomsbury Academic

An imprint of Bloomsbury Publishing Plc

50 Bedford Square	1385 Broadway
London	New York
WC1B 3DP	NY 10018
UK	USA

www.bloomsbury.com

BLOOMSBURY and the Diana logo are trademarks of Bloomsbury Publishing Plc

First published 2015

British Library Cataloguing-in-Publication Data
A catalogue record for this book is available from the British Library.

ISBN: HB: 978-1-4725-2947-3
PB: 978-1-4725-2341-9

Library of Congress Cataloging-in-Publication Data
A catalog record for this book is available from the Library of Congress.

Typeset by Deanta Global Publishing Services, Chennai, India
Printed and bound in India

CONTENTS

Introduction: Western Civilization in Global Context

The twin volumes in this anthology of sources are meant to serve two main purposes. The first is to acquaint the reader with (or to reinforce for him or her) a general outline of the course of Western Civilization within a broader context of world history through sources that are representative of each period. The second is to provide an opportunity for the student or reader to gain experience reading a variety of primary source documents, including works of literature and poetry and analyzing them from a historical perspective. Any topic covered in this text would, of course, require fuller research to gain a fuller understanding of that topic, but one has to start somewhere. My hope is that this text will serve as a useful place to start one's study of history. I also hope, however, that even those who already have some background in history will enjoy the range of sources covered and the approach taken here toward understanding Western Civilization in a global context.

For the most part, chapters appear in chronological order, with some overlap to allow for greater emphasis on particular themes and different aspects of the past. For example, the chapter in Volume I on the Scientific Revolution overlaps chronologically with chapters dealing with other aspects of the sixteenth and seventeenth centuries. I have attempted to select sources that deal with themes and topics traditionally covered by Western Civilization courses that deal with issues that lend themselves to class discussion. Many of the sources lend themselves to discussion because they are subject to varying interpretations. Thus, the encouragement of critical thinking and analysis represents another aim of this two-volume anthology.

TYPES OF SOURCES

By reading a variety of sources, students may perhaps gain a sense of the different approaches historians take in their attempt to understand the past. I have attempted to include in these volumes an interesting and provocative set of readings representing a wide range of primary source materials, including official documents, historical writings, literary works, letters, and other assorted written works and visual sources from each period of history from ancient times to the present.

In addition, individual chapters emphasize different aspects of history, drawing from a range that includes politics, intellectual and scientific thought, religion, society, women's experiences and perspectives, and popular culture. Both volumes include sources written by people of different backgrounds and nationalities, in addition to sources written by women as well as men. Different types of sources appear within the same chapters, as well as varying from chapter to chapter.

Finally, this particular collection of sources aims (a) to provide an understanding of the general course of historical development and the causal and chronological links between periods and sources; and (b) to emphasize such themes as changing values as a reflection of different civilizations; evolving views on religion, morality, and spirituality; attitudes toward political leadership, authority and the state; and the competing trends of freedom and individualism vs. community and conformity. While it was impossible to include every work of importance in the evolution of Western Civilization, this sourcebook does include excerpts from some of the major works of Western Civilization ranging from Homer to Marx and including writings by Herodotus, Virgil, Dante, Machiavelli, Luther, and Rousseau, to name a few. From each work, I have attempted to select passages of compelling interest and historical significance. Each chapter contains a general introduction, as well as introductions to individual sources or, in some instances, a set of sources. The chapter and source introductions do not provide an exhaustive treatment of the subject, but aim to provide the necessary historical context and background to help readers get the most out of the sources. Questions for thought or discussion appear after each source or set of sources, as well as at the end of each chapter.

READING AND UNDERSTANDING
PRIMARY SOURCES

Despite the fact that we live in an increasingly technologically and visually oriented society, reading and interpreting sources will remain a vital and valuable skill for academic and professional success, as well as for anyone committed to lifelong learning. In writing papers, in particular, one needs to know how to extract the most important or relevant information from whatever sources they use. When reading secondary books and articles, sometimes this task can seem relatively easy. When researching a paper on the British general election of 1918 following the First World War, it does not take much effort to find the relevant passages in a biography of David Lloyd George on that particular topic. However, when reading primary sources one needs to ask more questions and consider a range of factors so that one does not misuse them or take a quote out of context.

It helps, of course, to have some background on the author or artist and the particular historical context in which they composed their work. The chapter and source introductions help to serve that purpose to make it easier to read the sources in these texts. One question to always keep in mind is the purpose or intention of the work. Furthermore, does the source have a particular tone that indicates if the author means everything literally or employs metaphor to make her or his point? How does the style of writing relate to the content? Does an author exaggerate for effect or use understatement? How has the intended audience influenced the words selected and the tone of the work? Is the author telling the truth or does he or she have a reason to distort the truth or to deliberately lie? One of the most important things to keep in mind when reading primary sources from the past is that these sources cannot be considered true or factually reliable just because they are from the past. The questions raised here are just some of the questions that you might generally keep in mind as you begin to approach the task of reading the variety of sources included here.

In addition, because these texts include such a wide variety of sources not all questions apply equally to each source. Additional questions may come to mind besides these as you gain more experience with reading primary sources. If you are reading a letter or a personal memorandum, you will naturally ask different questions than you would of a poem or the lyrics to a song. Nevertheless, if you keep one central question in mind it can serve as a useful guide and starting point if you are at a loss: What is the most important point or message contained in this particular piece of writing?

Also, it is important to remember that in many instances there is not one single correct interpretation of a particular source. That does not mean that every interpretation possesses equal validity, however. You should aim to make an informed judgment in your analysis and interpretation. As with the papers that you write, you want to have the ability to defend your position with direct reference to the source, sound critical analysis, direct comparison or contrast with other sources, or some references to the historical background or context for the work. While in some instances the meaning of a text might emerge quickly on one reading, in other instances you might need to re-read a source to tease out its meaning or to form your interpretation of it.

In general, literary sources are more open to interpretation because literary works, especially poems, do not contain clear-cut factual statements. Still, even if they provide more opportunity for you to form your own interpretation, you want to develop the ability to explain why a particular work means what it does to you.

Having said this, I would also emphasize that reading a piece of literature as a historical source differs from reading it for the purposes of literary analysis or criticism. The same applies to the visual images that appear in the text, especially works of art. For example, historians might concern themselves less with literary style, plot, or character analysis, or the use of imagery, and more with the ways in which a novel or a play reflected or influenced its times. How people in the past responded to a painting or a poem becomes more important than what it means for us or our times. Here the most important question might be: what does this work tell us about the time in which the author wrote it? Still, we study the past because we believe it has some relevance to our world and our lives, so these considerations are not always mutually exclusive. By reading excerpts from works of literature, along with other types of primary sources, you should be able to hone your ability to interpret and explain the meaning and relevance of different kinds of writing for an understanding of history. The primary purpose of a poet or novelist is generally not to tell us about the past, at least not in any kind of straightforward way, but in some ways that makes their works all the more valuable to the historian; they do so more reliably because they do so unintentionally.

As historians and students of history, we have the benefit of hindsight when reading primary sources. We can misuse that gift or use it constructively. We misuse that gift if we fail to remember the famous dictum of the British historian F. W. Maitland that "what is now in the past was once in the future." We cannot assume that people in the past should have acted or thought a certain way based on what we know happened later. We can use the gift of hindsight, however, because we can better understand the meaning, effects, and consequences that followed from certain decisions, actions, or ideas. We can contextualize them better because we can see them in relation to other contemporary sources or forces of which they might not have been aware. Most importantly, we can see the way in which they relate to us and the world in which we live.

COMPARATIVE HISTORY

This sourcebook is based on the philosophy that it is increasingly important to include non-Western perspectives while still emphasizing the value of teaching Western Civilization. It emphasizes a comparative approach that seems well suited for the increasingly global society of the twenty-first century. Chapters generally contain at least one excerpt from a non-Western source that lends itself either to comparison or contrast with a selected source from Western Civilization or that will allow for a comparison of historical developments in general between different societies within a particular period. The study of non-Western sources not only provides an opportunity to consider different perspectives and broaden one's cultural awareness, but also has the potential to contribute to a better understanding of Western history and civilization by providing a basis for comparison. We all benefit from exposure to sources from other civilizations and understand both history and our own complex world better as a result.

Introduction to Volume II

This volume begins with the European Enlightenment of the eighteenth century and includes sources from as late as the early twenty-first century. The period began with a new sense of optimism reflected in Alexander Pope's poem, "An Essay on Man," the first source that appears in the collection that follows. Not everyone in the eighteenth century shared Pope's benign view of the world and the place of humanity within it, but the belief in progress and the possibility of an end to the evils that still plagued society emerged as dominant themes during that period. Hopes for change yielded to demands for it, which culminated in the American and French Revolutions. Key documents such as the American Declaration of Independence and the French Declaration of the Rights of Man and Citizen, both of which appear in Chapter 2, are not dry and dusty artifacts but rather compositions that express the vibrancy of the ideals that animated people to change the course of history.

Historical change takes many forms in the modern period, however, not all of it is seen as positive. Even the American and French Revolutions had their dark sides; the new United States of America preserved the institution of slavery even as it proclaimed a commitment to liberty and equality, while the French endured a Reign of Terror before their revolution yielded to the dictatorship of Napoleon. The sources in Chapter 3 reflect the ambivalence felt by many writers toward the Industrial Revolution and the dramatic social alterations that accompanied it. In her novel, *North and South*, for example, Elizabeth Gaskell juxtaposed the polite and humane values of rural England with the cold and calculating economic philosophy that dominated the growing manufacturing centers; an excerpt from this work of fiction merits inclusion alongside the poetry of Blake and Wordsworth and the socialist writings of Marx and Engels.

The Industrial Revolution provided Britain with the wealth to emerge as the world's greatest power in the nineteenth century. The British Empire became just one manifestation of increasing cross-cultural interaction at that time.

India, as the center of that empire, became a prime example of the impact of Western imperialism; both British and Indian sources help to illustrate the nature of that particular cross-cultural exchange. In particular, the writings of Rammohun Roy and Dadabhai Naoroji illustrate changing views of British rule within India during the course of the nineteenth century. Readers will encounter a diverse selection of Western perspectives on imperialism as well, from writers that include David Livingstone, Rudyard Kipling, Theodore Roosevelt, and Joseph Conrad. Two chapters on imperialism and cross-cultural exchange frame chapters on European nationalism and nineteenth-century reform movements, which include, for example, sources on the abolition of slavery in the United States and Brazil and the emancipation of the serfs in Russia. None of the important historical developments of the nineteenth century occurred in isolation from the rest. For example, Karl Marx wrote about British imperialism in India as well as the effects of the Industrial Revolution; thus his words can be found in both Chapters 3 and 7.

The twentieth century occupies approximately half of this volume, beginning with a chapter on the First World War. The sources in that chapter range from documents relating to the outbreak of the war to literary responses written by Erich Maria Remarque and Robert Graves a decade after the war's end. As important as the First World War is for an understanding of modern history, the twentieth century was such a complex age that a wide range of sources seemed necessary to convey the nature of it. Therefore, do not be surprised to find the words of the British writer Virginia Woolf in a chapter that includes excerpts from a novel about the Mexican revolution and the reflections of an American ambassador to Turkey. Each in their own way says something about the period under consideration and the changes affecting twentieth-century life, society, and politics.

No change affected twentieth-century history more than the rise of the Soviet Union out of the ashes of world war, revolution, and civil war. Each source dealing with Russian and Soviet history appears within its chronological framework, but the reader could also follow this theme across chapters, moving from an American's eyewitness account of the Russian Revolution in 1917 to Joseph Stalin's ruminations on the future of the Communist Party in the 1920s to a description of the role of women in postwar Soviet society in a novel by Alexander Solzhenitsyn written in the 1960s, in addition to other sources dealing with the Cold War between the Soviet Union and the United States. If more sources related to these two superpowers start to appear in the later chapters, this merely reflects their importance to the history of the second half of the twentieth century. Of course, works from other perspectives, both within and outside of Europe, continue to figure prominently, sometimes in relation to the actions of the superpowers. For example, the poetry of a Korean writer reacting to the atomic bombs dropped on Japan by the United States appear immediately following an excerpt from the memoirs of the US president, Harry Truman, dealing with the future of atomic energy. The passages from Solzhenitsyn's novel *Cancer Ward* are paired with reflections on gender by the French philosopher Simone de Beauvoir.

Likewise, the sources below reflect a diversity of perspectives even on subjects such as decolonization and the decline of imperialism. The sources in the chapter on the 1960s reflect responses to a rapidly changing era from individuals ranging from the famous French war hero and politician Charles de Gaulle to the Canadian singer-songwriter Joni Mitchell, from the leader of the Communist People's Republic of China, Mao Zedong, to the American Civil Rights leader Martin Luther King. Sources from Christian, Jewish, and Muslim writers appear in the chapter on modern religious fundamentalism, including a passage from Harold Bloom, who, although he was raised as a Jew, writes as a literary and religious critic.

In the 1970s and 1980s, political lines became redrawn as it seemed that future conflict would center on the struggle between democracy and dictatorship. The Cold War had frequently made democracies allies of dictatorships in the alignment against the spread of communism, and communists allies of democracy in places where they sought to overthrow dictatorships. Sources from this period include the memoirs of individuals involved in this struggle in El Salvador, Nicaragua, and China. However, the fall of communism in Eastern Europe and then the Soviet Union created visions in the West of a "new world order." While one political scientist, Francis Fukuyama, believed that these developments presaged the triumph of democracy worldwide and thus, in a sense, "the end of history," his counterpart Samuel Huntington foretold "a clash of civilizations" that would usher in the next historical period. Excerpts from both writers appear in Chapter 16. The final chapter, like much of this entire volume, reflects a continuing struggle to create a better and more peaceful world, as reflected in the title of the book by the Israeli politician Benjamin Netanyahu excerpted there, *A Durable Peace*. The reader will find much to ponder and learn from the sources in this volume, but one of the most important subjects that they might help to illuminate is why such a peace has proved so elusive over the past three centuries and does not yet appear to be forthcoming. Equally important, however, is the human spirit that keeps trying in the face of great obstacles; this, I believe, is reflected in some of the sources here as well.

CHAPTER ONE

The Enlightenment

INTRODUCTION

Historians sometimes use the designation of the eighteenth century in Europe as the period of "the Enlightenment" interchangeably with "the Age of Reason." Both terms can be misleading and the selection of any half-dozen or so sources would not suffice to do justice to an era that was as complex as this one was. Nevertheless, the sources in this chapter each reflect the themes of changing political, moral, and religious values that will receive special emphasis throughout this volume. The Enlightenment, like most intellectual and cultural movements, does not have an abrupt starting point, but in many ways it makes sense to begin this volume in the early eighteenth century when a new set of political, intellectual, and religious circumstances were already in place. King Louis XIV of France (r. 1643–1715) died in 1715, giving way to a regency that did not exercise the same stultifying influence over French society and culture. Isaac Newton (1642–1727) represented for many the culmination of the Scientific Revolution (see Volume I, Chapter 16) that inspired confidence among Europe's educated classes in humanity's ability to understand the world and the universe and the belief that the cosmos that they inhabited adhered to a rational plan or design. In addition, by the early eighteenth century, religious toleration was increasingly common in Europe, where widespread persecution and wars fought for religious purposes were largely outdated.

Religion, of course, continued to play an important role in the everyday lives of many people, while religious concerns were far from absent in Enlightenment thought. Religious thinkers known as Deists believed that the Newtonian system required a Creator and was compatible with a belief in God, but they rejected the supernatural aspects of Christianity and other "revealed" religions. They hoped that liberation from such superstitions would usher in a more enlightened age based on reason, common sense, and religious toleration. However, reason shows up in different thinkers during this period in some very different ways.

The poet Alexander Pope (1688–1744) used classical models of rhymed couplets to impose order on philosophy in an attempt to reveal profound truths that reflected a larger order to the universe and the place of humanity within that order. The French writer, Voltaire (1694–1788), embodied the type of Enlightenment thinker designated by the term *philosophe*. Philosophes engaged philosophically with the real world and used social criticism as a means toward improving society. In his short novel, *Candide*, Voltaire directly challenges the optimistic perspective of Pope and that of the earlier German philosopher, Gottfried Wilhelm Leibniz (1646–1716), without, however, totally abandoning his hope that the world can be made a better place. Another French thinker, Charles, the baron de Montesquieu (1689–1755), attempted to show Europeans the folly of some of their most cherished ideas and customs through the eyes of foreign visitors in his novel, *The Persian Letters*, prior to developing his political thought in the *Spirit of the Laws*, which influenced both the American and French revolutions. Both Voltaire and Montesquieu used satire as a way to expose what were, to them, irrational beliefs and practices. Even the American Calvinist theologian, Jonathan Edwards (1703–58), despite his own participation in the emotionally charged religious revival known in New England as the Great Awakening, thought reason an essential tool of theology and looked skeptically at those Christians who entirely gave themselves over to highly charged states of religious ecstasy.

The philosopher Immanuel Kant (1724–1804) serves well as a particularly prominent representative of the German Enlightenment, known in German as the *Aufklärung*. Tim Blanning, in his survey of eighteenth-century European history, identifies a "culture of feeling" that coexisted with a "culture of reason" throughout the period, challenging the view that Romanticism succeeded the Enlightenment as a later reaction to the latter's excessive reliance upon rationality.* The German Enlightenment better exemplifies Blanning's "culture of feeling" than its English or French counterparts, but exceptions to such a generalization exist among members of each nationality. In the case of Germany, Kant and his contemporary Gotthold Lessing (1729–81) placed a greater emphasis on reason, while Johann Wolfgang von Goethe (1749–1832) and Friedrich Schiller (1759–1805) are more associated with the *Sturm and Drang* ("Storm and Stress") movement within German literature that influenced the Romantic Movement. Kant's definition in the essay quoted below of "Enlightenment" as "man's release from his self-incurred tutelage" in many ways spoke for the movement as a whole. Yet, despite, or perhaps because of, Kant's hostile attitude toward established authority, he placed limits upon human reason and retained his belief in God as a necessary being in a moral universe.

The political radical Thomas Paine, best known in America for his political pamphlet *Common Sense* that provided a clear rationale for the independence of Britain's North American colonies, formulated his own views on religion in a book appropriately titled *The Age of Reason*. Paine's "Profession of Faith," which appears in this chapter, illustrates the way in which an enlightened Deist could preserve a belief in God while rejecting the power of churches to dictate their beliefs to others. Some scholars, such as Margaret Jacob and Jonathan Israel, who have written on the eighteenth-century phenomenon now known as the "Radical Enlightenment," would point out that there

---

*Tim Blanning (2007), *The Pursuit of Glory: The Five Revolutions that Made Modern Europe: 1648–1815*, New York: Penguin Books.

were others willing to go further and to embrace atheism, but such thinkers generally lacked the influence that "moderate thinkers" from Voltaire to Paine had at the time.

No eighteenth-century thinker was more influential that Jean-Jacques Rousseau (1712–78), who hailed originally from Geneva, Switzerland, but spent most of his life and career in France. Rousseau's ideas on philosophy, history, literature, politics, psychology, and education all had a profound influence on each of those fields. His educational treatise in the form of a novel, *Emile* (1762), is perhaps the work that most combined his interest in all of the subjects mentioned above. Despite some rather extreme or far-fetched notions on child-rearing, it is still in many ways his most practical work for guiding individual thought and action in the world.

If Europeans were becoming more enlightened during the eighteenth century, it was at least partly because they were becoming more aware of other cultures and alternative perspectives. The two sources that appear in this chapter written by non-Europeans include a treatise on the proper education for women, written by a Japanese man (or possibly a woman) and an excerpt from a biographical account by a former African-American slave, Olaudah Equiano. Equiano went on to become a highly respected writer and advocate for the abolition of the slave trade in eighteenth-century Britain.

ALEXANDER POPE, INTRODUCTION

Raised as a Catholic, Alexander Pope developed early in his life a passion for the study of ancient as well as modern languages and the classics. He was a prolific poet, who translated the Iliad *and the* Odyssey *of Homer into English in addition to his own creative works. He is perhaps most known for his epic poem* The Rape of the Lock *(1712–14), but arguably his most important poem was his* Essay on Man *(1733), which in both content and style is practically unrivaled by any other poem written in rhymed couplets. Pope's verses represent the culmination of the growing confidence of the English educated classes coming out of the turbulent seventeenth century with the political and social order slightly altered but largely intact. Pope also displays a total trust in God's wisdom, which contrasts sharply with the anxiety and fretfulness displayed by many seventeenth-century Puritans over the state of affairs in church and state. Pope's birth in 1688, the year of the so-called "Glorious Revolution," is thus highly symbolic, even though members of the political elite would have still considered Pope as an outsider because of his Catholicism. Pope's optimism is all the more striking because on a personal level he suffered almost continually from physical maladies, including a curved spine that restricted his height to less than 5 feet. Significantly, the serenity of mind necessary for composing the lines that follow also contrasts sharply with the number of literary enemies that Pope made in his lifetime and the bitter attacks that he was capable of leveling at his critics and fellow authors.*

Note here the extent to which Pope uses reason as he surveys the place occupied by human beings in the world and the cosmos.

Alexander Pope, "An Essay on Man"*

Awake, my St. John! leave all meaner things
To low ambition, and the pride of Kings.
Let us (since Life can little more supply
Than just to look about us and to die)
Expatiate free o'er all this scene of Man;
A mighty maze! but not without a plan;
A Wild, where weeds and flow'rs promiscuous shoot,
Or Garden, tempting with forbidden fruit.
Together let us beat this ample field,
Try what the open, what the covert yield;
The latent tracts, the giddy heights explore
Of all who blindly creep, or sightless soar;
Eye Nature's walks, shoot Folly as it flies,
And catch the Manners living as they rise;
Laugh where we must, be candid where we can;
But vindicate the ways of God to Man. (ll. 1–17)

Presumptuous Man! the reason would'st thou find,
Why form'd so weak, so little, and so blind!
First, if thou canst, the harder reason guess,
Why form'd no weaker, blinder, and no less!
Ask of the mother earth, why oaks are made
Taller or stronger than the weeds they shade? (ll. 35–40)

Of systems possible, if 'tis confest
That wisdom infinite must form the best,
Where all must full or not coherent be,
And all that rises, rise in due degree;
Then, in the scale of reas'ning life, 'tis plain
There must be, somewhere, such a rank as Man;

---

*Aubrey Williams, ed. (1969), *Poetry and Prose of Alexander Pope*, Boston: Hougton Mifflin Company, pp. 122–23, 125–30.

And all the question (wrangle e'er so long)
Is only this, if God has plac'd him wrong? (ll. 43–50)

    In Pride, in reas'ning Pride, our error lies;
All quit their sphere, and rush into the skies.
Pride still is aiming at the blest abodes,
Men would be Angels, Angels would be Gods.
Aspiring to be Gods, if Angels fell,
Aspiring to be Angels, Men rebel;
And who but wishes to invert the laws
Of ORDER, sins against th' Eternal Cause. (ll. 123–30)

    But errs not Nature from this gracious end,
From burning sun when livid deaths descend,
When earthquakes swallow, or when tempests sweep
Towns to one grave, whole nations to the deep?
"No ('tis reply'd) the first Almighty Cause
"Acts not by partial, but by gen'ral laws; . . .
If plagues or earthquakes break not Heav'n's design
Why then a Borgia, or a Catiline? . . .
From pride, from pride, our very reas'ning springs;
Account for moral as for nat'ral things:
Why charge we Heav'n in those, in these acquit?
    Better for Us, perhaps, it might appear,
Were there all harmony, all virtue here;
That never air or ocean felt the wind;
That never passion discompos'd the mind:
But ALL subsists by elemental strife;
And Passions are the elements of Life.
And gen'ral Order since the whole began,
Is kept in Nature, and is kept in Man. (ll. 141–46, 155–56, 162–74)

The bliss of Man (could Pride that blessing find)
Is not to act or think beyond mankind;
No pow'rs of body or of soul to share,
But what his nature and his state can bear.
Why has not Man a microscopic eye?
For this plain reason, Man is not a Fly. . . . (ll. 189–94)

Vast chain of being, which from God began,
Natures aethereal, human, angel, man,
Beast, bird, fish, insect! what no eye can see,
No glass can reach! from Infinite to thee,

From thee to Nothing!—On superior pow'rs
Were we to press, inferior might on ours:
Or in the full creation leave a void.
When one step broken, the great scale's destroy'd:
From Nature's chain whatever link you strike,
Ten or ten thousandth, breaks the chain alike. (ll. 237–47)

All Nature is but Art, unknown to thee;
All Chance, Direction, which thou canst not see;
All Discord, Harmony, not understood;
All partial Evil, universal Good:
And, spite of Pride, in erring Reason's spite,
One truth is clear, "Whatever IS, is RIGHT." (ll. 289–94)

Questions

1. Pope's poem is known as a "theodicy" or a justification of God. How successful is he at achieving his attempt "to justify the ways of God to man"?
2. Is Pope here merely preserving traditional ideas about the "Great Chain of Being" or is he developing new ideas suited for an age that is moving away from traditional justifications for religion?
3. When Pope concludes, "whatever is, is right," is he justifying evil? Is it possible to argue that evil and suffering are necessary, even in a perfect world?

VOLTAIRE, INTRODUCTION

Voltaire developed an extremely hostile attitude toward the Catholic Church and did not share Alexander Pope's acceptance of the imperfections of humanity or the natural order. However, Voltaire faced a difficult conundrum. While he rejected Catholicism and even any form of revealed religion, he found it impossible to embrace atheism, which he defined in his Philosophical Dictionary *as "a monstrous evil . . . that, even if it is not as baleful as fanaticism . . . is nearly always fatal to virtue."* He thus had to work out for himself a philosophy that did not rely on God as a reliable guide in human affairs but that did not deny his existence either. One such attempt came in his brief novel,* Candide. *In* Candide, *the title character undergoes a lengthy chain of trials and torments, witnessing many of the worst*

---

*Quoted in Karen Armstrong (1993), *A History of God: The 4,000-Year Quest of Judaism, Christianity and Islam*, New York: Ballantine Books, p. 311.

examples of human cruelty and caprice that were characteristic of the period. Along the way, the philosopher, Dr. Pangloss, a figure modeled on the German thinker Leibniz, accompanies him. Voltaire parodies Leibniz's philosophy through Pangloss's constant assertion that, no matter what happens, "all is for the best in this best of all possible worlds." Eschewing the comforts of either philosophy or religion, Candide and his small company end the novel in reflection about the meaning of their experiences and of life in general. The famous conclusion of the novel appears below. The practical solution that Voltaire offers here represents another important strain in Enlightenment thought and a direct response to Pope's satisfaction with the world as it is.

Voltaire, *Candide**

. . . It would be natural to suppose that when, after so many disasters, Candide was married to his mistress, and living with the philosopher Pangloss, the philosopher Martin, the prudent Cacambo and the old woman, having brought back so many diamonds from the country of the ancient Incas, he would lead the most pleasant life imaginable. But he was so cheated by the Jews that he had nothing left but his little farm; his wife, growing uglier every day, became shrewish and unendurable; the old woman was ailing and even more bad-tempered than Cunegonde [Candide's wife] . . . when they were not arguing, the boredom was so excessive that one day the old woman dared to say to them: "I should like to know which is worse, to be raped a hundred times by Negro pirates, to have a buttock cut off, to run the gauntlet among the Bulgarians, to be whipped and flogged in an *auto-da-fé*, to be dissected, to row in a galley, to endure all the miseries through which we have passed, or to remain here doing nothing?" "'Tis a great question," said Candide. These remarks led to new reflections, and Martin especially concluded that man was born to live in the convulsions of distress or the lethargy of boredom. Candide did not agree, but he asserted nothing. Pangloss confessed that he had always suffered horribly; but, having once maintained that everything was for the best, he had continued to maintain it without believing it. . . . In the neighborhood there lived a very famous Dervish, who was supposed to be the best philosopher in Turkey; they went to consult him; Pangloss was the spokesman and said: "Master, we have come to beg you to tell us why so strange an animal as man was ever created." "What has it to do with you?" said the Dervish. "Is it your business?" "But, reverend father," said Candide, "there is a horrible amount of evil in the world." "What does it matter," said the Dervish, "whether there is evil or good? When his highness sends a ship to Egypt, does he worry about the comfort or

---

*Voltaire, *Candide*, translated by Richard Aldington, in *The Portable Voltaire* (1949), edited by Ben Ray Redman, New York: Viking, pp. 324–28.

discomfort of the rats in the ship?" "Then what should we do?" said Pangloss. "Hold your tongue," said the Dervish. "I flattered myself," said Pangloss, "that I should discuss with you effects and causes, this best of all possible worlds, the origin of evil, the nature of the soul and pre-established harmony." At these words the Dervish slammed the door in their faces. During this conversation the news went round that at Constantinople two viziers and the mufti had been strangled and several of their friends impaled. . . . As Pangloss, Candide, and Martin were returning to their little farm, they came upon an old man who was taking the air under a bower of orange-trees at his door. Pangloss, who was as curious as he was argumentative, asked him what was the name of the mufti who had just been strangled. "I do not know," replied the old man. "I have never known the name of any mufti or of any vizier. I am entirely ignorant of the occurrence you mention; I presume that in general those who meddle in public affairs sometimes perish miserably and that they deserve it; but I never inquire what is going on in Constantinople; I content myself with sending there for sale the produce of the garden I cultivate." . . . "You must have a vast and magnificent estate?" said Candide to the Turk. "I have only twenty acres," replied the Turk. "I cultivate them with my children; and work keeps at bay three great evils: boredom, vice and need." As Candide returned to his farm he reflected deeply on the Turk's remarks. . . . "Let us work without theorizing," said Martin; "'tis the only way to make life endurable." The whole small fraternity entered into this praiseworthy plan, and each started to make use of his talents. The little farm yielded well. Cunegonde was indeed very ugly, but she became an excellent pastrycook; Pacquette embroidered; the old woman took care of the linen. Even Friar Giroflée performed some service; he was a very good carpenter and even became a man of honor; and Pangloss sometimes said to Candide: "All events are linked up in this best of all possible worlds; for, if you had not been expelled from the noble castle by hard kicks in your backside for love of Mademoiselle Cunegonde, if you had not been clapped into the Inquisition, if you had not wandered about America on foot, if you had not stuck your sword in the Baron, if you had not lost all your sheep from the land of Eldorado, you would not be eating candied citrons and pistachios here." "'Tis well said," replied Candide, "but we must cultivate our garden."

Questions

1. In what ways does Voltaire's conclusion to *Candide* challenge the prevailing optimism of Pope and the Enlightenment as a whole? In what ways does it preserve it?

2. In what other ways does this passage represent the thought of the Enlightenment? What would you conclude about the philosophy of Voltaire based solely on it?

3. What is symbolic about the image of the garden in Voltaire's story? What might the garden represent for the Enlightenment and Western Civilization generally?

MONTESQUIEU, INTRODUCTION

Montesquieu published his 1721 novel, The Persian Letters, *anonymously, presumably in part to maintain the illusion that these were actual letters written by real people. In addition, he hoped to avoid the wrath of the censors for the criticisms of the French political and social system and the Catholic Church contained therein. The Catholic Church, in particular, would have been sensitive to such criticisms given that it had already lost so much ground in Europe to the Protestant Reformation. Furthermore, the Church in France had to deal with a major reform movement among French Catholics called Jansenism, whose ideas bore a striking resemblance to Protestant theology. The adherents of Jansenism sought a more authentic and emotional faith than that provided by the institutionalized church. Montesquieu also had more to lose by revealing his identity since he belonged to the class of the nobility, the members of which might have regarded him as a traitor based on his critique of the status quo from which they had benefited immensely.* The Persian Letters *was an immense success, the equivalent of an eighteenth-century bestseller. Ten editions of the book appeared within a year of its initial publication. The exotic locale seems to have appealed to the reading public—the novel was partly set in a Persian harem—as did the strange customs and values of the Persian visitors to France. However, one of the main points of the novel is that European customs and values would have seemed just as strange to external observers, as suggested by the following passages. Unlike his contemporaries, scholars no longer regard Montesquieu's depiction of the Persians as entirely accurate, but it did show them in a generally favorable, if stereotypical, light.*

Montesquieu, *The Persian Letters**

Letter 24: Rica to Ibben, at Smyrna

The King of France is the most powerful ruler in Europe. He has no goldmines like the King of Spain, his neighbor, but his riches are greater, because he

---

*Montesquieu (1975), *The Persian Letters*, translated by C. J. Betts, Harmondsworth: Penguin Books, pp. 72–73, 151–52.

extracts them from his subjects' vanity, which is more inexhaustible than mines. He has been known to undertake or sustain major wars with no other funds but what he gets from selling honorific titles, and by a miracle of human vanity, his troops are paid, his fortresses supplied, and his fleets equipped.

Moreover, this king is a great magician. He exerts authority even over the minds of his subjects; he makes them think what he wants. If there are only a million crowns in the exchequer, and he needs two million, all he has to do is persuade them that one crown is worth two, and they believe it. If he is involved in a difficult war without any money, all he has to do is to get it into their heads that a piece of paper will do for money, and they are immediately convinced of it. He even succeeds in making them believe that he can cure them of all sorts of diseases by touching them, such is the force and power that he has over their minds.

You must not be amazed at what I tell you about this prince: there is another magician, stronger than he, who controls his mind as completely as he controls other people's. This magician is called the Pope. He will make the king believe that three are only one, or else that the bread one eats is not bread, or that the wine one drinks not wine, and a thousand other things of the same kind. . . .

Letter 75 Usbek to Rhedi, at Venice

I must admit to you that I have not observed among Christians the same lively faith in their religion that is to be found among Muslims. It is a long way with them from professing their religion to belief in it, from belief to being convinced, and from being convinced to practicing it. Religion does not so much provide an opportunity for regeneration as for controversy, in which everyone takes part. Courtiers, soldiers, women even, rise up in opposition to the clergy and ask for things to be proved, when they have resolved not to believe them. It is not that they have made up their minds rationally, and have taken the trouble to examine the truth or falsity of the religion that they are rejecting; they are rebels who, having felt the weight of their yoke, have shaken themselves free before becoming acquainted with it. Consequently, they are no more steadfast in their incredulity than in their faith, but live in an ebb and flow of belief which carries them ceaselessly from one to the other. One of them said to me one day: "I believe in the immortality of the soul periodically. My opinions depend entirely on my physical condition. According to whether I have greater vitality, or my digestion is functioning well or badly, or the atmosphere I breathe is thick or thin, or the food I eat is light or heavy, I am a Spinozist, a Socinian or a Catholic, unbelieving or devout. When the doctor is at my bedside, my confessor has the advantage. I know how to prevent religion from disturbing me when I am well, but I allow it to console me when I am ill: when I have no hope left in that respect, along comes religion and wins me over by its promises; I am quite willing to surrender myself to it so as to die with hope on my side."

A long time ago the Christian kings freed all the serfs in their states because, they said, Christianity makes all men equal. It is true that this act of religion was extremely useful to them: it was a means of diminishing the power of the nobles, by removing the lower classes from their control. Subsequently they made conquests in countries where they realized that it was advantageous to have slaves. They gave permission for them to be bought and sold, forgetting the religious principle which had affected them so deeply. Shall I tell you what I think?—what is true at one time is false at another. Why do we not do the same as Christians? It is very naïve of us to refuse to found colonies and make conquests in a favorable climate, when we could easily do so, because the water is not pure enough there for us to wash according to the precepts of the holy Koran.

I give thanks to Almighty God, whose envoy is the great prophet Ali, that I belong to a religion which has priority over all human interests and is as pure as Heaven, whence it descended.

Questions
1. What specific criticisms of French society does Montesquieu offer or imply here?
2. How might his European readers have reacted or responded to these observations on the part of Montesquieu's Persian characters? How might the king or his advisors have responded? The church?
3. Does Montesquieu make his criticisms more effectively because he voices them through non-European literary characters instead of addressing these issues head-on in a direct attack? What does Montesquieu contribute to Enlightenment thought in this work?

JONATHAN EDWARDS, INTRODUCTION

The New England clergyman Jonathan Edwards's best known sermon, "Sinners in the Hands of an Angry God," has come to symbolize the "fire and brimstone" approach prominent in certain strains of Protestant Christianity that attempt to scare or intimidate people into repentance of their sins and acceptance of Christ. Today such an approach is often reduced in fundamentalist churches to the thoughtless sound-bite "turn or burn." However, Edwards's thought and approach to religion was much more complex and nuanced than most stereotypical accounts of them. In the sermon excerpted below, Edwards stresses the love and mercy of God as he tried to remove any impediments for those who might think that they are too old to change. Edwards, a Calvinist, underwent his own conversion experience in 1727, at the relatively tender age of twenty-four. Nevertheless, here he stresses that God values equally any conversion in and of itself independent of one's age or how many years of service one can offer to the church. Pay particular attention to the way in which he develops his argument here and the implications of it for his overall theology.

Jonathan Edwards, "Pardon for the Greatest Sinners"*

The proper *use* of this subject is, to encourage sinners whose consciences are burdened with a sense of guilt, immediately to go to God through Christ for mercy. If you go in the manner we have described, the arms of mercy are open to embrace you. You need not be at all the more fearful of coming because of your sins, let them be ever so black. If you had as much guilt lying on each of your souls as all the wicked men in the world, and all the damned souls in hell; yet if you come to God for mercy, sensible of your own vileness, and seeking pardon only through the free mercy of God in Christ, you would not need to be afraid; the greatness of your sins would be no impediment to your pardon. Therefore, if your souls be burdened, and you are distressed for fear of hell, you need not bear that burden and distress any longer. If you are but *willing, you* may freely come and unload yourselves, and cast all your burdens on Christ, and rest in him.

But here I shall speak to some OBJECTIONS which some awakened sinners may be ready to make against what I now exhort them to.

1. Some may be ready to object, I have spent my youth and all the best of my life in sin, and I am afraid God will not accept of me, when I offer him only mine old age.—To this I would answer, 1. Hath God said any where, that he will not accept of *old sinners* who come to him? God hath often made offers and promises in universal terms; and is there any such exception put in? Doth Christ say, All that thirst, let them come to me and drink, *except* old sinners? Come to me, all ye that labour and are heavy laden, except old sinners, and I will give you rest? Him that cometh to me, I will in no wise cast out, if he be not an old sinner? Did you ever read any such exception any where in the Bible? and why should you give way to exceptions which you make out of your own heads, or rather which the devil puts into your heads, and which have no foundation in the word of God?—Indeed it is more rare that old sinners are willing to come, than others; but if they do come, they are as readily accepted as any whatever.

---

*http://www.ccel.org/ccel/edwards/sermons.pardon.html

2. When God accepts of young persons, it is not for the sake of the service which they are like to do him afterwards, or because youth is better worth accepting than old age. You seem entirely to mistake the matter, in thinking that God will not accept of you because you are old; as though he readily accepted of persons in their youth, because their youth is better worth his acceptance; whereas it is only for the sake of Jesus Christ, that God is willing to accept of any.

You say, your life is almost spent, and you are afraid that the best time for serving God is past; and that therefore God will not now accept of you; as if it were for the sake of the service which persons are like to do him, after they are converted, that he accepts of them. But a self-righteous spirit is at the bottom of such objections. Men cannot get off from the notion, that it is for some goodness or service of their own, either done or expected to be done, that God accepts of persons, and receives them into favor.—Indeed they who deny God their youth, the best part of their lives, and spend it in the service of Satan, dreadfully sin and provoke God; and he very often leaves them to hardness of heart when they are grown old. But if they are willing to accept of Christ when old, he is as ready to receive them as any others; for in that matter God hath respect only to Christ and his worthiness.

Questions
1. What is the tone of this sermon by Edwards? Is he preaching to the converted or are his arguments likely to persuade those Christians who might be lukewarm about their faith?
2. What role does reason play in Edwards's arguments?
3. Even though the Enlightenment is usually associated with criticisms of the Christian religion and the rise of Deism, could you consider this an Enlightenment work? What is the relationship of this work to the Enlightenment?
4. What are the implications of the ideas expressed here for Edwards's theology of salvation? Is he contradicting the Calvinist emphasis on predestination in which human beings are incapable of contributing to their own salvation?

IMMANUEL KANT AND THOMAS PAINE, INTRODUCTION

For someone who would encourage people to use their own understanding, Immanuel Kant certainly took his time putting his own ideas into print. He published his first book, The Critique of Pure Reason, *at the age of fifty-seven, after which he quickly made up for lost time, completing his important trilogy, with* The Critique of Practical Reason *and* The Critique of Judgment, *in addition to composing numerous other writings on history, morality, philosophy, and aesthetics. While his more philosophical writings can be almost impregnably dense for the average reader, his 1784 essay "What is Enlightenment?" is exceedingly clear. Kant has little use for established authority in any field, which is one of the reasons that he set out on his own quest to deal with the pressing philosophical and moral issues of his day in his future work. Writing toward the end of the period designated as the Enlightenment, Kant became its most successful advocate, whose defense of the movement's primary principles would long outlast the period, as would the middle ground that he staked out between excessive rationalism on the one hand and excessive empiricism on the other in the philosophical debates of the eighteenth century.*

In The Age of Reason, *Thomas Paine applied some of the same principles that underlay his political thought to the subject of religion. In* The Rights of Man, *Paine vehemently objected to any institution formulating rules and policies for a people until "the end of time." This objection even applied to constitutionally elected bodies such as parliaments or to the enlightened framers of eighteenth-century constitutions. He reserved the right of future generations to think for themselves. In Paine's "Profession of Faith" that appears below, he asserts his own determination to think for himself in matters of religion as well. But he does not presume to tell others how to think; he speaks only for himself. Like Kant, but in a different way, he is encouraging people to use their own understanding instead of bowing to political or religious authority.*

Immanuel Kant, "What is Enlightenment?"*

Enlightenment is man's release from his self-incurred tutelage. Tutelage is man's inability to make use of his understanding without direction from another. Self-incurred is this tutelage when its cause lies not in lack of reason but in lack of resolution and courage to use it without direction from another. *Sapere aude!* "Have courage to use your own reason!"—that is the motto of the enlightenment.

Laziness and cowardice are the reasons why so great a portion of mankind, after nature has long since discharged them from external direction . . ., nevertheless remains under lifelong tutelage, and why it is so easy for others to set themselves up as their guardians. It is so easy not to be of age. I have a book which understands for me, a pastor who has a conscience for me, a physician

---

*Immanuel Kant, "What is Enlightenment?" in Immanuel Kant (1963), *On History*, edited by Lewis White Beck, translated by Lewis White Beck, Robert E. Anchor, and Emil L. Fackenheim, Indianapolis: The Bobbs-Merrill Company, pp. 3–5, 9.

who decides my diet, and so forth, I need not trouble myself. I need not think, if I can only pay—others will readily undertake the irksome work for me.

For this enlightenment, however, nothing is required but freedom, and indeed the most harmless among all the things to which this term can properly be applied. It is the freedom to make public use of one's reason at every point. But I hear on all sides, "Do not argue!" The officer says: "Do not argue but drill!" The tax collector: "Do not argue but pay!" The cleric: "Do not argue but believe!" Only one prince in the world says, "Argue as much as you will, and about what you will, but obey!" Everywhere there is a restriction upon freedom.

Which restriction is an obstacle to enlightenment, and which is not an obstacle but a promoter of it? I answer: The public use of one's reason must always be free, and it alone can bring about enlightenment among men. The private use of reason, on the other hand, may often be narrowly restricted without particularly hindering the progress of enlightenment. By the public use of one's reason I understand the use which a person makes of it as a scholar before the reading public. Private use I call that which one may make of it in a particular civil post or office which is entrusted to him. Many affairs which are conducted in the interest of the community require a certain mechanism through which some members of the community must passively conduct themselves with an artificial unanimity, so that the government may direct them to public ends, or at least prevent them from destroying those ends. Here argument is certainly not allowed—one must obey. But so far as a part of the mechanism regards himself at the same time as a member of the whole community or of a society of world citizens, and thus in the role of a scholar who addresses the public (in the proper sense of the word) through his writings, he certainly can argue without hurting the affairs for which he is in part responsible as a passive member. . . .

I have placed the main point of enlightenment—the escape of men from their self-incurred tutelage—chiefly in the matters of religion because our rulers have no interest in playing the guardian with respect to the arts and sciences and also because religious incompetence is not only the most harmful but also the most degrading of all. . . .

Thomas Paine, "The Author's Profession of Faith," from *The Age of Reason**

It has been my intention, for several years past, to publish my thoughts upon religion; I am well aware of the difficulties that attend the subject, and from

---

*Thomas Paine, *The Age of Reason* in *Basic Writings of Thomas Paine* (1942), New York: Wiley Book Company, pp. 5–7.

that consideration, had reserved it to a more advanced period of life. I intended it to be the last offering I should make to my fellow-citizens of all nations, and that at a time when the purity of the motive that induced me to it could not admit of a question, even by those who might disapprove the work.

The circumstance that has now taken place in France, of the total abolition of the whole national order of priesthood, and of everything appertaining to compulsive systems of religion, and compulsive articles of faith, has not only precipitated my intention, but rendered a work of this kind exceedingly necessary, lest, in the general wreck of superstition, of false systems of government, and false theology, we lose sight of morality, of humanity, and of the theology that is true.

As several of my colleagues, and others of my fellow-citizens of France, have given me the example of making their voluntary and individual profession of faith, I also will make mine; and I do this with all that sincerity and frankness with which the mind of man communicates with itself.

I believe in one God, and no more; and I hope for happiness beyond this life.

I believe in the equality of man, and I believe that religious duties consist in doing justice, loving mercy, and endeavouring to make our fellow-creatures happy.

But, lest it should be supposed that I believe many other things in addition to these, I shall, in the progress of this work, declare the things I do not believe, and my reasons for not believing them.

I do not believe in the creed professed by the Jewish church, by the Roman church, by the Greek church, by the Turkish church, by the Protestant church, nor by any church that I know of. My own mind is my own church.

All national institutions of churches, whether Jewish, Christian, or Turkish, appear to me no other than human inventions set up to terrify and enslave mankind, and monopolize power and profit.

I do not mean by this declaration to condemn those who believe otherwise; they have the same right to their belief as I have to mine. But it is necessary to the happiness of man, that he be mentally faithful to himself. Infidelity does not consist in believing, or in disbelieving; it consists in professing to believe what he does not believe.

It is impossible to calculate the moral mischief, if I may so express it, that mental lying has produced in society. When a man has so far corrupted and prostituted the chastity of his mind, as to subscribe his professional belief to things he does not believe, he has prepared himself for the commission of every other crime. He takes up the trade of a priest for the sake of gain, and, in order to qualify himself for that trade, he begins with a perjury. Can we conceive anything more destructive to morality than this?

Soon after I had published the pamphlet *Common Sense*, in America, I saw the exceeding probability that a revolution in the system of government would be followed by a revolution in the system of religion. The adulterous connection of church and state, wherever it had taken place, whether Jewish, Christian, or Turkish, had so effectually prohibited, by pains and penalties, every discussion upon established creeds, and upon first principles of religion, that until the system of government should be changed, those subjects could not be brought fairly and openly before the world; but that whenever this should be done, a revolution in the system of religion would follow. Human inventions and priest-craft would be detected; and man would return to the pure, unmixed, and unadulterated belief of one God, and no more.

Questions

1. Why is freedom so important to Kant? What does freedom have to do with Enlightenment?
2. What are some specific connections between Kant's views on Enlightenment and Paine's "Profession of Faith"? What are the differences between these two works? What was the goal of each?
3. What do these sources reveal about the age in which they were writing? Should these views be considered moderate or radical for their time?

JEAN-JACQUES ROUSSEAU AND KAIBARA EKKEN, INTRODUCTION

In 1762, Jean-Jacques Rousseau defined the obligations of the state in The Social Contract *and defined, or rather redefined, the duties of the individual in* Emile. Emile *is predicated on the concept that the individual must stay true to his nature. Of course, he must become aware of his nature in order to know how to stay true to it. The problem for Rousseau was that eighteenth-century education generally used any means necessary in order to transform the child into someone who would be politically controllable, easily disciplined, and accepting of authority—in short, someone as far from his own true nature as possible. Rousseau was concerned equally with the contribution that each individual could make to society and the contributions that society could make to the individual. Unable to conceive of the reform of the French educational system as long as it was dominated by the Catholic Church, however, Rousseau has his fictional student Emile raised by a tutor who could guide him from infancy to maturity, aware of the child's unique tendencies and natural abilities. Rousseau based his ideas on education on the Enlightenment premise that human nature was essentially good. Unfortunately, by the time he introduces the main female character, Sophie, into the novel, the book takes a turn in the direction of romance and away from educational philosophy.*

It is not that Rousseau's ideas are not applicable to women, but he used a male for his model student and one could easily interpret his brief remarks on female education in Book V of Emile *as misogynistic. The same could perhaps be said of the Japanese treatise on women's education that was written either by the Japanese intellectual Kaibara Ekken (1630–1714) or his learned wife, Kaibara Token (1652–1713). Seventeenth-century Japan was a traditional society influenced by the socially conservative philosophy of Confucianism. In fact, Kaibara Ekken wrote other works targeted for specific audiences with advice on how to behave according to one's station in life and to adjust to their place within the Japanese social system. Taken in conjunction, the two sources below raise questions about the overall purpose of education. They both ask whether or not education should primarily prepare the individual for his or her expected role in society or to teach the pupil to look after his or her own well-being and personal development.*

Jean-Jacques Rousseau, *Emile**

The wise man can keep his own place; but the child who does not know what his place is, is unable to keep it. There are a thousand ways out of it, and it is the business of those who have charge of the child to keep him in his place, and this is no easy task. He should be neither beast nor man, but a child. He must feel his weakness, but not suffer through it; he must be dependent, but he must not obey; he must ask, not command. He is only subject to others because of his needs, and because they see better than he what he really needs, what may help or hinder his existence. No one, not even his father, has the right to bid the child do what is of no use to him.

When our natural tendencies have not been interfered with by human prejudice and human institutions, the happiness alike of children and of men consists in the enjoyment of their liberty. But the child's liberty is restricted by his lack of strength. He who does as he likes is happy provided he is self-sufficing; it is so with the man who is living in a state of nature. He who does what he likes is not happy if his desires exceed his strength; it is so with a child in like conditions. Even in a state of nature children only enjoy an imperfect liberty, like that enjoyed by men in social life. Each of us, unable to dispense with the help of others, becomes so far weak and wretched. We were

---

*Jean-Jacques Rousseau (1971), *Emile*, translated by Barbara Foxley, London: J.M. Dent and Sons, pp. 48–9.

meant to be men, laws and customs thrust us back into infancy. The rich and great, the very kings themselves are but children; they see that we are ready to relieve their misery; this makes them childishly vain, and they are quite proud of the care bestowed on them, a care which they would never get if they were grown men.

These are weighty considerations, and they provide a solution for all the conflicting problems of our social system. There are two kinds of dependence: dependence on things, which is the work of nature; and dependence on men, which is the work of society. Dependence on things, being non-moral, does no injury to liberty and begets no vices; dependence on men, being out of order, gives rise to every kind of vice, and through this master and slave become mutually depraved. If there is any cure for this social evil, it is to be found in the substitution of law for the individual; in arming the general will with a real strength beyond the power of any individual will. If the laws of nations, like the laws of nature, could never be broken by any human power, dependence on men would become dependence on things; all the advantages of a state of nature would be combined with all the advantages of social life in the commonwealth. The liberty which preserves a man from vice would be united with the morality which raises him to virtue.

Keep the child dependent on things only. By this course of education you will have followed the order of nature. Let his unreasonable wishes meet with physical obstacles only, or the punishment which results from his own actions, lessons which will be recalled when the same circumstances occur again. It is enough to prevent him from wrong doing without forbidding him to do wrong. Experience or lack of power should take the place of law. Give him, not what he wants, but what he needs. Let there be no question of obedience for him or tyranny for you. Supply the strength he lacks just so far as is required for freedom, not for power, so that he may receive your services with a sort of shame, and look forward to the time when he may dispense with them and may achieve the honor of self-help.

Kaibara Ekken, "Greater Learning for Women"

Seeing that it is a girl's destiny, on reaching womanhood, to go to a new home, and live in submission to her father-in-law and mother-in-law, it is even more incumbent upon her than it is on a boy to receive with all reverence her parents' instructions. Should her parents, through excess of tenderness, allow her to grow up self-willed, she will infallibly show herself capricious in her husband's house, and thus alienate his affection, while, if her father-in-law be a man of correct principles, the girl will find the yoke of these principles intolerable. . . .

More precious in a woman is a virtuous heart than a face of beauty. The vicious woman's heart is ever excited; she glares wildly around her, she vents her anger on others, her words are harsh and her accent vulgar. When she speaks it is to set herself above others, to upbraid others, to envy others, to be puffed up with individual pride, to jeer at others, to outdo others,— all things at variance with the "way" in which a woman should walk. The only qualities that befit a woman are gentle obedience, chastity, mercy, and quietness.

From her earliest youth, a girl should observe the line of demarcation separating women from men; and never, even for an instant, should she be allowed to see or hear the slightest impropriety. The customs of antiquity did not allow men and women to sit in the same apartment, to keep their wearing-apparel in the same place, to bathe in the same place or to transmit to each other anything directly from hand to hand. . . .

Let her never even dream of jealousy. If her husband be dissolute, she must expostulate with him, but never either nurse or vent her anger. If her jealousy be extreme, it will render her countenance frightful and her accents repulsive, and can only result in completely alienating her husband from her, and making her intolerable in his eyes. Should her husband act ill and unreasonably, she must compose her countenance and soften her voice to remonstrate with him; and if he be angry and listen not to the remonstrance, she must wait over a season, and then expostulate with him again when his heart is softened. Never set thyself up against thy husband with harsh features and a boisterous voice! . . .

The five worst maladies that afflict the female mind are: indocility, discontent, slander, jealousy, and silliness. Without any doubt, these five maladies infest seven or eight out of every ten women, and it is from these that arises the inferiority of women to men. A woman should cure them by self-inspection and self-reproach. The worst of them all, and the parent of the other four, is silliness.

Woman's nature is passive. This passiveness, being of the nature of the night, is dark. Hence, as viewed from the standard of man's nature, the foolishness of woman fails to understand the duties that lie before her very eyes, perceives not the actions that will bring down blame upon her own head, and comprehends not even the things that will bring down calamities on the heads of her husband and children. Neither when she blames and accuses and curses innocent persons, nor when, in her jealousy of others, she thinks to set up herself alone, does she see that she is her own enemy. . . . Again, in the education of her children, her blind affection induces an erroneous system. Such is the stupidity of her character that it is incumbent on her, in every particular, to distrust herself and to obey her husband.

Questions
1. What does the above passage from *Emile* indicate about Rousseau's views on the relationship between the individual and society?
2. What does Kaibara say about the main roles that Japanese society expected women to play?
3. Is the difference between these two writings that the first is idealistic and the second is realistic? Is it possible to make a case that the reverse is true? Or are they both based on ideals that are unlikely to succeed in actual practice?

OLAUDAH EQUIANO, INTRODUCTION

The European Enlightenment coexisted uneasily alongside the perpetuation of the institution of human slavery, in which European merchants participated through their involvement in the triangular slave trade that brought slaves from West Africa to the Americas in exchange for the cotton, coffee, sugar, and tobacco cultivated by slaves for export back to Europe. The English had become the preeminent country in the slave trade after their victory in the War of the Spanish Succession at the beginning of the eighteenth century. They benefited from their ability to manufacture goods and weapons that were in demand in Africa that they could exchange for slaves.

Olaudah Equiano was the African name of a slave (his owner gave him the Swedish name Gustavas Vassa for unknown reasons) who managed to secure his freedom after spending years as a slave. Equiano first served aboard a British naval ship, then as a procurer of slaves in the West Indies for his new owner, a Quaker merchant from Philadelphia named Robert King. After earning enough money to purchase his freedom (though not without considerable difficulty), he ended up in London where he became something of a celebrity as an advocate for the abolition of the slave trade and the author of a bestselling autobiography, written in 1789, an excerpt from which appears below. Equiano had every right to be outraged, not only by his own treatment, but also by the horrors associated with the slave trade that he witnessed and heard of during his time in the West Indies. He channeled his anger and his passion into an intelligent, rational, and persuasive account of his experiences. His autobiography fit in well with the spirit of the Enlightenment and played an influential role in moving public opinion toward abolition of the slave trade, which the British Parliament passed into law in 1807. In 1833, Britain abolished slavery throughout the British Empire altogether.

Olaudah Equiano, account of arrival in West Indies, 1756, from *The Interesting Narrative of the Life of Olaudah Equiano or Gustavus Vassa the African**

At last we came in sight of the island of Barbadoes, at which the whites on board gave a great shout, and made many signs of joy to us. We did not know what to think of this; but as the vessel drew nearer we plainly saw the harbour, and other ships of different kinds and sizes; and we soon anchored amongst them off Bridge Town. Many merchants and planters now came on board, though it was in the evening. They put us in separate parcels, and examined us attentively. They also made us jump, and pointed to the land, signifying we were to go there. We thought by this we should be eaten by those ugly men, as they appeared to us; and, when soon after we were all put down under the deck again, there was much dread and trembling among us, and nothing but bitter cries to be heard all the night from these apprehensions, insomuch that at last the white people got some old slaves from the land to pacify us. They told us we were not to be eaten, but to work, and were soon to go on land, where we should see many of our country people. This report eased us much; and sure enough, soon after we were landed, there came to us Africans of all languages. We were conducted immediately to the merchant's yard, where we were all pent up together like so many sheep in a fold, without regard to sex or age.

As every object was new to me everything I saw filled me with surprise. What struck me first was that the houses were built with stories, and in every other respect different from those in Africa: but I was still more astonished on seeing people on horseback. I did not know what this could mean; and indeed I thought these people were full of nothing but magical arts. While I was in this astonishment one of my fellow prisoners spoke to a countryman of his about the horses, who said they were the same kind they had in their country. I understood them, though they were from a distant part of Africa, and I thought it odd I had not seen any horses there; but afterwards when I came to converse with different Africans, I found they had many horses amongst them, and much larger than those I then saw. We were not many days in the merchant's custody before we were sold after their usual manner, which is this: On a signal given (as the beat of a drum), the buyers rush at once into the yard where the slaves are confined, and make choice of that parcel they like best. The noise and clamor with which this is attended, and the eagerness visible in the countenances of the buyers serve not a little to increase the apprehensions of the terrified Africans, who may well

---

The Interesting Narrative of the Life of Olaudah Equiano or Gustavus Vassa the African (1789), London, pp. 84–88. Available online at http://history.hanover.edu/texts/equiano/equiano_contents.html.

be supposed to consider them as the ministers of that destruction to which they think themselves devoted. In this manner, without scruple, are relations and friends separated, most of them never to see each other again. I remember in the vessel in which I was brought over, in the men's apartment, there were several brothers, who, in the sale, were sold in different lots; and it was very moving on this occasion to see and hear their cries at parting. O, ye nominal Christians! might not an African ask you, learned you this from your God, who says unto you, Do unto all men as you would men should do unto you? Is it not enough that we are torn from our country and friends to toil for your luxury and lust of gain? Must every tender feeling be likewise sacrificed to your avarice? Are the dearest friends and relations, now rendered more dear by their separation from their kindred, still to be parted from each other, and thus prevented from cheering the gloom of slavery with the small comfort of being together and mingling their sufferings and sorrows? Why are parents to lose their children, brothers their sisters, or husbands their wives? Surely this is a new refinement in cruelty, which, while it has no advantage to atone for it, thus aggravates distress, and adds fresh horrors even to the wretchedness of slavery.

FIGURE 1: Joseph Wright, *A Philosopher Lecturing with a Mechanical Planetary*. Courtesy of the Derby Art Museum and Gallery.

Questions

1. What techniques does Equiano use in this passage to condemn the slave trade? How effective are they?
2. What are the main abuses associated with the slave trade that are identified in this passage?
3. Does Equiano's account of the slave trade qualify as an "Enlightenment" work? Why or why not?

Joseph Wright (1734–97) was a well-known painter during his own lifetime whose works frequently dealt with subjects related to science and technology. He lived during the early stages of the Industrial Revolution, which thrived mainly in Northern England. He personally knew many of the leading scientists and manufacturers of his time and enjoyed the patronage of the inventor and factory owner, Richard Arkwright, and Josiah Wedgewood, renowned for his innovative pottery factories.

Questions

1. In what ways does this painting reflect the ideas and ideals of the Enlightenment?
2. What are the various poses and facial expressions in the painting meant to represent?
3. Why might the artist have included individuals of such diverse ages in the painting?

Chapter Questions

1. How have the above sources contributed to your understanding of the Enlightenment as a whole? What characteristics of the Enlightenment stand out or can be derived from a collective reading of these sources?
2. How do Paine's views on religion compare to those of Jonathan Edwards? Do they have anything in common? How might each have responded to the other?
3. Which source included here was likely to have the greater impact in effecting change in European society: Montesquieu's *Persian Letters*, Rousseau's *Emile*, or Equiano's autobiography? Why?

CHAPTER TWO

The American and French Revolutions

INTRODUCTION

Despite the challenges that the Enlightenment provided to established authority, and despite the precedents of the English revolutions of the seventeenth century, the American and French Revolutions came to many as dramatic surprises and sudden changes in the political order. It is true that the American crisis built over the course of a dozen years that followed the end of the Seven Years War—the French and Indian War in North America—in 1763 and that the crisis began with simple objections to new taxes imposed by Britain and the British government's attempt to adhere to the previously laxly enforced Navigation Acts that placed restrictions on American trade. Even so, the decision to challenge the king's authority to rule the American colonies and to renounce their allegiance to him turned those resisting George III from rebels into revolutionaries. Even in July 1776, the decision to declare independence was not made lightly and needed a strong rationale, which Thomas Jefferson provided in the Declaration of Independence.

Thirteen years later, when French writers composed the Declaration of the Rights of Man and Citizen, they clearly did so with the Declaration of Independence as a model. This makes a comparison between these two documents a valuable and instructive historical exercise. The French experience supporting the Americans in their fight for liberty against a king perceived as an oppressive monarch influenced them deeply, especially those such as Lafayette and Rochambeau who had fought in America. But transatlantic influence worked both ways, for the Americans were also influenced by the ideas of the French Enlightenment. The French revolutionaries, of course, were at least equally influenced by it and directly incorporated some of the ideas of Rousseau and the French philosophes in their declaration. It is important to note that at this point—August 1789—the French, unlike the Americans in their document, were not declaring their independence from the king, Louis XVI (r. 1774–93), but rather asserting that any government, including that of the king, had to respect certain fundamental human rights.

Like the Declaration of Independence, however, the Declaration of the Rights of Man and Citizen did not include women in its defense of equality and human rights. This could have been the result of remaining eighteenth-century prejudices during the "Age of Reason" that women were not the rational creatures that men were and that they were still governed too much by uncontrollable passions. Therefore, when the English novelist Mary Wollstonecraft (1759–97) set out to defend the "rights of women," she had to address these existing stereotypes at the same time that she made progressive, feminist arguments for women's equality. What her work has in common with the abovementioned documents is that they all remained influential long after their initial publication. But Wollstonecraft's *Vindication of the Rights of Women* also provides a powerful testament to the existence of feminist ideas at that time.

Critics of the French Revolution, of whom there were many almost from the very beginning, could eventually point to the fact that rule by the people carried its own set of dangers. As the situation in France deteriorated into civil war and the French revolutionary government became surrounded by internal and external foes, the emergency tribunal known as the Committee of Public Safety began a "Reign of Terror" in order to eliminate its enemies and preserve the Revolution. This episode in French history has troubled and exercised the minds of French historians and citizens ever since, among them a writer named Edmond Biré (1829–1907), who attempted to reconstruct how contemporaries viewed the event in *The Diary of a Citizen of Paris During the Terror*.

Civil disorder, foreign invasion or the threat of it, continued economic depression, and political instability all seemed to call for a strong leader who could stabilize France, provide order, and defend the country. Napoleon Bonaparte (1769–1821) was a French general who emerged out of the Directory, a five-member executive body charged with restoring order after the Terror. Napoleon rose to the position of emperor by 1804. In the course of the next two years, he defeated both Austria and Prussia, both of which had opposed the French Revolution almost from the very beginning, and had started to make himself master of Europe. Even Russia, which had entered the war against the French, acquiesced and signed a peace treaty (of Tilsit) with Napoleon in 1807. However, Napoleon still faced opposition from the British, who had destroyed his naval fleet at the Battle of Trafalgar in October 1805, and from Spanish rebels who resisted French occupation. When the British sent their army into Spain they started the Peninsular War, which became a major thorn in Napoleon's side and threatened to undo him, for all his military successes elsewhere. As long as Spain could resist French troops, France's other enemies might be encouraged to rise again.

Meanwhile, the Napoleonic occupation of Spain had led to the overthrow of the Bourbon monarchy there and provided an opportunity for Spain's Latin American colonies to declare their independence, just as Britain's North American colonies had done in 1776. This proved problematic in 1813 when Napoleon was forced to recognize King Ferdinand VII's return to the Spanish throne for Ferdinand expected to retain his American colonies. However, military leaders such as José de San Martin (1778–1850) in Argentina and Simón Bolívar (1783–1830) in northern South America proved successful in defending Spanish freedom. In South America, however, freedom proved to be a mixed blessing because not everyone supported the policies or personal aggrandizement of Bolívar, who fancied himself South America's Napoleon to its revolutions.

Democracy was even proving to be something of a mixed blessing in the newly formed United States of America in the early decades of the nineteenth century. Far from a peaceful, harmonious republic, the new nation was rife with inconsistencies, contradictions, and conflicts. But its people seemed to possess an abundance of energy, initiative, and vitality. Europeans, scarred by the violence and war that had accompanied the French Revolution and Napoleonic wars, looked askance at the American experiment with democracy. In the early 1830s, the French attorney, Alexis de Tocqueville (1805–59), traveled throughout the United States to observe the new nation firsthand, on the pretense of studying the American prison system on behalf of the French government. With the eye of an outsider, Tocqueville attempted to explain the nature of "democracy in America" to European readers and, to a large extent, to the Americans themselves.

THOMAS JEFFERSON, THE DECLARATION OF INDEPENDENCE, INTRODUCTION

In the summer of 1776, the Second Continental Congress, sitting in Philadelphia, with representatives from thirteen of Britain's American colonies, debated whether or not to cut the umbilical cord that still tied it to their mother country. When they decided to do so, they based their decision as much on practical considerations such as enticing French support, without which they would probably not win the war in which they were already engaged with Britain, as they did on high-minded republican principles. The French did enter the war, which was still to be won. It would take five more years and the surmounting of numerous setbacks, defeats, and obstacles to victory, but the Declaration of Independence changed the nature of the conflict and the course of history. It remains a controversial document, however, in large part because of its failure to condemn slavery and to include women and African-Americans in its proclamation that "all men are created equal." Therefore, the document should be read with an eye for what it does not say as much as for what it does.

Thomas Jefferson, The Declaration of Independence*

IN CONGRESS, July 4, 1776.

The unanimous Declaration of the thirteen united States of America,
When in the Course of human events, it becomes necessary for one people to dissolve the political bands which have connected them with another, and to

---

*http://www.archives.gov/exhibits/charters/declaration_transcript.html

assume among the powers of the earth, the separate and equal station to which the Laws of Nature and of Nature's God entitle them, a decent respect to the opinions of mankind requires that they should declare the causes which impel them to the separation.

We hold these truths to be self-evident, that all men are created equal, that they are endowed by their Creator with certain unalienable Rights, that among these are Life, Liberty and the pursuit of Happiness.—That to secure these rights, Governments are instituted among Men, deriving their just powers from the consent of the governed,—That whenever any Form of Government becomes destructive of these ends, it is the Right of the People to alter or to abolish it, and to institute new Government, laying its foundation on such principles and organizing its powers in such form, as to them shall seem most likely to effect their Safety and Happiness. Prudence, indeed, will dictate that Governments long established should not be changed for light and transient causes; and accordingly all experience hath shewn, that mankind are more disposed to suffer, while evils are sufferable, than to right themselves by abolishing the forms to which they are accustomed. But when a long train of abuses and usurpations, pursuing invariably the same Object evinces a design to reduce them under absolute Despotism, it is their right, it is their duty, to throw off such Government, and to provide new Guards for their future security.—Such has been the patient sufferance of these Colonies; and such is now the necessity which constrains them to alter their former Systems of Government. The history of the present King of Great Britain is a history of repeated injuries and usurpations, all having in direct object the establishment of an absolute Tyranny over these States. To prove this, let Facts be submitted to a candid world.

He has refused his Assent to Laws, the most wholesome and necessary for the public good.

He has forbidden his Governors to pass Laws of immediate and pressing importance, unless suspended in their operation till his Assent should be obtained; and when so suspended, he has utterly neglected to attend to them.

He has refused to pass other Laws for the accommodation of large districts of people, unless those people would relinquish the right of Representation in the Legislature, a right inestimable to them and formidable to tyrants only.

He has called together legislative bodies at places unusual, uncomfortable, and distant from the depository of their public Records, for the sole purpose of fatiguing them into compliance with his measures.

He has dissolved Representative Houses repeatedly, for opposing with manly firmness his invasions on the rights of the people.

He has refused for a long time, after such dissolutions, to cause others to be elected; whereby the Legislative powers, incapable of Annihilation, have returned to the People at large for their exercise; the State remaining in the mean time exposed to all the dangers of invasion from without, and convulsions within.

He has endeavoured to prevent the population of these States; for that purpose obstructing the Laws for Naturalization of Foreigners; refusing to pass others to encourage their migrations hither, and raising the conditions of new Appropriations of Lands.

He has obstructed the Administration of Justice, by refusing his Assent to Laws for establishing Judiciary powers.

He has made Judges dependent on his Will alone, for the tenure of their offices, and the amount and payment of their salaries.

He has erected a multitude of New Offices, and sent hither swarms of Officers to harrass our people, and eat out their substance.

He has kept among us, in times of peace, Standing Armies without the Consent of our legislatures.

He has affected to render the Military independent of and superior to the Civil power.

He has combined with others to subject us to a jurisdiction foreign to our constitution, and unacknowledged by our laws; giving his Assent to their Acts of pretended Legislation:

For Quartering large bodies of armed troops among us:

For protecting them, by a mock Trial, from punishment for any Murders which they should commit on the Inhabitants of these States:

For cutting off our Trade with all parts of the world:

For imposing Taxes on us without our Consent:

For depriving us in many cases, of the benefits of Trial by Jury:

For transporting us beyond Seas to be tried for pretended offences

For abolishing the free System of English Laws in a neighbouring Province, establishing therein an Arbitrary government, and enlarging its Boundaries so as to render it at once an example and fit instrument for introducing the same absolute rule into these Colonies:

For taking away our Charters, abolishing our most valuable Laws, and altering fundamentally the Forms of our Governments:

For suspending our own Legislatures, and declaring themselves invested with power to legislate for us in all cases whatsoever.

He has abdicated Government here, by declaring us out of his Protection and waging War against us.

He has plundered our seas, ravaged our Coasts, burnt our towns, and destroyed the lives of our people.

He is at this time transporting large Armies of foreign Mercenaries to compleat the works of death, desolation and tyranny, already begun with circumstances of Cruelty & perfidy scarcely paralleled in the most barbarous ages, and totally unworthy the Head of a civilized nation.

He has constrained our fellow Citizens taken Captive on the high Seas to bear Arms against their Country, to become the executioners of their friends and Brethren, or to fall themselves by their Hands.

He has excited domestic insurrections amongst us, and has endeavoured to bring on the inhabitants of our frontiers, the merciless Indian Savages, whose known rule of warfare, is an undistinguished destruction of all ages, sexes and conditions.

In every stage of these Oppressions We have Petitioned for Redress in the most humble terms: Our repeated Petitions have been answered only by repeated injury. A Prince whose character is thus marked by every act which may define a Tyrant, is unfit to be the ruler of a free people.

Nor have We been wanting in attentions to our British brethren. We have warned them from time to time of attempts by their legislature to extend an unwarrantable jurisdiction over us. We have reminded them of the circumstances of our emigration and settlement here. We have appealed to their native justice and magnanimity, and we have conjured them by the ties of our common kindred to disavow these usurpations, which, would inevitably interrupt our connections and correspondence. They too have been deaf to the voice of justice and of consanguinity. We must, therefore, acquiesce in the necessity, which denounces our Separation, and hold them, as we hold the rest of mankind, Enemies in War, in Peace Friends.

We, therefore, the Representatives of the united States of America, in General Congress, Assembled, appealing to the Supreme Judge of the world for the rectitude of our intentions, do, in the Name, and by Authority of the good People of these Colonies, solemnly publish and declare, That these United Colonies are, and of Right ought to be Free and Independent States; that they are Absolved from all Allegiance to the British Crown, and that all political connection between them and the State of Great Britain, is and ought to be totally dissolved; and that as Free and Independent States, they have full Power to levy War, conclude Peace, contract Alliances, establish Commerce, and to do all other Acts and Things which Independent States may of right do. And for the support of this Declaration, with a firm reliance on the protection of divine Providence, we mutually pledge to each other our Lives, our Fortunes and our sacred Honor.

Questions

1. What general principles does the Declaration seek to establish? In what ways do these reflect the ideals of the Enlightenment?
2. How much emphasis is devoted to specific abuses of the English government in relation to the colonies? What seem to have been the most objectionable practices, based on this document?

3. Thomas Jefferson was forced to compromise and to eliminate a passage that would have condemned slavery and blamed George III for its
   perpetuation in America. Since Jefferson himself owned slaves, was this
   hypocritical on his part? Does the document deserve its reputation as a
   foundation of liberty or should Jefferson and the members of the Continental Congress be blamed for not broadening its definitions of freedom
   and equality?

THE DECLARATION OF THE RIGHTS OF MAN AND CITIZEN, INTRODUCTION

*The French Revolution had started when a bankrupt Louis XVI was persuaded
to call back into existence the Estates-General, a national representative
assembly that had not met since the early seventeenth century. The Declaration
of the Rights of Man and Citizen, like the Declaration of Independence, was
a stepping stone and not a final outcome. The French did not abolish the
monarchy for another four years and the French government went through
several permutations, including the founding of the first French Republic and
the establishment of the French Empire under Napoleon, before the eventual
restoration of the Bourbon monarchy in 1815. However, this document
represented the original ideals on which the Revolution had been based, even
if those ideals became compromised in the course of the Revolution itself. It
remains a testament to those original ideals, which have survived long after the
end of the French Revolution.*

The Declaration of the Rights of Man and Citizen*

Articles:

1. Men are born and remain free and equal in rights. Social distinctions
   may be founded only upon the general good.
2. The aim of all political association is the preservation of the natural and
   imprescriptible rights of man. These rights are liberty, property, security,
   and resistance to oppression.

---

*http://avalon.law.yale.edu/18th_century/rightsof.asp

3. The principle of all sovereignty resides essentially in the nation. No body nor individual may exercise any authority which does not proceed directly from the nation.

4. Liberty consists in the freedom to do everything which injures no one else; hence the exercise of the natural rights of each man has no limits except those which assure to the other members of the society the enjoyment of the same rights. These limits can only be determined by law.

5. Law can only prohibit such actions as are hurtful to society. Nothing may be prevented which is not forbidden by law, and no one may be forced to do anything not provided for by law.

6. Law is the expression of the general will. Every citizen has a right to participate personally, or through his representative, in its foundation. It must be the same for all, whether it protects or punishes. All citizens, being equal in the eyes of the law, are equally eligible to all dignities and to all public positions and occupations, according to their abilities, and without distinction except that of their virtues and talents.

7. No person shall be accused, arrested, or imprisoned except in the cases and according to the forms prescribed by law. Any one soliciting, transmitting, executing, or causing to be executed, any arbitrary order, shall be punished. But any citizen summoned or arrested in virtue of the law shall submit without delay, as resistance constitutes an offense.

8. The law shall provide for such punishments only as are strictly and obviously necessary, and no one shall suffer punishment except it be legally inflicted in virtue of a law passed and promulgated before the commission of the offense.

9. As all persons are held innocent until they shall have been declared guilty, if arrest shall be deemed indispensable, all harshness not essential to the securing of the prisoner's person shall be severely repressed by law.

10. No one shall be disquieted on account of his opinions, including his religious views, provided their manifestation does not disturb the public order established by law.

11. The free communication of ideas and opinions is one of the most precious of the rights of man. Every citizen may, accordingly, speak, write, and print with freedom, but shall be responsible for such abuses of this freedom as shall be defined by law.

12. The security of the rights of man and of the citizen requires public military forces. These forces are, therefore, established for the good of all and not for the personal advantage of those to whom they shall be intrusted.

13. A common contribution is essential for the maintenance of the public forces and for the cost of administration. This should be equitably distributed among all the citizens in proportion to their means.

14. All the citizens have a right to decide, either personally or by their representatives, as to the necessity of the public contribution; to grant this freely; to know to what uses it is put; and to fix the proportion, the mode of assessment and of collection and the duration of the taxes.

15. Society has the right to require of every public agent an account of his administration.

16. A society in which the observance of the law is not assured, nor the separation of powers defined, has no constitution at all.

17. Since property is an inviolable and sacred right, no one shall be deprived thereof except where public necessity, legally determined, shall clearly demand it, and then only on condition that the owner shall have been previously and equitably indemnified.

Questions
1. How does this declaration compare to the American Declaration of Independence? Are there ways in which it goes further in its assertion of human rights and principles of popular sovereignty? Are there ways in which the Declaration of Independence goes further in these areas?
2. In what ways does this document reflect the ideals of the Enlightenment?
3. What are the specific rights guaranteed in the document? Are these rights guaranteed for Frenchmen or does the document state or imply that they are meant for all men?

Jacques-Louis David (1748–1825) began his career under the ancien régime of the Bourbon monarchy, but became the painter most associated with the French Revolution. His idealistic portraits of Napoleon would further reflect his continually evolving political views. Events moved so quickly during the Revolution, that David never finished the painting for which the following illustration was supposed to be the basis: David's rendering of the famous *Tennis Court Oath* of 1789 in which members of the Estates General declared themselves the National Assembly and vowed to meet until France had a new constitution.

FIGURE 2: Jacques Louis David, *The Tennis Court Oath*. Courtesy of Getty Images.

Questions
1. What are the key elements of David's artistic style that appear in this image?
2. Does David manage to capture the importance and excitement of the historical situation?
3. Does the drawing attempt to make a political statement itself or does it merely present an objective picture of what occurred?

MARY WOLLSTONECRAFT, *A VINDICATION OF THE RIGHTS OF WOMEN*, INTRODUCTION

Mary Wollstonecraft personally experienced the disadvantages of a woman trying to make it on her own in a society that considered her inferior on account of her sex. But she also shared in the Enlightenment critique of established authority in general as a religious nonconformist and a defender of the French Revolution against the likes of Edmund Burke, who valued tradition and continuity over abstract rights and sudden political change. Her earlier Vindication of the Rights of Men *positioned her on the side of Thomas Paine (see Chapter 1) and previous Enlightenment thinkers such as Jean-Jacques Rousseau. However, she took their arguments one step further in her* Vindication of the Rights of Women *to ensure that the "the rights of man" did not exclude the approximately 50 percent of the human race that was female. As the passages below indicate, however, she believed that women needed to be educated differently in order to be prepared to exercise those rights. Her arguments were persuasive and not openly attacked at the time, though they had little immediate impact on women's position; her influence was to be much greater over the long term than in her own lifetime.*

Mary Wollstonecraft, *A Vindication of the Rights of Women**

Another instance of that feminine weakness of character, often produced by a confined education, is a romantic twist of the mind, which has been very properly termed *sentimental*.

Women subjected by ignorance to their sensations, and only taught to look for happiness in love, refine on sensual feelings, and adopt metaphysical notions respecting that passion, which lead them shamefully to neglect the duties of life, and frequently in the midst of these sublime refinements they plump into actual vice.

These are the women who are amused by the reveries of the stupid novelists, who, knowing little of human nature, work up stale tales, and describe meretricious scenes, all retailed in sentimental jargon, which equally tend to corrupt the taste and draw the heart aside from its daily duties. . . .

Females, in fact, denied all political privileges, and not allowed, as married women, excepting in criminal cases, a civil existence, have their attention naturally drawn from the interest of the whole community to that of the minute parts, though the private duty of any member of society must be very imperfectly performed when not connected with the general good. The mighty business of female life is to please, and restrained from entering into more important concerns by political and civil oppression, sentiments become events, and reflection deepens what it should, and would, have effaced, if the understanding had been allowed to take a wider range.

But, confined to trifling employments, they naturally imbibe opinions which the only kind of reading calculated to interest an innocent, frivolous mind inspires. Unable to grasp any great thing, is it surprising that they find the reading

---

*Mary Wollstonecraft (1891), *Vindication of the Rights of Women*, New York: Humboldt, pp. 189–94.

of history a very dry talk, and disquisitions addressed to the understanding intolerably tedious and almost unintelligible? . . .

When, therefore, I advise my sex not to read such flimsy works, it is to induce them to read something superior. . . .

Besides, the reading of novels makes women, and particularly ladies of fashion, very fond of using strong expressions and superlatives in conversation; and, though the dissipated, artificial life which they lead prevents their cherishing any strong legitimate passion, the language of passion in affected tones slips forever from their glib tongues, and every trifle produces those phosphoric bursts which only mimic in the dark the flame of passion.

Ignorance and the mistaken cunning that Nature sharpens in weak heads as a principle of self-preservation, render women very fond of dress, and produce all the vanity which such a fondness may naturally be expected to generate, to the exclusion of emulation and magnanimity.

. . . And very natural it is—for they have not any business to interest them, have not a taste for literature, and they find politics dry, because they have not acquired a love for mankind by turning their thoughts to the grand pursuits that exalt the human race and promote general happiness.

Women are supposed to possess more sensibility, and even humanity, than men, and their strong attachments and instantaneous emotions of compassion are given as proofs; but the clinging affection of ignorance has seldom anything noble in it, and may mostly be resolved into selfishness, as well as the affection of children and brutes. I have known many weak women whose sensibility was entirely engrossed by their husbands; and as for their humanity, it was very faint indeed, or rather, it was only a transient emotion of compassion. Humanity does not consist "in a squeamish ear," says an eminent orator, "it belongs to the mind as well as the nerves."

But this kind of exclusive affection, though it degrades the individual, should not be brought forward as proof of the inferiority of the sex, because it is the natural consequence of confined views; for even women of superior sense, having their attention turned to little employments, and private plans, rarely rise to heroism, unless when spurred on by love! and love, as an heroic passion, like genius, appears but once in an age. I therefore agree with the moralist who asserts, "that women have seldom so much generosity as men;" and that their narrow affections, to which justice and humanity are often sacrificed, render the sex apparently inferior, especially as they are commonly inspired by men; but I contend that the heart would expand as the understanding gained strength, if women were not depressed from their cradles. . . .

Besides, how can women be just or generous, when they are the slaves of injustice?

Questions
1. How does Wollstonecraft deal with the stereotype that women are by nature more emotional or sentimental than men? What does she propose in order to remedy that stereotype?
2. What are her views on women's equality?
3. Does she view women as naturally superior to men in any way? Why or why not?

EDMOND BIRÉ, *THE DIARY OF A CITIZEN OF PARIS DURING THE TERROR*, INTRODUCTION

The Diary of a Citizen of Paris During the Terror *is a different kind of source from most that are included in this sourcebook. It is not technically a primary source for the Reign of Terror since it was written about a hundred years later. But it proves instructive nonetheless, partly because Biré relied heavily on primary sources for his reconstruction both of events and the reactions of French citizens at that time. Furthermore, Biré's work could be considered a primary source, not for the 1790s but for the 1890s, providing insight into how the Terror was viewed in retrospect and the extent to which the revolutionary period continued to exercise a hold on the French imagination. Biré said that he wrote the diary as "the sole means of ridding my mind of these dark visions." But he also wanted to convey a sense of the impression that the events surrounding the Terror had made on the common people of France at that time. Biré's achievement was recognized by the secretary of the Académie Francaise as possessing "all the interest of romance and all the value of real history. . . ." The entry below is set in the period between the arrest of Louis XVI in September 1792 for conspiring with the enemies, which he had been in fact doing, and his execution in January 1793.*

Edmond Biré, *The Diary of a Citizen of Paris During the Terror**

Monday, November 5, 1792

Since the opening of the Convention, and since the day on which we became a Republic, the public agitation and disturbance has continually increased; disorder and terror reigns supreme.

---

*Edmond Biré (1898), *The Diary of a Citizen of Paris During the Terror*, translated by John de Villiers, London: Chatto and Windus, pp. 127–28.

Walk through the streets, stop in the public squares, read the news-sheets and the placards that adorn the walls, attend the sectional assemblies, enter the clubs of the Cordeliers and the Jacobins, penetrate even into the National Convention—on all sides you will find shouts of death, rumors of rebellion, threats of murder.

On October 29, Roland, the Minister of the Interior, laid before the Convention a report on the state of Paris. "The principles of rebellion and bloodshed"—so runs this official document—"are openly professed and applauded in every assembly; murmurs are even heard against the Convention itself. I can no longer doubt that partisans of the old regime and enemies of the people, hiding their madness or their villainy under a mask of patriotism, have conceived a plan of a complete revolt, hoping to rise once more to power by the aid of bloodshed, atrocities, and gold. The worthy Roland is well aware that the villains he denounces are anything but partisans of the old regime, and rank, on the contrary, amidst the staunchest defenders of the Republic. But to recognize and proclaim this fact, to boldly attack those patriots who would sweep away him and his friends, more energy and honesty were required than may reasonably be looked for in the poor man who praised the zeal and patriotism displayed by Fournier, the American, the author of the "Massacre of the Prisoners of Orleans."

Meanwhile, the prisons that were emptied on September 2 are being daily refilled with fresh suspects. The arrests made by order of the Vigilance Committee of the Commune between October 10 and November 1 amounted to 1,032. The total number of prisoners at the beginning of the month was 1,375. . . .

. . . M. Target, President of one of the courts, and spokesman for the delegation, expressed himself in the following terms . . . : ". . . The motives for the arrest of so many citizens are unknown; the prison registers have been badly kept, and no complaint has been made to the courts by the police officers. The commune therefore reduces the court to inactivity, and hence it comes that the citizens of a Republic are more oppressed than they were under a despot."

Prisons overflowing with victims, rebellion in the public streets, anarchy everywhere, commerce suspended, work stopped, workshops deserted, misery and starvation in every home—such is the Paris which the Revolution has given us. Hear the avowal of the most ardent Republicans—Robespierre declaring in the Jacobin Club on October 29 that 100,000 Frenchmen are on the eve of starvation, Marat writing in his paper, "The trade of Paris is absolutely ruined and more than 100,000 of its inhabitants who were in comfortable circumstances before the fall of the Bastille are now in penury." Starvation stares us in the face, but though the people of Paris are without bread, they shall have their shows. The trial of Louis XVI begins tomorrow.

Questions

1. How well does Biré convey the impression of having been present at the events that he describes? What important historical information or insights are provided in the above passages?
2. Does he succeed in his stated objective of providing "a rough and simple sketch" of a complicated time?
3. What is the value of such a source for the understanding of history? Is it the same as that of a historical novel? Is all history—even nonfiction—nothing more than an imaginative recreation of the past?

THE CONFIDENTIAL CORRESPONDENCE OF NAPOLEON BONAPARTE WITH HIS BROTHER JOSEPH, INTRODUCTION

The following excerpts from the correspondence of Napoleon with his brother, Joseph, whom he had appointed king of Spain in 1807, are part of a larger story of his war with Britain and his attempt to cut Britain off from European trade through a blockade called the Continental System. But they also relate directly to how difficult the French found it to rule Spain in the face of Spanish opposition and guerilla warfare. The Spanish were not the only people under French rule who bristled under foreign domination, but they were the only people who had their hopes sustained by a foreign invasion by the British, who also wanted to drive Napoleon's armies out of Spain. In December 1808 the British had 20,000 troops in Spain and were threatening to oust the French army under the command of Marshal General Jean-de-Dieu Soult. This prompted Napoleon himself to cross the Pyrenees with an army, but he had to withdraw hurriedly under the threat of a renewed war with Austria. The French might have defeated the British on land in Spain and they might have crushed Spanish resistance, but they found it very difficult to do both. The French finally left Spain in 1813, after the disastrous failure of Napoleon's invasion of Russia in 1812. His correspondence with Joseph reflects both the specific situation that Napoleon faced in early 1809 and his general attitudes toward the lands that he conquered.

Napoleon Bonaparte, *The Confidential Correspondence of Napoleon Bonaparte with his Brother Joseph**

Napoleon to Joseph
Benevento, January 6, 1809

My Brother—I thank you for your new year's day wishes. I have no hopes for peace in Europe for this year at least. I expect it so little, that I signed yesterday a decree for raising 100,000 men. The fierce hatred of England, the events at Constantinople, all betoken that the hour of peace and repose has not yet struck. As for you, your kingdom seems to be settling into tranquility. The provinces, of Leon, of the Asturias, of New Castile, desire nothing but rest. I hope that Galicia will soon be at peace, and that the country will be evacuated by the English.

Saragossa must fall before long, and General St. Cyr, who has 30,000 men, ought to settle the affairs of Catalonia.

Napoleon to Berthier
Valladolid, January 9, 1809

My Cousin—Write to General Belliard to express my displeasure at the want of firmness displayed by his government: everyday Frenchmen are assassinated in Madrid, and he does nothing. Tell him that 30 of the worst characters of the town must be arrested and shot; that this is what I have done at Valladolid; and that I shall hold him responsible for the first assassination committed on a Frenchman, if the arrest of a Spaniard does not immediately follow. The behavior in Madrid is absurd.

Napoleon to Joseph
Valladolid, January 12, 1809

. . . I have sent word for you to make your entry into Madrid, and to assume the government, all with as much pomp as possible. I am anxious that it may be on the 14th, 15th, or 16th. I think these things now necessary and important. I have as yet heard no news of the English; our army was in presence of their rear-guard on the 8th. I have ordered a battalion of 600 men, which is at Soria, to repair to Madrid as soon as it is relieved. You may incorporate it in your guard. Numerous detachments of conscripts are on their way. Belliard did admirably. You must hang at Madrid a score of the worst characters. Tomorrow I intend to hang here seven notorious for their excesses. They have been severely

*Napoleon I, Emperor of the French (1856), *The Confidential Correspondence of Napoleon Bonaparte with his Brother Joseph*, Vol. II, New York: D. Appleton and Company, pp. 13, 18, 28.

denounced to me by respectable people whom their existence disturbed, and who will recover their spirits if they are got rid of. If Madrid is not delivered from at least 100 of these firebrands, you will be able to do nothing. Out of this 100, hang or shoot 12 or 15, and send the rest to France to the galleys. I had no peace in France, I could not restore confidence to the respectable portion of the community, until I had arrested 200 firebrand assassins of September, and sent them to the colonies. From that time the spirit of the capital changed as if by the waving of a wand.

Questions

1. What does the above correspondence reveal about the nature of Napoleonic rule in Spain?
2. How does Napoleon propose to deal with resistance to French rule there?
3. Do these letters seem to be exceptional or characteristic of Napoleonic rule in general?

HENRI LA FAYETTE VILLAUME DUCOUDRAY-HOLSTEIN, *MEMOIRS OF SIMÓN BOLÍVAR*, INTRODUCTION

Henri La Fayette Villaume Ducoudray-Holstein (1772–1839) was born in Prussia, but he served as an officer in Napoleon's army before fleeing to South America to serve under Simón Bolívar. Bolívar had emerged as a national hero throughout northern South America for leading the fight for independence, first in his native Venezuela and then in Ecuador, Colombia, and Bolivia. Like Napoleon, however, his blend of republican ideals and personal ambition led to opposition, and not just from former royalists. In his personal recollections, Ducoudray-Holstein does not paint a particularly flattering portrait of the general, while at the same time attempting to account for his success and the extent of his popularity throughout the region. Bolívar had a radical vision for the future of the continent, one that included the participation of both African-Americans and Indians who had suffered under centuries of Spanish rule. But because noble landowners who wanted freedom from Spain did not necessarily want social reform or land redistribution, some kind of a military dictatorship was likely going to be necessary in order to accomplish his vision. Nonetheless, the picture we get here is one of a choice between the lesser of two evils.

Henri La Fayette Villaume Ducoudray-Holstein,
*Memoirs of Simón Bolívar**

But how is it possible (the questions naturally arise) that general Bolívar should have liberated his country, and preserved in himself the supreme power, without superior talents?

If by "liberating the country" it is meant that he has given his country a free government, I answer, that he has not done so; and this question, I think, is thus fairly disposed of. If it be meant, that he has driven out the Spaniards, I answer, that he has done little, or nothing, towards this; far less, certainly, than the meanest of the subordinate chieftains. To the question, how can he have retained his power, without superior talents? I answer, in the first place, that the *reputation* of superior talents, goes a great ways. But I shall not desire the reader to be satisfied with this answer.

Before the revolution of Caracas April 19th 1810, and ever since that time, the Spaniards themselves have constantly and powerfully contributed to assist the patriots in all their enterprises; by forcing the inhabitants to withdraw themselves from an onerous and base submission; by leaving them no other alternative but to resist oppression, cruelty and death, by force of arms, or submit to them. Without any disposition to disparage the bravery, the constancy of the Colombian people, I say that the policy, and the whole behavior of the Spanish chieftains, during the war on Main, has operated powerfully toward the freedom and independence of the people. It has been a stimulus supplied with very little respite. Their obstinacy, their hypocrisy, their barbarous cruelties, their entire want of moderation, of even the semblance of liberal policy, of talents, and of courage, have contributed efficaciously to alienate them from the confidence and favorable opinion of the people. These inhabitants naturally chose to be under the dominion of their native chieftains, rather than to perish under the cruelties and vexations of the Spaniards. If these latter had adopted a liberal system for administering the provinces of Venezuela and New Granada, as soon as the Americans perceived the precarious situation of the mother country, I venture to boldly pronounce, that none of them would have thought of separating from Spain. This opinion is supported by the well-known fact, that not one of the patriotic juntas in 1810, had dreamed of detaching itself from the adored King Ferdinand. The stupid management of the Spanish authorities has facilitated all the operations of the patriots. The grievous faults of Bolívar, and some of his generals, have been exceeded by

---

*Henri La Fayette Villaume Ducoudray-Holstein (1829), *Memoirs of Simón Bolívar*, Boston: S.G. Goodrich and Company, pp. 335–36. Available online at http://archive.org/stream/memoirssimonbol00holsgoog#page/n11/mode/2up.

those of his adversaries. It is not strange, therefore, that Bolívar should have been able to do all he has done with very limited talents.

It has been said, long since, that oppression cannot be exercised upon any people beyond a certain point; that passing this point certainly produces resistance and, at last, revolt and revolution. The territory of Colombia has a vast extent of coast. It was impossible that it should be guarded by the Spanish troops that were sent out. Bolívar, when beaten and driven from one place, had only to go to another. The advantage in point of numbers, was vastly against the Spaniards. Their greatest number of troops never exceeded twenty thousand; whereas, on the part of the patriots, there was a great majority of people in the country containing about two millions of souls. Guixora's revolution in favor of the constitution of 1812, occupied Spain at home and prevented her sending powerful aid to Morillo. The Spaniards generally, and Morillo among the rest, became tired and worn out; their troops deserted by hundreds. If Morillo had sought to aid Bolívar, he could not have done it more effectually than by appointing La Torre his successor; for the drooping and sickly state of the Spaniards at that time, La Torre was but a poor physician. A powerful moral cause stood also in aid of Bolívar; I mean public opinion, which, if not unanimously in his favor, was certainly so against the cruel deeds of the Spaniards; and the Colombians, in their choice between two evils, very naturally took that which appeared to be the least.

Questions
1. What is the main reason that the author provides here for the success of Simón Bolívar in his efforts to liberate South America from Spanish rule?
2. Is this interpretation too biased to be taken as historically accurate? What might account for the biases of the author?
3. When the biases of the author are taken into account, does this passage still contribute to an understanding of the independence movement in South America? What other historical factors might have accounted for the success of Bolívar beyond those mentioned here?

ALEXIS DE TOCQUEVILLE, *DEMOCRACY IN AMERICA*, INTRODUCTION

In 1831 Tocqueville and his companion, Gustave de Beaumont, began their travels in the United States where they visited almost every state, as well as

Michigan, West Virginia, and Wisconsin, which were not yet states. Tocqueville came from an aristocratic background, but he took up a practical career as a lawyer and possessed a strong interest in history and politics. Living in a rapidly changing world, he believed that democracy might represent the wave of the political future and that it behooved Europeans to learn from the American example. In the passage, below, from his famous book, Democracy in America, *he provides a handy summary of the strengths and weaknesses of democracy when compared with aristocratic-led governments.*

Alexis de Tocqueville, *Democracy in America**

THE defects and weaknesses of a democratic government may readily be discovered; they can be proved by obvious facts, whereas their healthy influence becomes evident in ways which are not obvious and are, so to speak, hidden. A glance suffices to detect its faults, but its good qualities can be discerned only by long observation. The laws of the American democracy are frequently defective or incomplete; they sometimes attack vested rights, or sanction others which are dangerous to the community; and even if they were good, their frequency would still be a great evil. How comes it, then, that the American republics prosper and continue?

In the consideration of laws a distinction must be carefully observed between the end at which they aim and the means by which they pursue that end; between their absolute and their relative excellence. If it be the intention of the legislator to favor the interests of the minority at the expense of the majority, and if the measures he takes are so combined as to accomplish the object he has in view with the least possible expense of time and exertion, the law may be well drawn up although its purpose is bad; and the more efficacious it is, the more dangerous it will be.

Democratic laws generally tend to promote the welfare of the greatest possible number; for they emanate from the majority of the citizens, who are subject to error, but who cannot have an interest opposed to their own advantage. The laws of an aristocracy tend, on the contrary, to concentrate wealth and power in the hands of the minority; because an aristocracy, by its very nature, constitutes a minority. It may therefore be asserted, as a general proposition, that the purpose of a democracy in its legislation is more useful to humanity than that of an aristocracy. This, however, is the sum total of its advantages.

Aristocracies are infinitely more expert in the science of legislation than democracies ever can be. They are possessed of a self-control that protects them from the errors of temporary excitement; and they form far-reaching designs, which they know how to mature till a favorable opportunity arrives.

---

*http://xroads.virginia.edu/~Hyper/DETOC/1_ch14.htm.

Aristocratic government proceeds with the dexterity of art; it understands how to make the collective force of all its laws converge at the same time to a given point. Such is not the case with democracies, whose laws are almost always ineffective or inopportune. The means of democracy are therefore more imperfect than those of aristocracy, and the measures that it unwittingly adopts are frequently opposed to its own cause; but the object it has in view is more useful.

Questions

1. What are the main advantages and disadvantages of a democracy, according to Tocqueville?
2. Why might it take longer to observe the good qualities of a democracy than the negative ones?
3. Based on the above passage, does Tocqueville seem to favor democratic or aristocratic government? On what basis?

Chapter Questions

1. What do the collective sources in this chapter reveal about the relationship between democracy and authority in the late eighteenth and early nineteenth centuries?
2. What conflicting impressions are created by reading the above sources in tandem? Do they contribute to an understanding of why the developments to which they relate have been so controversial historically?
3. How had the standards for assessing the legitimacy of political authority changed during this period?

CHAPTER THREE

The Industrial Revolution: Reaction and Ideology

INTRODUCTION

The Industrial Revolution, which had originated in Britain during the eighteenth century, overlapped with the French Revolution in bringing about dramatic changes to European life and society during the nineteenth century. As the population expanded throughout this period, more workers became available to staff the workshops and factories whose products were now carried around the globe by European merchants. The growing population of Britain and Europe also increased demand for textiles and everyday household items. In order to take advantage of this demand, British entrepreneurs borrowed money at low interest rates and established factories that concentrated workers under a single roof where all aspects of production could be supervised and controlled. The result was not just a new type of work environment, but a new society in which workers were viewed as economic commodities and deemed expendable because other workers, including women and children, were capable of working the new machines that had dramatically expanded productive capacities.

The sources in this chapter largely deal with some of the reactions to the Industrial Revolution and the new kind of society that it produced. By the end of the eighteenth century, people had started to observe the impact of industrialization on society as a whole and became concerned about its overall effects on the human condition itself. In Britain, these changes were most evident in Northern England and the south of Scotland, where the abundance of coal and iron made the region a desirable location for the construction of factories close to the natural resources upon which they relied. Southern England possessed factories, too, while much of the North remained rural or untamed land, but the northern industrial cities that either arose or whose populations greatly expanded became strongly associated with industrialization and the changes it brought. Robert Owen (1771–1858) was a factory owner who attempted to convert his mill at New Lanark, Scotland, into a model that would negate the worst abuses of industrial capitalism. Friedrich Engels (1820–95) was the son of a German industrialist who co-owned a factory in Manchester. His experience at his father's factory led him to write his treatise exposing *The Condition of the English Working Class* in 1844, just a few years prior to his collaboration with the German socialist Karl Marx on their influential *Communist Manifesto*. Elizabeth Gaskell (1810–65) was born in London, but she married and moved to Manchester, where she witnessed firsthand the effects of the changes occurring around her in that northern town that led her to contrast them with a competing vision of society based on her experience in the south in novels such as *North and South* (1855).

Despite all of the criticisms of the Industrial Revolution and its social consequences, its proponents, including the factory owners themselves, defended it as the only basis for progress and prosperity. Despite the agricultural revolution of the eighteenth century that supported the larger population, it is clear that there were not sufficient jobs in agriculture (though these increased too) in order to provide for the growing numbers of workers. While some traditional workers, particularly those known as Luddites, did blame the new machines for the loss of their livelihood, most industrial workers knew that they depended on the factories. They did not want to destroy them, but merely wanted higher pay, healthier and safer working conditions, reasonable hours, and to be treated with a certain amount of dignity and respect. Marx and Engels did not demand the end of the factory-system, only the transference of its ownership from the capitalist bourgeois class to the proletariat, or working class. Elizabeth Gaskell's Mr. Thornton is an eloquent and persuasive spokesperson for the North and its economic values in *North and South*.

But none of this meant that the critics did not have valid points that at least had the potential to put a check on the unbridled embrace of technology and the exploitation of nature. The new cities exhibited protruding smokestacks belching out polluted air that made it difficult to breathe and colored the entire atmosphere around them a dreary gray. Workers seemed to exist to serve the machines, of which they practically became a part. Women and children as young as five or six years old were exploited and paid far less than would have been given to males doing the same job, while being shut indoors for as many as sixteen hours a day, six days a week. Romantic poets such as William Blake, William Wordsworth, Samuel Taylor Coleridge, and Lord Byron did not provide a monolithic response to industrialization, but they all reacted to it in thoughtful and imaginative ways. In addition, Mary Shelley's *Frankenstein* (1818) still represents the almost definitive cautionary tale about an amoral preoccupation with science, technology, knowledge, and the manipulation of nature run amuck.

Finally, the Industrial Revolution in England thrived largely on the cotton mills of Lancashire and the North that depended heavily on the supplies of cotton cultivated by African-American slaves in the American South. In this sense, while Britain had ended its participation in the slave trade in 1807 and abolished slavery throughout the British Empire in 1833, in America slaves were as much the victims of the Industrial Revolution, and the preoccupation with progress and profits that accompanied it, as the worst abused factory workers in Britain. Some would have said more so. These included Fanny Kemble (1809–93), a British actress and writer who spent several years married to a southern plantation owner and provided a firsthand account based on her observations on American slavery. Kemble rejected the comparison between American slaves and British factory workers, frequently made by slave owners who argued that their slaves were better off than British workers and that the British no right to chastise them regarding slavery, and argued that those who made it were deluding themselves. The chapter concludes with excerpts from her journal on this subject.

ROBERT OWEN, *THE BOOK OF THE NEW MORAL WORLD*, INTRODUCTION

Robert Owen is significant in history not primarily for his attempt to reform the conditions of life and work for his employees at his model mill in New Lanark, as commendable and well-intentioned as these efforts might have been. He is more significant as one of the leading "utopian socialists," along with the French reformers Claude Henrí de Rouvroy, the comte de Saint-Simon (1760–1825) and Charles Fourier (1772–1837), who proposed a wholly different, idealistic society as an alternative to that which had developed in Europe. Owen provided education for the children of his workers and tried to create a sense of community among them, but he soon lost patience with such piecemeal measures. In his introduction to The Book of the New Moral World, *he attempts to explain why a total reorientation of society is necessary to make life more fair, just, and meaningful for all of its members. Owen attempted to put his ideas into practice, first in Scotland, and then in the utopian community of New Harmony, Indiana.*

Robert Owen, *The Book of the New Moral World**

. . . the present classification of society will be not only useless, but it will be discovered to be unjust and productive of every kind of evil; necessarily destructive of sincerity, honesty, and of all the finest feelings, and most valuable sympathies of our nature. This artificial and most injurious classification will be superseded by one derived immediately from nature,—one that shall insure sincerity and honesty; that shall cultivate, foster, and encourage the finest feelings, the best sympathies, and continually calling into action the higher qualities of our nature, and that shall insure to everyone the full amount of happiness that his original constitution, under the most favorable circumstances, shall be capable of receiving. These effects can be obtained, only, by a natural classification into employments according to age and capacity. All, at the same

---

*Robert Owen (1840), *The Book of the New Moral World Containing the Rational System of Society, Founded on Demonstrable Facts, Developing the Constitution and Laws of Human Nature and Society*, Glasgow: H. Robinson and Co., pp. xiv–xv.

period of life, will pursue the same general occupations, for the public benefit, for which all, by their superior training and education, will be made more than competent; and all will have a large portion of each day to employ, according to their peculiar capacities and individual inclinations, without interfering with the happiness of others.

By these arrangements, and this classification, all will become superior, physically, intellectually, and morally; each will know all the duties of life, and will have the greatest desire to execute them in the best manner. In this classification, however, none will be trained to teach incongruities or mysteries, which must derange the mental faculties and disorder of all the transactions of mankind—none will be engaged in devising or administering laws in opposition to the laws of nature; or, in adjudging artificial rewards and punishments to counteract those of nature, which are all wise and efficient. It will be obvious, even to children, thus rationally educated, that all human laws must be either unnecessary, or in opposition to Nature's laws, that they must create disunion, produce crime incessantly, and involve all transactions in inextricable confusion. None will be trained in idleness and uselessness to waste extravagantly the productions of others, to which no just law can give them a shadow of right or title; and no unjust law will be admitted into the code of the NEW MORAL WORLD. None will be trained and set apart to attack, plunder, and murder their fellow-men; this conduct will be known to be irrational, and the very essence of wickedness; nor yet, will any be trained to bargain with, or even to attempt to take advantage of another, or to desire individual privileges or distinctions of any kind. The individual who is trained to buy cheap, sell dear, and seek for individual benefits above his fellows, is thereby degraded—is unfitted to acquire superior qualities—is deprived of the finest feelings of our nature, and rendered totally incompetent to experience the highest enjoyments of human existence. Nor will any be permitted, by society, to be trained in an *inferior manner*, or for *inferior purposes*;—but all will have the original powers and faculties of their nature directed and cultivated, in such a manner, as shall make it unavoidable, that each shall become, at maturity, superior in mind, manner, and conduct.

In this NEW WORLD, the sympathies of human nature will be rightly directed from infancy, and will engender a spirit of benevolence, confidence, and affection, which will pervade mankind.

The impurities of the present system, arising from human laws opposed to nature's laws, will be unknown. The immense mass or degradation of character, and of heart-rending suffering, experienced by both sexes, but especially by women, will be altogether prevented—and the characters of all women will, by a superior, yet natural training, be elevated to become lovely, good, and intellectual. Of this state of purity and felicity few of the present generation have been trained to form any correct or rational conception.

Questions

1. Are Owen's ideas an extension of the ideas of the Enlightenment or a departure from them?
2. What are some similarities and differences between the ideas expressed here and those expressed in the passages by Jean-Jacques Rousseau and Mary Wollstonecraft in the previous chapter?
3. What does Owen indicate is most necessary to create a better, more moral society? Is he totally unrealistic in his approach to social reform?

FRIEDRICH ENGELS, *THE CONDITION OF THE WORKING CLASS IN ENGLAND*, AND KARL MARX AND FRIEDRICH ENGELS, *THE COMMUNIST MANIFESTO*, INTRODUCTION

Friedrich Engels and his even more famous collaborator Karl Marx have long been tainted by their association with a communist ideology that in its twentieth-century manifestation has been associated with tyranny, totalitarianism, and an attack on the soul of humanity. For a proper historical understanding of their work and ideas, it is necessary to rescue them from these associations and to restore them to their original historical context. Marx and Engels set out to liberate human beings, not to enslave them. They responded to the conditions of their own age, but went beyond social criticism or the construction of pie-in-the-sky solutions such as those of the utopian socialists to advocate actual historical change, which at the time they believed could only be accomplished by revolution. They were not alone in this, as the Revolutions of 1848 that almost perfectly coincided with the publication of the Communist Manifesto, *would demonstrate; by no means were all of the revolutionaries of 1848 communists. The timing of the publication of their manifesto was no coincidence; the Communist League had asked Marx and Engels to finish their project earlier than expected once revolution had broken out in Naples and Sicily that January. Their works combined Engels's practical knowledge and experience, as evidenced in* The Condition of the Working Class in England *with Marx's philosophical concern with the human alienation that attended factory work, which can be seen in many of his writings, including the excerpt from* The Communist Manifesto *that appears below.*

Friedrich Engels, *The Condition of the Working Class in England**

If we briefly formulate the result of our wanderings, we must admit that 350,000 working-people of Manchester and its environs live, almost all of them, in wretched, damp, filthy cottages, that the streets which surround them are usually in the most miserable and filthy condition, laid out without the slightest reference to ventilation, with reference solely to the profit secured by the contractor. In a word, we must confess that in the working-men's dwellings of Manchester, no cleanliness, no convenience, and consequently no comfortable family life is possible; that in such dwellings only a physically degenerate race, robbed of all humanity, degraded, reduced morally and physically to bestiality, could feel comfortable and at home. . . .

. . . We must add that many families, who had but one room for themselves, receive boarders and lodgers in it, that such lodgers of both sexes by no means rarely sleep in the same bed with the married couple; and that the single case of a man and his wife and his adult sister-in-law sleeping in one bed was found, according to the "Report on the Sanitary Condition of the Labouring Population," six times repeated in Manchester. Common lodging-houses, too, are very numerous; Dr. Kay gives their number in 1831 as 267 in Manchester proper, and they must have increased greatly since then. Each of these receives from twenty to thirty guests, so that they shelter all told, nightly, from five to seven thousand human beings. The character of the houses and their guests is the same as in other cities. Five to seven beds in each room lie on the floor— without bedsteads, and on these sleep, mixed indiscriminately, as many persons as apply. What physical and moral atmosphere reigns in these holes I need not state. Each of these houses is a focus of crime, the scene of deeds against which human nature revolts, which would perhaps never have been executed but for this forced centralisation of vice. Gaskell gives the number of persons living in cellars in Manchester proper as 20,000. . . .

The whole clothing of the working-class, even assuming it to be in good condition, is little adapted to the climate. The damp air of England, with its sudden changes of temperature, more calculated than any other to give rise to colds, obliges almost the whole middle-class to wear flannel next to the skin, about the body, and flannel scarfs and shirts are in almost universal use. Not only is the working-class deprived of this precaution, it is scarcely ever in a position to use a thread of woollen clothing; and the heavy cotton goods, though thicker, stiffer, and heavier than woollen clothes, afford much less protection against cold and wet, remain damp much longer because of

---

*http://www.marxists.org/archive/marx/works/1845/condition-working-class/ch04.htm

their thickness and the nature of the stuff, and have nothing of the compact density of fulled woollen cloths. And, if a working-man once buys himself a woollen coat for Sunday, he must get it from one of the "cheap shops" where he finds bad, so-called "Devil's-dust" cloth, manufactured for sale and not for use, and liable to tear or grow threadbare in a fortnight, or he must buy of an old clothes'-dealer a half-worn coat which has seen its best days, and lasts but a few weeks. Moreover, the working-man's clothing is, in most cases, in bad condition, and there is the oft-recurring necessity for placing the best pieces in the pawnbroker's shop. But among very large numbers, especially among the Irish, the prevailing clothing consists of perfect rags often beyond all mending, or so patched that the original colour can no longer be detected. Yet the English and Anglo-Irish go on patching, and have carried this art to a remarkable pitch, putting wool or bagging on fustian, or the reverse—it's all the same to them. But the true, transplanted Irish hardly ever patch except in the extremest necessity, when the garment would otherwise fall apart. Ordinarily the rags of the shirt protrude through the rents in the coat or trousers. . . .

As with clothing, so with food. The workers get what is too bad for the property-holding class. In the great towns of England everything may be had of the best, but it costs money; and the workman, who must keep house on a couple of pence, cannot afford much expense. Moreover, he usually receives his wages on Saturday evening, for, although a beginning has been made in the payment of wages on Friday, this excellent arrangement is by no means universal; and so he comes to market at five or even seven o'clock, while the buyers of the middle-class have had the first choice during the morning, when the market teems with the best of everything. But when the workers reach it, the best has vanished, and, if it was still there, they would probably not be able to buy it. The potatoes which the workers buy are usually poor, the vegetables wilted, the cheese old and of poor quality, the bacon rancid, the meat lean, tough, taken from old, often diseased, cattle, or such as have died a natural death, and not fresh even then, often half decayed. . . .

Karl Marx and Friedrich Engels, *The Communist Manifesto**

. . . Modern bourgeois society with its relations of production, of exchange and of property, a society that has conjured up such gigantic means of production and of exchange, is like the sorcerer, who is no longer able to control the powers of the nether world whom he has called up by his spells. For many a decade past

---

*Karl Marx and Friedrich Engels, *Manifesto of the Communist Party* in Robert C. Tucker, ed. (1978), *The Marx-Engels Reader*, New York: W.W. Norton and Company, pp. 469–500, excerpts from pp. 478–79.

the history of industry and commerce is but the history of the revolt of modern productive forces against the modern conditions of production, against the property relations that are the condition for the existence of the bourgeoisie and of its rule. It is enough to mention the commercial crises that by their periodical return put on its trial, each time more threateningly, the existence of the entire bourgeois society. . . . Society suddenly finds itself put back into a state of momentary barbarism; it appears as if a famine, a universal war of devastation had cut off the supply of every means of subsistence; industry and commerce seem to be destroyed; and why? Because there is too much civilization, too much means of subsistence, too much industry, too much commerce. The productive forces at the disposal of society no longer tend to further the development of the conditions of bourgeois property; on the contrary, they have become too powerful for these conditions, by which they are fettered, and so soon as they overcome these fetters, they bring disorder into the whole of bourgeois society, endanger the existence of bourgeois property. The conditions of bourgeois society are too narrow to comprise the wealth created by them. And how does the bourgeois get over these crises? On the one hand by enforced destruction of a mass of productive forces; on the other, by the conquest of new markets, and by the more thorough exploitation of the old ones. That is to say. By paving the way for more extensive and more destructive crises, and by diminishing the means whereby crises are prevented.

The weapons with which the bourgeoisie felled feudalism to the ground are now turned against the bourgeoisie itself.

But not only has the bourgeoisie forged the weapons that bring death to itself; it has also called into existence the men who are to wield those weapons—the modern working class—the proletarians. . . .

Owing to the extensive use of machinery and to the division of labor, the work of the proletarians has lost all individual character, and consequently, all charm for the workman. He becomes an appendage of the machine, and it is only the most simple, most monotonous, and most easily acquired knack, that is required of him. Hence, the cost of production of a workman is restricted, almost entirely, to the means of subsistence that he requires for his maintenance, and for the propagation of his race. But the price of a commodity, and therefore also of labor, is equal to its cost of production. In proportion, therefore, as the repulsiveness of the work increases, the wage decreases. Nay more, in proportion as the use of machinery and division of labor increases, in the same proportion the burden of toil also increases, whether by prolongation of the working hours, by increase of the work exacted in a given time or by increased speed of the machinery, etc.

Modern industry has thus converted the little workshop of the patriarchal master into the great factory of the industrial capitalist. Masses of laborers, crowded into the factory, are organized like soldiers. As privates of the industrial army they are placed under the command of a perfect hierarchy of officers and sergeants. Not only are they slaves of the bourgeois class, and of the bourgeois State; they are daily and hourly enslaved by the machine, by the over-looker, and above all, by the individual bourgeois manufacturer himself. The more openly this despotism proclaims gain to be its end and aim, the more petty, the more hateful and the more embittering it is.

The less the skill and exertion of strength implied in manual labor, in other words, the more modern industry becomes developed, the more is the labor of men superseded by that of women. Differences of age and sex have no longer any distinctive social validity for the working class. All are instruments of labor, more or less expensive to use, according to their age and sex.

Questions

1. In the first passage by Engels, what are the main problems faced by the working class in Manchester in the mid-1840s? How would his readers have likely responded to such a description of the working and living conditions of the workers?
2. How does the information provided by Engels in *The Condition of the English Working Class* inform and influence the ideas put forth in *The Communist Manifesto*? In other words, what is the relationship between these two works?
3. What are the main problems with bourgeois capitalism according to Marx and Engels? Are any of their points still relevant?

This painting, by the French painter Eugène Delacroix (1798–1863), has become one of the most famous images from nineteenth-century art, at least prior to the works of the impressionists later in the century. In 1830, a revolution in France resulted in the overthrow of the last Bourbon king to rule France, Charles X (r. 1824–30). In 1831, the new government, headed by King Louis Philippe, who came from the Orleans branch of the royal family, purchased this painting to honor the revolution and give legitimacy to the new regime as representative of the French people. This was consistent with Louis Philippe referring to himself as "king of the French" instead of "king of France."

Questions

1. Is this painting meant to be a realistic portrayal of revolution or a symbolic justification for it?
2. How would you describe the style in which it is painted? How does the style relate to your answer to question #1?

FIGURE 3: Eugène Delacroix, *Liberty Leading the People,* 1834. Courtesy of Getty Images.

3. Is this a work of propaganda or does it represent a genuine commitment to the liberty and the rights of the people? Can a conservative regime appropriate revolutionary concepts and symbolism for its own purposes?

ELIZABETH GASKELL, *NORTH AND SOUTH,* INTRODUCTION

Elizabeth Gaskell and her contemporary literary critics of industrial society, such as Charles Dickens, approached their subjects from a humanistic rather than the theoretical perspective of Marx and Engels. Gaskell had already published several novels, including Mary Barton *(1848),* Cranford *(1853), and* Ruth *(1853), before she wrote* North and South *in 1854–5. Her novel* North and South *has frequently been compared to Dickens's novel* Hard Times, *written a few years earlier, which also creates a fictional northern industrial city and exposes, in a far more satirical way, the hypocrisy and inflated self-importance of the mill owners. Indeed, Dickens's Coketown and Gaskell's Milton bear many similarities. However, Gaskell's mill owner, Mr. Thornton, in contradistinction to Dickens's Josiah Bounderby, is not a stock character and his arguments are taken rather more seriously by Gaskell. Nonetheless, Gaskell still juxtaposes Thornton's "Northern" perspective with Margaret's "Southern" one, including in the dialogues contained in the excerpts taken from her novel that appear below.*

Elizabeth Gaskell, *North and South**

For several miles before they reached Milton, they saw a deep lead-colored cloud hanging over the horizon in the direction in which it lay. It was all the darker from contrast with the pale gray-blue of the wintry sky; for in Heston there had been the earliest signs of frost. Nearer to the town, the air had a faint taste and smell of smoke; perhaps, after all, more a loss of the fragrance of grass and herbage than any positive taste or smell. Quick they were whirled over long, straight, hopeless streets of regularly-built houses, all small and of brick. Here and there a great oblong many-windowed factory stoop up, like a hen among her chickens, puffing out black "unparliamentary" smoke, and sufficiently accounting for the cloud which Margaret had taken to foretell rain. As they drove through the larger and wider streets, from the station to the hotel, they had to stop constantly; great loaded lurries blocked up the not over-wide thoroughfares. Margaret had now and then been into the city in her drives with her aunt. But there the heavy lumbering vehicles seemed various in their purposes and intent; here every van, every wagon and truck, bore cotton, either in raw shape in bags, or the woven shape in bales of calico. People thronged the footpaths, most of them well-dressed as regarded the material, but with a slovenly looseness which struck Margaret as different from the shabby, threadbare smartness of a similar class in London. . . .

After a quiet life in a country parsonage for more than twenty years, there was something dazzling to Mr. Hale [Margaret's father] in the energy which conquered immense difficulties with ease; the power of the machinery of Milton, the power of the men of Milton, impressed him with a sense of grandeur, which he yielded to without caring to inquire into the details of its exercise. But Margaret went less abroad, among machinery and men; saw less of power in its public effect, and, as it happened, she was thrown with one or two of those who, in all measures affecting masses of people, must be acute sufferers for the good of many. The question always is, has everything been done to make the sufferings of these exceptions as small as possible? Or, in the triumph of the crowded procession, have the helpless been trampled on, instead of being gently lifted aside out of the roadway of the conqueror, whom they have no power to accompany on his march?

[Mr. Thornton speaking] . . . "I won't deny that I am proud of belonging to a town—or perhaps I should rather say a district—the necessities of which give birth to such grandeur of conception. I would rather be a man toiling, suffering—nay, failing and successless—here, than lead a dull prosperous life in the old worn grooves of what you call more aristocratic society down in the

---

*Elizabeth Gaskell (1973; first published 1855), *North and South*, Oxford: Oxford University Press, pp. 59, 69, 81, 85.

South, with their slow days of careless ease. One may be clogged with honey and unable to rise and fly."

"You are mistaken," said Margaret, roused by the aspersion on her beloved South to a fond vehemence of defense, that brought the color into her cheeks and the angry tears to her eyes. "You do not know anything about the South. If there is less adventure or less progress—I suppose I must not say less excitement—from the gambling spirit of trade, which seems requisite to force out these wonderful inventions, there is less suffering also. I see men here going about in the streets who look ground down by some pinching sorrow or care— who are not only sufferers but haters. Now, in the South we have our poor, but there is not that terrible expression in their countenances of a sullen sense of injustice which I see here." . . .

[Mr. Thornton speaking] . . . "Sixteen years ago, my father died under very miserable circumstances. I was taken from school, and had to become a man (as well as I could) in a few days. I had such a mother as few are blest with; a woman of strong power, and firm resolve. We went into a small country town, where living was cheaper than in Milton, and where I got employment in a draper's shop (a capital place, by the way, for obtaining a knowledge of goods). Week by week our income came to fifteen shillings, out of which three people had to be kept. My mother managed so that I put by three out of these fifteen shillings regularly. This made the beginning; this taught me self-denial. Now that I am able to afford my mother such comforts as her age, rather than her own wish, requires, I thank her silently on each occasion for the early training she gave me. Now when I feel that in my own case it is not good luck, nor merit, nor talent,—but simply the habits of life which taught me to despise indulgences not thoroughly earned,—indeed, never to think twice about them,—I believe that this suffering, which Miss Hale says is impressed on the countenances of the people of Milton, is but the natural punishment of dishonestly-enjoyed pleasure, at some former period of their lives,. I do not look on self-indulgent, sensual people as worthy of my hatred; I simply look upon them with contempt for their poorness of character."

Questions

1. What are the main arguments given by Thornton and Margaret here in defense of the North and the South respectively? Does Gaskell make one side more persuasive than the other or does she objectively present both viewpoints?
2. *North and South* was written about ten years after Engels's description of the working classes of Manchester. Is there any indication that conditions have changed during that time?

3. How significant is it that Gaskell chose a woman to represent the southern perspective and a man the northern? Are women more naturally inclined to be social reformers and men to promote the interests of business and industry?

SELECTED POEMS OF WILLIAM BLAKE, WILLIAM WORDSWORTH, SAMUEL TAYLOR COLERIDGE, AND GEORGE GORDON, LORD BYRON, INTRODUCTION

Although Germany also possesses strong associations with Romanticism, insofar as Romanticism represented a reaction not just to the Enlightenment but also to the Industrial Revolution, it is natural, and perhaps inevitable, that the leading Romantic poets of the late eighteenth and early nineteenth centuries would be English. William Wordsworth, for example, had initially been supportive of the French Revolution—enthusiastically so—but became one of the leading critics of the Industrial Revolution. Both he and Samuel Taylor Coleridge attempted to make human beings once again comfortable with nature. Unlike some of his fellow poets, William Blake was not an unbridled critic of industrialization. But he abhorred a materialistic approach to life and any philosophy that reduced human beings to an economic entity. He sought to preserve the freedom of the imagination and wrote poems on a wide range of subjects, in addition to being a painter and an engraver. The romantic poets may have been fighting a futile rearguard action against the inevitable march of progress, but their times were enhanced and characterized as much by their vision as they were by the changes to which they were reacting.

William Blake, "The Chimney Sweeper"*

When my mother died I was very young,
And my Father sold me while yet my tongue
Could scarcely cry "'weep! 'weep! 'weep! 'weep!"
So your chimneys I sweep and in soot I sleep.

There's little Tom Dacre, who cried when his head,
That curled like a lamb's back, was shaved: so I said,

---

*Richard Abcarian and Marvin Klotz, eds (1973), *Literature: The Human Experience*, New York: St. Martin's Press, p. 79.

"Hush, Tom! never mind it, for when your head's bare
You know that the soot cannot spoil your white hair."

And so he was quiet and that very night
As Tom was a-sleeping, he had such a sight!
That thousands of sweepers, Dick, Joe, Ned, and Jack,
Were all of them locked up in coffins of black.

And by came an Angel who had a bright key,
And he opened the coffins and set them all free;
Then down a green plain leaping, laughing, they run,
And wash in a river, and shine in the Sun.

Then naked and white, all their bags left behind,
They rise upon clouds and sport in the wind;
And the Angel told Tom, if he'd be a good boy,
He'd have God for his father, and never want joy.

And so Tom awoke; and we rose in the dark,
And got with our bags and our brushes to work.
Though the morning was cold, Tom was happy and warm;
So if all do their duty they need not fear harm.

William Wordsworth, "The World is Too Much With Us"*

The world is too much with us; late and soon,
Getting and spending, we lay waste our powers:
Little we see in Nature that is ours;
We have given our hearts away, a sordid boom!
This Sea that bares her bosom to the moon;
The winds that will be howling at all hours,
And are up-gathered now like sleeping flowers;
For this, for everything, we are out of tune;
It moves us not.—Great God! I'd rather be
A Pagan suckled in a creed outworn;
So might I, standing on this pleasant lea,
Have glimpses that would make me less forlorn;
Have sight of Proteus rising from the sea;
Or hear old Triton blow his wreathed horn.

*Oscar Williams, ed. (1963), *The Mentor Book of Major British Poets*, New York: Mentor Books, p. 68.

William Wordsworth, "Composed upon Westminster Bridge"*

Earth has not anything to show more fair;
Dull would he be of soul who could pass by
A sight so touching in its majesty;
This City now doth, like a garment, wear
The beauty of the morning; silent, bare,
Ships, towers, domes, theatres, and temples lie
Open unto the fields, and to the sky;
All bright and glittering in the smokeless air.
Never did sun more beautifully steep
In his first splendor, valley, rock, or hill;
Ne'er saw I, never felt, a calm so deep!
The river glideth at his own sweet will:
Dear God! the very houses seem asleep;
And all that mighty heart is lying still!

Samuel Taylor Coleridge, "Kubla Khan: Or, A Vision in a Dream"**

In Xanadu did Kubla Khan
A stately pleasure-dome decree:
Where Alph, the sacred river, ran
Through caverns measureless to man
    Down to a sunless sea.
So twice five miles of fertile ground
With walls and towers that were girdled round:
And there were gardens bright with sinuous rills,
Where blossomed many an incense-bearing tree;
And here were forests ancient as the hills,
Enfolding sunny spots of greenery.

But oh! that deep romantic chasm which slanted
Down the green hill athwart a cedarn cover!
A savage place! as holy and enchanged

---

*Oscar Williams, ed. (1963), *The Mentor Book of Major British Poets*, New York: Mentor Books, pp. 68–69.
**Oscar Williams, ed. (1963), *The Mentor Book of Major British Poets*, New York: Mentor Books, pp. 79–80.

As e'er beneath a waning moon was haunted
By woman wailing for her demon-lover!
And from this chasm, with ceaseless turmoil seething,
As if this earth in fast thick pants were breathing,
A mighty fountain momently was forced:
Amid whose swift half-intermitted burst
Huge fragments vaulted like rebounding hail,
Or chaffy grain beneath the thresher's flail:
And 'mid these dancing rocks at once and ever
It flung up momently the sacred river.
Five miles meandering with a mazy motion
Through wood and dale the sacred river ran,
Then reached the caverns measureless to man,
And sank in tumult to a lifeless ocean:
And 'mid this tumult Kubla heard from far
Ancestral voices prophesying war!
    The shadow of the dome of pleasure
    Floated midway on the waves;
    Where was heard the mingled measure
    From the fountain and the caves.
It was a miracle of rare device,
A sunny pleasure-dome with caves of ice!

    A damsel with a dulcimer
    In a vision once I saw:
    It was an Abyssinian maid,
    And on her dulcimer she played,
    Singing of Mount Abora.
    Could I revive within me
    Her symphony and song,
    To such a deep delight 'twould win me,
That with music loud and long,
I would build that dome in air,
That sunny dome! those caves of ice!
And all who heard should see them there,
And all should cry, Beware! Beware!
His flashing eyes, his floating hair!
Weave a circle round him thrice,
And close your eyes with holy dread,
For he on honey-dew hath fed,
And drunk the milk of Paradise.

George Gordon, Lord Byron, "The Ocean," from *Childe Harold's Pilgrimage*, Canto IV*

There is a pleasure in the pathless woods,
There is a rapture on the lonely shore,
There is a society, where none intrudes,
By the deep Sea, and music, in its roar:
I love not Man the less, but Nature more,
From these our interviews, in which I steal
From all I may be, or have been before,
To mingle with the Universe, and feel
What I can ne'er express, yet cannot all conceal.

Roll on, thou deep and dark blue Ocean—roll!
Ten thousand fleets sweep over thee in vain;
Man marks the earth with ruin—his control
Stops with the shore; upon the watery plain
The wrecks are all thy deed, nor doth remain
A shadow of man's ravage, save his own,
When, for a moment, like a drop of rain,
He sinks into thy depths with a bubbling groan,
Without a grave, unknelled, uncoffined, and unknown.

His steps are not upon thy paths,—thy fields
Are not a spoil for him,—thou dost arise
And shake him from thee; the vile strength he wields
For earth's destruction thou dost all despise,
Spurning him from thy bosom to the skies,
And sends'st him, shivering in thy playful spray
And howling, to his Gods, where haply lies
His petty hope in some near port or bay,
And dashest him again to earth:—there let him lay.

The armaments which thunderstrike the walls
Of rock-built cities, bidding nations quake,
And monarchs tremble in their capitals,
The oak leviathans, whose huge ribs make
Their clay creator the vain title take
Of lord of thee, and arbiter of war—
These are thy toys, and, as the snowy flake,

---

*Oscar Williams, ed. (1963), *The Mentor Book of Major British Poets*, New York: Mentor Books, pp. 133–34.

They melt into thy yeast of waves, which mar
Alike the Armada's pride or spoils of Trafalgar.

Thy shores are empires, changed in all save thee—
Assyria, Greece, Rome, Carthage, what are they?
Thy waters washed them power while they were free,
And many a tyrant since; their shores obey
The stranger, slave, or savage; their decay
Has dried up, realms to deserts:—not so thou;—
Unchangeable, save to thy wild waves' play,
Time writes no wrinkle on thine azure brow:
Such as creation's dawn beheld, thou rollest now.

Thou glorious mirror, where the Almighty's form
Glasses itself in tempests; in all time,—
Calm or convulsed, in breeze, or gale, or storm,
Icing the pole, or in the torrid clime
Dark-heaving—boundless, endless, and sublime,
The image of eternity, the throne
Of the Invisible; even from out thy slime
The monsters of the deep are made; each zone
Obeys thee; thou goest forth, dread, fathomless, alone.

And I have loved thee, Ocean! and my joy
Of youthful sports was on thy breast to be
Borne, like the bubbles, onward: from a boy
I wantoned with thy breakers—they to me
Were a delight; and if the freshening sea
Made them a terror—t'was a pleasing fear,
For I was as it were a child of thee,
And trusted to thy billows far and near,
And laid my hand upon thy mane—as I do here.

Questions

1. In "The Chimney Sweeper," what is Blake trying to say about the plight of
   the boys employed as chimney sweepers? Does he really expect them to be
   happy at their work? What imagery does he use to convey his message? Is
   the poem a microcosm for his larger attitudes toward industrialization?
2. How would you describe the attitude toward nature reflected in the poems
   here by Wordsworth, Coleridge, and Byron? In what ways does this represent a response to industrial society?

3. How do the two poems by Wordsworth differ from one another? In "The World is Too Much With Us" does he exaggerate his position in order to make a point? How are those attitudes tempered in the second selection?
4. Coleridge's poem "Kubla Khan" is based on a dream, but it creates a certain image of nature juxtaposed with human achievement. Is the poem merely meant to evoke a feeling or to put forth a certain world view? Which is the case with the other poems in this section?

MARY SHELLEY, *FRANKENSTEIN*, INTRODUCTION

Mary Shelley was the daughter of two famous parents, the writers William Godwin and Mary Wollstonecraft (see Chapter 2 of this volume). Mary Wollstonecraft, however, died shortly after giving birth to her daughter, leaving young Mary emotionally neglected. The early death of her mother surely must have played a role in her leaving home at the age of sixteen to be with a married man, the poet Percy Bysshe Shelley. She had, however, received a good education and received encouragement from her lover/husband to take up writing. Mary Shelley wrote Frankenstein *at the age of twenty-one as part of a competition among her literary social circle proposed by Lord Byron to see who could write the best "ghost story."* Frankenstein *was her first and most enduring novel, as well as an immediate literary sensation. It was only in the second edition published in 1823, however, that she was revealed as the author of the work, catching many reviewers off guard who had assumed that the novel had been written by a man. The novel is actually named for the doctor who brought to life a human being composed of the body parts of dead corpses rather than for the monster he created. The novel takes a tragic turn when Frankenstein rejects his own creation, who determines to enact revenge on his creator and his loved ones for being brought into the world without love. In the passages below, Dr. Frankenstein describes his thoughts immediately prior to and immediately after the consummation of his great experiment.*

Mary Shelley, *Frankenstein**

No human being could have passed a happier childhood than myself. My parents were possessed by the very spirit of kindness and indulgence. We felt

---

*Mary Shelley (1985; first published 1818), *Frankenstein*, London: Penguin, pp. 39, 42, 58–59.

that they were not the tyrants to rule our lot according to their caprice, but the agents and creators of all the many delights which we enjoyed. When I mingled with other families, I distinctly discerned how peculiarly fortunate my lot was, and gratitude assisted the development of filial love.

My temper was sometimes violent, and my passions vehement; but by some law in my temperature they were turned not towards childish pursuits but to an eager desire to learn, and not to learn all things indiscriminately. I confess that neither the structure of languages, nor the code of governments, nor the politics of various states possessed attractions for me. It was the secrets of heaven and earth that I desired to learn; and whether it was the outward substance of things, or the inner spirit of nature and the mysterious soul of man that occupied me, still my enquiries were directed to the metaphysical, or in its highest sense, the physical secrets of the world. . . .

. . . My father was not scientific, and I was left to struggle with a child's blindness, added to a student's thirst for knowledge. Under the guidance of my new preceptors, I entered with the greatest diligence into the search of the philosopher's stone and the elixir of life; but the latter soon obtained my undivided attention. Wealth was an inferior object; but what glory would attend the discovery, if I could banish disease from the human frame and render man invulnerable to anything but a violent death! . . .

It was on a dreary night of November, that I beheld the accomplishment of my toils. With an anxiety that almost amounted to agony, I collected the instruments of life around me, that I might infuse a spark of being into the lifeless thing that lay at my feet. It was already one in the morning; the rain pattered dismally against the panes, and my candle was nearly burnt out, when, by the glimmer of the half-extinguished light, I saw the dull yellow eye of the creature open; it breathed hard, and a convulsive motion agitated its limbs.

How can I describe my emotions at this catastrophe, or how delineate the wretch whom with such infinite pains and care I had endeavored to form? His limbs were in proportion, and I had selected his features as beautiful. Beautiful!—Great God! His yellow skin scarcely covered the work of muscles and arteries beneath; his hair was of a lustrous black, and flowing; his teeth of pearly whiteness; but these luxuriances only formed a more horrid contrast with his watery eyes, that seemed almost of the same color as the dun-white sockets in which they were set, his shriveled complexion and straight black lips.

The different accidents of life are not so changeable as the feelings of human nature. I had worked hard for nearly two years, for the sole purpose of infusing life into an inanimate body. For this I had deprived myself of rest and health. I had desired it with an ardor that far exceeded moderation; but now that I had finished, the beauty of the dream vanished, and breathless horror and disgust filled my heart. Unable to endure the aspect of the being I had created, I rushed out of the room, and continued a long time traversing my bedchamber, unable to compose my mind to sleep. . . .

Questions

1. What effect did his quest for knowledge and the creation of life through artificial means have on the personality and psyche of the doctor?
2. How did he feel once he brought his new creation to life?
3. Why might Mary Shelley have depicted the doctor and his emotions this way?

FANNY KEMBLE, *JOURNALS*, INTRODUCTION

Fanny Kemble rose to fame as an actress early in her life, best known for playing the role of Juliet in Shakespeare's Romeo and Juliet. *At the age of twenty-one she traveled with her father to America, where she met and married Pierce Mease Butler, whose Georgia plantations housed hundreds of slaves to grow the tobacco, rice, and cotton from which the family profited. The marriage lasted only until 1848, when she returned to England to resume her acting career. The journal, from which the following excerpt appears, although known to some abolitionists, was not published until the 1860s at the time of the American Civil War. It contains her reflections on slavery and reflects her personal experience living on a plantation in the American South during the late 1830s. Although there is some question about the accuracy of some of the specific information in her journals, the arguments below are not dependent on this and stand on their own as a view of slavery from someone who had lived on a slave plantation.*

Fanny Kemble, *Journals**

But I do not admit the comparison between your slaves and even the lowest class of European free laborers, for the former are allowed the exercise of no faculties but those which they enjoy in common with the brutes that perish. The just comparison is between the slaves and the useful animals to whose level your

---

*Fanny Kemble, *Journal of a Residence on a Georgian Plantation: 1838-1839*, http://www.gutenberg.org/catalog/world/readfile?fk_files=1484761&pageno=3.

laws reduce them; and I will acknowledge that the slaves of a kind owner may be as well cared for, and as happy, as the dogs and horses of a merciful master; but the latter condition—i.e. that of happiness—must again depend upon the complete perfection of their moral and mental degradation. Mr. ——, in his letter, maintains that they are an inferior race, and, compared with the whites, "animals, incapable of mental culture and moral improvement:" to this I can only reply, that if they are incapable of profiting by instruction, I do not see the necessity for laws inflicting heavy penalties on those who offer it to them. If they really are brutish, witless, dull, and devoid of capacity for progress, where lies the danger which is constantly insisted upon of offering them that of which they are incapable. We have no laws forbidding us to teach our dogs and horses as much as they can comprehend; nobody is fined or imprisoned for reasoning upon knowledge, and liberty, to the beasts of the field, for they are incapable of such truths. But these themes are forbidden to slaves, not because they cannot, but because they can and would seize on them with avidity—receive them gladly, comprehend them quickly; and the masters' power over them would be annihilated at once and for ever. But I have more frequently heard, not that they were incapable of receiving instruction, but something much nearer the truth—that knowledge only makes them miserable: the moment they are in any degree enlightened, they become unhappy. In the letter I return to you Mr. —— says that the very slightest amount of education, merely teaching them to read, "impairs their value as slaves, for it instantly destroys their contentedness, and since you do not contemplate changing their condition, it is surely doing them an ill service to destroy their acquiescence in it"; but this is a very different ground of argument from the other. The discontent they evince upon the mere dawn of an advance in intelligence proves not only that they can acquire but combine ideas, a process to which it is very difficult to assign a limit; and there indeed the whole question lies, and there and nowhere else the shoe really pinches. A slave is ignorant; he eats, drinks, sleeps, labors, and is happy. He learns to read; he feels, thinks, reflects, and becomes miserable. He discovers himself to be one of a debased and degraded race, deprived of the elementary rights which God has granted to all men alike; every action is controlled, every word noted; he may not stir beyond his appointed bounds, to the right hand or to the left, at his own will, but at the will of another he may be sent miles and miles of weary journeying—tethered, yoked, collared, and fettered—away from whatever he may know as home, severed from all those ties of blood and affection which he alone of all human, of all living creatures on the face of the earth may neither enjoy in peace nor defend when they are outraged. If he is well treated, if his master be tolerably humane or even understand his own interest tolerably, this is probably all he may have to endure: it is only to the consciousness of these evils that knowledge and reflection awaken him. But how is it if his master be severe, harsh, cruel—or even only careless—leaving his creatures to the delegated dominion of some overseer, or agent, whose love of power, or other evil dispositions, are checked by no considerations of personal interest? Imagination shrinks from the possible result of such a state of things; nor must you, or Mr. ——, tell me that the horrors thus suggested exist only in imagination. The Southern newspapers, with their advertisements of negro sales and personal descriptions of fugitive slaves, supply details of misery that it would be difficult for imagination to exceed. Scorn, derision, insult, menace— the handcuff, the lash—the tearing away of children from parents, of husbands from wives—the weary trudging in droves along the common highways, the labor of body, the despair of mind, the sickness of heart—these are the realities which belong to the system, and form the rule, rather than the exception, in the slave's experience. And this system exists here in this country of yours, which boasts itself the asylum of the oppressed, the home of freedom, the one place in all the world where all men may find enfranchisement from all thraldoms of mind, soul, or body—the land elect of liberty.

Questions

1. What reasons does Kemble give for rejecting the aptness of the comparison between the lowest factory workers and slaves?
2. Why does she suggest that education would be detrimental to slaves, as long as they remain slaves?
3. On what basis does she reject the argument that slaves might benefit from working for a lenient and paternalistic owner?

Chapter Questions

1. What specific evidence exists in the sources in this chapter that the Industrial Revolution was changing the world and the ways in which people lived and thought beyond the impact that it had on working conditions?
2. What is the value of using literary sources to understand a complex economic and social phenomenon such as the Industrial Revolution? What are the limitations?
3. Which of the above sources, if any, actually proposes solutions to the social problems created by the Industrial Revolution? Were those solutions viable?

CHAPTER FOUR

Cultural Interaction Between Europe and the World, 1815–75

INTRODUCTION

Most European history textbooks concentrate on European imperialism after 1875 when European nations began to expand their influence and number of colonies to such an extent that this movement has been dubbed the "New Imperialism." However, developments in the preceding decades greatly altered the relationship that Europeans had with India, China, Japan, and Africa and helped to prepare the way for the intensification of imperial activities in the last quarter of the nineteenth century. In India, this period saw the British government take control from the East India Company and begin to govern British territories there directly. In China, British vested interests in the opium trade led to war in 1839 and a series of treaties beginning with the Treaty of Nanking (1842) that completely altered the relationship and balance of power between China and Europe. In Japan, the United States exerted its military power to pressure the Japanese to grant access to trade there and brought Japan back within the orbit of Western civilization. In Africa, British explorers such as Richard Burton and David Livingstone were the first Europeans to set sight on the wonders of the continent's interior and in the process render its vast expanses suddenly more accessible to other European interests.

The British had emerged from the Napoleonic wars as the dominant world power, thanks largely to their unchallenged naval supremacy. As the leading industrial nation in the world, the British also had a competitive technological and economic advantage that allowed them to largely ignore European politics and concentrate on their overseas interests in India and China. However, their relationship with India and China could hardly have been more different. In India, the British tended to believe that they had a mission to govern well and to bring India the benefits of European civilization. There was also the practical matter of needing the general support of the Indian population because the British were in such a minority there. In China, the British seemed to have felt that they could be more ruthless and base their policies solely on their own economic interests. Therefore, while the British Raj in India attracted the support of Indian soldiers willing to serve in the army, Indian civil servants willing to participate in administration, and Indian intellectuals who recognized some of the benefits that Britain brought to India, in China, the government became increasingly resentful of the heavy handed way in which the British demanded the right to import opium, with all of its toxic effects on Chinese society, into the country. The first two sources of this chapter represent two very different kinds of appeal to the British: the first a letter by the Indian intellectual Rammohun Roy to a British official regarding British educational policy in India, the second a letter to Queen Victoria from the Chinese official, Lin Zexu, appealing on moral grounds for a change in British policy regarding the opium trade.

The British victory in the Opium War (1839–42) did nothing to decrease resentment by the Chinese, but rendered China powerless to do much about the British presence there. Britain had gained formal control over Hong Kong and Kowloon, in addition to securing trading privileges in the Treaty of Nanking. Meanwhile, resentment toward the British was growing in India because from the 1830s the British had started to introduce reforms intended to change Indian society and culture. Indian resentment at this policy of social engineering culminated in the Great Indian Mutiny of 1857, which is described below by an American journalist. After the Mutiny, the British government relieved the East India Company of its control in India and refrained from policies that might alienate the Indians, concentrating instead on building railroads and governing more efficiently. But some Indians, such as Dadabhai Naoroji, began to advocate for a greater degree of self-government for India, recognizing that British rule had provided some advantages for Indians but stressing that there were also disadvantages that could only be overcome by India eventually gaining its independence.

In many respects the issue for India, China, and Japan was much the same: how much and to what extent to embrace Western influence and how much to resist that influence to preserve their own unique culture and traditions. In general, the Chinese were the most resistant to Western influence, Indians embraced some aspects of Western progress while clinging to their religious and cultural heritage, and Japan went the furthest in embracing Westernization as a means of modernizing and allowing it to compete with the West on its own terms. In this chapter, an American provides his observations on Japan just prior to the change in government known as the Meiji Restoration (1868), which embraced Westernization.

Finally, it is true that in 1875 Africa was still the least known and least affected by Western influence of the parts of the world considered here. But it was in Africa that later European colonists would perhaps bring about the greatest changes, one of the main reasons why the period after 1875 is associated with a "new" imperialism. This would not have been possible without the benefit of the experience of explorers such as David Livingstone in the immediately preceding period covered by this chapter. In the passage below from the journal of David Livingstone, we get an early glimpse of European attitudes toward Africans. Although his observations are perhaps biased, as any such must be to some extent, at least they are based on firsthand experience with Africans from the interior of the country, which no previous European could have said.

RAMMOHUN ROY, "LETTER TO LORD AMHERST," INTRODUCTION

Rammuhon Roy (1772–1833) was among the first generation of Indians to receive the benefits of a British education. His writings and educational and cultural activities have been credited with beginning a "Hindu Renaissance" among well-educated Indians who sought to preserve India's cultural heritage, but at the same time sought to move beyond it. They desired to balance the advantages that they recognized in the English educational system with the preservation of their own cultural identity. Roy was an educational leader who published his ideas in books and journals and founded schools that taught in English. At the time when Roy wrote this letter, the British were still exercising caution in interfering too much with Indian customs, generally leaving Indians to practice most of their traditions, with a few exceptions, such as the practice of suttee, or widow burning, which was also opposed by Indians such as Roy. Toward the end of his life, Roy placed more emphasis on the importance of an understanding of Indian philosophy and the principles on which Indian civilization had been built, founding the Society of God (Brahmo Samaj) in 1828. But Roy remained a critic of many Indian traditions, including polygamy and the caste system, and favored a monotheistic religion instead of polytheism. He died in 1833, the year in which the British abolished slavery throughout the British Empire.

Rammohun Roy, "Letter to Lord Amherst"*

RAMMOHUN ROY

CALCUTTA

The 11th December 1823

To His Excellency the Right Hon'ble William Pitt, Lord Amherst

My Lord,

Humbly reluctant as the natives of India are to obtrude upon the notice of Government the sentiments they entertain on any public measure there are circumstances when silence would be carrying this respectful feeling to culpable excess. The present Rulers of India, coming from a distance of many thousand miles to govern a people whose language, literature, manners, customs, and ideas are almost entirely new and strange to them, cannot easily become

---

*Bureau of Education. Selections from Educational Records, Part I (1781–1839). Edited by H. Sharp. Calcutta: Superintendent Government Printing, 1920. Reprint. Delhi: National Archives of India, 1965, 98–101. Available online at http://www.sdstate.edu/projectsouthasia/loader.cfm?csModule=security/getfile&PageID=853836.

so intimately acquainted with their real circumstances, as the natives of the country are themselves. We should therefore be guilty of a gross dereliction of duty to ourselves, and afford our Rulers just ground of complaint at our apathy, did we omit on occasions of importance like the present to supply them with such accurate information as might enable them to devise and adopt measures calculated to be beneficial to the country, and thus second by our local knowledge and experience their declared benevolent intentions for its improvement.

The establishment of a new Sangscrit School in Calcutta evinces the laudable desire of Government to improve the Natives of India by Education,—a blessing for which they must ever be grateful; and every well wisher of the human race must be desirous that the efforts made to promote it should be guided by the most enlightened principles, so that the stream of intelligence may flow into the most useful channels.

When this Seminary of learning was proposed, we understood that the Government in England had ordered a considerable sum of money to be annually devoted to the instruction of its Indian Subjects. We were filled with sanguine hopes that this sum would be laid out in employing European Gentlemen of talents and education to instruct the natives of India in Mathematics, Natural Philosophy, Chemistry, Anatomy and other useful Sciences, which the Nations of Europe have carried to a degree of perfection that has raised them above the inhabitants of other parts of the world.

While we looked forward with pleasing hope to the dawn of knowledge thus promised to the rising generation, our hearts were filled with mingled feelings of delight and gratitude; we already offered up thanks to Providence for inspiring the most generous and enlightened of the Nations of the West with the glorious ambitions of planting in Asia the Arts and Sciences of modern Europe.

We now find that the Government are establishing a Sangscrit school under Hindoo Pundits to impart such knowledge as is already current in India. This Seminary (similar in character to those which existed in Europe before the time of Lord Bacon) can only be expected to load the minds of youth with grammatical niceties and metaphysical distinctions of little or no practicable use to the possessors or to society. The pupils will there acquire what was known two thousand years ago, with the addition of vain and empty subtilties [sic] since produced by speculative men, such as is already commonly taught in all parts of India.

The Sangscrit language, so difficult that almost a life time is necessary for its perfect acquisition, is well known to have been for ages a lamentable check on the diffusion of knowledge; and the learning concealed under this almost impervious veil is far from sufficient to reward the labour of acquiring it. But if it were thought necessary to perpetuate this language for the sake of the portion of the valuable information it contains, this might be much more easily accomplished by other means than the establishment of a new Sangscrit College; for there have been always and are now numerous professors of Sangscrit in the different parts of the country, engaged in teaching this language as well as the other branches of literature which are to be the object of the new Seminary. Therefore their more diligent cultivation, if desirable, would be effectually promoted by holding out premiums and granting certain allowances to those most eminent Professors, who have already undertaken on their own account to teach them, and would by such rewards be stimulated to still greater exertions.

From these considerations, as the sum set apart for the instruction of the Natives of India was intended by the Government in England, for the improvement of its Indian subjects, I beg leave to state, with due deference to your Lordship's exalted situation, that if the plan now adopted be followed, it will completely defeat the object proposed; since no improvement can be expected from inducing young men to consume a dozen of years of the most valuable period of their lives in acquiring the niceties of the Byakurun or Sangscrit Grammar. For instance, in learning to discuss such points as the following: Khad signifying to eat, khaduti, he or she or it eats. Query, whether does the word khaduti, taken as a whole, convey the meaning he, she, or it eats, or are separate parts of this meaning conveyed by distinct portions of the word? As if in the English language it were asked, how much meaning is there in the eat, how much in the s? and is the whole meaning of the word conveyed by those two portions of it distinctly, or by them taken jointly?

Neither can much improvement arise from such speculations as the following, which are the themes suggested by the Vedant:—In what manner is the soul absorbed into the deity? What relation does it bear to the divine essence? Nor will youths be fitted to be better members of society by the Vedantic doctrines, which teach them to believe that all visible things have no real existence; that as father, brother, etc., have no actual entirety, they consequently deserve no real affection, and therefore the sooner we escape from them and leave the world the better. Again, no essential benefit can be derived by the student of the Meemangsa from knowing what it is that makes the killer of a goat sinless on pronouncing certain passages of the Veds, and what is the real nature and operative influence of passages of the Ved, etc.

Again the student of the Nyaya Shastra cannot be said to have improved his mind after he has learned from it into how many ideal classes the objects in the Universe are divided, and what speculative relation the soul bears to the body, the body to the soul, the eye to the ear, etc.

In order to enable your Lordship to appreciate the utility of encouraging such imaginary learning as above characterized, I beg your Lordship will be pleased to compare the state of science and literature in Europe before the time of Lord Bacon, with the progress of knowledge made since he wrote.

If it had been intended to keep the British nation in ignorance of real knowledge the Baconian philosophy would not have been allowed to displace the system of the schoolmen, which was the best calculated to perpetuate ignorance. In the same manner the Sangscrit system of education would be the best calculated to keep this country in darkness, if such had been the policy of the British Legislature. But as the improvement of the native population is the object of the Government, it will consequently promote a more liberal and enlightened system of instruction, embracing mathematics, natural philosophy, chemistry and anatomy, with other useful sciences which may be accomplished with the sum proposed by employing a few gentlemen of talents and learning educated in Europe, and providing a college furnished with the necessary books, instruments and other apparatus.

In representing this subject to your Lordship I conceive myself discharging a solemn duty which I owe to my countrymen and also to that enlightened Sovereign and Legislature which have extended their benevolent cares to this distant land actuated by a desire to improve its inhabitants and I therefore humbly trust you will excuse the liberty I have taken in thus expressing my sentiments to your Lordship. I have, etc.,

RAMMOHUN ROY CALCUTTA;
The 11th December 1823

Questions
1. What is the purpose of Roy's letter?
2. What does it reflect about Indian attitudes toward British rule? What does it reflect about British attitudes toward Indians?
3. What does Roy see as the values of a British education for Indians? How does he define the type of education that he wishes his fellow countrymen to receive?
4. What does he see as the disadvantages of an education that stresses Indian philosophy and religious traditions? What might have led Roy to revise his position stated here regarding the learning of Sanskrit and the study of Indian philosophy?

Eugène Delacroix painted the *Women of Algiers* in 1834 around the time that Algiers became a French colony. Delacroix had traveled to Morocco two years earlier, where he made sketches on which this painting is likely based. The painting is not only famous and one of Delacroix's best known works,

FIGURE 4: Eugène Delacroix, *Women of Algiers in their Apartment*, 1834.
Courtesy of Getty Images.

residing in the Louvre Museum, but it also is one of the more controversial
works in Western art because of its portrayal of Muslim women in such a
way that many would have found offensive. Nineteenth-century Europeans
might have been shocked by the drug paraphernalia in the foreground and
the sexually charged atmosphere conveyed by the painting, while Muslims
generally did not permit women to be portrayed artistically at all, much less
in such revealing poses.

Questions
1. What does the painting convey about Delacroix's view of his subjects? Is it
   a favorable depiction of them?
2. What might the painting indicate more generally about Western attitudes
   toward the Islamic culture of northern Africa at that time?
3. How does this painting compare to Delacroix's "Liberty Leading the
   People," which appears in the previous chapter?

LIN ZEXU, "LETTER TO QUEEN VICTORIA," 1839, INTRODUCTION

The opium trade increased in China in the 1830s, when an end to the monopoly of the British East India Company opened the trade up to independent merchants, many of whom saw an opportunity to get rich from it. Lin Zexu (1775–1850) was an imperial commissioner who in 1838 was given by the Emperor Daoguang (r. 1821–50) the responsibility of almost single-handedly putting an end to the opium trade. Lin and others objected to the trade not only because of the enervating effects that opium use had on those who became addicted to the drug, but also because of the amount of silver bullion leaving the country to pay for it. Lin took a number of forceful measures in an attempt to achieve this aim, including the confiscation and destruction of several million pounds of raw opium in Guanghzhou in 1839. But he also took the step of appealing directly to Britain's young and recently anointed Queen Victoria (r. 1837–1901). Lin had enough copies of his letter made to distribute to every European ship leaving China in the hopes that his message would be conveyed successfully. If the letter ever did reach Queen Victoria, it obviously had no effect on British policy, given the Opium War that immediately ensued. But it does represent a telling and unique form of cultural interaction and goes a long way toward providing the Chinese side of the story in this ignominious episode in the history of Western imperialism. A postscript: After Britain's victory in the Opium War, the Chinese government, acquiescing to the demands of the British, had Lin exiled to western China far from the Qing court, to which, however, he returned three years later to take up another administrative position.

Lin Zexu, "Letter to Queen Victoria," 1839*

A communication: magnificently our great Emperor soothes and pacifies China and the foreign countries, regarding all with the same kindness. If there is profit, then he shares it with the peoples of the world; if there is harm, then he removes it on behalf of the world. This is because he takes the mind of heaven and earth as his mind.

The kings of your honorable country by a tradition handed down from generation to generation have always been noted for their politeness and submissiveness. We have read your successive tributary memorials saying, "In general our countrymen who go to trade in China have always received

---

*Ssuyu Teng and John Fairbank, *China's Response to the West* (Cambridge, MA: Harvard University Press, 1954), repr. in Mark A. Kishlansky, ed. (1995), *Sources of World History*, *Volume II*, New York: HarperCollins College Publishers, pp. 266–69.

His Majesty the Emperor's gracious treatment and equal justice" and so on. Privately we are delighted with the way in which the honorable rulers of your country deeply understand the grand principles and are grateful for the Celestial grace. For this reason the Celestial Court in soothing those from afar has redoubled its polite and kind treatment. The profit from trade has been enjoyed by them continuously for two hundred years. This is the source from which your country has become known for its wealth.

But after a long period of commercial intercourse, there appear among the crowd of barbarians both good persons and bad, unevenly. Consequently there are those who smuggle opium to seduce the Chinese people and so cause the spread of the poison to all provinces. Such persons who only care to profit themselves, and disregard their harm to others, are not tolerated by the laws of heaven and are unanimously hated by human beings. His Majesty the Emperor, upon hearing of this, is in a towering rage. He has especially sent me, his commissioner, to come to Kwangtung, and together with the governor-general and governor jointly to investigate and settle this matter.

All those people in China who sell opium or smoke opium should receive the death penalty. We trace the crime of those barbarians who through the years have been selling opium, then the deep harm they have wrought and the great profit they have usurped should fundamentally justify their execution according to law. We take into consideration, however, the fact that the various barbarians have still known how to repent their crimes and return to their allegiance to us by taking the 20,183 chests of opium from their storeships and petitioning us, through their consular officer [superintendent of trade], Elliot, to receive it. It has been entirely destroyed and this has been faithfully reported to the Throne in several memorials by this commissioner and his colleagues.

Fortunately we have received a specially extended favor from His Majesty the Emperor, who considers that for those who voluntarily surrender there are still some circumstances to palliate their crime, and so for the time being he has magnanimously excused them from punishment. But as for those who again violate the opium prohibition, it is difficult for the law to pardon them repeatedly. Having established new regulations, we presume that the ruler of your honorable country, who takes delight in our culture and whose disposition is inclined towards us, must be able to instruct the various barbarians to observe the law with care. It is only necessary to explain to them the advantages and disadvantages and then they will know that the legal code of the Celestial Court must be absolutely obeyed with awe.

We find your country is sixty or seventy thousand li [three li make one mile, ordinarily] from China. Yet there are barbarian ships that strive to come here for trade for the purpose of making a great profit. The wealth of China is used to profit the barbarians. That is to say, the great profit made by barbarians is all taken from the rightful share of China. By what right do they then in return use the poisonous drug to injure the Chinese people? Even though the barbarians may not necessarily intend to do us harm, yet in coveting profit to an extreme, they have no regard for injuring others. Let us ask, where is your conscience? I have heard that the smoking of opium is very strictly forbidden by your country; that is because the harm caused by opium is clearly understood. Since it is not permitted to do harm to your own country, then even less should you let it be passed on to the harm of other countries—how much less to China! Of all that China exports to foreign countries, there is not a single thing which is not beneficial to people: they are of benefit when eaten, or of benefit when used, or of benefit when resold: all are beneficial. Is there a single article from China which has done any harm to foreign countries? Take tea and rhubarb, for example; the foreign countries cannot get along for a single day without them. If China cuts off these benefits with no sympathy for those who are to suffer, then what can the barbarians rely upon to keep themselves alive? Moreover the woolens, camlets, and longells [i.e., textiles] of foreign countries cannot be woven unless they obtain Chinese silk. If China, again, cuts off this beneficial export, what profit can the barbarians expect to make? As for other foodstuffs, beginning with candy, ginger, cinnamon, and so forth, and articles for use, beginning with silk, satin, chinaware, and so on, all the things that must be had by foreign countries are innumerable. On the other hand, articles coming from the outside to China can only be used as toys. We can take them or get along without them. Since they are not needed by China, what difficulty would there be if we closed our frontier and stopped the trade? Nevertheless, our Celestial Court lets tea, silk, and other goods be shipped without limit and circulated everywhere without begrudging it in the slightest. This is for no other reason but to share the benefit with the people of the whole world. The goods from China carried away by your country not only supply your own consumption and use, but also can be divided up and sold to other countries, producing a triple profit. Even if you do not sell opium, you still have this threefold profit. How can you bear to go further, selling products injurious to others in order to fulfill your insatiable desire?

Suppose there were people from another country who carried opium for sale to England and seduced your people into buying and smoking it; certainly your honorable ruler would deeply hate it and be bitterly aroused. We have heard heretofore that your honorable ruler is kind and benevolent. Naturally you would not wish to give unto others what you yourself do not want. We have also heard that the ships coming to Canton have all had regulations promulgated and given to them in which it is stated that it is not permitted to carry contraband goods. This indicates that the administrative orders of your honorable rule have been originally strict and clear. Only because the trading ships are numerous, heretofore perhaps they have not been examined with care. Now after this communication has been dispatched and you have clearly understood the strictness of the prohibitory laws of the Celestial Court, certainly you will not let your subjects dare again to violate the law.

We have further learned that in London, the capital of your honorable rule, and in Scotland, Ireland, and other places, originally no opium has been produced. Only in several places of India under your control such as Bengal, Madras, Bombay, Patna, Benares, and Malwa has opium been planted from hill to hill, and ponds have been opened for its manufacture. For months and years work is continued in order to accumulate the poison. The obnoxious odor ascends, irritating heaven and frightening the spirits. Indeed you, O King, can eradicate the opium plant in these places, hoe over the fields entirely, and sow in its stead the five grains [millet, barley, wheat, etc.]. Anyone who dares again attempt to plant and manufacture opium should be severely punished. This will really be a great, benevolent government policy that will increase the common weal and get rid of evil. For this, Heaven must support you and the spirits must bring you good fortune, prolonging your old age and extending your descendants. All will depend on this act.

As for the barbarian merchants who come to China, their food and drink and habitation, all received by the gracious favor of our Celestial Court. Their accumulated wealth is all benefit given with pleasure by our Celestial Court. They spend rather few days in their own country but more time in Canton. To digest clearly the legal penalties as an aid to instruction has been a valid principle in all ages. Suppose a man of another country comes to England to trade, he still has to obey the English laws; how much more should he obey in China the laws of the Celestial Dynasty?

Now we have set up regulations governing the Chinese people. He who sells opium shall receive the death penalty and he who smokes it also the death penalty. Now consider this: if the barbarians do not bring opium, then how can the Chinese people resell it, and how can they smoke it? The fact is that the wicked barbarians beguile the Chinese people into a death trap. How then can we grant life only to these barbarians? He who takes the life of even one person still has to atone for it with his own life; yet is the harm done by opium limited to the taking of one life only? Therefore in the new regulations, in regard to those barbarians who bring opium to China, the penalty is fixed at decapitation or strangulation. This is what is called getting rid a harmful thing on behalf of mankind.

Moreover we have found that in the middle of the second month of this year [April 9] Consul [Superintendent] Elliot of your nation, because the opium prohibition law was very stern and severe, petitioned for an extension of the time limit. He requested an extension of five months for India and its adjacent harbors and related territories, and ten months for England proper, after which they would act in conformity with the new regulations. Now we, the commissioner and others, have memorialized and have received the extraordinary Celestial grace of His Majesty the Emperor, who has redoubled his consideration and compassion. All those who from the period of the coming one year (from England) or six months (from India) bring opium to China by mistake, but who voluntarily confess and completely surrender their opium, shall be exempt from their punishment. After this limit of time, if there are still those who bring opium to China then they will plainly have committed a willful violation and shall at once be executed according to law, with absolutely no clemency or pardon. This may be called the height of kindness and the perfection of justice.

Our Celestial Dynasty rules over and supervises the myriad states, and surely possesses unfathomable spiritual dignity. Yet the Emperor cannot bear to execute people without having first tried to reform them by instruction. Therefore he especially promulgates these fixed regulations. The barbarian merchants of your country, if they wish to do business for a prolonged period, are required to obey our statutes respectfully and to cut off permanently the source of opium. They must by no means try to test the effectiveness of the law with their lives. May you, O King, check your wicked and sift your wicked people before they come to China, in order to guarantee the peace of your nation, to show further the sincerity of your politeness and submissiveness, and to let the two countries enjoy together the blessings of peace. How fortunate, how fortunate indeed! After receiving this dispatch will you immediately give us a prompt reply regarding the details and circumstances of your cutting off the opium traffic; be sure not to put this off. The above is what has to be communicated.

Questions

1. What is the tone of Lin Zexu's letter? What would have been the likely effect of the letter and its tone if it had been read by a European at that time?
2. Does Lin make a compelling case for the end of the opium trade? What are his main points against it?
3. On what basis does Lin suggest that China deserves special preference from the British government?
4. What are some of his underlying assumptions about China and the West?

CHARLES CREIGHTON HAZEWELL, "THE INDIAN REVOLT," INTRODUCTION

The eruption of the Great Mutiny in the Bengal Army in May 1857 had as its immediate cause the rumor that new cartridges greased with either pork or beef fat needed to be bitten by Muslim and Hindu soldiers who would have considered one or the other to be a gross violation of their religious values. But the Mutiny was symbolic of mounting grievances over the subversion of the Indian textile industry by the import of inexpensive cloth goods from British factories and regarding what Indians perceived as a growing insensitivity on the part of the British to Indian culture and economic interests alike. British tax collectors had started to assess lands that had previously been tax-exempt and in general showed an increasing disregard for Indian sensibilities. For this reason, the Mutiny drew significant support from the civilian populations of north and central India, even as it spread through the armies of the East India Company. Charles Creighton Hazewell (1814–83) was an experienced American journalist with a deep knowledge of world affairs at the time that he provided this account of the Mutiny.

Charles Creighton Hazewell, "The Indian Revolt"*

For the first time in the history of the English dominion in India, its power has been shaken from within its own possessions, and by its own subjects. Whatever attacks have been made upon it heretofore have been from without, and its career of conquest has been the result to which they have led. But now no external enemy threatens it, and the English in India have found themselves suddenly and unexpectedly engaged in a hand-to-hand struggle with a portion of their subjects, not so much for dominion as for life. There had been signs and warnings, indeed, of the coming storm; but the feeling of security in possession and the confidence of moral strength were so strong, that the signs had been neglected and the warnings disregarded. . . .

One day toward the end of January last, a workman employed in the magazine at Barrackpore, an important station about seventeen miles from Calcutta, stopped to ask a Sepoy for some water from his drinking-vessel. Being refused, because he was of low caste, and his touch would defile the vessel, he said, with a sneer, "What caste are you of, who bite pig's grease and cow's fat on your cartridges?" Practice with the new Enfield rifle had just been introduced, and the cartridges were greased for use in order not to foul the gun. The rumor spread among the Sepoys that there was a trick played upon them,—that this was but a device to pollute them and destroy their caste, and the first step toward a general and forcible conversion of the soldiers to Christianity. The groundlessness of the idea upon which this alarm was founded afforded no hindrance to its ready reception, nor was the absurdity of the design attributed to the ruling powers apparent to the obscured and timid intellect of the Sepoys. The consequences of loss of caste are so feared,—and are in reality of so trying a nature,—that upon this point the sensitiveness of the Sepoy is always extreme, and his suspicions are easily aroused. Their superstitious and religious customs

---

*Charles Creighton Hazewell (1857), "The Indian Revolt," *The Atlantic Monthly*, December: 217–22.

"interfere in many strange ways with their military duties." "The brave men of the 35th Native Infantry," says Sir Charles Napier, "lost caste because they did their duty at Jelalabad; that is, they fought like soldiers, and ate what could be had to sustain their strength for battle." But they are under a double rule, of religious and of military discipline,—and if the two come into conflict, the latter is likely to give way.

. . . On the 26th of February, the 19th regiment, then stationed at Berhampore, refused to receive the cartridges that were served out, and were prevented from open violence only by the presence of a superior English force. After great delay, it was determined that this regiment should be disbanded. The authorities were not even yet alarmed; they were uneasy, but even their uneasiness does not seem to have been shared by the majority of the English residents in India. It was not until the 3rd of April that the sentence passed upon the 19th regiment was executed. The affair was dallied with, and inefficiency and dilatoriness prevailed everywhere.

But meanwhile the disaffection was spreading. The order for confining the use of the new cartridges to the Europeans seems to have been looked upon by the native regiments as a confirmation of their suspicions with regard to them. The more daring and evil-disposed of the soldiers stimulated the alarm, and roused the prejudices of their more timid and unreasoning companions. No general plan of revolt seems to have been formed, but the materials of discontent were gradually being concentrated; the inflammable spirits of the Sepoys were ready to burst into a blaze. Strong and judicious measures, promptly put into action, might even now have allayed the excitement and dissipated the danger. But the imbecile commander-in-chief was enjoying himself and shirking care in the mountains; and Lord Canning and his advisers at Calcutta seem to have preferred to allow the troops to take the initiative in their own way. Generally throughout Northern India the common routine of affairs went on at the different stations, and the ill-feeling and insubordination among the Sepoys scarcely disturbed the established quiet and monotony of Anglo-Indian life. But the storm was rising. . . .

The course of English life in those stations where the worst cruelties and the bitterest sufferings have been inflicted on the unhappy Europeans has been for a long time so peaceful and undisturbed, it has gone on for the most part in such pleasant and easy quiet and with such absolute security, that the agony of sudden alarm and unwarned violence has added its bitterness to the overwhelming horror. It is not as in border settlements, where the inhabitants choose their lot knowing that they are exposed to the incursions of savage enemies,—but it is as if on a night in one of the most peaceful of long-settled towns, troops of men, with a sort of civilization that renders their attack worse than that of savages, should be let loose to work their worst will of lust and cruelty. The details are too recent, too horrible, and as yet too broken and irregular, to be recounted here.

. . .

The struggle of the trained and ambitious classes against the English power will but have served to confirm it. The revolt overcome, the last great danger menacing English security in India will have disappeared. England will have learnt much from the trials she has had to pass through, and that essential changes will take place within a few years in the constitution of the Indian government there can be no doubt. But it is to be remembered that for the past thirty years, English rule in India has been, with all its defects, an enlightened and beneficient rule. The crimes with which it has been charged, the crimes of which it has been guilty, are small in amount, compared with the good it has effected. Moreover, they are not the result of inherent vices in the system of government, so much as of the character of exceptional individuals employed to carry out that system, and of the native character itself.—But on these points we do not propose now to enter.

If the close of this revolt be not stained with retaliating cruelties, if English soldiers remember mercy, then the whole history of this time will be a proud addition to the annals of England. For though it will display the incompetency and the folly of her governments, it will show how these were remedied by the energy and spirit of individuals; it will tell of the daring and gallantry of her men, of their patient endurance, of their undaunted courage,—and it will tell, too, with a voice full of tears, of the sorrows, and of the brave and tender hearts, and of the unshaken religious faith supporting them to the end, of the women who died in the hands of their enemies. The names of Havelock and Lawrence will be reckoned in the list of England's worthies, and the story of the garrison of Cawnpore will be treasured up forever among England's saddest and most touching memories.

Questions
1. What does Hazewell see as the main historical significance of the Mutiny?
2. What explanations does he offer for the causes of the Mutiny?
3. In what ways does he suggest that the British might benefit from the Mutiny?
4. Does Hazewell exhibit any biases in this account?

DADABHAI NAOROJI, *POVERTY AND UNBRITISH RULE IN INDIA*, INTRODUCTION

After the Mutiny, the British continued to outlaw suttee and female infanticide, but they generally steered clear of interfering with other Indian customs, even allowing polygamy and the arranged marriages of children. However, this was no longer enough to appease all Indians, especially those intellectuals who increasingly wondered why political representation and balanced government were good for the British but not good for India. Dadabhai Naoroji (1825–1917) was one who took matters into his own hands, moving to London where he could advocate for Indian political rights and greater opportunities for advancement within the civil service. He was elected to the British Parliament in 1892. His writing below preceded his participation in the founding of the Indian National Congress in 1885, whose main goal was to promote Indian self-government. The works and example of political activism set by Naoroji had an important influence on Gandhi and other Indian nationalist leaders of the twentieth century.

Dadabhai Naoroji, *Poverty and Unbritish Rule in India**

November 16, 1880

The Moral Poverty of India and Native Thoughts on the Present British Indian Policy

In my last paper I confined myself to meeting Mr. Danvers' line of argument on the question of the material destruction and impoverishment of India by the present British Indian policy. I endeavored to show that this destruction and impoverishment of India was mainly caused by the unnatural treatment it received at the hand of its British rulers, in the way of subjecting it to a large variety of expenditure upon a crushing foreign agency both in India and England, whereby the children of the country were displaced and deprived of their natural rights and means of subsistence in their own country; that, by what was being taken and consumed in India itself, and by what was being continuously taken away by such agency clean out of the country, an exhaustion of the very life-blood of the country was unceasingly going on; that not till this disastrous drain was duly checked, and not till the people of India were restored to their natural rights in their own country, was there any hope for the material amelioration of India.

In this memorandum I desire to submit for the kind and generous consideration of his Lordship the Secretary of State for India, that from the same cause of the deplorable drain, besides the material exhaustion of India, the moral loss to her is no less sad and lamentable.

---

*Dadabhai Naoroji (1901), *Poverty and Unbritish Rule in India*, London: Swan Sonnenschein, pp. 203–5. http://books.google.com/books/about/Poverty_and_Un_British_Rule_in_India.html?id=oqwCAAAAMAAJ.

With the material wealth go also the wisdom and experience of the country. Europeans occupy almost all the high places in every department of Government directly or indirectly under its control. While *in* India, they acquire India's money, experience, and wisdom; and when they go, they carry both away with them, leaving India so much poorer in material and moral wealth. Thus India is left without, and cannot have those elders in wisdom and experience who in every country are the natural guides of the rising generations in their national and social conduct, and of the destinies of their country; and a sad, sad loss is this!

Every European is isolated from the people around him. He is not their mental, moral, or social leader or companion. For any mental or moral influence or guidance or sympathy with the people he might just as well be living on the moon. The people know him not, and he knows not, nor cares for the people. Some honorable exceptions do, now and then, make an effort to do some good if they can, but in the very nature of things these efforts are always feeble, exotic, and of little permanent effect. These men are not always in the place, and their works die away when they go.

The Europeans are not the natural leaders of the people. They do not belong to the people; they cannot enter their thoughts or feelings; they cannot join or sympathize with their joys or griefs. On the contrary, every day the estrangement is increasing. Europeans deliberately and openly widen it more and more. There may be very few social institutions started by Europeans in which Natives, however fit and desirous to join, are not deliberately and insultingly excluded. The Europeans are, and make themselves, strangers in every way. All they effectually do is to eat the substance of India, material and moral, while living there, and when they go, they carry away all they have acquired, and their pensions and future usefulness besides.

The most deplorable loss to India needs most serious consideration, as much in its political as in its national aspect. Nationally disastrous as it is, it carries politically with it its own Nemesis. Without the guidance of elderly wisdom and experience of their own natural leaders, the education which the rising generations are now receiving is naturally leading them (or call it misleading them if you will) into directions which bode no good to the rulers, and which, instead of being the strength of the rulers, as it ought to and can be, will turn out to be their great weakness. The fault will be of the rulers themselves for such a result. The power that is now being raised by the spread of education, though yet slow and small, is one that in time must, for weal or woe, exercise great influence; in fact, it has already begun to do so. However strangely the English rulers, forgetting their English manliness and moral courage, may, like the ostrich, shut their eyes, by gagging acts or otherwise, to the good or bad influences they are raising around them, this good or evil is rising nevertheless. The thousands that are being sent out by the universities every year find themselves in an anomalous position. There is no place for them in their mother-land. They may beg in the streets or break stones on the road for aught the rulers seem to care for their natural rights, position and duties in their own country. They may perish or do what they like or can, but scores of Europeans must go from this country to take up what belongs to them, and that in spite of every profession, for years and years past and up to the present day, of English statesmen that they must govern India for India's good, by solemn Acts and declarations of Parliament, and, above all, by the words of the august sovereign herself. For all practical purposes all these high promises have been hitherto almost wholly, the purest romance, the reality being quite different.

Questions

1. What does Naoroji mean here by "unBritish rule"? What are his major criticisms of British policy in India at this time?
2. Why does Naoroji say that it is important for Indians to have a say in their own governance?
3. Why are the British unsuited to rule India, according to Naoroji?

JAPAN THROUGH AMERICAN EYES: THE JOURNAL OF FRANCIS HALL, INTRODUCTION

In 1854, Matthew Perry prepared the way for the opening of Japan to American trade, using the threat of military force to get the Japanese to acquiesce in granting trading privileges to the United States and to establishing diplomatic relations between the two countries. One of the beneficiaries of the opening of Japan to American business was Francis Hall (1822–1902), who cofounded Walsh, Hall, and Company, a trading business based in Yokohama and Kanagawa on the Japanese coast. During his stay in Japan from 1859 to 1866, in addition to writing articles for the New York Tribune, *Hall kept the journal in which the following entries appeared. Overall, Hall was impressed by the Japanese, no doubt because they were in the process of adapting themselves to the Western values that Hall, as an American businessperson, cherished. Hall's journal reflects his own cultural biases, while at the same time showing the interest that Westerners displayed during this period toward other cultures. However, as the entries below indicate, all was not smooth sailing, and as late as 1863, Hall despaired of not only the future of his business enterprise, but also of his own personal safety. Hall's journal was published for the first time in 1992, thanks mainly to the initiative of its editor, Professor Francis G. Notehelfer, director of the Center for Japanese Studies at UCLA.*

Japan Through American Eyes: The Journal of Francis Hall*

Wednesday, May 6, 1863

Today a regular panic has seized the town; the native population are fleeing in the utmost haste. Everyone believes war is inevitable and is hastening to escape from the vicinity of the sea. Scarcely a native merchant has the nerve to remain, but all offer their wares at any price they can get. The excitement among the foreigners is hardly less. All day long the wharves are crowded with merchandise to go off to the shipping. Any price is paid for boats or coolies here. The transportation of a package that would usually cost two *tempos* has gone to three, four, and six times that price. This excitement is intensified by the fact of several assaults having been made in order to collect claims. Mr. Robertson was seized in his bedroom while dressing this morning and carried off to the rear for the settlement, for what purposes of violence we do not know; he was fortunately rescued. Mr. Schoyer was likewise beset by a large gang of laborers and had to pay them money, which he says was not due, but in all these cases the Japanese had some claims. Servants left their masters robbing them as they went. Macaulay, a landlord, was knocked down by his own servants and robbed. A Portuguese was similarly treated. The confusion grew hourly greater, and when about noon it was heard that Dupontes, a Frenchman, had shot a man for making a similar demand on him, the excitement reached its height. The town was full of coolies whose burden poles would have been dangerous weapons, had they had the courage and determination to use them. All dreaded the coming of night.

At this time a consultation, or conference was being had on the *Euryalus*, Admiral Kuper's flagship, at which were present the English and French authorities, and on the side of the Japanese the Governor of Yokohama and Takamoto, one of the Governors of Foreign Affairs from Yedo. At this interview the French admiral was present as he had just arrived in the *Semiramis* from China. The Japanese asked for more time on the ground that the Tycoon had not yet returned: that he was on the way back and might now be expected in a few days more. The French admiral took the just ground that the reasons assigned for the delay were good, and that when the Japanese recently asked

*Francis Hall (2001), *Japan Through American Eyes: The Journal of Francis Hall*, edited by Francis G. Notehelfer, Boulder, CO: Westview Press, pp. 332–35.

for thirty days extension of time it ought to have been promptly granted for the just cause given, the emperor's absence. Takomoto, the emperor's envoy, disclosed that orders had come from the Mikado at Miako not to meet the English demands, but to fight rather for the expulsion of the foreigners. He further said that this anti-foreign party was so powerful that it was doubtful if the Tycoon's government could effectually resist it. He was then asked if the Tycoon would accept the assistance of the Allies to put down this hostile faction. His reply was, that was a question he could not decide, he must first submit it to the Goroju.

It was finally concluded at this conference that the Japanese should be allowed fifteen days from that day, the 6th, for their final answer and that in the meantime the Governor should restore the old order in Yokohama, that the merchants should return to their shops, and the servants to their place. Moreover that the Allies should in the meantime be permitted to take such measures for the protection of the settlement by landing troops, or otherwise as seemed advisable.

Accordingly in the afternoon the Governor issued an *ofoori* to that intent enjoining upon all the native population to return to their customary avocations. The potent influence of this government was at once seen in the quiet that was suddenly restored.

The Japanese have received a further delay, but there can be little hope any longer of a peaceful solution. The declarations of the Governor at the conference show that the Tycoon seems to have only a choice between a civil and a foreign war, and it hardly seems possible that he would escape the latter by a choice of the former.

Friday, May 22, 1863

We have news from Nagasaki yesterday and today. The panic and confusion at Nagasaki was even worse than here. The merchants generally removed their property to the shipping and many of themselves went thither also. The English Consul was among those who left the shore. There was the same panic among the towns people who fled as here selling their stocks of goods for what they could get. This fright was much contributed to by the outspoken Governor of that city, who said that if he heard that the Yedo government refused to meet the English demands he should consider war inaugurated and take the offensive. He advised all foreigners without regard to nationality to leave the place; promising them however 24 Japanese hours notice before hostile acts were commenced by him.

Monday, June 1, 1863

Early this morning I found General Pruyn, his son, and his secretary had arrived from Yedo. It appears also that yesterday afternoon he had been solicited to leave Yedo in so urgent a way that his volition was hardly left to him. The officials of his household guard informed him that a conspiracy of seven hundred *ronins* to take his life that night had been discovered that he *must* go. Early this morning mission families began to move, and now Yedo and Kanagawa are at last evacuated. A large body of guards came down from Yedo to protect the Kanagawa families during the night and nobody was allowed to move without an escort.

Today imperial soldiers armed with muskets, swords, and spears are filing through our streets and taking up guard stations at different points. We must accept these native guards, while we distrust them, since the fleet in the bay will not land for our defense.

I saw a letter in the hands of General Pruyn today, a translation from a Japanese document to the government officers at Yedo and emanating from the Mikado. The Mikado says that it is understood that all the daimos will retire (from Miako) to their provinces and put everything in order preparatory to the work of exterminating the foreigners which his faithful Siogoon or General in Chief has undertaken to accomplish.

I saw also a second document which stated that if the Siogoon failed in this work he would set upon its execution himself. These documents being shown to the Japanese officials with whom General Pruyn has frequent communication they pronounced the first genuine, the second they knew nothing about.

One cannot help feeling at times that we are surrounded with wily foes and treacherous friends and that the fate of the Portuguese in the 17th century threatens us.

Questions
1. What were the alternatives open to the Japanese leaders in regard to accepting the presence of American and European businesses on their soil?
2. What do these entries reveal about the nature of cultural interaction between the Japanese and Westerners at this time?
3. Do these entries suggest that the Westernization of Japan was not a foregone conclusion? What insights do they provide into the developments leading to the Meiji Restoration?

DAVID LIVINGSTONE, *AFRICAN JOURNAL, 1853–1856*, INTRODUCTION

David Livingstone (1813–73) grew up in Lanarkshire near the site of Robert Owen's model factory at New Lanark and was himself employed as a mill worker when he was only ten years old. As an adult, Livingstone was determined to become a missionary, which provided the initial impetus for his first trip to Africa in 1851. He is best known for his discovery of Victoria Falls in 1855 and other lakes and rivers previously unknown to Europeans and for his dramatic encounter with the American journalist Henry Stanley, who, in the employ of the New York Herald, *set off on a quest to find the missing Livingstone in 1871. But perhaps more important were the people he discovered in Africa and his determination to save them from the evils of slavery and abuse. Based on his experiences in Africa, Livingstone became convinced by the time of his death in 1873 that only direct colonization, bringing along with it the benefits of commerce and Christianity, could put an end to the slave trade and improve the lives of the African people, thus linking him directly with the imperial enterprises in Africa that followed in his wake. In this passage, Livingstone discusses his observations on the people with whom he lived on his first trip to Africa.*

David Livingstone, *African Journal, 1853–1856**

October 23, 1855. It would not be fair, in estimating the moral status of this people, to enumerate their bad actions only. If the same were done in England, the lower classes of that country would appear worse than they are here. It seems better to compare the actual amount of goodness in each class, the badness in both being rather exceptional than otherwise. From intimate knowledge of the poorer classes in England and Scotland, I have no hesitation in ascribing to them a very admirable amount of kindly feeling towards each other, which is manifested on all occasions of real necessity. There is a constant stream of benevolence flowing from the rich to the poor, but this, large as it is, cannot be compared with the unostentatious attentions of the poor to each other. Of this disinterested kindness of the native poor to each other there exists only a vestige here. If one gives food or anything else to a poor person, it is always with the hope of being repaid with interest, & should no hope of payment appear in the borrower (we may call him) falling sick, the lender would without blushing take back what he could.

The poor of this country might be fairly compared with the Jewish money-lenders of England, and by no means with the common run of the poorer classes. A poor person who has no relatives will seldom be supplied with water in illness, and when death ensues will certainly be dragged out to be devoured by the hyenas, instead of being buried. Food is given to servants in consideration only of services expected. Boys and girls may be seen undergoing absolute starvation when their masters or rather owners are scarce of food. No one else will give a morsel to the poor wretched skeletons, public opinion being that such generosity without hope of an equivalent is stark folly.

---

*David Livingstone (1963), *African Journal 1853–1856*, edited by I. Schapira, pp. 318–21.

An interesting-looking girl came to my wagon in a state of entire nudity, almost a skeleton. Giving her a little clothing and food I enquired after her owner, and offered to provide for her if he would allow her to come and live near us. He would "allow me to feed her and make her fat, and then take her away". I protested against his heartlessness in expecting service from one whom he refused to feed. She did not again appear clothed, and in a day or two was lost sight of. She had gone out a little way from the town and, too weak to return, had been cruelly left to perish.

In another case a poor boy appeared going to the water for a drink. On enquiry, I found the master belonged to a party notorious for starving their dependents. He proposed that I should fatten this one too for his private benefit. I expatiated in public on the meanness of wishing me to do what he would not from humanity or self-interest do for himself, and said that though I was willing to assist the poor skeleton with the little I could spare, I could not submit to do it only to prolong his misery, as on his return he would certainly be starved again. If he wished to kill the boy, let it be known as his act. Sekeletu (King of Barotseland in western Zambia, c. 1835–63) decided that the owner should give up his alleged right rather than destroy the child. He was so far gone as to be in the cold stage of starvation, but soon came round on a little milk three or four times a day, and other food when I have it; and I shall be able to hand him over to Sekeletu when I depart, certain he will receive at least enough food.

This act, little as it may seem, would assuredly not be performed by a single individual in the tribe, and the majority look upon it as proof of a soft corner in my cranium. I might keep him as my own servant, or slave rather, but I have invariably declined such, even when offered as presents from chiefs, believing it better to give a negative and state my objections to the entire system than to take a protégé by giving the slave liberty afterwards. . . .

In confounding proximity to these vices, which are really not too darkly drawn, a little child just able to walk never goes near a company of men without getting a handful, and, in eating meat, pieces are handed generally to all the company, as if they were a most generous disposition.

There is a wonderful mixture of good and evil. They have been remarkably kind to me. The conclusion I have come to is that they are a strange mixture of good and evil, as everywhere else, the evil predominating. [They] show great forbearance and justice sometimes, yet sometime also will kill the parents of children, in order that the latter may not desert service and flee to the former. But this happens only among Makololo.

The servitude rendered from time immemorial by the poorer to the richer classes cannot be called slavery, though akin to it. The poor man is called a child of the rich man, and their intercourse is on a sort of equality. . . . The rich man lends the inferior his cattle, and gives or lends him and his wife clothes, but the poor man can leave the master and transfer his services to another, and all that can be done is to resume possession of the cattle and clothes. . . . It is like slavery only in no specified wages being paid, but the obligations are well understood.

Questions
1. Is it a valid comparison to compare the poor of one society to the poor of a completely different society, as Livingstone does here?
2. What do the entries above reveal about Livingstone's own cultural biases?
3. What do they reveal about his interaction with the Africans? Are they a valuable or reliable source of information about the people whom he discusses here?
4. What conclusions might his readers at the time have drawn from Livingstone's account?

Chapter Questions

1. What tentative conclusions might be reached on the basis of the sources in this chapter about the nature of cross-cultural interaction between Europeans and non-Westerners during the nineteenth century? What other kinds of sources might be helpful in developing a deeper understanding of that relationship?
2. What might the three sources by Roy, Hazewell, and Naroji indicate about the larger history of British rule in India and the direction of Indian history in the nineteenth century?
3. To what extent can indications of the expansion of European imperialism toward the end of the nineteenth century be found in these sources from the preceding period?

CHAPTER FIVE

Europe and the West in an Age of Nationalism

INTRODUCTION

Modern nationalism had begun to a very large degree as a response to the French Revolution and the Napoleonic conquests that affected much of the European continent. In the first half of the nineteenth century it evolved from a defensive response to foreign invasion to become a more positive ideal that inspired people who believed that the nation was the primary means through which human progress could occur and human greatness could be achieved. Leading liberals and revolutionaries from this period saw nationalism more as a means to an end than an end in itself. They saw the nation as the means through which each individual could fulfill his or her destiny, as the source of benefits for society as a whole, that included the protection or guarantee of individual rights, and as a source of pride based on its own unique cultural characteristics. If nations came into conflict, the more just cause belonged to the one fighting for liberation or independence as opposed to a nation bent on dominating another people.

These early ideals ran through the mind of Giuseppe Garibaldi (1807–82), who cut his nationalistic teeth in the Young Italy movement spearheaded by the Italian nationalist, Giuseppe Mazzini. Young Italy advocated the unification of Italy and the expulsion of foreign rulers such as the Austrians from Italian territories. Garibaldi was a soldier, a man of action, who, on being forced to flee Italy after an aborted revolution in the 1830s, traveled to South America to join the cause of nationalists there fighting for their own independence. To Garibaldi's mind, the cause of one nation was the cause of every nation. He later gained status as a national military hero who played a critical role in the unification of Italy. In his memoirs, he reflected back on his time in South America and what it meant to him.

As important as Garibaldi was to the cause of Italian unification, it could not have been achieved without the leadership supplied by Count Camilo di Cavour, the leading statesman of the northern kingdom of Piedmont-Sardinia. Garibaldi and Mazzini had collaborated during the Revolutions of 1848 in an attempt to establish a Roman Republic, which promised to remove at least one obstacle to Italian unification by eliminating the papacy from its role in the politics and governance of Italy. However, the Republic collapsed under the threat of French intervention, demonstrating that revolutionaries alone could not fulfill the nationalist agenda; a unified Italy required a leader capable of handling the practical negotiations to bring it about and experienced enough to govern on a day-to-day basis. By 1860, the growing number of fervent nationalists in Italy were willing to compromise the liberal agenda of Mazzini and Garibaldi in order to achieve their goal of unification.

The history of German unification followed a similar pattern. The failure of the Revolutions of 1848 and the collapse of the Frankfurt Assembly, which had convened in that year to work out a plan for unification, left German nationalists in need of a practical leader possessing the power and intelligence required to solve the seemingly intractable obstacles in the way of a united Germany. They found their leader in the Prussian aristocrat, Otto von Bismarck. After becoming chief minister of Prussia in 1862, Bismarck first outmaneuvered the Prussian liberals in the Reichstag to collect taxes that allowed him to strengthen the Prussian military. He then launched a series of three wars that by 1871 had neutralized opposition from Denmark, Austria, and France and resulted in the unification of Germany. His reflections on his policies and thinking in these years provide important insights into a period that culminated in the declaration of the German Empire in the Hall of Mirrors in Versailles following the defeat of France in the Franco-Prussian War. An account of this event, which turned out to be a key turning point in European history, appears in this chapter.

Nineteenth-century nationalism manifested itself in different ways, as is reflected by the remaining sources in this chapter. The speeches of the Irish Protestant landlord and politician Charles Stewart Parnell (1846–91) date from a time in which Irish nationalists were putting increasing pressure on the British for home rule, a form of independence that would have kept Ireland within the British Commonwealth. Ireland had officially become a part of the United Kingdom in 1801, but Irish nationalist leaders such as Daniel O'Connell viewed Ireland as a nation that deserved its own parliament and the right to govern itself. Resentment toward the British had grown as the century wore on, fueled by the inadequate response of the government to the Great Famine of the 1840s, which resulted in the deaths of about a million Irish and the emigration of about a million more, and the poverty and insecurity of many of the tenant farmers who remained. Parnell took up the cause as the leader of the Irish Party in the British Parliament. Through speeches like those that appear in this chapter, he gave voice to the oppressed while going a long way toward defining what nationalism meant for Ireland.

A different kind of nationalist vision appears in the writings of Theodore Roosevelt, a believer in American "exceptionalism," who bought into the idea that the United States had a "manifest destiny" to play an active role in world affairs and expand its territory and influence throughout the Western Hemisphere and beyond. In a way, his views represent how far ideas about nationalism had departed from the liberal and revolutionary causes with which it was associated earlier in the nineteenth century. He played an active role in the Spanish-American War in Cuba in 1898, even organizing his own private regiment, the "Roughriders." As president from 1901 to 1909, he pursued an active foreign policy, which is best known for the "Roosevelt Corollary to the Monroe Doctrine," in which he asserted the US right to intervene in other American states in order to preserve US interests. Yet Roosevelt did remain a liberal in some ways, busting trusts and monopolies, supporting reform legislation on social matters, and even running for president (and losing) in 1908 under the banner of the Progressive Party after having served as a Republican president.

Finally, we turn our attention to China, which was still an independent nation at the end of the nineteenth century but one that seemed to be increasingly losing its grip on power over its own affairs because of the power and influence wielded by Westerners inside the country. Chinese intellectuals began to question how China could reassert itself as an independent country; many looked to Japan which had more success at doing so since the Meiji Restoration. Chinese defeat in the Sino-Japanese War and the failure of the Boxer Rebellion, a nationalist uprising in 1898, both fueled a higher level of desperation and hopelessness among Chinese nationalists. In this context, Liang Qichao proposed a program for "renewing the people" that would have a great influence on revolutionaries such as Sun Yat-sen, who would eventually overthrow the weak Qing dynasty and establish a Chinese republic in an effort to restore China to the status of a powerful and independent nation.

GIUSEPPE GARIBALDI, MEMOIRS, INTRODUCTION

Garibaldi was welcomed by the revolutionary leaders to whose causes he offered his services in South America, where he spent about a dozen years and gained valuable experience that would help him in his military struggles in Sicily and Italy years later. He suffered innumerable hardships there, including being shot in the neck, but his sojourn there also seems to have strengthened his resolve and commitment to the cause of nationalism in general. When he wrote this autobiography he was no doubt looking as much to the future as he was to the past, looking back with pride on what he had accomplished in South America but with anticipation of seeing his dream for a united Italy fulfilled. Garibaldi remained a soldier, his legend untarnished by participation in politics after his military exploits had helped to bring about the creation of a new Italian nation.

Giuseppe Garibaldi, Memoirs*

I have served the cause of the people in America, and served it with sincerity, as I everywhere fought against absolutism. Being warmly attached to the system corresponding with my convictions, I was equally opposed in my feelings to the opposite system. I have always rather pitied than hated men who have been led to selfishness by misfortune; and, when now viewing the scenes I passed through, from a far distant country, and long after their occurrence, the accounts contained in the succeeding pages may be regarded as impartial, with the care which has been taken in recording facts, reviewing occurrences, and making allowances for men and circumstances. . . .

In the camp of Republicans there was a scarcity of meat, and the infantry were especially famishing. But, what was still more insupportable, thirst also prevailed, for there was no water. But that people are hardened by a life of privations. No lamentations were heard, except for the want of permission to fight. Oh Italians! oh, for the day when you shall be united and enduring like those children of the desert. The stranger shall not then trample upon your soil; he shall not contaminate your air. Italy will then take her proper place among the first nations of the earth. . . .

There were many Italians in Montevideo, whose condition and feelings I soon learned to appreciate. They were regarded with scorn by many of the other foreign residents, especially the French, who were in much greater numbers, and seemed to take pleasure in humiliating my poor and injured countrymen.

This was not the first case, though one of the most marked and unrighteous, in which the wronged and suffering party were made to bear the reproach of those very traits of character displayed by their strong and false-hearted conquerors. In exile and poverty, under the bitter and hourly personal experience of their national misfortunes, and reproached by the world with having brought them upon themselves, the Italians in South America were depressed and disheartened by their gloomy recollections, their present sorrows and their cloudy future. Many of them were occupying themselves with such labors and business as they could find or invent, to obtain the means of subsistence, and laying the foundations of the fortunes which they have since accumulated by industry and economy; but few formed any sanguine expectations of gaining that distinction for military prowess, which the more numerous and vaunting Frenchmen around them then arrogated to themselves. I however, ere long, began to indulge in more daring anticipations. . . .

---

*Giuseppe Garibaldi (1860), *The Life of General Garibaldi Written by Himself with the Sketches of His Companions in Arms*, translated by Theodore Dwight, New York: A.S. Barnes and Burr, pp. 81, 88, 114–15.

I resolved to find employment for some of them, and to raise the courage and hopes of all, and at the same time to prepare them for future service as soldiers in Italy, by bringing them into the service which was offered to myself. . . .

Questions

1. What do these passages reveal about Garibaldi's view of nationalism and what he hopes to accomplish by it in Italy?
2. How does he regard his experiences in South America? Does he achieve his objective of providing an "objective" account of this period of his life?
3. What impression might these passages have left on Italian readers of the nineteenth-century? Did Garibaldi contribute to his own legend? How might people of other nations have viewed these passages?

OTTO VON BISMARCK AND GERMAN UNIFICATION, INTRODUCTION

In the excerpt below, Bismarck refers to his oft-quoted phrase of "blood and iron" as the decisive factors in the quest for the unification of Germany. This did not necessarily make Bismarck a warmonger, but he did seem to understand that Prussia was going to need to use force in order to exercise its leadership in German affairs. Bismarck, in fact, was more motivated by a desire that Prussia take the lead in any future unified German state than by any idealistic commitment to German unification similar to that possessed by Garibaldi with regard to Italian unification. Bismarck used his military buildup to crush Austria in the Austro-Prussian War of 1866, ensuring Prussian leadership of any future unified Germany. However, the military victory over Austria left Prussia only in control of the northern states, which quickly became amalgamated into the North German Confederation. So Bismarck next set his sights on overcoming both the resistance of France and that of the states of southern Germany to Prussian leadership over the largely Catholic south. The Franco-Prussian War succeeded on both counts: Prussia defeated the French and removed them as an obstacle to German unification, while the war stimulated a wave of German patriotism throughout the south. Of the two sources included here, the first contains Bismarck's reflections about German unification, while the second involves a description of the sentiments surrounding the scene when German unity became official in January 1871. In the second account, however, the author, in the excitement over what this victory meant for Germany, left out what it meant for France—the loss of Alsace-Lorraine and a humiliating defeat that left a desire for revenge on the part of the French, who would remain enemies of Germany for the foreseeable future.

Otto Von Bismarck, Memoirs*

Retrospect of Prussian Policy

. . . Prussia—such was the point of my speech—as a glance at the map will show, could no longer wear unaided on its long narrow figure the panoply which Germany required for its security; it must be equally distributed over all the German peoples. We should get no nearer the goal by speeches, associations, decisions of majorities; we should be unable to avoid a serious contest, a contest which could only be settled by blood and iron. In order to secure our success in this, the deputies must place the greatest possible weight of blood and iron in the hands of the King of Prussia, in order that according to his judgment he might throw it into one scale or the other. . . .

As I continued to speak in this sense, the King grew more and more animated, and began to assume the part of an officer fighting for kingdom and fatherland. In presence of external and personal danger he possessed a rare and absolutely natural fearlessness, whether on the field of battle or in the face of attempts on his life; his attitude in any external danger was elevating and inspiring. . . . Hitherto, on his journey, he had only asked himself whether, under the superior criticism of his wife and public opinion in Prussia, he would be able to keep steadfast on the road on which he was entering with me. The influence of our conversation in the dark railway compartment counteracted this sufficiently to make him regard the part which the situation forced upon him more from the standpoint of the officer. He felt as though he had been touched in his military honor, and was in the position of an officer who has orders to hold a certain position to the death, no matter whether he perishes in the task or not. . . .

Dynasties and Stocks

Never, not even at Frankfurt, did I doubt that the key to German politics was to be found in princes and dynasties, not in publicists, whether in parliament and the press, or on the barricades. The opinion of the cultivated public as uttered in parliament and the press might promote and sustain the determination of the

---

*Otto von Bismarck (1899), *Bismarck: The Man and the Statesman*, New York: Harper and Brothers, Vol. I, pp. 313–24, Vol. II, pp. 99–101.

dynasties, but perhaps provoked their resistance more frequently than it urged them forward in the direction of national unity. The weaker dynasties leant for shelter upon the national cause, rulers and houses that felt themselves more capable of resistance mistrusted the movement, because with the promotion of Germany unity there was the prospect of the diminution of their independence in favor of the central authority or the popular representative body. The Prussian dynasty might anticipate that the hegemony in the future German Empire would eventually fall to it, with an increase of consideration and power. It could foresee its own advantage, so far as it were not absorbed by a national parliament, in the lowering of status so much dreaded by the other dynasties. . . .

In order that German patriotism should be active and effective, it needs as a rule the middle term of dependence on a dynasty; independent of dynasty it rarely comes to the rising point, though in theory it daily does so, in parliament, in the press, in public meeting; in practice the German needs either attachment to a dynasty or the goad of anger, hurrying him into action: the latter phenomenon, however, by its own nature is not permanent. . . . The German's love of Fatherland has need of a prince on whom it can concentrate its attachment. . . .

The other nations of Europe have no such go-between for their patriotism and national sentiment. Poles, Hungarians, Italians, Spaniards, Frenchmen would under any or without any dynasty preserve their homogeneous national unity. The Teutonic stocks of the north, the Swedes and the Danes, have shown themselves pretty free from dynastic sentiment; and in England, though external respect for the Crown is demanded by good society, and the formal maintenance of monarchy is held expedient by all parties that have hitherto had any share in government, I do not anticipate the disruption of the nation, or that such sentiments were common in the time of the Jacobites would attain to any practical form, if in the course of its historical development the British people should come to deem a change of dynasty or the transition to a republican form of government necessary or expedient. The preponderance of dynastic attachment, and the use of a dynasty as the indispensable cement to hold together a definite portion of the nation calling itself by the name of the dynasty is a specific peculiarity of the German Empire. . . .

Official Account of the Reestablishment of the German Empire, January 18, 1871*

In the palace of Louis XIV, in that ancient center of a hostile power which for centuries has striven to divide and humiliate Germany, the solemn proclamation of the German Empire was made on January 18, exactly one

---

*James Harvey Robinson and Charles A. Beard (1909), *Readings in Modern European History*, Boston: Ginn and Company, pp. 163–65.

hundred and seventy years after the assumption of the royal dignity by the Prussian sovereigns at Königsberg. Though the German people, owing to the necessities of the times, were represented at the ceremony only by the German army, the eyes of the entire nation were gratefully turned to the place where, surrounded by sovereigns, generals, and soldiers, King William announced to the world the assumption by himself and his heirs of a title for the reestablishment of which we have been yearning during the sixty long years it has been in abeyance.

As yet the infatuation of the enemy does not permit us to throw aside the weapons we have taken up in self-defense; and as our unity arose out of the first part of the campaign, so will our empire be strengthened by the remaining feats of arms. By the self-sacrificing devotion of all classes of society, the nation has proved that it still possesses that warlike prowess which distinguished our ancestors. It has recovered its ancient position in Europe; and, neither fearing an adversary nor envying any neighbor, discreet and temperate in its acts and aims, it accepts the destiny prophesied for it in the proclamation of its new emperor. This destiny is to add to its power not by conquest but by promoting culture, liberty, and civilization. As far as the German people are concerned, there will be no more wars in Europe after the termination of the present campaign. . . .

Owing to the unfavorable weather, the festive procession which was to conduct his Majesty from the prefecture to the palace did not take place. The crown prince, with Lieutenant General Blumenthal, his chief of staff, and an escort of Prussians, Würtembergers, Badeners, and Bavarians, drove to the palace to receive his royal father at the eastern portal in front of the Princes' Stairway. In the courtyard of the palace a company of the king's own troops was drawn up as a guard of honor. . . .

At a quarter past twelve his Majesty entered the hall, when a choir consisting of men of the Seventh, Forty-Seventh, and Fifty-Eighth regiments intoned the choral, "Let all the world rejoice in the Lord." . . . When the choir ceased, the congregation sang one verse of the choral, "Praise and honor unto the Lord." The ordinary military liturgy was then read by the clergymen and a sermon preached by the Reverend A. Rogge. Alluding to the well known inscription on the ceiling of the hall, "*Le roi governe par lui-même*," the preacher observed that the kings of Prussia had risen to greatness by adopting a different and more religious motto, namely "The kings of the earth reign under me, saith the Lord." The *Te Deum Laudamus* closed the service.

The king then walked up to where the colors were displayed, and, standing before them, read the document proclaiming the reestablishment of the German Empire. Count Bismarck having read the king's proclamation to the German nation, the grand duke of Baden stepped forth and exclaimed, "Long live his

Majesty the emperor!" The cheers of the assembly were taken up by the bands playing the national anthem.

Questions

1. What do the views expressed by Bismarck in these passages from his memoirs reveal about his political beliefs? What kind of government does he favor for Prussia/Germany? Why?
2. Is Bismarck a pragmatist or a political idealist? Cite examples from the source to illustrate or support your answer.
3. What justifications does the account of the declaration of the German Empire provide for the unification of Germany and German nationalism?
4. Which of the two sources above is more reflective of German nationalism? Why?

Anton von Werner (1843–1915) accompanied the German army during its invasion of France in the Franco-Prussian War of 1870–1. This painting represents the French surrender after the Battle of Sedan on September 1, 1870, which resulted in the German capture of the French Emperor Napoleon

FIGURE 5: Anton von Werner, *The Capitulation of Sedan on 1st September 1870.* Courtesy of Getty Images.

III. Otto von Bismarck is seated to the right; the figure standing next to him is General von Moltke, the chief of the German general staff. Werner also did a painting depicting the proclamation of the German Empire in January 1871.

Questions

1. In what ways does this painting supplement the account of the proclamation of the German Empire that appears earlier in the chapter?
2. Is this painting meant to convey a position or a certain attitude toward the event it depicts? If so, what is that position or attitude? Why choose this subject for a painting instead of a battlefield or action scene?
3. Is the painting reflective of German nationalism? How does it portray Bismarck? How might this painting have been viewed by people of other nationalities, for example the French or the English?

CHARLES STEWART PARNELL, INTRODUCTION

In 1879, Ireland was embroiled in a "Land War" in which Direct Action Nationalists engaged in acts of terrorism and the destruction of landlords' property in order to gain concessions that would give Irish tenant farmers fairer rents and more rights, such as the right to sell their stake in the land or to be compensated for improvements they made to their property if they should be evicted for any reason. In addition, rural poverty remained widespread and the memory of the Great Famine lingered. Parnell appealed both to the desire for land reform among the Irish and to aspirations for Irish independence that practically dated back to the 1801 Act of Union itself but that had intensified in the course of the nineteenth century. Parnell sought change through political legislation, but he supported direct action as a means of putting additional pressure on the British to make concessions. The strategy worked to a degree; the 1881 Land Act was just one in a series of reforms passed by the British Parliament in an attempt to appease Irish radicals. But these did not end demands for home rule. Under pressure from Parnell and his Irish party, the British Prime Minister, William Gladstone, would introduce a Home Rule Bill in 1885. It would be defeated, but Irish home rule would remain a central issue in British politics until the Anglo-Irish Treaty of 1921 finally established the Irish Free State in all but the six counties of Northern Ireland, which remained a part of the United Kingdom.

Charles Stewart Parnell, Speech at Limerick, August 31, 1879, and Speech at a Banquet in Wexford, October 10, 1881*

The Land for the People

I firmly believe that, bad as are the prospects of this country, out of that we will obtain good for Ireland. . . . It is the duty of the Irish tenant farmers to combine amongst themselves and ask for a reduction of rent, and if they get no reduction where a reduction is necessary, then I say that it is the duty of the tenant to pay no rent until he gets it. And if they combined in that way, if they stood together, and if being refused a reasonable and just reduction, they kept a firm grip of their homesteads, I can tell them that no power on earth could prevail against the hundreds of thousands of the tenant farmers of this country. Do not fear. You are not to be exterminated as you were in 1847, and take my word for it, it will not be attempted. You should ask for concessions that are just. Ask them in the proper manner, and good landlords will give these conditions. But for the men who had always shown themselves regardless of right and justice in their dealings with these questions, I say it is necessary for you to maintain a firm and determined attitude. If you maintain that attitude victory must be yours. If when a farm was tenantless, owing to any cause, you refuse to take it, and the present most foolish competition amongst farmers came to an end, as undoubtedly it now must, these men who are forgetful of reason and of common sense must come to reconsider their position. I believe that the land of a country ought to be owned by the people of the country. And I think we should center our exertions upon attaining that end. . . . When we have the people of this country prosperous, self-reliant, and confident of the future, we will have an Irish nation which will be able to hold its own amongst the nations of the world. We will have a country which will be able to speak with the enemy in the gate—we will have a people who understand their rights, and knowing those rights, will be resolved to maintain them. We must all have this without injustice to any individual.

At a Banquet in Wexford

I am frequently disposed to think that Ireland has not yet got through the troubled waters of affliction to be crossed before we reach the promised land of prosperity to Ireland. If we had no one but our own selves to deal with, we should soon arrive at prosperity; but we have, unfortunately another, a

---

*Charles Stewart Parnell (2009; originally published 1892), *Words of the Dead Chief*, Dublin: University Dublin College Press, pp. 31–32, 67.

stronger and more powerful nation outside our own nation, who assume to control our destinies, and we do not know what interference, what meddlesome interference we will have to meet from time to time in the future to retard our prosperity and prevent the attainment of that which we all hope and wish for. . . . But I have every confidence that even the most bigoted Saxon will come to recognize that he is asking the great English nation to perform an impossibility when he asks that nation to attempt to rule our nation from England soil. . . .

Questions

1. How are the land issue and Irish nationalism linked in these speeches by Parnell?
2. What do these passages reveal about the nature of nineteenth-century nationalism in general?
3. What does Parnell expect to be the benefits of Irish home rule, as indicated by these speeches?

THEODORE ROOSEVELT, *AMERICAN IDEALS AND OTHER ESSAYS*, INTRODUCTION

The passage in this essay by Theodore Roosevelt provides some of the background and ideological context for the Roosevelt Corollary to the Monroe Doctrine, which Roosevelt pronounced on December 2, 1904, in response to an economic crisis in the Dominican Republic. As president, Roosevelt was also a strong proponent of sea power and supported the construction of the Panama Canal. His commitment to US involvement in world affairs even led him to propose himself as a mediator in the Russo-Japanese War; his brokering of a peace treaty ending that conflict earned him the Nobel Peace Prize for 1906. He took a proactive approach in domestic matters as well, throwing his energy behind conservation of natural resources, a larger role for government in the economy, and looking out for the best interests of US citizens through his support for such legislation as the Pure Food and Drug Act. Roosevelt was also a prolific author and a voracious reader who must have slept very little considering all that he undertook. The following excerpt from one of his essays provides a unique look at the ways in which nationalism factored into his larger views and political and foreign policy programme.

Theodore Roosevelt, *American Ideals and Other Essays**

The Monroe Doctrine should not be considered from any purely academic standpoint, but as a broad, general principle of living policy. It is to be justified not by precedent merely, but by the needs of the nation and the true interests of Western civilization. It, of course, adds strength to our position at this moment to show that the action of the national authorities is warranted by the actions of their predecessors on like occasions in the past, and that the line of policy we are now pursuing is that which has been pursued by all other statesmen of note since the Republic grew sufficiently powerful to make what it said of weight in foreign affairs. But even if in time past we had been as blind to the national honor and welfare as are the men who at the present day champion the anti-American side of the Venezuelan question, it would now be necessary for statesmen who were both far-sighted and patriotic to enunciate the principles for which the Monroe Doctrine stands. In other words, if the Monroe Doctrine did not already exist, it would be necessary forthwith to create it. . . .

The Monroe Doctrine may briefly be defined as forbidding European encroachment on American soil. It is not desirable to define it so rigidly as to prevent our taking into account the varying degrees of national interest in varying cases. The United States has not the slightest wish to establish a universal protectorate over other American States, or to become responsible for their misdeeds. If one of them becomes involved in an ordinary quarrel with a European power, such quarrel must be settled between them by any one of the usual methods. But no European state is to be allowed to aggrandize itself on American soil at the expense of any American State. Furthermore, no transfer of an American colony from one European State to another is to be permitted, if, in the judgment of the United States such transfer would be hostile to its own interests.

John Quincy Adams, who, during the presidency of Monroe, first clearly enunciated the doctrine, which bears his chief's name, asserted it as against both Spain and Russia. In the clearest and most emphatic terms he stated that the United States could not acquiesce in the addition of new territory within the limits of any independent American State, whether in the Northern or Southern Hemisphere, by any European power. He took his position against Russia when Russia threatened to take possession of what is now Oregon. He took this position against Spain when, backed by other powers of Continental Europe, she threatened to conquer certain of the Spanish-American States. . . .

---

*Theodore Roosevelt (1903), *American Ideals and Other Essays*, Philadelphia: Green and Company, pp. 45–46, 47–48, 50–51.

Primarily, our action is based on national self-interest. In other words, it is patriotic. A certain limited number of persons are fond of decrying patriotism as a selfish virtue, and strive with all their feeble might to inculcate in its place a kind of milk-and-water cosmopolitanism. These good people are never men of robust character or of imposing personality, and the plea itself is not worth considering. Some reformers may urge that in the ages distant future patriotism, like the habit of monogamous marriage, will become a needless and obsolete virtue; but just at present the man who loves other countries as much as he does his own is quite as noxious a member of society as the man who loves other women as much as he loves his wife. Love of country is an elemental virtue, like love of home, or like honesty or courage. No country will accomplish very much for the world at large unless it elevates itself. The useful member of the community is a man who first and foremost attends to his own rights and his own duties, and who therefore becomes better fitted to do his share in the common duties of all. The useful member of the brotherhood of nations is the nation which is most thoroughly saturated with the national idea, and which realizes most fully its rights as a nation and its duties to its own citizens. This is in no way incompatible with a scrupulous regard for the rights of other nations, or the desire to remedy the wrongs of suffering peoples.

Questions
1. What do you think that Roosevelt means here by "the true interests of Western Civilization"?
2. What does Roosevelt suggest here about the extent of the rights and responsibilities of the United States toward other American states? What does he suggest about the limits of US power in regard to them?
3. In what ways does this passage by Roosevelt reflect American nationalism? What is his definition of nationalism?

LIANG QICHAO, "THE MEANING OF 'RENEWING THE PEOPLE,'" INTRODUCTION

Like Garibaldi, Liang Qichao (1873–1929) participated in a reform movement in his native country led by a fellow countryman, only to be forced into exile when that initial attempt at reform went awry. Kang Youwei (1858–1927) briefly led a reform movement in 1898 ("the Hundred Days of Reform") that landed Liang a position as a bureaucrat in the Chinese government until the Empress Dowager Cixi (1835–1908) ousted the reformers in an attempt to return China to autocratic rule. Liang fled to Japan, from where he launched a journal called Renewing the People. *The publication only lasted from 1902 to 1905, but had a profound influence on a new generation of Chinese intellectuals searching for new ideas and solutions to China's subservience to Western influence. Here Liang explains his use of the term "renewing the people," a traditional neo-Confucian concept that Liang has co-opted in the service of Chinese nationalism.*

Liang Qichao, "The Meaning of 'Renewing the People'"*

The term *renewing the people* does not mean that our people must give up entirely what is old in order to follow others. There are two meanings of *renewing*. One is to improve what is original in the people and so renew it; the other is to adopt what is originally lacking in the people and so make a new people. Without both of these, there will be no success. . . .

When a nation can stand up in the world its citizens must have a unique character. From morality and laws to customs, habits, literature, and the arts, these all possess a certain unique spirit. Then the ancestors pass them down and their descendants receive them. The group becomes unified and a nation is formed. This is truly the wellspring of nationalism. Our people have been established as a nation on the Asian continent for several thousand years, and we must have some special characteristics that are grand, noble, and perfect, and distinctly different from those of other races. We should preserve these characteristics and not let them be lost. What is called preserving, however, is not simply to let them exist and grow by themselves and then blithely say, "I am preserving them, I am preserving them." It is like a tree: unless some new buds come out every year, its withering away may soon be expected. Or like a well: unless there is always some new spring bubbling, its exhaustion is not far away.

Is it enough merely to develop what we already have? No, it is not. The world of today is not the world of yesterday. In ancient times, we Chinese were people of villages instead of citizens. This is not because we were unable to form a citizenry but due to circumstances. Since China majestically used to be the predominant power in the East, surrounded as we were by

---

*Wm. Theodore de Bary and Richard Lufrano, eds (2000), *Sources of the Chinese Tradition*, New York: Columbia University Press, pp. 289–91.

small battalion groups, and lacking any contact with other large states, we Chinese generally considered our state to encompass the whole world. All the messages we received, all that influenced our minds, all the instructions of our sages, and all that our ancestors passed down qualified us to be citizens of a state. Although the qualifications of citizenship are not necessarily much superior to these other characteristics, in an age of struggle among nations for the survival of the fittest while the weak perish, if the qualities of citizens are wanting, then the nation cannot stand up independently between Heaven and earth.

If we wish to make our nation strong, we must investigate extensively the methods followed by other nations in becoming independent. We should select their superior points and appropriate them to make up for our own shortcomings. Now with regard to politics, academic learning, and technology, our scribes know how to take the superior points of others to make up for our own weakness; but they do not know that the people's virtue, the people's wisdom, and the people's vitality are the great basis of politics, academic learning, and techniques. If they do not take the former but adopt the latter, neglect the roots but tend the branches, it will be no different from seeing the luxuriant growth of another tree and wishing to graft its branches onto our withered trunk, or seeing the bubbling flow of another well and wishing to draw its water to fill our dry well. Thus, how to adopt and make up for what we originally lacked so that people may be renewed should be deeply and carefully considered.

. . . Thus, what I mean by "renewing the people" does not refer to those who are infatuated with Western ways and, in order to keep company with others, throw away our morals, learning, and customs of several thousand years' standing. Nor does it refer to those who stick to old paper and say that merely embracing the morals, learning, and customs of these thousands of years will be sufficient to enable us to stand upon the great earth.

Questions
1. What does Liang Qichao mean here by the phrase "renewing the people"?
2. What does Liang say is distinctive about Chinese nationalism? On what is Chinese nationalism based?
3. What is Liang's attitude toward the West? Why does he say that China needs to do in order to compete with the West?

Chapter Questions

1. Using the sources in this chapter, would it be possible to construct a narrative of the history of nineteenth-century nationalism? In other words, is there a connecting thread among the sources here or are they isolated based on their own time period and setting?

2. Does nationalism have a single meaning or different meanings, depending on the time and place?

3. For example, is there something particularly unique about American or Chinese nationalism compared to European nationalism? What do the sources by Roosevelt and Liang have in common with the other sources in this chapter? What specific differences do they reveal?

CHAPTER SIX

Reform Movements of the Nineteenth Century

INTRODUCTION

While revolutionary leaders such as Garibaldi and political leaders such as Bismarck focused on fulfilling the nationalist aspirations of the Italian and German people, respectively, others concentrated their efforts on making the hopes raised by the thinkers of the Enlightenment and the leaders of the French Revolution a reality by creating a better world. First and foremost on the agenda of those interested in reform was the abolition of slavery, which was still widespread in the nineteenth century and constituted the most obvious affront to liberal and enlightened thinkers in Europe and the Americas. Slavery was too entrenched in the United States, South America, and the Caribbean to be eradicated all at once, so reformers at first set their sights on the abolition of the slave trade. Britain took the lead, with the Parliament voting to end British participation in the slave trade in 1807, which was followed by the abolition of slavery throughout the British Empire in 1833. In 1844 the French followed suit and ended slavery throughout their empire, a measure that the government of King Louis Phillipe had announced six years earlier.

The issue of slavery in the United States at that time, however, seemed as intractable as it had been when the new nation was formed in the eighteenth century. Neither the abolitionists nor the defenders of slavery felt happy about the Missouri Compromise of 1820, which had restricted slavery in the United States to those states south of the 36°30' parallel. The British government attempted to put pressure on Texas to abolish slavery after it had declared its independence from Mexico in 1836, but to no avail; at the outbreak of the American Civil War in 1861 approximately one-fourth of families in Texas (about 22,000) owned slaves.

Two years after Texas gained its independence, Frederick Douglass (c.1817–95) escaped from slavery in Maryland, fleeing north where five years later he joined the Massachusetts Anti-Slavery Society, one of a number of abolitionist organizations springing up throughout the North in the middle decades of the nineteenth century. During the Civil War, he became a consultant for Abraham Lincoln (1809–65), who had been elected the sixteenth president of the United States in 1860 because of—and despite—his anti-slavery views. His election led a number of southern states to secede from the Union to form a new nation of Confederate States, which, had it been successful, would likely have perpetuated the institution of slavery indefinitely. Lincoln knew he could not abolish slavery in the southern states if they left the United States, so he fought to keep the Union together. At the same time he could not at first make the war just about slavery, for fear of alienating pro-slavery sympathizers in the northern states. However, on January 1, 1863, Lincoln declared the emancipation of slaves throughout the south, leading many to flee their farms and plantations to seek a new life in the North or to enlist in the Union army to play a role in the defeat of the Confederacy. This had been preceded by his famous Gettysburg Address, a powerful evocation of the reasons why the sacrifice of thousands of lives at the decisive battle that occurred near the tiny Pennsylvania hamlet was justified by a larger cause.

After the Union victory in the American Civil War and the end of slavery in the United States, only a few bastions of slavery in the Western Hemisphere remained. Even after the Spanish ended slavery in Cuba in 1886 and even though Brazil outlawed the slave trade in 1871, Brazilian plantation owners remained obstinate in their defense of slavery. But Brazil also had a strong abolition movement, led by the stately and popular Joaquim Nabuco (1848–1910). Nabuco and the Brazilian abolitionists did not merely condemn slavery on moral grounds but also as an obstacle to the modernization of the Brazilian economy. Some Brazilian provinces that did not grow coffee, and thus had little to lose, declared an end to slavery even before nationwide abolition. In other provinces, slaves simply took matters into their own hands and began fleeing plantations in droves. With public opinion veering sharply in the direction of abolition, Brazil officially emancipated its slaves in 1888.

The largest numbers of people affected by the emancipation movement of the nineteenth century were the Russian serfs, who received their freedom from Tsar Alexander II (r. 1855–81) in 1861. Alexander, who became known as the "Tsar-Liberator," gained a reputation as a reformer, but his motivations had stemmed from Russia's military defeat in the Crimean War, which was ongoing at the time of his accession to the throne. Like the "enlightened despots" of the eighteenth century, Alexander continued to govern as an absolute ruler and to strengthen his military, introducing universal conscription in 1874. He pursued a policy of expanding Russian territory and his continuation of autocratic measures provoked the rise of revolutionary organizations, including one called the "People's Will," which was responsible for Alexander's assassination in 1881. Nonetheless, he will always be most remembered for the emancipation of the serfs, the effects of which would be felt for decades after.

Having ended slavery in the British Empire in 1833, British politicians then turned their attention to the need for political and social reform at home and throughout the British Isles. The passage of the First Great Reform Act in 1832 had expanded the electorate by about 300,000, but still left the vast majority of the population disenfranchised. The enactment of some preliminary social legislation, such as the First Factory Act in 1833 and the New Poor Law in 1834, indicated a willingness on the part of government to address social issues, but did little to actually ameliorate the frequently abysmal working and living conditions of the working classes. By the 1860s the need for further reform was so pressing that a Conservative government actually passed a Second Great Reform Act in 1867, further expanding the electorate. The main sponsor of that bill was the Tory politician, Benjamin Disraeli (1804–81), who became prime minister the following year and again from 1874 to 1880. Disraeli had hoped that by embracing reform, the Conservatives could steal the thunder of the Liberal Party, led at the time by William E. Gladstone (1809–98), a former Conservative with a lengthy political résumé. Despite their differences, reform became the hallmark of the administration of both men. In addition to the Reform Act of 1867, Disraeli's government passed a wide array of social legislation, including measures dealing with public health and working class residences. In addition to the Liberal Party's landmark Education Act of 1870, making primary education compulsory throughout the United Kingdom, Gladstone turned his attention to the grievances of the Irish, especially the issue of land reform in a country that was still recovering from the devastating famine that struck the island in the 1840s.

FREDERICK DOUGLASS, *NARRATIVE OF THE LIFE OF FREDERICK DOUGLASS*, INTRODUCTION

The opening of Frederick Douglass's famous autobiography serves as a valuable introduction not only to the life of this important abolitionist but to the issue of slavery in general in the United States in the mid-nineteenth century. His matter-of-fact description of his upbringing and experience reveal the ability to calmly and dispassionately examine his life and situation that many would find morally repellent. The eloquence of his autobiography and his speeches in defense of emancipation did not conform to most people's images of former slaves during his lifetime. However, Douglass was only willing to temper his language so far; he took a strong stance in favor of abolition, including his eventual defense of the use of violence to bring about an end to the South's "peculiar institution."

Frederick Douglass, *Narrative of the Life of Frederick Douglass**

My father was a white man. He was admitted to be such by all I ever heard speak of my parentage. The opinion was also whispered that my master was

---

*Frederick Douglass (1845), *Narrative of the Life of Frederick Douglass*, Boston: The Antislavery Office, pp. 2–3, 4–5. Available online at http://www.ibiblio.org/ebooks/Douglass/Narrative/Douglass_Narrative.pdf.

my father; but of the correctness of this opinion, I know nothing; the means of knowing was withheld from me. My mother and I were separated when I was but an infant—before I knew her as my mother. It is a common custom, in the part of Maryland from which I ran away, to part children from their mothers at a very early age. Frequently, before the child has reached its twelfth month, its mother is taken from it, and hired out on some farm a considerable distance off, and the child is placed under the care of an old woman, too old for field labor. For what this separation is done, I do not know, unless it be to hinder the development of the child's affection toward its mother, and to blunt and destroy the natural affection of the mother for the child. This is the inevitable result.

I never saw my mother, to know her as such, more than four or five times in my life; and each of these times was very short in duration, and at night. She was hired by a Mr. Stewart, who lived about twelve miles from my home. She made her journeys to see me in the night, travelling the whole distance on foot, after the performance of her day's work. She was a field hand, and a whipping is the penalty of not being in the field at sunrise, unless a slave has special permission from his or her master to the contrary—a permission which they seldom get, and one that gives to him that gives it the proud name of being a kind master. I do not recollect of ever seeing my mother by the light of day. She was with me in the night. She would lie down with me, and get me to sleep, but long before I waked she was gone. Very little communication ever took place between us. Death soon ended what little we could have while she lived, and with it her hardships and suffering. She died when I was about seven years old, on one of my master's farms, near Lee's Mill. I was not allowed to be present during her illness, at her death, or burial. She was gone long before I knew anything about it. Never having enjoyed, to any considerable extent, her soothing presence, her tender and watchful care, I received the tidings of her death with much the same emotions I should have probably felt at the death of a stranger.

Called thus suddenly away, she left me without the slightest intimation of who my father was. The whisper that my master was my father, may or may not be true; and, true or false, it is of but little consequence to my purpose whilst the fact remains, in all its glaring odiousness, that slaveholders have ordained, and by law established, that the children of slave women shall in all cases follow the condition of their mothers; and this is done too obviously to administer to their own lusts, and make a gratification of their wicked desires profitable as well as pleasurable; for by this cunning arrangement, the slaveholder, in cases not a few, sustains to his slaves the double relation of master and father. . . .

I have had two masters. My first master's name was Anthony. I do not remember his first name. He was generally called Captain Anthony—a title which, I presume, he acquired by sailing a craft on the Chesapeake Bay. He was not considered a rich slaveholder. He owned two or three farms, and about thirty slaves. His farms and slaves were under the care of an overseer. The overseer's name was Plummer. Mr. Plummer was a miserable drunkard, a profane swearer, and a savage monster. He always went armed with a cowskin and a heavy cudgel. I have known him to cut and slash the women's heads so horribly, that even master would be enraged at his cruelty, and would threaten to whip him if he did not mind himself. Master, however, was not a humane slaveholder. It required extraordinary barbarity on the part of an overseer to affect him. He was a cruel man, hardened by a long life of slaveholding. He would at times seem to take great pleasure in whipping a slave. I have often been awakened at the dawn of day by the most heart-rending shrieks of an own aunt of mine, whom he used to tie up to a joist, and whip upon her naked back till she was literally covered with blood. No words, no tears, no prayers, from his gory victim, seemed to move his iron heart from its bloody purpose. The louder she screamed, the harder he whipped; and where the blood ran fastest, there he whipped longest. He would whip her to make her scream, and whip her to make her hush; and not until overcome by fatigue, would he cease to swing the blood-clotted cowskin. I remember the first time I ever witnessed this horrible exhibition. I was quite a child, but I well remember it. I never shall forget it whilst I remember anything. It was the first of a long series of such outrages, of which I was doomed to be a witness and a participant. It struck me with awful force. It was the bloodstained gate, the entrance to the hell of slavery, through which I was about to pass. It was a most terrible spectacle. I wish I could commit to paper the feelings with which I beheld it.

Questions

1. How do Douglass's personal experiences reflect larger issues related to slavery and abuses excoriated by the abolitionists? What specific abuses did Douglass experience or witness as a young slave?

2. How would you describe the tone of Douglass's writing? Was this intentional? What effect does it have on the reader?

3. In what ways does the tone reinforce the contents or the rhetorical message that Douglass attempts to convey to the reader? In other words, what is the purpose of Douglass in recording the details and facts recounted here?

FIGURE 6: Anti-slavery illustration from *Uncle Tom's Cabin*.
Courtesy of Getty Images.

Harriet Beecher Stowe (1811–96) published her novel *Uncle Tom's Cabin* in 1852, largely in response to the Fugitive Slave Law, which required law enforcement officers in the North to assist in the capture and return of escaped slaves who fled the South in search of freedom. The book may not have adhered to contemporary literary standards in its undisguised political message, but it gained such enormous popularity that Lincoln later referred to Stowe as "the little woman who wrote the book that made this great [Civil] war." Stowe created memorable figures and scenes that seared the horrors of slavery onto the public imagination, reinforced by images that appeared in the book, such as the one above. The illustration is by E. F. Skinner and was accompanied by the caption, "Tom is sold by auction and taken off in fetters." In the book, Tom's new master, Simon Legree, would become synonymous with cruel and sadistic abuse of power and authority.

Questions
1. How important are illustrations in reinforcing the message of a book?
2. Do illustrations have the ability to change the impact of a text on the reader? What might have been the impact of this illustration?
3. What is the value of book illustrations as a historical source, independent of the text itself? What is the historical value of this particular illustration?

ABRAHAM LINCOLN, SELECTED WRITINGS, INTRODUCTION

Abraham Lincoln started his political career as a country lawyer who was first elected to the US House of Representatives in 1846; his stint as a Congressman was brief, however, lasting only one two-year term. His motivation to return to the political fray stemmed from the passage of the 1852 Kansas-Nebraska Act, which violated the Missouri Compromise by allowing the voters in those states to determine whether they would permit slavery or not. He addresses this issue in a letter to an old friend, Joshua Speed, an excerpt from which appears below. Lincoln's aggressive campaign denouncing the Act brought him national attention and quickly catapulted him to the leadership of the newly formed Republican Party. Just two years after he joined it, he became its nominee for President. His simple eloquence and passionate commitment to his ideals served him well on the campaign trail and as President, as can be seen from the passages below from his Gettysburg Address and his second inaugural address of March 4, 1865, which followed his reelection in 1864. On April 14, 1865, Lincoln himself became yet another victim of the Civil War, shot to death by a frustrated actor and Southern sympathizer named John Wilkes Booth while attending a play at Ford's Theatre in Washington.

Abraham Lincoln, Letter to Joshua Speed, August 24, 1855[*]

I do oppose the extension of slavery, because my judgment and feelings so prompt me; and I am under no obligation to the contrary. If for this you and I must differ, differ we must. You say if you were President, you would send an army and hang the leaders of the Missouri outrages upon the Kansas elections; still, if Kansas fairly votes herself a slave state, she must be admitted, or the Union must be dissolved. But how if she votes herself a slave State *unfairly*—that is, by the very means for which you say you would hang men? Must she still be admitted, or the Union be dissolved? That will be the phase of the question when it first becomes a practical one. In your assumption that there may be a *fair* decision of the slavery question in Kansas, I plainly see you and I would differ about the Nebraska-law. I look upon that enactment not as a *law*, but as *violence* from the beginning. It was conceived in violence, passed in violence, is maintained in violence, and is being executed in violence. I say it was *conceived* in violence, because the destruction of the Missouri Compromise, under the circumstances,

---

[*]http://www.abrahamlincolnonline.org/lincoln/speeches/speed.htm

was nothing less than violence. It was *passed* in violence, because it could not have passed at all but for the votes of many members in violence of the known will of their constituents. It is *maintained* in violence because the elections since, clearly demand its repeal, and this demand is openly disregarded. *You* say men ought to be hung for the way they are executing that law; and *I* say the way it is being executed is quite as good as any of its antecedents. It is being executed in the precise way which was intended from the first; else why does no Nebraska man express astonishment or condemnation? Poor Reeder is the only public man who has been silly enough to believe that anything like fairness was ever intended; and he has been bravely undeceived.

That Kansas will form a Slave Constitution, and, with it, will ask to be admitted into the Union, I take to be an already settled question; and so settled by the very means you so pointedly condemn. By every principle of law, ever held by any court, North or South, every negro taken to Kansas is free; yet, in utter disregard of this—in the spirit of violence merely—that beautiful Legislature gravely passes a law to hang men who shall venture to inform a negro of his legal rights. This is the substance, and real object of the law. If, like Haman, they should hang upon the gallows of their own building, I shall not be among the mourners for their fate.

Abraham Lincoln, "Gettysburg Address"*

Fourscore and seven years ago our fathers brought forth on this continent a new nation, conceived in liberty and dedicated to the proposition that all men are created equal. Now we are engaged in a great civil war, testing whether that nation or any nation so conceived and so dedicated can long endure. We are met on a great battlefield of that war. We have come to dedicate a portion of that field as a final resting-place for those who here gave their lives that that nation might live. It is altogether fitting and proper that we should do this. But in a larger sense, we cannot dedicate, we cannot consecrate, we cannot hallow this ground. The brave men, living and dead who struggled here have consecrated it far above our poor power to add or detract. The world will little note nor long remember what we say here, but it can never forget what they did here. It is for us the living rather to be dedicated here to the unfinished work which they who fought here have thus far so nobly advanced. It is rather for us to be here dedicated to the great task remaining before us—that from these honored dead we take increased devotion to that cause for which they gave the last full measure of devotion—that we here highly resolve that these dead shall not have died in vain, that this nation under God shall have a new birth

---

*http://avalon.law.yale.edu/19th_century/gettyb.asp

of freedom, and that government of the people, by the people, for the people shall not perish from the earth.

Abraham Lincoln, Second Inaugural Address*

On the occasion corresponding to this four years ago, all thoughts were anxiously directed to an impending civil war. All dreaded it—all sought to avert it. While the inaugural address was being delivered from this place, devoted altogether to saving the Union without war, insurgent agents were in the city seeking to destroy it without war—seeking to dissolve the Union, and divide effects, by negotiation. Both parties deprecated war; but one of them would make war rather than let the nation survive; and the other would accept war rather than let it perish. And the war came.

One-eighth of the whole population were colored slaves, not distributed generally over the Union, but localized in the Southern part of it. These slaves constituted a peculiar and powerful interest. All knew that this interest was, somehow, the cause of the war. To strengthen, perpetuate, and extend this interest was the object for which the insurgents would rend the Union, even by war; while the government claimed no right to do more than to restrict the territorial enlargement of it.

Neither party expected for the war the magnitude or the duration which it has already attained. Neither anticipated that the cause of the conflict might cease with, or even before, the conflict itself should cease. Each looked for an easier triumph, and a result less fundamental and astounding. Both read the same Bible, and pray to the same God; and each invokes his aid against the other. It may seem strange that any men should dare to ask a just God's assistance in wringing their bread from the sweat of other men's faces; but let us judge not, that we be not judged. The prayers of both could not be answered—that of neither has been answered fully.

The Almighty has his own purposes. "Woe unto the world because of offenses! for it must needs be that offenses come; but woe to that man by whom the offense cometh." If we shall suppose that American slavery is one of those offenses which, in the providence of God, must needs come, but which, having continued through his appointed time, he now wills to remove, and that he gives to both North and South this terrible war, as the woe due to those by whom the offense came, shall we discern therein any departure from those divine attributes which the believers in a living God always ascribe to him? Fondly do we hope—fervently do we pray—that this mighty scourge of war

---

*http://www.lbl.gov/IT/CIS/dp/samples/lincoln-2nd-inaug.pdf

may speedily pass away. Yet, if God wills that it continue until all the wealth piled by the bondsman's two hundred and fifty years of unrequited toil shall be sunk, and until every drop of blood drawn by the lash shall be paid by another drawn with the sword, as was said three thousand years ago, so still it must be said, "The judgments of the Lord are true and righteous altogether."

With malice toward none; with charity for all; with firmness in the right, as God gives us to see the right, let us strive on to finish the work we are in; to bind up the nation's wounds; to care for him who shall have borne the battle, and for his widow, and his orphan—to do all which may achieve and cherish a just and lasting peace among ourselves, and with all nations.

Questions

1. What does Lincoln's letter to Speed reveal about his position with regard to the Kansas-Nebraska act? Does it contain an outright condemnation of slavery? Why do you think he frames his argument in the way he does?

2. In his Gettysburg Address, Lincoln says that "the world will little note nor long remember what we say here. . . ." Instead, it has become one of the most famous and remembered speeches of all time. Why?

3. How does Lincoln frame the Civil War, its causes, and its significance in his Second Inaugural Address? Based on the passage above, what rhetorical purposes was this speech meant to serve? What is the historical importance of this speech? How does it compare to the other two documents included above?

PAULA SOUZA, "A PLANTER'S ACCOUNT OF THE ENDING OF SLAVERY IN BRAZIL," INTRODUCTION

Even before the formal abolition of slavery in Brazil, its end had been a foregone conclusion for some time. Still, when the Brazilian slaves were freed in 1888 and their owners received no compensation from the Brazilian government, some planters had to wonder if they could survive economically. In the letter below, one plantation owner, Paula Souza, explains why emancipation might not be such a bad thing for them after all. After all, the liberated slaves would still need jobs and most would continue to work at tasks for which they had the knowledge and experience. In fact, some planters had already freed their slaves in exchange for a specified length of continued service that usually lasted at least several years. This firsthand account is one of the most valuable sources for understanding the transitional period in Brazilian history that followed the emancipation of the slaves. The author was a former opponent of abolition; the abolitionist member of Brazil's Chamber of Deputies had the letter published in a São Paulo newspaper in April 1888 within a month of its composition.

Paula Souza, "A Planter's Account of the Ending of Slavery in Brazil"*

Remanso, March 19, 1888

Since the first of January I have not possessed a single slave! I liberated all of them, and bound them to the property by means of a contract identical to the one that I have with the foreign colonists and that I intend to have with those whom I will hire. You can see that my slavocratic tendencies are moderate and tolerable.

I joyfully inform you that my new colonists have not yet given me the least reason for complaint. I am living happy and content among them, and they shower me with attention and respect.

I granted them total and unconditional freedom, and in the short speech which I made to them when I passed out their letters, I spoke to them of the grave responsibilities that freedom imposed upon them, and I spoke some words to them that came from my heart and were completely different from those that I had prepared for the occasion. From the literary point of view it was a total fiasco, because I also wept. I ended up granting them a week to make the arrangements that would suit them best, while at the same time informing them that my place would always remain open to those among them who wished to work and behave themselves.

With the exception of three, who went to search for their sisters in São Paulo, and of two others, including an *ingênuo*, who joined their father, whom I freed ten years ago, all stayed with me, and they are the same whom I find about me, and with whom I am now happy and content as I said above.

And now to the information that will benefit the planters in the north, who soon will be faced by that social necessity: the total and immediate emancipation of the slave.

Tell the others in your province not to fool themselves with a half-measure of freedom in the hope of not disorganizing work that has already been started. With conditional liberation they will get nothing from the slaves. They want to feel free, and to work under a new system only, and with total responsibility.

---

*Robert Edward Conrad (2000), *Children of God's Fire: A Documentary History of Black Slavery in Brazil*, State College: Penn State University Press, pp. 476–78.

Conditional liberation, even with a very short period of continuing obligations, does not have any effect upon those people who have been tormented by such a long captivity. They suspect—and with reason in regard to some—that that kind of freedom is a mere trick to keep them in that slavery from which circumstances have now freed them. They work, but lazily and with a poor attitude. The body functions, but not the spirit.

When they are completely free they cause a bit of trouble, but in the end they establish themselves at one place or another. What does it matter? What difference does it make if my ex-slaves go in search of another patron, if at least they work, and others come to take their place!

We here in São Paulo have a complete experience with the matter and a total understanding of every form of liberation. There is only one reasonable and profitable kind of freedom, and that is total, immediate, and unconditional freedom. The liberated people must themselves take responsibility for the error of leaving the place where they were slaves. It is obvious that there are masters who have lost all their workers, and the only reason for this is that they did not deserve to possess them. But the great majority will be settled someplace within a month.

Questions
1. What has convinced this former defender of slavery of the merits of abolition?
2. What is the purpose of the letter?
3. Is the author sympathetic to the freed slaves? Is he more concerned for their interests or those of the planters? What effects were such attitudes likely to have on the future of owner-labor relations on Brazilian coffee plantations?

ALEKSANDR NIKOLAEVICH ENGELGARDT, *LETTERS FROM THE COUNTRY, 1872–1887,* INTRODUCTION

In 1871 the government of Tsar Alexander II sought to punish Aleksandr Nikolaevich Engelgardt, a chemist employed in the capital city of St. Petersburg, for his radical political associations by exiling him from the capital. Allowed to choose the location of his exile, Engelgardt chose the remote country village of Batischevo in Smolensk Province. This occurred ten years after the emancipation of the serfs in Russia. In his new location, Engelgardt took up the administration of his estate and writing, the latter of which led to a series of letters "from the country," which were published in a journal called Notes from the Fatherland *between 1872 and 1882. The excerpts below are indicative of the kind of revealing information and insightful analysis contained in the letters, which provide a great source of information on the effects of emancipation in the ensuing decades. Cathy A. Frierson, who edited the letters and translated them into English, described them as offering "valuable access to history from below, from the village street, the gentry manor, the local court of justice, the train station, and the tavern." What most distinguished the emancipation of the serfs from the freedom of the slaves in places like the United States and Brazil was that the newly-freed Russian peasants received land at the expense of the aristocracy, even if they were expected to reimburse the former landowners through a complex formula that placed responsibility on the* mir, *or village as a whole, rather than on individual peasants. The advantages of such a system form a starting point for the excerpts below.*

Aleksandr Nikolaevich Engelgardt, *Letters from the Country, 1872–1887**

Anyone who understands the *essence* of our agriculture will understand how important it is for agriculturalists to gather together for farming together and what enormous wealth could then be realized. Only through *joint* farming is it possible to plant feed grasses, which makes it possible to mow earlier and to make more profitable use of the harvest season. Only with joint farming is it possible to purchase the most important farm machinery, namely machinery that *speeds up* the harvesting of hay and grain; only with joint farming is it possible to release a significant number of people for work elsewhere. Given the rapidity of railroad transportation, these people could go to the south, where the harvest season starts sooner, and, having done their work there, they could return home to their own harvest. On the other hand, it becomes clear how important it is to suspend any other production which takes hands away from the fieldwork during the harvest season. All factories should shut down their operations during this time. Again, the enormous number of free hands points to the necessity of developing small-scale domestic production. We do not need factories or mills, but *small* village distilleries, dairies, tanneries, weaving mills, and so on, whose refuse can also be used profitably in farming.

*Aleksandr Nikolaevich Engelgardt (1993), *Letters from the Country, 1872–1887*, translated and edited by Cathy A. Frierson, New York: Oxford University Press, pp. 172, 239–40.

The divisions of land into small plots for individual use, the settlement of separate farmers on these plots, living in their own households and cultivating their plots separately, is senseless in agricultural terms. Only agronomists who have been "translated from German" can defend this manner of farming by individual farmers on separate small pieces of land. Farming can *truly advance only when the land is under joint use and cultivation.* . . . I said above that several diggers' villages purchased land as their collective property after the Emancipation. I need to clarify this a bit, because some might think that the purchase of land by peasants may be more and more widespread among the peasants. But that is not the case at all. . . .

A branch of the Peasant Land Bank has opened here also. In our "Happy Little Corner" the peasants are also buying land with the bank's assistance. The five villages which border my estate have already purchased a rather large amount of land.

And it is turning out well.

The landowners are happy they can sell the land they don't need, land they don't know what to do with, from which they don't get any income, for which it is difficult to find any buyers other than peasants. For the most part it is cutoff lands that are being sold, land beyond the fields, wastelands, separate abandoned homesteads, and so on.

The peasants are happy they can buy the land they need "for eternity." They can put the land they have purchased "to good use." Purchased land is always absolutely essential for peasants; many of them, for the most part, even before—and others since the Emancipation itself—had made use of them, paying for them with the labor for the landowners, usually they worked plots of gentry land in *krugs*. But these jobs were extremely oppressive for the peasants. Only necessity, because there "was no place to move," forces the peasants to work these plots for the use of these lands.

Now, thanks to the assistance of the Peasant Land Bank, the question is being resolved splendidly to the satisfaction of both landowners and peasants. The landowners are receiving the money they need, the peasants are acquiring the land they need. Both sides are happy. It is turning out well. . . .

Questions
1. What are the advantages of collective farming, according to Engelgardt?
2. What is Engelgardt's attitude toward industrialization?
3. Writing from the vantage point of the 1870s, is he optimistic about the future? Why or why not?

BENJAMIN DISRAELI AND WILLIAM GLADSTONE, INTRODUCTION

Benjamin Disraeli was a charismatic and popular politician whose political philosophy was based in part on the argument that the aristocracy represented the interests of society as a whole whereas the middle-class supporters of the Liberal Party were mainly interested in furthering their own economic interests. Disraeli was also a political pragmatist, however. When proposing the Second Great Reform Act in 1867, which approximately doubled the size of the electorate, Disraeli persuaded his fellow party members that it would be better to have a more moderate reform measure sponsored by them than a more radical one passed by the Liberal Party. Still, Disraeli made no secret of his own political views, which one can discern from his novels and other writings, including voluminous correspondence. The letter below is particularly indicative of Disraeli's views on the working classes and other matters related to the passage of the Second Reform Act.

Disraeli believed, among other things, that the working classes would be willing to support a Conservative Party agenda, even one that included imperial expansion and an aggressive foreign policy, both of which Disraeli pursued as prime minister from 1874 to 1880. In 1879, campaigning to convince the public to oust the Conservatives and Disraeli from power, Gladstone laid out his case against them in a passionate plea related to his commitment to get an Irish Land Act through Parliament. His series of speeches, excerpts from one of which appears below, given in Scotland over the period of about two weeks, are considered a critical turning point in turning the electorate against Disraeli and securing a landslide victory for Gladstone and the Liberals in the next general election. Gladstone would indeed go on to pass an Irish Land Act in 1881 and a third Great Reform Act in 1884, but his government would founder on his support for a home rule bill for Ireland in 1885–6. The two documents below, written by bitter rivals, perhaps provide some indication of why the British electorate vacillated between the two over a two-decade period.

Benjamin Disraeli, Letter, November 11, 1867*

To: W. Cotter

Sir,—

I regret that I cannot dine with the London and Westminster working men today. I should have been honored and gratified by being their guest; but it is

---

*Benjamin Disraeli (2013), *Benjamin Disraeli Letters*, Volume IX, edited by Michel W. Pharand and Ellen L. Hawran, Toronto: University of Toronto Press, p. 409.

impossible. I approve the purpose of the association, of which you are chairman, and of the means by which they are effecting it. None are so interested in maintaining the institutions of the country as the working classes. The rich and the powerful will not find much difficulty, under any circumstances, in maintaining their rights, but the privileges of the people can only be defended and secured by national institutions. There is also another reason why I am glad to see among the working classes an organization in favor of the laws and constitution of the country. There are some symptoms of a lawless spirit amongst us at the moment which the light-headed may be inclined to admire as the proofs of the spirit of freedom. Nothing can be more fallacious. Their tendency is hostile to freedom, and their consequence must be detrimental to our common rights. In old days it was our pride that the constable's staff had more authority in this realm than the sabres and muskets of the police of the continent. It will be bad for us all if that constitutional conviction ceases to influence this country. It was a homage to law, which is the foundation of all freedom. He who wars against order wars against liberty.

I remain yours truly,
B. DISRAELI

William Gladstone, Speech in St. Andrew's Hall, Glasgow, December 5, 1879*

. . . What is the general upshot? Let us look at it together. I will use the fewest words. We have finance in confusion; we have legislation in intolerable arrear; we have honor compromised by the breach of public law; we have public distress aggravated by the destruction of confidence; we have Russia aggrandized yet estranged; we have Turkey befriended as we say, but mutilated, and sinking every day; we have Europe restless and disturbed—Europe, which after the Treaty of Paris, at all events so far as the Eastern Question was concerned, had something like the rest for a period approaching twenty years, has, almost ere the ink of the Treaty of Berlin is dry, been agitated from end to end with rumors and alarms, so that on the last 10th of November we were told that the Prime Minister thought that peace might be preserved, but on the previous 9th of November—namely, four months after the Treaty—it had been much more doubtful. In Africa you have before you the memory of bloodshed, of military disaster, the record of 10,000 Zulus—such is the computation of Bishop Colenso—slain for no other offence than their attempt to defend against your artillery with their naked bodies their hearths and homes, their wives and families. You have the invasion of a free people in the Transvaal; and you have,

---

*William Gladstone (1971), *Midlothian Speeches*, New York: Humanities Press, pp. 209–10.

I fear, in one quarter or another,—I will not enter into details, which might be injurious to the public interest,—prospects of further disturbance and shedding of blood. You have Afghanistan ruined; you have India not advanced, but thrown back in government, subjected to heavy and unjust charges, subjected to what may well be termed, in comparison with the mild government of former years, a system of oppression; and with all this you have had at home, in matters which I will not detail, the law broken, and the rights of Parliament invaded. Gentlemen, amidst the whole of this pestilent activity,—for I must call it,—this distress and bloodshed which we have either produced or largely shared in producing, not in one instance down to the Treaty of Berlin, and down to the war in Afghanistan,—not in one instance did we either do a deed, or speak an effectual word, on behalf of liberty. Such is the upshot, gentlemen, of the sad enumeration. To call this policy Conservative is, in my opinion, a pure mockery, and an abuse of terms. Whatever it may be in its motive, it is in its result disloyal, it is in its essence thoroughly subversive. There is no democrat, there is no agitator, there is no propounder of anti-rent doctrines, whatever mischief he may do, who can compare in mischief with possessors of authority who thus invert, and who thus degrade, the principles of free government in the British Empire. Gentlemen, I wish to end as I began. Is this the way, or is this not the way, in which a free nation, inhabiting these islands, wishes to be governed? Will the people, be it now or be it months hence, ratify the deeds that have been done, and assume upon themselves that tremendous responsibility? The whole humble aim, gentlemen of my proceedings has been to bring home, as far as was in my power, this great question to the mind and to the conscience of the community at large. If I cannot decide the issue,—and of course I have no power to decide it,—I wish at least to endeavor to make it understood by those who can. And I cherish the hope that

    "When the hurly-burly's done,

    When the battle's lost and won,"

I may be able to bear home with me, at least, this consolation, that I have spared no effort to mark the point at which the roads divide,—the one path which plunges into suffering, discredit, and dishonor, the other which slowly, perhaps, but surely, leads a free and high-minded people towards the blessed ends of prosperity and justice, of liberty and peace.

Questions

1. Why does Disraeli stand up for the interests of the working classes in the above letter?
2. How is this letter indicative of a larger political philosophy on his part? What can be deduced about that philosophy on the basis of this letter?

3. What are Gladstone's main criticisms of the Disraeli-led government in 1879? Is he mainly attacking Disraeli's actions, the consequences of his actions, or his philosophical approach to government?
4. On the basis of the above speech, why do you think that Gladstone's speeches against Disraeli and his government were so successful?

Chapter Questions

1. How does Souza's discussion of the effects of emancipation in Brazil compare to Engelgardt's treatment of the Russian peasantry after emancipation? What might account for the differences? Are there any similarities?
2. How does the illustration from *Uncle Tom's Cabin* reinforce the description of life under slavery provided by Frederick Douglass?
3. To what extent can one detect the legacies of the Enlightenment and the French Revolution in the abolitionist and reform movements of the nineteenth century? What specific references in the documents above speak to those legacies?

CHAPTER SEVEN

The New Imperialism

INTRODUCTION

The British acquired a huge empire in the course of the nineteenth century without much of a specific plan or purpose behind it. Once they had acquired it, however, they came to regard it as important—even essential—to sustaining Britain's economy and position as a great power. In addition, imperial expansion captured the imagination of the reading public, fascinated by the tales of adventures in exotic locales so different from those of their native land. In the closing decades of the century, however, fascination had turned to anxiety. The Russians encroached on India, while the construction of the Suez Canal in Egypt shortened the sea route to India and made Africa seem more important from a strategic standpoint.

India provided a sense of unity and identity to the British Empire as a whole. The British could take pride in their ability to maintain their rule in India with a minimum of expense and manpower because of the massive amount of support that they received from the native Indian population, either through active participation in the army or civil service or through the passive acceptance of the millions of inhabitants who vastly outnumbered the British who served there. The pride they took in the administration of the empire made the Russian threat to India seem all the more nefarious and far more dangerous than it really warranted. In his novel, *Kim*, Rudyard Kipling captured some of the anxieties associated with the Russian threat and the espionage carried out on both sides in what became known as "the Great Game."

Passages from the novel *Kim* appear below, along with Kipling's most famous poem, "The White Man's Burden," written on the occasion of the US occupation of the Philippines in the aftermath of the Spanish-American War in 1898. To many readers, Kipling's poem provided a thinly veiled attempt to defend Western imperialism on the grounds that it served a higher purpose of bringing non-Western populations the benefits of Western technology and civilization. However, the socialist philosopher Karl Marx had also provided just such a justification a few years earlier in several articles that he wrote on British imperialism in India. Marx may not have liked imperialism any more than he liked capitalism, but he thought that both served world-historical purposes. Most historians would probably place Marx and Kipling at opposite ends of the political spectrum, but neither of their writings deserves simple dismissal as ideological claptrap. Both men raised complicated questions about the role and purposes of late nineteenth-century imperialism in India and elsewhere.

If British interest in India remained at a high level through the end of the nineteenth century, from mid-century stories from Africa seemed to prove equally compelling. Westerners went to Africa in the nineteenth century for a variety of reasons: to convert the natives to Christianity, to abolish slavery, to open up new markets for goods, to secure valuable raw materials for industrial enterprises in Europe, to search for gold or diamond mines in the hopes of becoming instantly and immensely rich, or simply as a place to settle and start a new life. David Livingstone had spent years as a missionary in Africa for humanitarian reasons (see Chapter 4). His disappearance provided the central motive for the first trip to Africa by the American journalist, Henry Morton Stanley, who, upon finding the missing Englishman, uttered the immortal words, "Dr. Livingstone, I presume?" An excerpt from Stanley's popular account, *How I Found Livingstone*, appears below. However, Stanley developed an interest in Africa that went far beyond his search for a missing person, as evidenced in the subsequent journeys he took there and the role that he played in some of the most important European discoveries related to what Europeans referred to as the "Dark Continent."

European imperialism in Africa certainly had its dark side, a theme explored in Joseph Conrad's famous short novel, *Heart of Darkness*. The worst abuses of Europeans in Africa occurred in the Belgian Congo, where Conrad served as a captain aboard a steamboat in 1890. The Belgians virtually enslaved the natives and forced them to work on the rubber plantations without regard for human life or comfort; millions died as the Belgians virtually robbed the colony of its resources and its people. No wonder that Conrad's experience there soured him on the whole imperial enterprise. By comparison, the Englishman Cecil Rhodes had more interest in exploiting the wealth of southern Africa than its people and appears as a veritable saint next to the Belgian King Leopold. Still, Rhodes had no moral qualms about benefiting from investments in African diamond mines and growing enormously wealthy from resources that might have gone to benefit the native inhabitants of the regions containing them. A man of enormous political ambition, Rhodes sought to protect his investments and economic interests by exercising political control over the territories connected to them, including the eponymous state of Rhodesia. His "Last Will and Testament" provides a glimpse into his attitudes toward his wealth and the areas of Africa that he controlled.

China always reacted differently to European imperialism and Western influence than did either India or Africa, mainly because of its long history as an independent nation and sovereign empire. When Indians mutinied in 1857, they did so not because they wished to free themselves of British influence so much as because they wanted the British to respect native Indian traditions. While the Indians did develop their own independence movement in the late nineteenth and early twentieth century, it came largely as a result of the introduction of Western influence and ideas about nationalism and popular sovereignty. The same held for the African independence movements after the Second World War. However, China had a long and proud history as an independent nation, which mattered in the late nineteenth century when the Chinese saw the ruling

Qing dynasty increasingly losing control over the country's affairs because of the "spheres of influence" established by Western powers. In the period of the "New Imperialism" Chinese resentment of Western influence culminated in the Boxer Rebellion of 1900. Many Western residents and missionaries with innocuous motives for being in China found themselves caught up in the violent rebellion that portended darker times for China in the following century.

RUDYARD KIPLING, "THE WHITE MAN'S BURDEN" AND *KIM*, INTRODUCTION

No English writer familiarized more people with British India than Rudyard Kipling (1865–1936). Born in Bombay, his parents sent him to England at the age of five, where he went to school until the age of seventeen. He returned to India in 1882, where he spent the next seven years. In his many novels set in India, Kipling provided his readers with a sense of the place; the title character in his novel Kim *straddled both worlds, feeling as if he belonged to both—and neither. "Kim" is short for Kimball O'Hara, a child who grows up thinking he is Indian before discovering that his father is an Irish soldier who has left instructions for Kim to attend an English school. At first repulsed by the idea, Kim embarks on a search for his personal identity in the company of an Indian holy man, who encourages his pupil to embrace both parts of his identity. Yet, Kim's personal growth also helps to prepare him for participation in the "Great Game" of anti-Russian espionage. The novel thus embraces complexity and deals with British India from a variety of perspectives. Although* Kim *is a fairly well-known novel, more people likely know Kipling as the jingoistic author of "The White Man's Burden," a poem that today reads as a patronizing homage to white European superiority. While a rereading of the poem in its historical context might prove valuable on its own, so might a comparison with several key passages from* Kim, *which show another side of Kipling.*

Rudyard Kipling, "The White Man's Burden,"*

TAKE up the White Man's burden—
Send forth the best ye breed—
Go bind your sons to exile
To serve your captives' need;
To wait in heavy harness

---

*http://www.kipling.org.uk/poems_burden.htm

On fluttered folk and wild—
Your new-caught sullen peoples,
Half devil and half child.
Take up the White Man's burden—
In patience to abide
To veil the threat of terror
And check the show of pride;
By open speech and simple,
An hundred times made plain,
To seek another's profit,
And work another's gain.
Take up the White Man's burden—
The savage wars of peace—
Fill full the mouth of famine
And bid the sickness cease;
And when your goal is nearest
The end for others sought,
Watch Sloth and heathen Folly
Bring all your hopes to nought.
Take up the White Man's burden—
No tawdry rule of kings,
But toil of serf and sweeper—
The tale of common things.
The ports ye shall not enter,
The roads ye shall not tread,
Go make them with your living,
And mark them with your dead!
Take up the White Man's burden—
And reap his old reward,
The blame of those ye better,
The hate of those ye guard—
The cry of hosts ye humour
(Ah slowly!) towards the light:-
"Why brought ye us from bondage,"
"Our loved Egyptian night?"
Take up the White Man's burden—
Ye dare not stoop to less—
Nor call too loud on Freedom
To cloak your weariness;
By all ye cry or whisper,
By all ye leave or do,
The silent sullen peoples

Shall weigh your Gods and you.
Take up the White Man's burden—
Have done with childish days—
The lightly proffered laurel,
The easy, ungrudged praise.
Comes now, to search your manhood
Through all the thankless years,
Cold-edged with dear-bought wisdom,
The judgement of your peers.

Rudyard Kipling, *Kim**

. . . The Englishman is not, as a rule, familiar with the Asiatic, but he would not strike across the wrist a kindly Babu who had accidentally upset a kilta with a red oilskin top. On the other hand, he would not press drink upon a Babu were he never so friendly, nor would he invite him to meat. The strangers [Russians] did all these things, and asked many questions,—about women mostly,—to which Huree returned gay and unstudied answers. They gave him a glass of whitish fluid like to gin, and then more; and in a little time his gravity departed from him. He became thickly treasonous, and spoke in terms of sweeping indecency of a Government which had forced upon him a white man's education and neglected to supply him with a white man's salary. He babbled tales of oppression and wrong till the tears ran down his cheeks for the miseries of his land. Then he staggered off, singing love-songs of Lower Bengal, and collapsed upon a wet tree-trunk. Never was so unfortunate a product of English rule in India more unhappily thrust upon aliens. . . .

When he presented himself again he was racked with a headache—penitent, and volubly afraid that in his drunkenness he might have been indiscreet. He loved the British Government—it was the source of all prosperity and honor, and his master at Rampur held the very same opinion. Upon this the men began to deride him and to quote past words, still step by step, with deprecating smirks, oily grins, and leers of infinite cunning, the poor Babu was beaten out of his defenses and forced to speak—truth! When Lurgan was told the tale later, he mourned aloud that he could not have been in the place of the stubborn, inattentive coolies, who with grass mats over their heads and the raindrops puddling in their foot-prints, waited on the weather. All the Sahibs of their acquaintance—rough-clad men joyously returning year after year to

---

*Rudyard Kipling (1983, © 1901), *Kim*, New York: Bantam Books, pp. 214–15.

their chosen gullies—had servants and cooks and orderlies, very often hillmen. These Sahibs travelled without any retinue. Therefore they were poor Sahibs, and ignorant; for no Sahib in his senses would follow a Bengali's advice. But the Bengali, appearing from somewhere, had given them money, and would make shift with their dialect. Used to comprehensive ill-treatment from their own color, they suspected a trap somewhere, and stood by to run if occasion offered.

Then through the new-washed air, steaming with delicious earth-smells, the Babu led the way down the slopes—walking ahead of the coolies in pride; walking behind the foreigners in humility. His thoughts were many and various. The least of them would have interested his companions beyond words. But he was an agreeable guide, ever keen to point out the beauties of his royal master's domain. He peopled the hills with anything they had a mind to slay—thar, ibex, or markhor, and bear by Elisha's allowance. He discoursed of botany and ethnology with unimpeachable inaccuracy, and his store of local legends— he had been a trusted agent of the State for fifteen years, remember—was inexhaustible.

"Decidedly this fellow is an original," said the taller of the two foreigners. "He is like the nightmare of a Viennese courier."

"He represents in petto India in transition—the monstrous hybridism of East and West," the Russian replied. "It is we who can deal with Orientals."

"He has lost his own country and has not acquired any other. But he has a most complete hatred of his conquerors. Listen. He confides to me last night," etc.

Questions

1. What does Kipling mean by "the white man's burden"? Why do you think he wrote it?
2. Is the poem a pro-imperialist work or a warning to take the responsibilities of colonial rule seriously?
3. Why would Huree speak so badly about the British when he was drunk and repent of it when he was sober? What is Kipling trying to say here about British rule in India?
4. How do the reading of the poem and the passages from the novel affect each other? Would you interpret the poem differently in light of the reading from *Kim*? Would you interpret the reading from *Kim* differently in light of the poem than you otherwise might have?
5. Is it important to know about Kipling's background and political views in order to ascertain the meaning of his writings?

KARL MARX, "ON IMPERIALISM IN INDIA," INTRODUCTION

Karl Marx recognized what many Indians themselves knew: that the British with their railroads, an educational system that taught the subjects of the Raj English as a common language, and their political ideas of representative government and natural rights, had already done much to make India a more unified and progressive (by Western standards) political entity. Whatever the British intent in India, or that of those Indians who chose to serve the empire, British rule had the effect of modernizing India in a relatively short time. To Marx, these developments had helped to prepare them for the next phase of their history. However, resistance still came from hereditary princely rulers determined to keep their peasant subjects in a state of submission, as well as those committed to preserving the traditional Indian caste system. Marx held that socialism depended on industrialization and the emergence of the two classes whose clash would determine the future: the bourgeoisie (middle class) and the proletariat (working class). His writings on British imperialism in India provide an opportunity to study the way in which Marx applied his historical theory of dialectical materialism to an actual historical situation unfolding outside of Europe during his own lifetime. Marx wrote the articles below for The New York Daily Tribune *in 1853.*

Karl Marx, "On Imperialism in India"*

The British Rule in India
London, Friday, June 10, 1853

These small stereotype forms of social organism have been to the greater part dissolved, and are disappearing, not so much through the brutal interference of the British tax-gatherer and the British soldier, as to the working of English steam and English free trade. Those family-communities were based on domestic industry, in that peculiar combination of hand-weaving, hand-spinning, and hand-tilling agriculture which gave them self supporting power. English interference having placed the spinner in Lancashire and the weaver in Bengal, or sweeping away both Hindoo spinner and weaver, dissolved these small semi-barbarian, semi-civilized communities, by blowing up their economical basis, and thus produced the greatest, and, to speak the truth, the only *social* revolution ever heard of in Asia.

---

*Karl Marx and Friedrich Engels, "The British Rule in India" and "The Future Results of British Rule in India," in Robert C. Tucker, ed. (1978), *The Marx-Engels Reader*, New York: W.W. Norton and Company, pp. 653–64, excerpts from pp. 657–59, 662–64.

Now, sickening as it must be to human feeling to witness those myriads of industrious patriarchal and inoffensive social organizations disorganized and dissolved into their units, thrown into a sea of woes, and their individual members losing at the same time their ancient form of civilization, and their hereditary means of subsistence, we must not forget that these idyllic village communities, inoffensive though they may appear, had always been the solid foundation of Oriental despotism, that they restrained the human mind within the smallest possible compass, making it the unresisting tool of superstition, enslaving it beneath traditional rules, depriving it of all grandeur and historical energies. . . . We must not forget that these little communities were contaminated by distinctions of caste and by slavery, that they subjugated man to external circumstances instead of elevating man to be the sovereign of circumstances, that they transformed a self-developing social state into a never changing natural destiny, and thus brought about a brutalizing worship of nature, exhibiting its degradation in the fact that man, the sovereign of nature, fell down on his knees in adoration of *Hanuman*, the monkey, and *Sabbala*, the cow.

England, it is true, in causing a social revolution in Hindostan, was actuated only by the vilest interests, and was stupid in her manner of enforcing them. But that is not the question. The question is, can mankind fulfill its destiny without a fundamental revolution in the social state of Asia? If not, whatever may have been the crimes of England she was the unconscious tool of history in bringing about that revolution.

The Future Results of British Rule in India
London, July 22, 1853

. . . If we knew nothing of the past history of Hindostan, would there not be the one great and incontestable fact, that even at this moment India is held in English thralldom by and Indian army maintained at the cost of India? India, then, could not escape the fate of being conquered, and the whole of her past history, if it be anything, is the history of the successive conquests she has undergone. Indian society has no history at all, at least no known history. What we call its history, is but the history of the successive intruders who founded their empires on the passive basis of that unresisting and unchanging society. The question therefore, is not whether the English had a right to conquer India, but whether we are to prefer India conquered by the Turk, by the Persian, by the Russian, to India conquered by the Briton.

England has to fulfill a double mission in India: one destructive, the other regenerating—the annihilation of old Asiatic society, and the laying of the material foundations of Western society in Asia.

Arabs, Turks, Tartars, Moguls, who had successively overrun India, soon became *Hindooized*, the barbarian conquerors being, by an eternal law of history, conquered themselves by the superior civilization of their subjects.

The British were the first conquerors superior, and therefore, inaccessible to Hindoo civilization. . . .

I know that the English millocracy intend to endow India with railways with the exclusive view of extracting at diminished expenses the cotton and other raw materials for their manufactures. . . . You cannot maintain a net of railways over an immense country, without introducing all those industrial processes necessary to meet the immediate and current wants of railway locomotion, and out of which there must grow the application of machinery to those branches of industry not immediately connected with railways. The railway-system will therefore become, in India, truly the forerunner of modern industry. This is the more certain as the Hindoos are allowed by British authorities themselves to possess particular aptitude for accommodating themselves to entirely new labor, and acquiring the requisite knowledge of machinery. Ample proof of this fact is afforded by the capacities and expertness of the native engineers in the Calcutta mint, where they have been for years employed in working the steam machinery, by the natives attached to the several steam engines in the Hurdwar coal districts, and by other instances. . . . Modern industry, resulting from the railway system, will dissolve the hereditary division of labor, upon which rest the Indian castes, those decisive impediments to Indian progress and Indian power.

All the English bourgeoisie may be forced to do will neither emancipate nor materially mend the social condition of the mass of the people, depending not only on the development of the productive powers, but on their appropriation by the people. But what they will not fail to do is to lay down the material premises for both. Has the bourgeoisie ever done more? Has it ever affected a progress without dragging individuals and peoples through blood and dirt, through misery and degradation?

The Indians will not reap the fruits of the new elements of society scattered among them by the British bourgeoisie, till in Great Britain itself the now ruling classes shall have been supplanted by the industrial proletariat, or till the Hindoos themselves shall have grown strong enough to throw off the English yoke altogether. . . .

The bourgeois period of history has to create the material basis of the new world—on the one hand the universal intercourse founded upon the mutual dependency of mankind, and the means of that intercourse; on the other hand the development of the productive powers of man and the transformation of material production into a scientific domination of natural agencies. Bourgeois industry and commerce create these material conditions of a new world in the same way as geological revolutions have created the surface of the earth. When a great social revolution shall have mastered the results of the bourgeois epoch, the market of the world and the modern powers of production, and subjected them to the common control of the most advanced peoples, then only will human progress cease to resemble that hideous pagan idol, who would not drink the nectar but from the skulls of the slain.

Questions

1. What does Marx regard as the overall impact of British rule in India? What specific effects of British rule there does he mention in these articles?
2. Why does Marx say that he has mixed feelings about the effects of British rule in India? Must human suffering always accompany human progress?
3. What is the role of the bourgeoisie in India, as elsewhere, according to Marx?
4. What does Marx say must happen in order for India to benefit from the socialist stage of historical development?

HENRY M. STANLEY, *HOW I FOUND LIVINGSTONE* AND *EXPLORATION DIARIES*, INTRODUCTION

In 1871 The New York Herald *funded Henry Morton Stanley's trip to central Africa for the express purpose of discovering the location or fate of Dr. David Livingstone, who had gone missing and whom many feared had died. His legendary encounter with Livingstone at Ujiji on Lake Tanganyika made him famous. He wrote about his first trip to Africa in his book,* How I Found Livingstone. *Stanley returned to Africa in 1874; on his second trip he spent three years crossing the continent from east to west. Starting in Zanzibar, he ended his journey in the former slave market of Boma in what was soon to become the Belgian Congo. In fact, Stanley's explorations helped to pave the way for King Leopold of Belgium to take control of the region, although that was not his primary intention. Europeans still remained ignorant about the source of the Nile, the size of Lake Tanganyika, the course of the Congo River, and about the nature of many of the lands through which Stanley passed. Stanley and his sponsors also sought to continue Livingstone's work of discovering and eradicating the sources of slave trade. He made a number of important geographical discoveries and observations in his travels, but he does not deserve all of the credit; Stanley had with him on this second expedition a significant military escort and an entourage of over a hundred people to do the heavy lifting. Nevertheless, he encountered and overcame many difficulties, his life threatened more than once by hostile natives. He published the journal that he kept during these years as a second book, his* Exploration Diaries, *excerpts from which appear below. Stanley returned to Africa for yet another—his third—expedition in 1887 on a state-sponsored mission to rescue the ruler of the southern Sudan, Emin Pasha.*

Henry M. Stanley, *How I Found Livingstone**

One day's life at Zanzibar made me thoroughly conscious of my ignorance respecting African people and things in general. I imagined I had read Burton and Speke through, fairly well, and that consequently I had penetrated the meaning, the full importance and grandeur, of the work I was about to be engaged upon. But my estimates, for instance, based upon book information, were simply ridiculous, fanciful images of African attractions were soon dissipated, anticipated pleasures vanished, and all crude ideas began to resolve themselves into shape.

I strolled through the city. My general impressions are of crooked, narrow lanes, white-washed houses, mortar-plastered streets, in the clean quarter;—of seeing alcoves on each side, with deep recesses, with a fore-ground of red-turbaned Banyans, and a back-ground of flimsy cottons, prints, calicoes, domestics and what not; or of floors crowded with ivory tusks; or of dark corners with a pile of unginned and loose cotton; or of stores of crockery, nails, cheap Brummagem ware, tools, &c., in what I call the Banyan quarter;—of streets smelling very strong—in fact, exceedingly, malodorous, with steaming yellow and black bodies, and woolly heads, sitting at the doors of miserable huts, chatting, laughing, bargaining, scolding, with a compound smell of hides, tar, filth, and vegetable refuse, in the negro quarter;—of streets lined with tall, solid-looking houses, flat roofed, of great carved doors with large brass knockers, with baabs sitting cross-legged watching the dark entrance to their masters' houses; of a shallow sea-inlet, with some dhows, canoes, boats, an odd steam-tub or two, leaning over on their sides in a sea of mud which the tide has just left behind it; of a place called "M'nazi-Moya," "One Cocoa-tree," whither Europeans wend on evenings with most languid steps, to inhale the sweet air that glides over the sea, while the day is dying and the red sun is sinking westward; of a few graves of dead sailors, who paid the forfeit of their lives upon arrival in this land; of a tall house wherein lives Dr. Tozer, "Missionary Bishop of Central Africa," and his school of little Africans; and of many other things, which got together into such a tangle, that I had to go to sleep, lest I should never be able to separate the moving images, the Arab from the African; the African from the Banyan; the Banyan from the Hindi; the Hindi from the European, &c.

---

*Henry M. Stanley (1872), *How I Found Livingstone*, London: Marston Low, Sampson, Low, and Searle, pp. 6–7, 9. Available online at http://www.gutenberg.org/catalog/world/readfile?fk_files=3223710&pageno=1.

Zanzibar is the Bagdad, the Ispahan, the Stamboul, if you like, of East Africa. It is the great mart which invites the ivory traders from the African interior. To this market come the gum-copal, the hides, the orchilla weed, the timber, and the black slaves from Africa. Bagdad had great silk bazaars, Zanzibar has her ivory bazaars; Bagdad once traded in jewels, Zanzibar trades in gum-copal; Stamboul imported Circassian and Georgian slaves; Zanzibar imports black beauties from Uhiyow, Ugindo, Ugogo, Unyamwezi and Galla.

Though I had lived some time among the negroes of our Southern States, my education was Northern, and I had met in the United States black men whom I was proud to call friends. I was thus prepared to admit any black man, possessing the attributes of true manhood or any good qualities, to my friendship, even to a brotherhood with myself; and to respect him for such, as much as if he were of my own color and race. Neither his color, nor any peculiarities of physiognomy should debar him with me from any rights he could fairly claim as a man. "Have these men—these black savages from pagan Africa," I asked myself, "the qualities which make man loveable among his fellows? Can these men—these barbarians—appreciate kindness or feel resentment like myself?" was my mental question as I travelled through their quarters and observed their actions. Need I say, that I was much comforted in observing that they were as ready to be influenced by passions, by loves and hates, as I was myself; that the keenest observation failed to detect any great difference between their nature and my own?

Henry M. Stanley, *Exploration Diaries**

February 13th (1877)
Voyage continues.

We have all the pleasures as well as the terrors of river life. We glide down narrow streams, between palmy and spicy islands, whose sweet fragrance and vernal color cause us to forget for a moment our dangerous life. We have before us the winding shores of islands, crowned with eternal spring life and verdure. Teak and Cotton-wood, Guinea and the Ware-Palm, the tall cane with its drooping feathery leaves, the bushy and many rooted Mangrove which flourishes by the water side, here and there a low grassy bank from which the crocodile plunges into the brown depths, the snorting and watchful Behemoth whose roar, echoed between tall banks of woods, has its volume redoubled. The terrors are rocks and rapids, the roaring plunging dreadful cataract, the sudden storms which wrinkle the river's face into a dangerous aspect, the savages which howled after us and required us for meat. . . .

---

*Henry M. Stanley (1961), *The Exploration Diaries of H.M. Stanley*, edited by Richard Stanley and Alan Nearne, New York: Vanguard Press, pp. 163–64.

I had just penned the above, inspired to it by a slight sense of enjoyment, when lo! We came in sight of a village, and immediately war drums and horns sounded their defiance. As we approached, we lay on our oars and permitted some dozen large canoes loaded with menacing savages to wheel and paddle about, expecting every moment war to begin, for such a surly scowling set I have seldom seen. In response to our friendly greetings, they aimed at us with their muskets, and there were probably 60 or 70 muskets pointed at us at one time. We pulled quietly by, and we were followed by six canoes, containing probably about 80 men, who exercised themselves in blowing a sonorous war horn. We descended this way for 2 miles, when suddenly I heard a musket shot and then another, and as I turned my head, I saw shot skipping over the water toward us. Of course we replied quick sharp and fatal, and [they] were driven back in a panic with three or four killed, while we, thank God, had not suffered a scratch. Not even a canoe had been struck. . . .

February 14th:
Voyage continues.

The fight of fights occurred today. It lasted from noon until 5 p.m. on the river. Up to near noon, we had rowed quietly down, then we sighted a village— whether on the main or an island I cannot say—and immediately we were announced with war cries and war drums. I halted behind a small island near the village to take meridian altitude and then set off [76°.7'30"]. From that spot to the end of the district, a distance of 10 miles, we maintained a running fight between 54 canoes and us. In each canoe there were from 10-20 men, so that we had over 500 men opposed to us. No one was hurt on our side, but the savages suffered more severely than ever I supposed they were capable of bearing. But truth must be told, some of them showed great courage and aptitude for war. Others again fired their guns at an enormous distance from us. The hostility with which these people bear for us is most strange, for as soon as they see us, without a word being spoken on either side, they man their canoes and fire away at us as if we were lawful game. By 5 p.m. we had run the gauntlet. I should not omit to state that in the middle of the fight some of our people saw food on shore, landed and seized it, which was small though valuable spoil to us.

Questions

1. What impression does Stanley convey of Africa and Africans in the passages from these two works?

2. Is there a difference in that impression between the passage from the first book and that from the second? If so, what might account for that difference?

3. On the basis of these passages, would you consider Stanley a racist? If not a racist, in what ways does he display his Western biases?
4. How well does Stanley capture the excitement or importance of his travels to Africa? Do these passages inspire you to want to read more in his books?

JOSEPH CONRAD, *HEART OF DARKNESS*, INTRODUCTION

Joseph Conrad's travels around the world as a member of the British merchant navy in the decade from 1886 to 1896 coincided with the height of the "New Imperialism" and made him a witness to numerous encounters between Europeans and peoples of other cultures. The son of Polish parents who had immigrated to the Ukraine (where Conrad was born) before migrating to Britain, Conrad had shortened and anglicized his original name (Józef Teodor Konrad Korzenlowski) and become a British citizen before joining the navy. His Polish heritage may have helped him see imperialism from the vantage point of the outsider, or at least given him an objectivity that allowed him to see imperialism from both sides. According to the historian Thomas Pakenham, Conrad based one of the main characters in his novel, Kurtz, on Arthur Hodester, a Belgian trader in ivory who had a more complex relationship with the natives than those who simply brutalized them.* Still, as the passages below indicate, Conrad did not sugarcoat his account of the European treatment of the native Africans. Written nine years after his time in the Congo, in Heart of Darkness *Conrad attempts to come to terms with his experiences there and in the process the nature of the imperial enterprise in general.*

Joseph Conrad, *Heart of Darkness***

"I got my appointment—of course; and I got it very quick. It appears the Company had received news that one of their captains had been killed in a scuffle with the natives. This was my chance, and it made me the more anxious to go. It was only months and months afterwards, when I made the attempt to recover what was left of the body, that I heard the original quarrel arose from

---

*Thomas Pakenham (1991), *The Scramble for Africa*, New York: Random House, p. 435.
**http://www.gutenberg.org/catalog/world/readfile?fk_files=3273932&pageno=1

a misunderstanding about some hens. Yes, two black hens. Fresleven—that was the fellow's name, a Dane—thought himself wronged somehow in the bargain, so he went ashore and started to hammer the chief of the village with a stick. Oh, it didn't surprise me in the least to hear this, and at the same time to be told that Fresleven was the gentlest, quietest creature that ever walked on two legs. No doubt he was; but he had been a couple of years already out there engaged in the noble cause, you know, and he probably felt the need at last of asserting his self-respect in some way. Therefore he whacked the old nigger mercilessly, while a big crowd of his people watched him, thunderstruck, till some man,—I was told the chief's son,—in desperation at hearing the old chap yell, made a tentative jab with a spear at the white man—and of course it went quite easy between the shoulder-blades. Then the whole population cleared into the forest, expecting all kinds of calamities to happen, while, on the other hand, the steamer Fresleven commanded left also in a bad panic, in charge of the engineer, I believe. Afterwards nobody seemed to trouble much about Fresleven's remains, till I got out and stepped into his shoes. I couldn't let it rest, though; but when an opportunity offered at last to meet my predecessor, the grass growing through his ribs was tall enough to hide his bones. They were all there. The supernatural being had not been touched after he fell. And the village was deserted, the huts gaped black, rotting, all askew within the fallen enclosures. A calamity had come to it, sure enough. The people had vanished. Mad terror had scattered them, men, women, and children, through the bush, and they had never returned. What became of the hens I don't know either. I should think the cause of progress got them, anyhow. However, through this glorious affair I got my appointment, before I had fairly begun to hope for it.

"Black shapes crouched, lay, sat between the trees, leaning against the trunks, clinging to the earth, half coming out, half effaced within the dim light, in all the attitudes of pain, abandonment, and despair. Another mine on the cliff went off, followed by a slight shudder of the soil under my feet. The work was going on. The work! And this was the place where some of the helpers had withdrawn to die.

"They were dying slowly—it was very clear. They were not enemies, they were not criminals, they were nothing earthly now,—nothing but black shadows of disease and starvation, lying confusedly in the greenish gloom. Brought from all the recesses of the coast in all the legality of time contracts, lost in uncongenial surroundings, fed on unfamiliar food, they sickened, became inefficient, and were then allowed to crawl away and rest. These moribund shapes were free as air—and nearly as thin. I began to distinguish the gleam of eyes under the trees. Then, glancing down, I saw a face near my hand. The black bones reclined at full length with one shoulder against the tree, and slowly the eyelids rose and the sunken eyes looked up at me, enormous and vacant, a kind of blind, white flicker in the depths of the orbs, which died out slowly. The man seemed young—almost a boy—but you know with them it's hard to tell. I found nothing else to do but to offer him one of my good Swede's ship's biscuits I had in my pocket. The fingers closed slowly on it and held—there was no other movement and no other glance. He had tied a bit of white worsted round his neck—Why? Where did he get it? Was it a badge—an ornament—a charm—a propitiatory act? Was there any idea at all connected with it? It looked startling round his black neck, this bit of white thread from beyond the seas."

Questions

1. What is the significance and meaning of the first passage from the novel quoted above? What does it say about cross-cultural attitudes between Europeans and the Africans described here?
2. Why does the narrator say that it did not surprise him to hear that Fresleven had attacked the village chief with a stick but "at the same time to be told that Fresleven was the gentlest, quietest creature that ever walked on two legs"?
3. What is the significance and meaning of the second passage? Why does Conrad end the final paragraph of this passage the way he does?
4. What points do these passages combined make about "the new imperialism"?

THE LAST WILL AND TESTAMENT OF CECIL RHODES, INTRODUCTION

Cecil Rhodes (1853–1902) served as Prime Minister of Cape Colony, South Africa, from 1890 to 1896, after acquiring enormous wealth through his interests in a number of diamond mines, whose companies he also sought to control. He specialized in buying and consolidating smaller companies into larger ones, which he did by convincing all parties involved in the process that he would make them richer as a result. An extremely persuasive individual, Rhodes convinced political leaders at home to make the territory of Bechuanaland a British protectorate in 1884 and to grant him his own charter for the colony in South Africa that would acquire the name of Rhodesia. He used his connections in the British government to benefit his financial interests, and his financial interests motivated him to further the territory controlled by the British Empire. He remained on the lookout for new territories ripe for acquisition, seeking to expand northward to take advantage of still untapped mines, raising the possibility of linking Britain's North African colonies with its South African possessions through a "Cape to Cairo railroad." His ultimate dream consisted of a unified South Africa under the British flag, but the Dutch descendants known as Afrikaners, including the Boers, stood in the way. Rhodes died in 1902, the same year in which the Boer War between the British and the Afrikaners ended with his dream unfulfilled.

The Last Will and Testament of Cecil Rhodes*

I am a natural-born British subject and I now declare that I have adopted and acquired and I hereby adopt and acquire and intend to retain Rhodesia as my domicile.

I admire the grandeur and loneliness of the Matoppos in Rhodesia and I therefore desire to be buried in the Matoppos on the hill which I used to visit and which I call the "View of the World" in a square to be cut in the rock on the top of the hill covered with a plain brass plate with these words thereon—"Here lie the remains of Cecil John Rhodes" and accordingly I direct my Executors at the expense of my estate to take all steps and do all things necessary or proper to give effect to this desire and afterwards to keep my grave in order at the expense of the Matoppos and Bulawayo fund hereinafter mentioned.

I direct my Trustees on the hill aforesaid to erect or complete the monument to the men who fell in the first Matabele War at Shangani in Rhodesia the bas-reliefs for which are being made by Mr. John Tweed and I desire the said hill to be preserved as a burial place but no person is to be buried there unless the Government for the time being of Rhodesia until the various states of South Africa or any of them shall have been federated and after such federation the Federal Government by a vote of two-thirds of its governing body says that he or she has deserved well of his or her country.

I give free of all duty whatsoever my landed property near Bulawayo in Matabeleland Rhodesia and my landed property at or near Inyanga near Salisbury in Mashonaland Rhodesia to my Trustees herein named upon trust that my Trustees must in some manner as in their uncontrolled discretion they shall think fit cultivate the same respectively for the instruction of the people of Rhodesia.

I give free of all duty whatsoever to my Trustees herein named such a sum of money as they shall carefully ascertain and in their uncontrolled discretion consider ample and sufficient by its investments to yield income amounting to the sum of £4,000 sterling per annum and not less than I direct my Trustees to invest the same sum and the said sum and the investments for the time being representing it I hereafter refer to as "the Matoppos and Bulawayo Fund." And I direct that my Trustees shall ever apply in such manner as in their uncontrolled

---

*W. T. Stead, ed. (1902), *The Last Will and Testament of Cecil Rhodes with Elucidatory Notes . . .*, London: "Review of Reviews" Office, pp. 3–6. Available online at http://books.google.com/book s?id=QRgUAAAAIAAJ&printsec=frontcover&source=gbs_ge_summary_r&cad=0#v=onepage &q&f=false.

discretion they shall think fit the income of the Matoppos and Bulawayo Fund in preserving protecting maintaining adorning and beautifying the said burial-place and hill and their surroundings and shall for ever apply in such manner as in their uncontrolled discretion they shall think fit the balance of the income of the Matoppos and Bulawayo Fund and any rents and profits of my said landed properties near Bulawayo in the cultivation as aforesaid of such property. . . .

Questions

1. How much does a will reveal about the person to whom it belongs? What does this will reveal about Cecil Rhodes as a person?
2. What does the will reveal about Rhodes's attitude toward Africa and Africans?
3. People do not generally consider themselves hypocrites. What elements of sincerity exist in the will? Does the will possess contradictions that might lead one to label Rhodes a hypocrite?
4. What can Rhodes's will tell us about British imperialism or imperialistic attitudes in general, recognizing that not everyone would have shared his views?

FEI CH'I-HAO AND EVA JANE PRICE ON THE BOXER REBELLION, INTRODUCTION

Chinese discontent with the inability of the Qing government to contain Western influence or the spread of Christianity in China came to a head in 1898. In November the Yellow River flooded its banks, its waters covering 2,000 square miles of the Shandong district, leaving an estimated million people temporarily homeless. Additional misery followed as a severe drought afflicted much of the rural population of the region. That same year, a martial arts organization calling itself "the Society of Harmonious Fists" began training its members to defend traditional Chinese values in the face of Western influence. These "Boxers," as they became known, soon began openly intimidating Western and Chinese Christians, whom they associated with the larger Western agenda of weakening China by teaching the virtues of peace and submissiveness. At first, Qing officials tolerated the group and even hoped that they might serve as added muscle for the crumbling dynasty, but Westerners rightly feared them and pressured the Chinese government to repress the Boxers activities. With the tacit support of the Qing court, the Boxers openly rebelled in 1900. They targeted the Western neighborhoods in Beijing and Tianjin, placing both under siege. Although Western powers stepped in to crush the rebellion, the immediate threat deeply impacted those living in China at the time. The Chinese Christian Fei Qihao provides one account of these developments; another came from the pen of his friend, the American missionary, Eva Jane Price. Both reveal some of the effects and consequences of the "new imperialism" in China. Hundreds of foreign residents, a large number of them missionaries, died in the rebellion. Soldiers captured a group of missionaries that included Fei, who would have died too had not one of them warned him that they planned to kill them all. He made his escape and walked 400 miles to Tianjin, where he informed the American consul of the slaughter. In total, the Boxers killed approximately 30,000 Chinese during the rebellion in addition to more than 200 foreigners, many of them missionaries. Eva Jane Price and her husband, Charles, were among them.

Fei Qihao, on the Boxer Rebellion*

The people of Shanghai are naturally timid and gentle, not given to making disturbances, being the most peaceable people in China. So our Shansi Christians were hopeful for themselves, even when the reports from the coasts grew more alarming. But there was one thing which caused us deep apprehension, and that was the fact that the wicked, cruel Yü Hsien, the hater of foreigners, was the newly appointed governor of Shansi. He had previously promoted the Boxer movement in Shantung, and had persuaded the Empress Dowager that the Boxers had supernatural powers and were true patriots.

Early in June my college friend K'ung Hsiang Hsi came back from T'ungchou from his vacation, reporting that the state of affairs there and at Peking was growing worse, that the local officials were powerless against the Boxers, and that the Boxers, armed with swords, were consistently threatening Christians scattered in the country.

From this time we had no communication with Tientsin [Tianjin] or Peking [Beijing]. All travelers were searched, and if they were discovered bearing foreign letters they were killed. So though several times messengers were started out to carry our letters to the coast, they were turned back by the Boxers before they had gone far. It was not long before the Boxers, like a pestilence, had spread all over Shansi. School had not closed yet in Fen Chou Fu, but as the feeling of alarm deepened, fathers came to take their boys home, and school was dismissed before the end of June.

One day as I sat brooding in the yard a man came up suddenly and said, "Why don't you go to see the Boxers drill?"

"Where are they? I asked."

"Inside the East Gate."

---

*Luella Miner, ed. (1903), *Two Heroes of Cathay*, New York: Fleming H. Revell Company, pp. 63–65. Available online at http://archive.org/stream/twoheroescathay00feigoog#page/n6/mode/2up.

So I started at once to see what their drill was like. In a large vacant space inside the city gate, I saw twenty or more ragged boys in their teens, naked to their waists, standing with their faces to the southeast. After muttering a rhymed jargon they bowed toward the southeast, then fell into a trance. Soon they rose, and showing their teeth, brandished their arms, and kicked about wildly for a while, then fell again on their backs. Thus they lay until other boys tapped lightly on their foreheads, when they would get up and go about as usual. There were rowdies standing by with swords and spears, and four or five hundred spectators. I asked afterward the meaning of the rhyme the boys had muttered, and learned that it was the invocation to the gods to come down and possess their bodies. After they had repeated it the gods would lead them away and train them as soldiers. Hearing this, I laughed at their foolishness, and sighed because of their ignorance. . . .

About the middle of June the friends at Tai Ku had received a letter from Mr. Pitkin at Pao Ting Fu, stating that a number of French railroad engineers and employees had been killed by the Boxers, and that the college at T'ungchou had been destroyed. When I heard this I went to my own room, overwhelmed with grief for my dear college home, and with fear for my father, mother, and beloved teachers and friends, for I did not know whether they were living or dead. I wanted to start at once for T'ungchou, but Mr. and Mrs. Price said that it was too dangerous, and that it would be very difficult for me to make my way through.

Eva Jane Price, *China Journal, 1889–1900: An American Missionary Family during the Boxer Rebellion**

February 14th, 1900

Do you hear of the trouble the Christians are having in two provinces just east of us? There is a native secret society called the "Boxers" who say they are going to overthrow the Protestant religion in China. They are persecuting the Catholics too. Just how far they will be allowed to persecute missionaries and their converts is not easy to say. They have ruined the homes of some forty church members where our friends, Arthur Smith and his wife, live, and they have killed one missionary belonging to an English society. But the last report was that they were to be taken in hand and a stop put to that kind of business, but one can't trust the reports that come from the Chinese themselves. So far in Shansi we have had no reason to fear any trouble. The people who come about us are friendly and this province is considered the quietest and its people the gentlest of any province in the empire.

---

*Eva Jane Price (1989), *China Journal, 1889–1900: An American Missionary Family during the Boxer Rebellion*, New York: Scribner, pp. 216, 225–26.

The winter has been cold and dry with very little prospect of rain or snow. Food takes another rise today because of the continued drought. One wonders what these people will do if it continues.

Today is the thirteenth of the Chinese new year, and tonight is the parade of lanterns. The streets are all decorated with tissue paper banners and hangings of different colors and look very gay. We don't often go out at such times. There is always such a crowd that we feel safer at home.

June 28th, 1900

After our meeting, Miss Partridge was the first to go back to her station and sent word from Taiku: "'Boxers' within five li of Li Man. I am warned not to go on." That was our first introduction to these present dangers. About the middle of May, the "little fire" had kindled simultaneously in different districts throughout the province. The first serious reports were brought by the C.I.M. friends who had attended the Ping Yang fu conference. Near Hung T'ung several Christians were attacked and robbed of all their household goods. The leading elder of the church there was nearly murdered as well as plundered, and others received bodily hurt in connection with the robberies. Still it seemed "far away" to us. Within a few weeks we heard they were in our city in several places drilling and drawing large crowds of restless adventurers. Daily within the past two weeks we have had fresh causes for uneasiness. We have learned what . . .

June 29th

Just what we have learned that I was going to write I shall never remember, I fear, for since the words were written we have learned what it is to meet danger, to have the feeling that we were facing death itself, and to realize as never before the power and majesty of our great Heavenly Father. Two weeks ago friends came to us for a visit partly, and partly to be in a safer place. Miss Eldred came from the district where the greatest outbreak has been, Hug T'ung, and Mr. and Mrs. Lundgren from Chieh Hsiu, sixty li away. Since they have been here we have thought and been able to talk of little besides the dangers around us. We tried to even pass a rule that we would not talk about it, but our hearts have been too full. Often just at nightfall disturbing letters or rumors have come in until for several nights we have not slept as usual. Last Sunday the most distressing rumors came that all foreigners in Peking had been killed. Our mail has been shut off, so we have not been able to learn anything authentic. Later in the day the Kuan [a local magistrate] posted a notice in favor of the "Boxers." Again, later, he put up another saying foreigners must be respected. Every day since there have been such conflicting rumors that one has been all but dissected. Our hearts have grown faint one hour to be lifted again the next.

On Wednesday evening we took the precaution to pack two trunks with most necessary things, and the next day they were secretly buried in the chicken house with a box containing most of our money. We seemed to be momentarily expecting an attack in which we would at least be robbed if nothing worse. To put out of sight the most necessary things seemed wise. This was done without the knowledge of the servants so far as we know.

Questions

1. Despite their obvious biases, what do these two sources tell us about the Boxer movement?
2. Although both sources come from the pens of Christian authors hostile to the Boxers, do they vary at all in their tone or attitude toward them?
3. How valuable are these writings as historical sources? What do they tell us about the period in which they were written? What role should they play in a history of the Boxer Rebellion?
4. To what extent do Fei Qihao and Eva Jane Price seem prepared for the rebellion and the fate that might possibly befall each of them?

FIGURE 7: The Battle of Isandlwana, Anglo-Zulu War, 1879. Courtesy of Getty Images.

The Anglo-Zulu War of 1879 began when the British invaded the Zulu kingdom in South Africa. In the Battle of Isandlwana, depicted here, the Zulus attacked a technologically superior but numerically inferior British force with an army of about 20,000 Zulu warriors, armed mainly with traditional weapons such as spears and shields. The Zulus suffered heavy casualties, but ultimately their numbers overwhelmed the British and temporarily halted their attempt to take over their kingdom. In the end, however, a larger invading force did succeed at defeating the Zulus, raising issues about the superiority of European military technology and the morality of using it against people who did not possess the technology to fight back on equal terms. In 1906, Winston Churchill, then under-secretary of the colonies, said of imperialism in Africa that "the whole enterprise is liable to be misrepresented by persons unacquainted with imperial terminology as the murdering of natives and the stealing of their lands."

Questions

1. Is this nineteenth-century painting a pro-imperialist or anti-imperialist painting? Would people have looked at this painting differently in the nineteenth century than they would today?
2. Compare this painting to the illustration from *Uncle Tom's Cabin* in Chapter 6. Are there any similarities? Are there any differences?
3. How can the artwork of a period add to our understanding of contemporary perceptions of events or issues? To what extent do they reflect those perceptions? To what extent do they shape them?

Chapter Questions

1. Kipling wrote the works included in this chapter about fifty years after Marx wrote his articles about India. Do his writings support or challenge Marx's analysis of the effects of British imperialism? Are Marx and Kipling complementary or contradictory sources on British imperialism?
2. How would you contrast Stanley's writing on Africa with that of Conrad? What factors account for the differences in their perspectives? Are there any similarities?
3. The New Imperialism took on different forms in India, Africa, and China. What do the sources in this chapter reveal about the different effects of imperialism in different places? Are there any common themes that emerge from the sources in this chapter?

CHAPTER EIGHT

First World War

INTRODUCTION

In the early twentieth century, a series of international crises brought the European powers to the brink of a general war. German and French interests clashed over the French occupation of Morocco, while the Russians and Austrians competed for influence in the Balkan states that had recently gained their independence from the Ottoman Empire. In 1908, the Austro-Hungarian Empire unilaterally annexed the states of Bosnia-Herzegovina. This act alienated the Balkan nation of Serbia in particular, which sought the territories for itself because of the significant number of Serbs living in them. In 1912, the Serbs took some of their frustration out on the Ottoman Empire in a conflict known as the First Balkan War. In conjunction with Bulgaria, Greece, and Montenegro, Serbia defeated the Ottomans, only to have its access to the sea blocked by the creation of an independent Albania in a peace settlement brokered by the great powers in 1913. Then, on June 28, 1914, a Serbian nationalist still upset over the Austrian annexation of Bosnia assassinated the heir to the Austrian throne, the Archduke Franz Ferdinand. As it turned out, this act of terrorism set in motion a chain of events that led to the outbreak of the First World War.

One can question, however, whether or not this act caused, or in other words, needed to lead to, a general European war based on the assumption that the diplomats and statesmen who made the decision to go to war in 1914 could have acted differently. One would need to study a wide range of sources to make that determination, but many historians have and even they have frequently come to radically different conclusions. The two documents that begin this chapter do at least offer a starting point for a consideration of that question based on the perspectives of two major participants in the crisis: General Helmuth von Moltke, the chief of the German general staff and Prince Lichnowsky, the German ambassador to Britain.

Germany became involved in the crisis over the assassination of the archduke almost immediately because a system of alliances had left Germany isolated from Russia, France, and Britain with Austria as its only ally among the great powers. Germany feared Russian intervention and wanted to prevent a major Austrian defeat at the hands of Russia. With confidence that they had German support, Austria declared war on Serbia on July 28, 1914. With Russia mobilizing for war, Germany declared war on Russia on August 1. This made Germany seem the aggressor, a decision that would come back to haunt the Germans at the end of the war. The memorandum from Moltke of July 29 reprinted below thus came at a crucial moment in the course of events leading up to the war. Meanwhile, Lichnowsky tried to ascertain Britain's position from some rather cryptic conversations with the British foreign secretary Lord Edward Grey.

We now know that the rulers themselves, especially Tsar Nicholas II of Russia and Kaiser Wilhelm II of Germany, wished to pull back from the brink despite two decades of diplomatic maneuvering, especially on Wilhelm's part, which made war among the great powers more likely. Lichnowsky recalls his sense of the course of events leading up to the war in the excerpt below.

Recent historians have blamed Russia for mobilizing first, forcing Germany into a war it would have preferred to avoid.* However, shortly after Germany declared war on Russia, it declared war on France (August 3) and invaded neutral Belgium because of a military strategy that called for a quick strike on Paris to knock France out of the war. Not only did this military strategy fail to work, the war bogged down in France with both sides maintaining heavily defended positions while their armies lived in trenches dug for the purpose of holding their line. The horrors of trench warfare became seared into the memories of European readers through works such as the novel *All Quiet on the Western Front* by the German Erich Maria Remarque and memoirs such as that by the Englishman, Robert Graves, excerpts from both of which appear below. In addition, poets such as Rupert Brooke, Siegfried Sassoon, and Wilfrid Owen responded to the war in complex ways as they sought a creative outlet for their outer experiences in the war and its effects upon them.

The fighting on the Eastern Front proved just as deadly, with the Russians experiencing enormously heavy losses. Russia, despite its immense size and large population, lacked the resources to sustain the war beyond 1917. A revolution in February 1917 overthrew the tsar and replaced him with a provisional government, which decided that continuing the war remained preferable to surrendering to the Germans. Additional defeats, massive shortages of food and essential supplies and materials, and growing urban unrest among the workers of Petrograd (St. Petersburg) led to the Bolshevik Revolution of October 1917. This second Russian Revolution represented another decisive turning point in the history of the twentieth century. The American journalist John Reed witnessed the events that accompanied it firsthand and wrote about them in his book, *Ten Days That Shook the World*. In general, the sources in this chapter not only reflect some of the important realities of the cataclysmic experience of the First World War, but also became important in shaping how the events of the war would be remembered in the years to come.

The First World War had many consequences, some of which the succeeding chapters will explore. The United States entered the war in 1917, but refused

---

*See especially Christopher M. Clark (2012), *The Sleepwalkers: How Europe Went to War in 1914*, London: Allen Lane; and Sean McMeekin (2013), *July 1914: Countdown to War*, New York: Basic Books.

to participate in the League of Nations agreed to at the Paris Peace Conference that followed the war. China and Italy had also both entered the war on the side of the Allies (Britain, France, and Russia), but disappointment with the peace settlement that followed led to the emergence of radical new movements in both places that would shape their respective histories. The war completely destroyed the remnants of both the Ottoman and the Austro-Hungarian Empires. In addition, a letter written by the British foreign secretary Arthur Balfour had long-range repercussions for the history of the Middle East. The chapter concludes with this "Balfour Declaration," which promised British support for the creation of a Jewish national homeland in Palestine.

HELMUTH VON MOLTKE, *MEMORANDUM TO THEOBALD VON BETHMANN HOLLWEG*, JULY 29, 1914, AND PRINCE LICHNOWSKY, "THE SERBIAN CRISIS," INTRODUCTION

General Helmuth von Moltke did not share the confidence of some of his colleagues that Germany could easily win a war with France that would allow it to avoid the perils of a prolonged two-front war. However, by 1913 it appeared as if he might not have any choice but to attempt it, given the rising tensions in Europe and the existence of the Triple Entente among Britain, France, and Russia. He also knew that Germany's promises of support to defend Austria against Russia would ring hollow if Germany became embroiled in a lengthy war with France. In the last days of July, he had to hope that the Triple Entente would not hold in the midst of the crisis. In the source below, printed in its entirety, Moltke provides his own personal analysis of the political situation in Europe on the eve of the First World War.

The Austrians hoped as well that Russia would refrain from intervening in their war with Serbia. They nonetheless declared war on Serbia, knowing that they had the backing of Germany, should Russia intervene. In retrospect, it seems delusional, given Russian interests in the Balkans and Russia's alliance with France and Britain, for the Austrians to have thought that they could keep an Austro-Serbian war localized. Edward Grey may not have made British interests entirely clear to Lichnowsky, but Russian mobilization had set in motion the chain of events that made war seem increasingly inevitable. Grey had at least warned Lichnowsky of what might happen. When Germany invaded Belgium, the scales, already heavily weighted toward a general European war, tipped in favor of Britain's entry into it. In the second source below, Lichnowsky recollects how he experienced the events leading up to the war.

Helmuth von Moltke, *Memorandum to Theobald von Bethmann Hollweg*, July 29, 1914[*]

The Grand General Staff to the Imperial Chancellor

Berlin, *July 29, 1914*

SUMMARY OF THE POLITICAL SITUATION

It goes without saying that no nation of Europe would regard the conflict between Austria and Serbia with any interest except that of humanity, if there did not lie within it the danger of general political complications that today already threaten to unchain a world war. For more than five years Serbia has been the cause of a European tension which has been pressing with simply intolerable weight on the political and economic existence of nations. With a patience approaching weakness, Austria has up to the present borne the continuous provocations and the political machinations aimed at the disruption of her own national stability by a people which proceeded from regicide at home to the murder of princes in a neighboring land. It was only after the last despicable crime that she took to extreme measures, in order to burn out with a glowing iron a cancer that has constantly threatened to poison the body of Europe. One would think that all Europe would be grateful to her. All Europe would have drawn a breath of relief if this mischief-maker could have been properly chastised, and peace and order thereby have been restored to the Balkans; but Russia placed herself at the side of this criminal nation. It was only then that the Austro-Serbian affair became the thunder-cloud which may at any moment break over Europe.

Austria has declared to the European cabinets that she intends neither to make any territorial acquisitions at Serbia's expense nor to infringe upon her status as a nation: that she only wants to force her unruly neighbor to accept the conditions that she considers necessary if they are to continue to exist side by side, and which Serbia, as experience has proved, would never live up to, despite solemn assurances, unless compelled by force. The Austro-Serbian affair is a purely private quarrel in which, as has been said, nobody in Europe would have a profound interest and which would in no way threaten the peace of Europe, but, on the contrary, would establish it more firmly, if Russia had not injected herself into it. This was what first gave the matter its menacing aspect.

Austria has only mobilized a portion of her armed forces, eight army corps, against Serbia—just enough with which to be able to put through her punitive expedition. As against this, Russia has made all preparations to enable her to

[*]Max Monteglas and Walther Shücking, eds (1924), *Outbreak of the War: German Documents Collected by Karl Kautsky*, New York: Oxford University Press, no. 349, pp. 306–8.

mobilize the army corps of the military districts of Kiev, Odessa and Moscow, twelve army corps in all, within the briefest period, and is providing for similar preparatory measures in the north also, along the German border and the Baltic Sea. She announces that she intends to mobilize when Austria advances into Serbia, as she cannot permit the destruction of Serbia by Austria, though Austria has explained that she intends nothing of the sort.

What must and will the further consequences be? If Austria advances into Serbia she will have to face not only the Serbian army but also the vastly superior strength of Russia; thus she cannot enter a war with Serbia without securing herself against an attack by Russia. That means that she will be forced to mobilize the other half of her Army, for she cannot possibly surrender at discretion to a Russia all prepared for war. At the moment, however, in which Austria mobilizes her whole Army, the collision between herself and Russia will become inevitable. But that, for Germany, is the *casus foederis*. If Germany is not to be false to her word and permit her ally to suffer annihilation at the hands of Russian superiority, she, too, must mobilize. And that would bring about the mobilization of the rest of Russia's military districts as a result. But then Russia will be able to say: I am being attacked by Germany. She will then assure herself of the support of France, which, according to the compact of alliance, is obliged to take part in the war, should her ally, Russia, be attacked. Thus the Franco-Russian alliance, so often held up to praise as a purely defensive compact, created only in order to meet the aggressive plans of Germany, will become active, and the mutual butchery of the civilized nations of Europe will begin.

It cannot be denied that the affair has been cunningly contrived by Russia. While giving continuous assurances that she was not yet "mobilizing," but only making preparations "for an eventuality," that "up to the present" she had called no reserves to the colors, she has been getting herself so ready for war that, when she actually issues her mobilization orders, she will be prepared to move her armies forward in a very few days. Thus she puts Austria in a desperate position and shifts the responsibility to her, inasmuch as she is forcing Austria to secure herself against a surprise by Russia. She will say: You, Austria, are mobilizing against us, so you want war with us. Russia assures Germany that she wishes to undertake nothing against her; but she knows perfectly well that Germany could not remain inactive in the event of a belligerent collision between her ally and Russia. So Germany, too, will be forced to mobilize, and again Russia will be enabled to say to the world: I did not want war, but Germany brought it about. After this fashion things must and will develop, unless, one might say, a miracle happens to prevent at the last moment a war which will annihilate for decades the civilization of almost all Europe.

Germany does not want to bring about this frightful war. But the German Government knows that it would be violating in ominous fashion the deep-rooted feelings of fidelity which are among the most beautiful traits of German character and would be setting itself against all the sentiments of the nation, if it did not come to the assistance of its ally at a moment which was to be decisive of the latter's existence.

According to the information at hand, France, also, appears to be taking measures preparatory to an eventual mobilization. It is apparent that Russia and France are moving hand in hand as far as regards their preparations.

Thus, when the collision between Austria and Russia becomes inevitable, Germany, also, will mobilize, and will be prepared to take up the fight on two fronts.

With relation to the military preparations we have in view, should the case arise, it is of the greatest importance to ascertain as soon as possible whether Russia and France intend to let it come to a war with Germany. The further the preparations of our neighbors are carried, the quicker they will be able to complete their mobilization. Thus the military situation is becoming from day to day more unfavorable to us, and can, if our prospective opponents prepare themselves further, unmolested, lead to fateful consequences for us.

Prince Lichnowsky, "The Serbian Crisis" from his Memoirs*

"The Serbian Crisis"

At the end of June I went to Kiel by command of the Kaiser. A few weeks prior to this I had been made an honorary D.C.L. of Oxford, an honor which had not been conferred on any German Ambassador since Herr von Bunsen. Whilst on board the *Meteor* we learned of the death of the Archduke. His Majesty regretted that his efforts to win the Archduke over to his way of thinking had thus been rendered vain. I do not know whether the plan of an active policy against Serbia had already been decided on at Konopischt.

As I was not instructed about views and events in Vienna, I did not attach very great importance to this occurrence. Later on I could only remark that amongst Austrian aristocrats a feeling of relief outweighed all other sentiments. [On board the *Meteor* there was also an Austrian guest of the Emperor's, Count Felix Thun. He had remained in his cabin all the time, suffering from sea sickness, in spite of the splendid weather; but on receiving the news he was well. The fright or joy had cured him.]

On my arrival in Berlin I saw the Chancellor and told him that I considered the state of our foreign relations very satisfactory, as we were on better terms

---

*Karl Max, fürst von Lichnowsky (Prince Lichnowsky) (1928), *Heading for the Abyss: Reminiscences*, translated by Sefton Delmer, New York: Payson and Clark, pp. 71–75.

with England than we had been for a long time, whilst in France also the government was in the hands of a pacifist Ministry.

Herr von Bethmann Hollweg did not appear to share my optimism, and complained about Russian armaments. I sought to reassure him, emphasizing the fact that Russia had no interest in attacking us, and that such an attack would never receive Anglo-French support, as both countries wanted peace. Thereupon I went to Dr. Zimmermann, who was acting for Herr von Jagow, and he told me that Russia was about to raise 900,000 additional troops. His language betrayed unmistakable annoyance with Russia, which was "everywhere in our way." There were also difficulties in economic policy. Of course I was not told that General von Moltke, Chief of the General Staff, was pressing for war; but I learned that Herr von Tschirschky had been reprimanded because he reported that he had counseled moderation in Vienna towards Serbia.

On my return from Silesia to London I stopped only a few hours in Berlin, where I heard that Austria intended to take steps against Serbia in order to put an end to an impossible situation.

[I am sorry that at the moment I underestimated the importance of the news. I thought that nothing would come of it this time either and that matters could easily be settled, even if Russia became threatening. I now regret that I did not stay in Berlin and at once declare that I would not co-operate in a policy of this kind.]

Subsequently I ascertained that, at the decisive conference at Potsdam on the 5th July, the Vienna enquiry received the unqualified assent of all the leading people, [and with the rider that no harm would be done if a war with Russia should result. Thus it was expressed, at any rate, in the Austrian protocol which Count Mensdorff received in London. Soon afterwards Herr von Jagow was in Vienna to consult Count Berchtold about all these matters.]

At that time I received instructions to induce the British Press to adopt a friendly attitude should Austria administer the *coup de grâce* to the "Great Serbia" movement, and to exert my personal influence to prevent public opinion from becoming inimical to Austria. If one remembered England's attitude during the annexation crisis of 1908, when public opinion showed sympathy for the Serbian rights in Bosnia, as well as her benevolent furtherance of national movements in the days of Lord Byron and Garibaldi, the probability that she would support the intended punitive expedition against the murderers of the prince was so remote, that I found myself obliged to give an urgent warning. But I also warned my Government against the whole plan, which I characterized as adventurous and dangerous, and advised them to counsel the Austrians to *moderation*, as I did not believe that the conflict could be localized.

Herr von Jagow replied to me that "Russia was not ready; there would probably be some fuss and noise, but the more firmly we took sides with Austria the more would Russia give way. As it was, Austria was accusing us of weakness and therefore we dare not leave her in the lurch. Public opinion in Russia, on the other hand, was becoming more and more anti-German, so we must just risk it."

In view of this attitude, based, as I found later, on reports [from Count Pourtalès] that Russia would not move under any circumstances, and which caused us to spur Count Berchtold on to the utmost energy—I hoped for salvation through British mediation, as I knew that Sir E. Grey's great influence in Petrograd could be used in the direction of peace. I therefore availed myself of my friendly relations with the Minister to request him in confidence to advise moderation in Russia in case Austria, as seemed likely, demanded satisfaction from Serbia.

At first the English Press preserved calm and was friendly to Austria, because the murder was generally condemned. But gradually more and more voices were heard insisting emphatically that, however much the crime merited punishment, its exploitation for political purposes could not be justified. Austria was strongly exhorted to use moderation.

When the ultimatum was published, all the papers with the exception of the *Standard* [—the ever-necessitous, which had apparently been bought by Austria—] were unanimous in condemnation. The whole world, excepting Berlin and Vienna, realized that it meant war—indeed, "the world-war." The British Fleet, which happened to have assembled for a naval review, was not demobilized.

My efforts were in the first place directed towards obtaining as conciliatory a reply from Serbia as was possible, since the attitude of the Russian Government left room for no doubts about the gravity of the situation.

Serbia responded favorably to the British efforts, M. Pashitch had really agreed to everything, except two points, about which, however, he declared his willingness to negotiate. If Russia and England had wanted the war, in order to attack us, a hint to Belgrade would have been enough, and the unprecedented Note would not have been answered.

Sir E. Grey went through the Serbian reply with me, and pointed out the conciliatory attitude of the Belgrade Government. Thereupon we discussed his proposal of mediation, which was to include a formula acceptable to both parties for clearing up the two points. His proposal was that a committee, consisting of M. Cambon, the Marquis Imperiali and myself, should assemble under his presidency, and it would have been an easy matter for us to find an acceptable formula for points at issue, which mainly concerned the collaboration of Austrian Imperial officials at the investigations in Belgrade. Given goodwill everything could have been settled at one or two sittings, and the mere acceptance of the British proposal would have brought about relaxation of the tension, and would have further improved our relations with England. I therefore strongly backed the proposal, on the ground that otherwise there was danger of a world-war, through which we stood to gain nothing and lose all; but in vain. It was derogatory to the dignity of Austria—we did not intend to interfere in Serbian matters—we left these to our ally. I was to work for "the localization of the conflict."

Needless to say a mere hint from Berlin would have decided Count Berchtold to content himself with diplomatic success, and to accept the Serbian reply. The hint was not given; on the contrary they urged in the direction of war. It would have been such a splendid success.

After our refusal Sir Edward requested us to submit a proposal. [We insisted on war with Serbia.] I could not obtain any reply but that Austria had shown an exceedingly "accommodating spirit" by not demanding an extension of territory.

Sir Edward rightly pointed out that even without an extension of territory it is possible to reduce a state to a condition of vassalage, and that Russia would see a humiliation in this, and would not suffer it.

The impression grew stronger and stronger that we wanted war under any circumstances. It was impossible to interpret our attitude on a question which did not directly concern us in any other way. The urgent requests and definite assurances of M. Sazonow, followed by the Czar's positively humble telegrams, the repeated proposals of Sir E. Grey, the warnings of the Marquis San Giuliano and Signor Bollati, my urgent counsels, all were of no avail. Berlin insisted that Serbia must be chastised.

The more I pressed, the less were they inclined to come round, [if only that I in conjunction with Sir Edward Grey might not have the success of averting war.]

Finally, on the 29th, Sir E. Grey decided on the famous warning. I replied that I had invariably reported that we should have to reckon with English opposition if it came to a war with France. Repeatedly the Minister said to me: "If war breaks out, it will be the greatest catastrophe the world has ever seen."

After that, events followed each other rapidly. When at last Count Berchtold, who up till then had, at the behest of Berlin, played the strong man, decided to come round, [and when Herr von Bethmann, too, grew afraid], we replied to the Russian mobilization, after Russia had negotiated and waited for a whole week in vain, with our ultimatum and the declaration of war.

Questions

1. What light do these two sources shed on the origins and outbreak of the First World War?
2. How does Lichnowsky's later recollection of the events leading to war compare to Moltke's analysis of the situation at the time?

3. What does Moltke's letter reveal about the German position in the critical days of late July 1914? If Moltke had possessed decision-making power, would Germany have followed the same course of action that it did? Would war have broken out anyway?

4. To what degree does Lichnowsky provide a balanced and objective view of the chain of events? Did he support Austria's position at the time? To what extent do you think the outcome of the war might have affected his interpretation of its origins?

ERICH MARIA REMARQUE, *ALL QUIET ON THE WESTERN FRONT*, AND ROBERT GRAVES, *GOODBYE TO ALL THAT*, INTRODUCTION

Remarque's novel and Graves's autobiography have much in common, even though Remarque fictionalized his war experience and Graves wrote about his as nonfiction. Both appeared in 1929, a decade after the end of the war along with a number of additional war memoirs. They both raise issues about the extent to which individualized accounts can represent the general experiences of millions of men. They both convey an aggressive antiwar attitude that served to remind people ten years later of the horror that the war had inflicted upon its participants and the drastic changes it had wrought in them.

All Quiet on the Western Front *became the most successful and best-known antiwar novel of all time. Because of that, it has drawn scrutiny as an inaccurate representation of Remarque's own war experience by critics who apparently did not understand that novels by definition do not need to adhere to strict biographical accuracy. Remarque's experience may not have matched exactly that of his novel's protagonist or mirrored the experience of every soldier who fought in the war, but one could argue that it did convey some broad and important truths about the war. One of those truths involved the huge gap that the war created between those who had experienced combat and those who had not. Robert Graves made that one of the themes of his own biographical account of his war experience. In their own ways, both of the books quoted below attempted to bridge that gap and to give the reading public some idea of the experience of war and what it had done to the men who fought it.*

Erich Maria Remarque, *All Quiet on the Western Front**

We see men living with their skulls blown open; we see soldiers run with their two feet cut off, they stagger on their splintered stumps into the next shell-hole; a lance-corporal crawls a mile and a half on his hands dragging his smashed knee after him; another goes to the dressing station and over his clasped hands bulge his intestines; we see men without mouths, without jaws, without faces; we find one man who has held the artery of his arm in his teeth for two hours in order not to bleed to death. The sun goes down, night comes, the shells whine, life is at an end.

Still the little piece of convulsed earth in which we lie is held. We have yielded no more than a few hundred yards of it as a prize to the enemy. But on every yard there lies a dead man.

What is leave?—A pause that only makes everything after it so much worse. Already the sense of parting begins to intrude itself. My mother watches me silently; I know she counts the days; every morning she is sad. It is one day less. She has put away my pack, she does not want to be reminded by it.

A man cannot realize that above such shattered bodies there are still human faces in which life goes its daily round. And this is only one hospital, one single station; there are hundreds of thousands in Germany, hundreds of thousands in France, hundreds of thousands in Russia. How senseless is everything that can be written, done, or thought, when such things are possible. It must all be lies and of no account when the culture of a thousand years could not prevent this stream of blood being poured out, these torture-chambers in their hundreds of thousands. A hospital alone shows what war is.

I am young, I am twenty years old; yet I know nothing of life but despair, death, fear, and fatuous superficiality cast over an abyss of sorrow. I see how peoples are set against one another, and in silence, unknowingly, foolishly, obediently, innocently slay one another. I see that the keenest brains in the world invent weapons and words to make it yet more refined and enduring. And all men of my age, here and over there, throughout the whole world see these things; all my generation is experiencing these things with me. What would our fathers do if we suddenly stood up and came before them and proffered our account? What do they expect of us if a time ever comes when the war is over? Through the years our business has been killing;—it was our first calling in life. Our knowledge of life is limited to death. What will happen afterwards? And what shall come out of us?

---

*Erich Maria Remarque (1956), *All Quiet on the Western Front*, translated by A. W. Wheen, New York: Fawcett Crest, pp. 134–35, 179, 263–64.

Robert Graves, *Goodbye to All That**

At least one in three of my generation at school died; because they all took commissions as soon as they could, most of them in the infantry and Royal Flying Corps. The average life expectancy of an infantry subaltern on the Western Front was, at some stages of the War, only about three months; by which time he had been either wounded or killed. The proportions worked out at about four wounded to every one killed. Of these four, one got wounded seriously, and the remaining three more or less lightly. The three lightly wounded returned to the front after a few weeks or months of absence, and again faced the same odds. Flying casualties were even higher. Since the War lasted for four and a half years, it is easy to see why most of the survivors, if not permanently disabled, collected several wound stripes.

In the trenches a few months later, I happened to belong to a company mess in which four of us young officers out of five had, by a coincidence, either German mothers or naturalized German fathers. One of them said: "I'm glad I joined when I did. If I'd put it off for a month or two, they'd have accused me of being a German spy. As it is, I have an uncle interned in Alexandra Palace, and my father's only been allowed to retain the membership of his golf club because he has two sons in the trenches." I told him: "Well, I have three or four uncles sitting somewhere opposite, and a number of cousins, too. One of those uncles is a general. But that's all right. I don't brag about them. Instead, I advertise my uncle Dick Poore, the British admiral commanding at Nore."

I am beginning to realize how lucky I was in my gentle introduction to the Cambrin trenches. We are now in a nasty salient, a little to the south of the brickstacks, where casualties are always heavy. The Company had seventeen casualties yesterday from bombs and grenades. The front trench averages thirty yards from the Germans. Today, at one part, which is only twenty yards away from an occupied German sap, I went along whistling "The Farmer's Boy", to keep up my spirits, when suddenly I saw a group bending over a man lying at the bottom of the trench. He was making a snoring noise mixed with animal groans. At my feet lay the cap he had worn, splashed with his brains. I had never seen human brains before; I somehow regarded them as a poetical figment. One can joke with a badly-wounded man and congratulate him on being out of it. One can disregard a dead man. But even a miner can't make a joke that sounds like a joke over a man who takes three hours to die, after the top part of his head has been taken off by a bullet fired at twenty yards' range.

---

*Robert Graves (1957, © 1929), *Goodbye to All That*, Garden City, NY: Doubleday and Company, pp. 59, 68, 114, 132–33.

Like everyone else, I had carefully worked out a formula for taking risks. In principle, we would take any risk, even the certainty of death, to save a life or to maintain an important position. To take life we would run, say, a one-in-five risk, particularly if there was some wider object than merely reducing the enemy's manpower; for instance, picking off a well-known sniper, or getting fire ascendancy in trenches where the lines came dangerously close. I only once refrained from shooting a German I saw, and that was at Cuinchy, about three weeks after this. While sniping from a knoll in the support line, where we had a concealed loop-hole, I saw a German, about seven hundred yards away, through my telescopic sights. He was taking a bath in the German third line. I disliked the idea of shooting a naked man, so I handed the rifle to the sergeant with me. "Here, take this. You're a better shot than I am." He got him; but I had not stayed to watch.

About saving the lives of enemy wounded there was disagreement; the convention varied with the division. Some divisions, like the Canadians and a division of Lowland Territorials, who claimed that they had atrocities to avenge, would not only avoid taking risks to rescue enemy wounded, but go out of their way to finish them off. The Royal Welch were gentlemanly: perhaps a one-in-twenty risk to get a wounded German to safety would be considered justifiable. An important factor in calculating risks was our own physical condition. When exhausted and wanting to get quickly from one point in the trenches to another without collapse, we would sometimes take a short cut over the top, if the enemy were not nearer than four or five hundred yards. In a hurry, we would take a one-in-two-hundred risk; when dead-tired even a one-in-fifty risk. In some battalions where morale was low, one-in-fifty risks were often taken in laziness or despair. The Munsters of the First Division were said by the Welsh to "waste men wicked" by not keeping properly under cover while in the reserve lines. The Royal Welch never allowed wastage of this sort. At no time in the War did any of us believe that hostilities could possibly continue more than another nine months or a year, so it seemed almost worth while taking care; there might even be a chance of lasting until the end absolutely unhurt.

Questions

1 What impact do the descriptions of war in these two sources have on the reader? Does the fictional or nonfictional nature of the two accounts affect the impact that they have?

2. To what extent can any writing, whether fiction or nonfiction, explain the war experience to noncombatants?

3. How much should we factor in the individual nature of these works when assessing their historical significance? Are people who enjoy combat, by nature, less likely to write about it?
4. In what ways do these two sources speak to the particular nature of the First World War and the fighting on the Western Front? In what ways do they speak to the nature of war in general?

SELECTED POEMS BY RUPERT BROOKE, WILFRID OWEN, SIEGFRIED SASSOON, AND ROBERT FROST, INTRODUCTION

The war provoked a variety of reactions even among those who experienced combat, as illustrated through the work of some of Britain's best known "war poets." Rupert Brooke, educated at Rugby and King's College, Cambridge, belonged to the elite group of writers known as the Bloomsbury Group before the war. Like many of his social class, he supported the war and prepared to do his duty. He wrote his best-known poem, "The Soldier," in 1914 and died a year later on a French hospital ship off the coast of Greece after contracting a disease caused by a mosquito bite. Siegfried Sassoon (1886–1967) and Wilfrid Owen (1893–1918) met in a Scottish rehabilitation hospital during the war, where the older Sassoon encouraged Owen to pursue his poetry. Their poems not only reflected their experiences and perspectives on the war, but did much to shape the way in which the postwar generations would remember it. The American poet, Robert Frost (1874–1963), lived in England from 1913 to 1915. Literary scholars have analyzed his short poem "Fire and Ice" in a variety of ways, but it appears here because Frost also felt the effects of the war and wrote this poem in its immediate aftermath in 1920.

Rupert Brooke, "The Soldier"*

If I should die, think only this of me:
That there's some corner of a foreign field
That is for ever England. There shall be
In that rich earth a richer dust concealed;
A dust whom England bore, shaped, made aware,
Gave, once, her flowers to love, her ways to roam,
A body of England's, breathing English air,

The Collected Poems of Rupert Brooke (1915 edition), available online at http://www.gutenberg.org/files/262/262-h/262-h.htm#link2H_4_0059.

Washed by the rivers, blest by suns of home.
And think, this heart, all evil shed away,
A pulse in the eternal mind, no less
Gives somewhere back the thoughts by England given;
Her sights and sounds; dreams happy as her day;
And laughter, learnt of friends; and gentleness,
In hearts at peace, under an English heaven.

Wilfrid Owen, "Dulce et Decorum Est"*

Bent double, like old beggars under sacks,
Knock-kneed, coughing like hags, we cursed through sludge,
Till on the haunting flares we turned our backs
And towards our distant rest began to trudge.
Men marched asleep. Many had lost their boots
But limped on, blood-shod. All went lame; all blind;
Drunk with fatigue; deaf even to the hoots
Of tired, outstripped Five-Nines that dropped behind.
Gas! Gas! Quick, boys!—An ecstasy of fumbling,
Fitting the clumsy helmets just in time;
But someone still was yelling out and stumbling,
And flound'ring like a man in fire or lime . . .
Dim, through the misty panes and thick green light,
As under a green sea, I saw him drowning.
In all my dreams, before my helpless sight,
He plunges at me, guttering, choking, drowning.
If in some smothering dreams you too could pace
Behind the wagon that we flung him in,
And watch the white eyes writhing in his face,
His hanging face, like a devil's sick of sin;
If you could hear, at every jolt, the blood
Come gargling from the froth-corrupted lungs,
Obscene as cancer, bitter as the cud
Of vile, incurable sores on innocent tongues,
My friend, you would not tell with such high zest
To children ardent for some desperate glory,
The old Lie; Dulce et Decorum est
Pro patria mori.

---

*http://www.warpoetry.co.uk/owen1.html

Siegfried Sassoon, "Attack"*

AT dawn the ridge emerges massed and dun
In the wild purple of the glow'ring sun,
Smouldering through spouts of drifting smoke that shroud
The menacing scarred slope; and, one by one,
Tanks creep and topple forward to the wire.
The barrage roars and lifts. Then, clumsily bowed
With bombs and guns and shovels and battle-gear,
Men jostle and climb to meet the bristling fire.
Lines of grey, muttering faces, masked with fear,
They leave their trenches, going over the top,
While time ticks blank and busy on their wrists,
And hope, with furtive eyes and grappling fists,
Flounders in mud. O Jesus, make it stop!

Robert Frost, "Fire and Ice"**

Some say the world will end in fire,
Some say in ice.
From what I've tasted of desire
I hold with those who favor fire.
But if it had to perish twice,
I think I know enough of hate
To say that for destruction ice
Is also great
And would suffice.

Questions
1. Compare the perspectives offered on the war in the poems above by Brooke, Sassoon, and Owen. What does each of the poems say about the personality of the author? What is the central message of each of the poems? Is the date of each poem significant?
2. What effect does Frost's poem "Fire and Ice" have when read alongside the others included in this section compared to how one might interpret it by reading it in isolation?

---

*http://www.best-poems.net/siegfried_sassoon/poem-18323.html
**http://www.poetryfoundation.org/poem/173527

FIGURE 8: Stretcher bearers giving aid to a soldier lying wounded in a trench on the Somme. Courtesy of Getty Images.

FIGURE 9: Saint Etienne machine gunners in firing position, August 2, 1917. Courtesy of Getty Images.

3. Does poetry ever have a single meaning or does the meaning of a poem shift depending on the context in which one reads it? What do the poems in this section mean to you?
4. What do these poems collectively contribute to an understanding of the experience and effects of the First World War?

Questions

1. In what ways do these images reinforce the sources included in this chapter? In what ways do they add to the sources included in this chapter?
2. How do these images combine to reflect the unique nature of fighting that occurred in the First World War?
3. What role do images such as these play in the reconstruction of history? Does the selective nature of the images included weaken their historical significance or does each image represent a valuable historical source in its own right?

JOHN REED, *TEN DAYS THAT SHOOK THE WORLD*, INTRODUCTION

At the beginning of 1917, the leader of the Russian Bolshevik Party, Vladimir Lenin, resided in Switzerland with little hopes that his revolutionary goals would be fulfilled in his lifetime. The February revolution and the abdication of Tsar Nicholas II provided new hope; with assistance from the Germans who wished to further chaos and instability within Russia, Lenin left Switzerland for Petrograd where he immediately began to advocate for a communist revolution to overthrow the Provisional Government. He joined the Petrograd Soviet, one of a number of local revolutionary councils that had sprung up all over Russia. For months, Lenin had difficulty persuading his colleagues that Russia met the criteria that Marx had established for a communist revolution; Lenin replied that they needed to revise Marx if necessary but seize the opportunity when it came to grab power. That opportunity finally came in October. In the passage below, John Reed attempts to capture the revolutionary atmosphere that accompanied the Bolshevik seizure of power and the second Russian Revolution of 1917.

John Reed, *Ten Days That Shook the World**

The order of the day, said Kamenev, was first Organization of Power; second, War and Peace; and third, the Constitutional Assembly. Lozovsky, rising, announced that upon agreement of the bureau of all factions, it was proposed to hear and discuss the report of the Petrograd Soviet, then to give the floor to members of Tsay-ee-kah and the different parties, and finally to pass to the order of the day.

But suddenly a new sound made itself heard, deeper than the tumult of the crowd, persistent, disquieting—the dull shock of guns. People looked anxiously towards the clouded windows, and a sort of fever came over them. Martov, demanding the floor, croaked hoarsely, "The civil war is beginning, comrades! The first question must be a peaceful settlement of the crisis. On principle and from a political standpoint we must urgently discuss a means of averting civil war. Our brothers are being shot down in the streets! At this moment, when before the opening of the Congress of Soviets the question of Power is being settled by means of a military plot organized by one of the revolutionary parties—"for a moment he could not make himself heard above the noise, "All of the revolutionary parties must face the fact!

The first *vopros* (question) before the Congress is the question of power, and this question is already being settled by force of arms in the streets! . . . We must create a power which will be recognized by the whole democracy. If the Congress wishes to be the voice of the revolutionary democracy it must not sit with folded hands before the developing civil war, the result of which may be a dangerous outburst of counter-revolution. . . . The possibility of a peaceful outcome lies in the formation of a united democratic authority. . . . We must elect a delegation to negotiate with the other Socialist parties and organizations. . . ."

So Lenin and the Petrograd workers had decided on insurrection, the Petrograd Soviet had overthrown the Provisional Government, and thrust the *coup d'etat* upon the Congress of Soviets. Now there was all great Russia to win—and then the world! Would Russia follow and rise? And the world—what of it? Would the peoples answer and rise, a red world-tide?

Although it was six in the morning, night was yet heavy and chill. There was only a faint unearthly pallor stealing over the silent streets, dimming the watch-fires, the shadow of a terrible dawn grey-rising over Russia. . . .

---

*John Reed (1977, © 1919), *Ten Days That Shook the World*, Harmondsworth: Penguin Books, pp. 100, 116.

Questions

1. Reed suggests here that the outbreak of violence in the city took the Petrograd Soviet by surprise. How does this affect the interpretation of the Russian Revolution?
2. What issues did the Soviets face upon the seizure of power? Were these the same issues that had faced the Provisional Government?
3. What attitude does Reed convey toward the events he describes? Is he a neutral observer?
4. If Reed's writing, like some of the others included in this chapter, helped to shape future perceptions of the events he describes, what lasting impression did he leave of the Bolshevik takeover in 1917?

THE BALFOUR DECLARATION, 1917, INTRODUCTION

Lord Balfour expressed his support for a Jewish national homeland in a letter written to Lord Rothschild, an outspoken supporter of the Zionist movement that sought to create a Jewish state. After the war, the League of Nations granted Britain a mandate over Palestine. Had the British government ignored or repudiated the Balfour Declaration, its historical significance would have been significantly lessened, but instead it became the basis for British policy in the region.

The Balfour Declaration, 1917*

Foreign Office
November 2nd, 1917

Dear Lord Rothschild:

I have much pleasure in conveying to you on behalf of His Majesty's Government, the following declaration of sympathy with Jewish Zionist aspirations which has been submitted to, and approved by, the Cabinet:

His Majesty's Government view with favor the establishment in Palestine of a national home for the Jewish people, and will use their best endeavors to facilitate the achievement of this object, it being clearly understood that nothing

---

London Times, November 9, 1917.

shall be done which may prejudice the civil and religious rights of existing non-Jewish communities in Palestine, or the rights and political status enjoyed by Jews in any other country.

I should be grateful if you would bring this declaration to the knowledge of the Zionist Federation.

Yours,
Arthur James Balfour

Questions
1. What tone does Balfour use in the letter? Why is that significant?
2. What indication do the contents of the letter give that this represented more than just a private correspondence?
3. Why do you think that Balfour chose to announce his support for a Jewish national homeland in this way?

Chapter Questions

1. Which of the sources in this chapter did you find most valuable as a historical source? Which did you find most insightful? If you answered these two questions differently, what distinction would you make between the value of a source for understanding history and the value of a source for understanding humanity? Is there a difference?
2. Do the literary sources in this chapter represent thoughtful reflection and the processing of information or a more immediate response to direct personal experience? Or do they differ in that regard? If so, which sources belong in which category?
3. What conclusions might you draw from these sources as a group about the effects of the First World War?

CHAPTER NINE

Revolution and Cultural Change in the Early Twentieth Century

INTRODUCTION

The First World War was surrounded on both sides by revolutions and social upheaval that did as much as the war to shape the future of the twentieth century. In Mexico, the government of Porfirio Díaz, who had served as president for all but four years since 1876, faced growing demands for political and social reform as he faced reelection in 1910. Though Mexico was nominally a democracy, Díaz ruled with a heavy hand and largely excluded representatives of the middle class from a voice in government, much less the peasants and working classes. Opponents of the regime found a leader in Francisco Madero, who first challenged Díaz in the election and then supported his overthrow when his campaign to unseat Díaz failed, as a result of massive corruption at the polls. Seeing the writing on the wall, Díaz resigned in 1911, with Madero replacing him. However, Madero's election only furthered the growth of revolutionary sentiment when the wealthy landowner proved no more interested in true reform than his predecessor. General Victoriano Huerta had Madero assassinated in 1913 in a military coup, while separate revolutionary movements emerged under the leadership of men such as Emiliano Zapata (1878–1919) and Pancho Villa (1878–1923). The Mexican revolution attracted widespread popular support from the peasants, workers, and some members of the middle class, but by 1915 divisions among the revolutionaries and widespread violence and banditry led to the kind of disillusion and despair that the Mexican writer Mariano Azuela captured so well in his novel of that year, *Los de Abajo* or *The Underdogs*.

Disenchantment and demands for reform afflicted the crumbling Ottoman Empire prior to the outbreak of the First World War as well. Long referred to as "the sick man of Europe," the Ottomans sealed their fate by allying with Germany and Austria—the losing side—during the First World War. While Britain and France, via the newly-formed League of Nations, carved up the former Ottoman provinces in the Middle East into protectorates under their control, Turkey experienced a revolution led by Mustafa Kemal (1881–1938), who came to be better known by his chosen name of Atatürk (Father of the Turks). After establishing a provisional government in 1921, Kemal officially overthrew the ruling dynasty in 1922 and established a republic a year later, with himself as president. Over the course of the next dozen years or so, he secularized many aspects of Turkish society and converted the country into a Westernized, European nation. Among other changes, he replaced the Turkish alphabet with Latin characters and gave greater freedoms to women. Kemal emphasized the importance of Turkish nationalism and maintained a strict separation between politics and religion. In doing so, he alienated Muslims throughout the Arab world, even as he inspired those Arabs with nationalist aspirations who admired Kemal's defiance of the European powers.

Although Turkey had been officially declared a republic in 1923, Kemal ruled over an authoritarian-style government, as was becoming common in many other countries in the aftermath of the First World War. The American diplomat and politician, Charles Hitchcock Sherrill (1867–1936), served as ambassador to Turkey in 1932–3, recording his impressions of the Turkish leader and his altered country in a book published the following year.

Revolutionary change was not just confined to politics in the early twentieth century, however. Cultural and literary values underwent radical shifts during this period as well. Perhaps no single individual was more associated with changing views on life, society, and European civilization than the venerable psychologist Sigmund Freud (1856–1939). Freud began his medical career in the 1880s and made his name studying nervous disorders, eventually suggesting that patients could overcome their neuroses by discovering the roots of their fears and anxieties in repressed memories and unconscious feelings of which they needed to be made aware. In his later writings, he focused on the ways in which whole societies were subject to the same psychological maladies of repression and unconscious desires, culminating in his landmark work, *Civilization and Its Discontents*, written in 1929. The First World War had called forth in Freud a psychological explanation for the war similar to his concept of a death wish that he had identified in individuals incapable of coping with reality. The concept of a death wish could also help to explain the annihilation of the individual that accompanied the totalitarian communist and fascist regimes of the interwar period as well (see Chapter 10).

In a world that seemed to lose its moorings in the chaos of revolutions and world war, literature frequently became unhinged from any connection with absolute values or any kind of concrete reality. Virginia Woolf was among those writers pioneering new directions in literature in the 1920s and 1930s. Although best known as a novelist, Woolf wrote in a variety of genres, including poetry. In novels such as *To the Lighthouse* and *Mrs. Dalloway*, she used experimental techniques that placed a greater emphasis on personal experience than third-person narration of an objective reality. But for a serious intellectual such as Woolf, the rise of fascism and the impending threat of a second world war represented realities that needed confrontation, leading her in a way to reconnect with the external world in her 1936 nonfiction book, *Three Guineas*, an excerpt from which concludes this chapter.

MARIANO AZUELA, *THE UNDERDOGS*, INTRODUCTION

Mariano Azuela (1873–1952) is one of the most important Mexican novelists of the twentieth century and The Underdogs, *written in 1915 and translated into*

English in 1929, is his most important work. Trained as a doctor, he became inspired by the ideals of the Revolution of 1910; he joined the revolutionary army of Pancho Villa. In his novel, Demetrio Macías is the leader of a peasant band of rebels. The other main characters include Luis Cervantes, a former opponent of the revolution and member of the middle class who had supported the military coup of Huerta in 1913, and Alberto Solís, a revolutionary who, like Azuela, has become disillusioned with the revolution but is at a loss to think of any viable alternative. It is perhaps noteworthy that Macías dies at the end of the novel without having advanced the revolution in any significant way. The two passages below explore both the ideals of the revolution and the frustration among those like Solís who have fought for any period of time.

Mariano Azuela, *The Underdogs**

"As I was saying," Luis Cervantes resumed, "when the revolution is over, everything is over. Too bad that so many men have been killed, too bad there are so many widows and orphans, too bad there was so much bloodshed.

"Of course, you are not selfish; you say to yourself: 'All I want to do is go back home.' But I ask you, is it fair to deprive your wife and kids of a fortune which God himself places within reach of your hand? Is it fair to abandon your motherland in this solemn moment when she most needs the self-sacrifice of her sons, when she most needs her humble sons to save her from falling again in the clutches of her eternal oppressors, executioners, and *caciques*? You must not forget that the thing a man holds most sacred on earth is his motherland."

Macias smiled, his eyes shining.

"Will it be all right if we go with Natera?"

"Not only all right," Venancio said insultingly, "but I think it absolutely necessary."

"Now Chief," Cervantes pursued, "I took a fancy to you the first time I laid eyes on you and I like you more and more every day because I realize what you are worth. Please let me be utterly frank. You do not yet realize your lofty noble function. You are a modest man without ambitions, you do not wish to realize the exceedingly important role you are destined to play in the revolution. It is not true that you took up arms simply because of Señor Mónico. You are under arms to protest against the evils of all the *caciques* who are overrunning the whole nation. We are the elements of a social movement which will not rest until it has enlarged the destinies of our motherland. We are the tools Destiny makes use of to reclaim the sacred rights of the people. We are not

*Mariano Azuela (1963), *The Underdogs: A Novel of the Mexican Revolution*, translated by E. Munguía, Jr., New York: Penguin, pp. 55–56, 72–73.

fighting to dethrone a miserable murderer, we are fighting against tyranny itself. What moves us is what men call ideals; our action is what men call fighting for principle. A principle! That's why Villa and Natera and Carranza are fighting; that's why we, every man of us, are fighting."

"Yes . . . yes . . . exactly what I've been thinking myself," said Venancio in a climax of enthusiasm.

"Hm," Solis went on, offering Cevantes a chair, "since when have you turned rebel?"

"I've been a rebel the last two months!"

"Oh, I see! That's why you speak with such faith and enthusiasm about things we all felt when we joined the revolution."

"Have you lost your faith or enthusiasm?"

"Look here, man, don't be surprised if I confide in you right off. I am so anxious to find someone intelligent among this crowd, that as soon as I get hold of a man like you, I clutch at him as eagerly as I would at a glass of water, after walking mile after mile through a parched desert. But frankly, I think you should do the explaining first. I can't understand how a man who was correspondent of a Government newspaper during the Madero regime, and later editorial writer on a Conservative journal, who denounced us as bandits in the most fiery articles, is now fighting on our side."

"I tell you honestly: I have been converted," Cervantes answered.

"Are you absolutely convinced?"

Solís sighed, filled the glasses; they drank.

"What about you? Are you tired of the revolution?" asked Cervantes sharply.

"Tired? My dear fellow, I'm twenty-five years old and I'm fit as a fiddle! But am I disappointed? Perhaps!"

"You must have sound reasons for feeling that way."

"I hoped to find a meadow at the end of the road, I found a swamp. Facts are bitter; so are men. That bitterness eats your heart out; it is poison, dry rot. Enthusiasm, hope, ideals, happiness—vain dreams, vain dreams. . . . When that's over, you have a choice. Either you turn bandit, like the rest, or the timeservers will swamp you. . . ."

Cervantes writhed at his friend's words; his argument was quite out of place . . . painful. . . . To avoid being forced to take issue, he invited Solís to cite the circumstances that had destroyed his illusions.

"Circumstances? No—it's far less important than that. It's a host of silly, insignificant things that no one notices except yourself . . . a change of expression, eyes shining—lips curled in a sneer—the deep import of a phrase that is lost! Yet take these things together and they compose the mask of our race . . . terrible . . . grotesque . . . a race that awaits redemption!"

He drained another glass. After a long pause, he continued:

"You ask me why I am still a rebel? Well, the revolution is like a hurricane: if
you're in it, you're not a man . . . you're a leaf, a dead leaf, blown by the wind."
  Demetrio reappeared. Seeing him, Solís relapsed into silence.

Questions
1. Why has Cervantes joined the Revolution? Do these passages provide an
   adequate answer to that question?
2. If Solís is so disillusioned by the revolution, why does he remain with the
   forces of Macías? What does he mean when he compares the revolution to a
   hurricane? Is this an apt comparison for revolution in general?
3. Are these passages from Azuela, which generally reflect the novel as a whole,
   meant to be prescriptive or merely descriptive? If the former, what message
   is he trying to get across? If the latter, what purpose is the novel meant to
   serve?

FIGURE 10: Diego Rivera, *The Rural School Teacher,* 1932. Courtesy of the Granger
Collection, New York City.

Diego Rivera (1886–1957) was roughly a contemporary of Mariano Azuela who lived through the Mexican Revolution and its relative failure to bring about meaningful social and political reform in Mexico. However, for much of the period of the revolution, Rivera was in Europe, only returning to Mexico in 1921 after ten years abroad. Like Azuela, he became committed to social change, joining the Communist Party and even visiting the Soviet Union at one point. His paintings reflected his commitment to causes of social justice and the eradication of poverty.

Questions

1. What is the message that this mural is meant to convey? How might it reflect the political ideals of the painter?
2. What does the figure with the gun represent? Why place him in such close proximity to the schoolteacher and her pupils?
3. Based on your knowledge of European art, what influence did Rivera's stay in Europe have on his painting? (If you have trouble answering this question, look at some examples of paintings, particularly those associated with the style known as Cubism, from the period between 1911 and 1921 when Rivera was in Europe.)

CHARLES HITCHCOCK SHERRILL, *A YEAR'S EMBASSY TO MUSTAFA KEMAL*, INTRODUCTION

Charles Hitchcock Sherrill had a diplomatic career that took him from Argentina to Turkey. More than just an eyewitness, Sherrill commented on the political developments of the twentieth century, noting with approval the emergence of strong leaders such as Mussolini and Hitler, which he believed the times called for. Like many others in the aftermath of the First World War, Sherrill had become disenchanted with parliamentary democracy, which he believed had become a historical anachronism. Such views must have surely affected his attitude toward Mustafa Kemal, the strongman who had dominated the new Turkish republic since its inception in 1923.

Charles Hitchcock Sherrill, *A Year's Embassy to Mustafa Kemal**

At no time during his strenuous efforts to give Turkish sovereignty back to the Turks and to free Turkey from all foreign enemies did Mustafa Kemal work harder than during the eleven months (September, 1921 to August, 1922) intervening between the end of the long battle of Sakarya and the beginning of the shorter one of Dumlu Punar. . . . More than once he has announced that all of Turkish territories must be freed from all invaders. . . . Turkey's man power as much as possible, launches no destructive battle campaign until every peaceful means of freeing the land has been tried and failed. While his agents are working to that end abroad, he too is energetically engaged at home, so as to conserve by effective preparation the lives of his soldiers when the hour strikes for his ultimate attack. . . .

Of all the stories I know dealing with Mustafa Kemal's political acumen, there are two in particular which especially reveal his statesmanship in striking fashion. . . .

Upon arriving in Turkey, it seemed well for me as a foreign ambassador to visit her battlefields, just as foreigners are accustomed to do in France. When I intimated this intention to the Turkish authorities, there came the reply that President Mustafa Kemal greatly preferred Turkey's present cordial relations with Greece, her former enemy on those very battlefields, to reviving memories of victories gained there! . . .

This broad-visioned attitude of mind impressed me deeply, but perhaps not so much as the following; when I sought to learn why Turkey, after her overwhelming defeat of the Greeks, had not insisted on receiving from them reparations in some form, they told me that Mustafa Kemal had then decided that renewed and perhaps increased commercial relations with the Greeks would pay Turkey better than irksome annual collections, which possibly might later be discontinued in some such way as to cause friction between the two nations. Show me another statesman in Europe, who, at the end of the Great War, displayed such farsighted statesmanship!

These two stories reveal a distinguished battle leader who is at heart such a practical pacifist that he prefers to substitute friendships with all Turkey's neighbors for the animosities of former times. And by so doing, he has abolished the former isolation of Turkey. This, the Gazi's eleventh revolution, had a wider repercussion abroad than at home.

---

*Charles Hitchcock Sherrill (1934), *A Year's Embassy to Mustafa Kemal*, New York: C. Scribner's Sons, pp. 121–22, 227–28.

Among the very few things the world learned from the Great War was that treaties which are not backed by common friendships and points of view possessed by both the two signatory nations become mere "scraps of paper."

The Gazi was the first of the great statesman who survived the war to realize and utilize this outstanding fact.

If the liberated and regenerated Turkey was to utilize the opportunities—commercial, cultural, and national—of the new era of world peace, Turkey must establish friendships with all her neighbors—friendships that would serve their mutual interests far better than signed treaties. To that great end the Gazi labored unceasingly, and his labors benefited those neighbors as well as his beloved homeland.

Questions

1. Based on the above excerpts, on what was Sherrill's admiration of Mustafa Kemal based?
2. How was his evaluation of Kemal specifically influenced by the First World War?
3. Might Mustafa Kemal had other reasons for seeking friendly relationships with Turkey's neighbors beyond those cited by Sherrill?
4. Given his obvious bias, how valuable is Sherrill's treatment of Kemal's regime as a historical source? What are its limitations? In what ways does it illuminate, not just Kemal's regime, but the period in which he is writing in general?

SIGMUND FREUD, *CIVILIZATION AND ITS DISCONTENTS*, INTRODUCTION

Freud sought to replace religion with science, but he was left to fall back on civilization—despite regarding (in his 1913 book Totem and Taboo) *the drives that created it as artificial—as the hope for keeping the baser instincts of humanity in check. Freud compared the life of a civilization to the life of a human being and saw in society as a whole the same instinct to kill one's father and establish one's own identity that he identified with the Oedipus complex in the individual. Furthermore, just as an individual internalizes guilt over these primordial desires, so civilization imposes laws and cultural restraints to compensate for the violence that brought it into existence in the first place. Civilization thus leads to a substitution of guilt for happiness, one of the main principles of his book, Civilization and Its Discontents. Freud, in fact, had raised the question of whether it made rational sense to serve civilization, given its fraudulent and psychologically repressive origins. However, Freud would have been the first to admit that the downfall of civilization would represent a disaster for humankind. Freud was no advocate of anarchy. Furthermore, like other existentialist philosophers of the twentieth century, Freud believed that humans could create their own values and give life meaning based on the rules of its own existence, and that this was only possible within the bounds of civilized society.*

Sigmund Freud, *Civilization and Its Discontents**

. . . Our patients do not believe us when we attribute an "unconscious sense of guilt" to them. In order to make ourselves at all intelligible to them, we tell them of an unconscious need for punishment, in which the sense of guilt finds expression. But its connection with a particular form of neurosis must not be over-estimated. Even in obsessional neurosis there are types of patients who are not aware of their sense of guilt, or who only feel it as a tormenting uneasiness, a kind of anxiety, if they are prevented from carrying out certain actions. It ought to be possible eventually to understand these things; but as yet we cannot. Here perhaps we may be glad to have it pointed out that the sense of guilt is at bottom nothing else but a topographical variety of anxiety; in its later phases it coincides completely with *fear of the super-ego*. And the relations of anxiety to consciousness exhibit the same extraordinary variations. Anxiety is always present somewhere or other behind every symptom; but at one time it takes noisy possession of the whole of consciousness, while at another it conceals itself so completely that we are obliged to speak of unconscious anxiety or, if we want to have a clearer psychological conscience, since anxiety is in the first instance simply a feeling, of possibilities of anxiety. Consequently it is very conceivable that the sense of guilt produced by civilization is not perceived as such either, and remains to a large extent unconscious, or appears as a sort of *malaise*, a dissatisfaction for which people seek other motivations. Religions, at any rate, have never overlooked the part played in civilization by a sense of guilt. Furthermore—a point which I failed to appreciate elsewhere—they claim to redeem mankind from this sense of guilt, which they call sin. From the manner in which, in Christianity, this redemption is achieved—by the sacrificial death of a single person, who in this manner takes upon himself a guilt that

---

*Sigmund Freud (1961), *Civilization and Its Discontents*, translated by James Strachey, New York: W.W. Norton and Company, pp. 333–34.

is common to everyone—we have been able to infer what the first occasion may have been on which this primal guilt, which was also the beginning of civilization, was acquired.

Questions

1. Do you think that Freud was right about general anxiety having its roots in an unconscious sense of guilt?
2. Is Freud implying that guilt exists within the individual, within humanity as a whole, or both?
3. How does he reach his conclusion about the origins of civilization from his observation about Christian redemption?
4. Do you think Freud is being too reductionist here? What impact do you think these ideas had on readers who had experienced the calamity of the First World War?

VIRGINIA WOOLF, *THREE GUINEAS*, INTRODUCTION

Most biographies of Virginia Woolf (1882–1941) begin with her famous father, Leslie Stephen, the author of English Literature and Society in the Eighteenth Century *(1903). In addition, her husband, Leonard Woolf, had a strong influence on her life; together they founded the Hogarth Press in 1917. However, Woolf surpassed both of them as a writer and a literary and intellectual influence both through her writings, especially her novels, and her leadership role in a circle of writers and artists in London known as the Bloomsbury Group. In addition to the novels mentioned in the chapter introduction, experimental works such as* Jacob's Room *(1922) and* Orlando *(1928) include disconnected impressions and events that readers need to piece together, time travel, and gender shifts in the same character. By 1936, however, the Spanish Civil War was raging; many opponents of fascism—including Woolf's own nephew, Julian Bell, who volunteered and died in the conflict—viewed Spain as a place where they could do something to stop its advance in Europe. Meanwhile, Hitler had torn up the Versailles Treaty and marched his troops into the Rhineland and the Italian dictator Mussolini (see Chapter 10) defied the League of Nations by launching an invasion of Abyssinia (Ethiopia). Woolf originally intended* Three Guineas *as part of a literary experiment in which she would interweave a fictional story with chapters that would be entirely nonfiction. In the end, she decided against this and published two separate books,* The Years *(fiction) and* Three Guineas *(nonfiction). In* Three Guineas, *Woolf responds to a letter that she receives from an unnamed man who asks for her assistance in preventing war from breaking out in Europe. A confirmed pacifist, Woolf nevertheless dodges the question because, as a woman, she has no desire to engage with men on their own terms at the risk of becoming like them or giving legitimacy to their perspective, which, she starts out by saying in the passage below, she cannot fully understand.*

Virginia Woolf, *Three Guineas**

How then are we to understand your problem, and if we cannot, how can we answer your question, how to prevent war? The answer based upon our experience and our psychology—Why fight?—is not an answer of any value. Obviously there is for you some glory, some necessity, some satisfaction in fighting which we have never felt or enjoyed. Complete understanding could only be achieved by blood transfusion and memory transfusion—a miracle still beyond the reach of science. But we who live now have a substitute for blood transfusion and memory transfusion which must serve at a pinch. There is that marvellous, perpetually renewed, and as yet largely untapped aid to the understanding of human motives which is provided in our age by biography and autobiography. Also there is the daily paper, history in the raw. There is thus no longer any reason to be confined to the minute span of actual experience which is still, for us, so narrow, so circumscribed. We can supplement it by looking at the picture of the lives of others. It is of course only a picture at present, but as such it must serve. It is to biography then that we will turn first, quickly and briefly, in order to attempt to understand what war means to you. Let us extract a few sentences from a biography. First, this from a soldier's life:

I have had the happiest possible life, and have always been working for war, and have now got into the biggest in the prime of life for a soldier. . . . Thank God, we are off in an hour. Such a magnificent regiment! Such men, such horses! Within ten days I hope Francis and I will be riding side by side straight at the Germans.

To which the biographer adds: From the first hour he had been supremely happy, for he had found his true calling. To that let us add this from an airman's life:

We talked of the League of Nations and the prospects of peace and disarmament. On this subject he was not so much militarist as martial. The

---

*Virginia Woolf (1938), *Three Guineas*, available online at http://gutenberg.net.au/ebooks02/0200931h.html.

difficulty to which he could find no answer was that if permanent peace were ever achieved, and armies and navies ceased to exist, there would be no outlet for the manly qualities which fighting developed, and that human physique and human character would deteriorate.

Here, immediately, are three reasons which lead your sex to fight; war is a profession; a source of happiness and excitement; and it is also an outlet for manly qualities, without which men would deteriorate. But that these feelings and opinions are by no means universally held by your sex is proved by the following extract from another biography, the life of a poet who was killed in the European war: Wilfred Owen.

Already I have comprehended a light which never will filter into the dogma of any national church: namely, that one of Christ's essential commands was: Passivity at any price! Suffer dishonour and disgrace, but never resort to arms. Be bullied, be outraged, be killed; but do not kill. . . . Thus you see how pure Christianity will not fit in with pure patriotism.

And among some notes for poems that he did not live to write are these:

The unnaturalness of weapons. . . . Inhumanity of war. . . . The insupportability of war. . . . Horrible beastliness of war. . . . Foolishness of war.

From these quotations it is obvious that the same sex holds very different opinions about the same thing. But also it is obvious, from today's newspaper, that however many dissentients there are, the great majority of your sex are today in favor of war. The Scarborough Conference of educated men, the Bournemouth Conference of working men are both agreed that to spend £300,000,000 annually upon arms is a necessity. They are of opinion that Wilfred Owen was wrong; that it is better to kill than to be killed. Yet since biography shows that differences of opinion are many, it is plain that there must be some one reason which prevails in order to bring about this overpowering unanimity. Shall we call it, for the sake of brevity, "patriotism"? What then, we must ask next, is this "patriotism" which leads you to go to war? Let the Lord Chief Justice of England interpret it for us:

Englishmen are proud of England. For those who have been trained in English schools and universities, and who have done the work of their lives in England, there are few loves stronger than the love we have for our country. When we consider other nations, when we judge the merits of the policy of this country or of that, it is the standard of our own country that we apply. . . . Liberty has made her abode in England. England is the home of democratic institutions. . . . It is true that in our midst there are many enemies of liberty— some of them, perhaps, in rather unexpected quarters. But we are standing firm. It has been said that an Englishman's Home is his Castle. The home of Liberty is in England. And it is a castle indeed—a castle that will be defended to the last. . . . Yes, we are greatly blessed, we Englishmen.

That is a fair general statement of what patriotism means to an educated man and what duties it imposes upon him. But the educated man's sister—what does "patriotism" mean to her? Has she the same reasons for being proud of England, for loving England, for defending England? Has she been "greatly blessed" in England? History and biography when questioned would seem to show that her position in the home of freedom has been different from her brother's; and psychology would seem to hint that history is not without its effect upon mind and body. Therefore her interpretation of the word "patriotism" may well differ from his. And that difference may make it extremely difficult for her to understand his definition of patriotism and the duties it imposes. If then our answer to your question, "How in your opinion are we to prevent war?" depends upon understanding the reasons, the emotions, the loyalties which lead men to go to war, this letter had better be torn across and thrown into the waste-paper basket. For it seems plain that we cannot understand each other because of these differences. It seems plain that we think differently according as we are born differently; there is a Grenfell point of view; a Knebworth point of view; a Wilfred Owen point of view; a Lord Chief Justice's point of view and the point of view of an educated man's daughter. All differ. But is there no absolute point of view? Can we not find somewhere written up in letters of fire or gold, "This is right. This wrong"?—a moral judgment which we must all, whatever our differences, accept? Let us then refer the question of the rightness or wrongness of war to those who make morality their profession—the clergy. Surely if we ask the clergy the simple question: "Is war right or is war wrong?" they will give us a plain answer which we cannot deny. But no—the Church of England, which might be supposed able to abstract the question from its worldly confusions, is of two minds also. The bishops themselves are at loggerheads. The Bishop of London maintained that "the real danger to the peace of the world today were the pacifists. Bad as war was dishonor was far worse." On the other hand, the Bishop of Birmingham described himself as an "extreme pacifist . . . I cannot see myself that war can be regarded as consonant with the spirit of Christ." So the Church itself gives us divided counsel—in some circumstances it is right to fight; in no circumstances is it right to fight. It is distressing, baffling, confusing, but the fact must be faced; there is no certainty in heaven above or on earth below. Indeed the more lives we read, the more speeches we listen to, the more opinions we consult, the greater the confusion becomes and the less possible it seems, since we cannot understand the impulses, the motives, or the morality which lead you to go to war, to make any suggestion that will help you to prevent war.

Questions

1. Woolf says that, although she does not have direct access to the world of men, she does have indirect access through biographies and autobiographies.

What does she say that these teach her? Do they help her to understand men better?

2. Why is she pessimistic about the efforts to prevent war?
3. Are women naturally more pacifistic than men? Is Woolf right about the gap between the sexes?

Chapter Questions

1. Compare and contrast the portrayal of revolutionary Mexico in the painting and in the passages from Azuela's novel above.
2. Do Freud's ideas shed any light on Hitchcock's treatment of Mustafa Kemal? In other words, is it possible that unconscious factors lay behind his admiration for the Turkish strongman?
3. In what ways do the excerpts from Virginia Woolf included here reflect larger themes or truths about the post–First World War period?

CHAPTER TEN

The Crisis of the Interwar Years

INTRODUCTION

During the period between the two world wars, a number of nations turned to more extreme political solutions, especially fascism and communism, first in response to the failure of the Western democracies to prevent the devastating experience of the First World War, then in response to the collapse of the world economy during the Great Depression, which started in 1929. Both of these movements also appealed to members of the working and middle classes seeking a more egalitarian society after the First World War but disillusioned with the liberal focus on the right to vote and the emphasis on personal freedoms and other civil rights. Instead, they sought to sublimate their personal identity to a larger cause, possibly as a result of a sense of the meaninglessness of life given the obliteration of so many millions of personal identities during the war. Italy and Germany were not the only European states that saw the rise of fascist or authoritarian governments between the wars, but they were the most important.

In Italy, Benito Mussolini (1883–1945) emerged as a fascist dictator who appealed to his followers through a particularly militant form of Italian nationalism, a corporate vision of Italian society, and a hero worship of sorts in which Mussolini himself, "Il Duce," (the Leader) embodied Italian strength and power. By 1924, Mussolini had taken over control of the Italian state through a combination of force and intimidation, but without much opposition from a king and parliament willing to overlook his rough manner and bullying tactics because they viewed him as a bulwark against the socialists. It took Hitler longer to gain power in Germany, despite having founded his Nazi party (originally the German Workers' Party) immediately after the end of the First World War. Although he attracted a loyal following that included some of the key figures of the future Nazi regime in the 1920s, Hitler's ideas did not take hold among a significant portion of the German population until after the Depression struck in the early 1930s. He had, however, written down some key aspects of his philosophy and his future plans for Germany in 1923 in a rambling and frequently incoherent autobiography that he called *Mein Kampf* ("My Struggle").

In the Soviet Union, which had replaced the old tsarist autocracy following the Russian Revolution and Civil War, a power struggle emerged in the early 1920s between two communist leaders with different visions of how best to carry on the movement and run the country following the death of Lenin, which occurred in 1924. Josef Stalin (1879–1953) emerged victorious over his main rival, Leon Trotsky, mostly as a result of intimidation and manipulation. However, he still felt the need to distinguish his ideas from those of the more intellectual Trotsky, something which he attempted to do in the source included in this chapter. Stalin was never regarded as a great Marxist thinker or theoretician; theory always took a back seat to power for him. He was better versed in communist ideology than he is sometimes given credit for, however. The first three sources in this chapter, therefore, provide an opportunity to become more familiar with the ideas of three of the most powerful dictators of the twentieth century in their own words.

While drastic changes in government characterized Italy, Germany, and Russia following the First World War, and France and Britain emerged from the war as weaker and poorer powers, the United States seemed poised to assume its position as the leading political and economic power in the world. However, American society had its own problems, including racial and social inequality, endemic rural poverty, especially in the south, and an increasing crime rate directly linked to new laws prohibiting the legal consumption of alcohol. Any illusions that these problems might be transcended in the near future were shattered by the onset of the Great Depression, which began in the United States in 1929 with the crash of the stock market on Wall Street. Problems of racial and social inequality became the focus of some of the great works of American literature that appeared during this period, including the poetry of Langston Hughes and the novels of John Steinbeck, in particular his 1939 classic, *The Grapes of Wrath*.

In China, conditions continued to deteriorate and Western influence continued to expand following the failure of the Boxer Rebellion at the turn of the century. The Chinese Revolution of 1911, led by the republican Sun Yat-sen, provided renewed hope, but did not bring the promised social changes that those who had supported the revolution anticipated. A weak central government led to the imposition of warlord rule in many regions and in most cases the privileged classes retained their power and prestige. Meanwhile, China had entered the First World War on the side of the victorious Allies, as had Japan, only to be disappointed when Japan was rewarded for its support with territorial gains—at China's expense! For many Chinese intellectuals, this was the last straw, leading to the revolutionary May 4 movement, which had both a political and a literary dimension. Lu Xun (1881–1936), one of the leading Chinese writers and intellectuals of the twentieth century, became one of the leading literary voices of this movement. One of the political leaders was Mao Zedong, founder and future leader of the Chinese Communist Party. However, the Chinese nationalist party, known as the Guomindang, emerged in control in the 1920s. A short-lived alliance with the Chinese Communists ended in 1927, followed by a civil war that plagued China off and on for the next two decades. The only lull in the civil war came as a result of the Japanese invasion of China in the 1930s. Japanese atrocities, such as those committed at Nanjing in 1937, convinced both the Guomindang and the Chinese Communist Party that they needed to work together to oust the Japanese before determining China's political future. The "Rape of Nanjing" led to full-scale warfare between China and Japan, a prelude to the larger world war that erupted two years later.

BENITO MUSSOLINI, ENCYCLOPEDIA ARTICLE ON FASCISM, INTRODUCTION

Benito Mussolini, like Adolf Hitler, had been a soldier during the First World War who actually reveled in the military discipline and camaraderie of army life. He had begun his career as a socialist-minded journalist before the war, but underwent a political transformation that turned him into a crusader against Bolshevism by 1921. This may have been as much a matter of convenience as conviction, since Mussolini shrewdly sensed the direction toward which the political winds in Italy were shifting. Posing as a defender of law and order, he secured election to the Italian parliament in that year. Within three years, he had secured the support of the monarchy, which he promised to preserve once in power. Mussolini wrote the following article defining his fascist principles in 1932, after he had already been in power for eight years.

Benito Mussolini, Encyclopedia article on Fascism*

Fascism, the more it considers and observes the future and the development of humanity quite apart from political considerations of the moment, believes neither in the possibility nor the utility of perpetual peace. It thus repudiates the doctrine of Pacifism—born of a renunciation of the struggle and an act of cowardice in the face of sacrifice. War alone brings up to its highest tension all human energy and puts the stamp of nobility upon the peoples who have courage to meet it. All other trials are substitutes, which never really put men into the position where they have to make the great decision—the alternative of life or death. . . .

. . . The Fascist accepts life and loves it, knowing nothing of and despising suicide: he rather conceives of life as duty and struggle and conquest, but above all for others—those who are at hand and those who are far distant, contemporaries, and those who will come after. . . .

. . . Fascism [is] the complete opposite of . . . Marxian Socialism, the materialist conception of history of human civilization can be explained simply through the conflict of interests among the various social groups and by the

---

*http://www.fordham.edu/halsall/mod/mussolini-fascism.asp

change and development in the means and instruments of production. . . . Fascism, now and always, believes in holiness and in heroism; that is to say, in actions influenced by no economic motive, direct or indirect. And if the economic conception of history be denied, according to which theory men are no more than puppets, carried to and fro by the waves of chance, while the real directing forces are quite out of their control, it follows that the existence of an unchangeable and unchanging class-war is also denied—the natural progeny of the economic conception of history. And above all Fascism denies that class-war can be the preponderant force in the transformation of society. . . .

After Socialism, Fascism combats the whole complex system of democratic ideology, and repudiates it, whether in its theoretical premises or in its practical application. Fascism denies that the majority, by the simple fact that it is a majority, can direct human society; it denies that numbers alone can govern by means of a periodical consultation, and it affirms the immutable, beneficial, and fruitful inequality of mankind, which can never be permanently leveled through the mere operation of a mechanical process such as universal suffrage. . . .

. . . Fascism denies, in democracy, the absur[d] conventional untruth of political equality dressed out in the garb of collective irresponsibility, and the myth of "happiness" and indefinite progress. . . .

. . . Given that the nineteenth century was the century of Socialism, of Liberalism, and of Democracy, it does not necessarily follow that the twentieth century must also be a century of Socialism, Liberalism and Democracy: political doctrines pass, but humanity remains, and it may rather be expected that this will be a century of authority . . . a century of Fascism. For if the nineteenth century was a century of individualism it may be expected that this will be the century of collectivism and hence the century of the State. . . .

The foundation of Fascism is the conception of the State, its character, its duty, and its aim. Fascism conceives of the State as an absolute, in comparison with which all individuals or groups are relative, only to be conceived of in their relation to the State. The conception of the Liberal State is not that of a directing force, guiding the play and development, both material and spiritual, of a collective body, but merely a force limited to the function of recording results: on the other hand, the Fascist State is itself conscious and has itself a will and a personality—thus it may be called the "ethic" State. . . .

. . . The Fascist State organizes the nation, but leaves a sufficient margin of liberty to the individual; the latter is deprived of all useless and possibly harmful freedom, but retains what is essential; the deciding power in this question cannot be the individual, but the State alone. . . .

. . . For Fascism, the growth of empire, that is to say the expansion of the nation, is an essential manifestation of vitality, and its opposite a sign of decadence. Peoples which are rising, or rising again after a period of decadence, are always imperialist; and renunciation is a sign of decay and of death. Fascism is the doctrine best adapted to represent the tendencies and the aspirations of a people, like the people of Italy, who are rising again after many centuries of abasement and foreign servitude. But empire demands discipline, the coordination of all forces and a deeply felt sense of duty and sacrifice: this fact explains many aspects of the practical working of the regime, the character of many forces in the State, and the necessarily severe measures which must be taken against those who would oppose this spontaneous and inevitable movement of Italy in the twentieth century, and would oppose it by recalling the outworn ideology of the nineteenth century—repudiated wheresoever there has been the courage to undertake great experiments of social and political transformation; for never before has the nation stood more in need of authority, of direction and order. If every age has its own characteristic doctrine, there are a thousand signs which point to Fascism as the characteristic doctrine of our time. For if a doctrine must be a living thing, this is proved by the fact that Fascism has created a living faith; and that this faith is very powerful in the minds of men is demonstrated by those who have suffered and died for it.

Questions

1. What is Mussolini's definition of fascism?
2. What difference might Mussolini's years of experience in power have made to his definition of fascism here?
3. To whom does the appeal of fascism seem primarily directed in this article?
4. Find a definition of fascism in a textbook, dictionary, encyclopedia or other source. How does it compare to Mussolini's definition? What can Mussolini's definition tell us about his political views?

ADOLF HITLER, *MEIN KAMPF*, INTRODUCTION

Adolf Hitler grew up in Austria at a time when Vienna was still the capital of the Habsburg Empire. There he learned to identify himself as a German in contradistinction to the Slavs who predominated in other parts of the Empire and the Jews by which he felt surrounded in the capital. He moved to Munich before the war and returned to the city after the war, making an ill-fated attempt to seize control of the government there during his infamous "Beer Hall Putsch" in 1923. This blatant act of treason landed him in prison, where he served nine months of a five-year term. He used this brief period of incarceration to compose his autobiography. Although Mein Kampf *cannot be taken as an infallible guide to Hitler's future policies (though some have attempted to do so), any attempt to understand the mind of the man who rose to power, caused the deaths of millions, and brought Germany to ruin must start here. One must also keep in mind that people joined the Nazi movement and supported Hitler for a variety of reasons and not necessarily because of the extremist views expressed here; it is unlikely that very many Nazis had actually read the book from cover to cover, if at all. But the views Hitler expressed in* Mein Kampf *do not stray very far from those expressed in his speeches, which were heard on radio or in person by millions of Germans. They therefore cannot be ignored when assessing the appeal of Nazism any more than they can be when considering the life and mind of Adolf Hitler. As the brief passages below suggest, he had an agenda for the German nation far different than that conceived of by the German nationalists of the nineteenth century.*

Adolf Hitler, *Mein Kampf**

. . . The art of all truly great national leaders has at all times primarily consisted of this: not to divide the attention of a people, but to concentrate that attention on a single enemy. The more unified the fighting spirit of a nation, the greater the magnetic attraction of a movement, the more forceful the power of its thrust. It is part of the genius of a great leader to make it appear as though even the most distant enemies belonged in the same category; for weak and fickle characters, if faced by many different enemies, will easily begin to have doubts about the justness of their cause.

As soon as the vacillating masses see themselves in a battle against too many enemies, they will immediately succumb to an objective view, and ask whether it can really be true that everybody else is wrong, and that only their own people or their own movements are right.

But if that happens, the first paralysis of your own strength sets in. Therefore, a great number of basically different enemies must always be described as belonging to the same group, so that as far as the mass of your followers is concerned, the battle is being waged against a single enemy. This strengthens the belief in the rightness of your cause, and increases the bitterness against those who would attack it. . . .

. . . Everything that we admire today on this earth, science and art, technology and inventions, is the creative product of but a few nations and perhaps originally but of one race. It is on them that the existence of all culture depends. Should they perish, the beauty of this earth will perish with them.

---

*Joachim Remak, ed. (1969), *The Nazi Years: A Documentary History*, Englewood Cliffs, NJ: Prentice Hall, pp. 33–35, excerpted from Adolf Hitler (1939), *Mein Kampf*, New York: Reynal and Hitchcock, pp. 129, 316–18, 329, 332, 334, 361–62, 378–79.

. . . All great cultures of the past were destroyed only because the originally creative race died from blood poisoning.

The final cause of such decline was always the failure to remember that all culture is created by men, and not vice versa, so that if a certain culture is to be saved, the men creating it must be saved. Their preservation, however, is tied to the iron law of necessity, and to the right to victory on the part of the best and the stronger.

Therefore, he who would live, let him fight, and he who would not fight in this world of struggle is not deserving of life.

. . . If one were to divide mankind into three species: the culture-creators, the culture-bearers, and the culture-destroyers, only the Aryan would be likely to fit the first definition. It is to him that we must trace the foundations and the walls of all that human beings have created.

. . . The most powerful antipode to the Aryan is the Jew. . . . No, the Jew possesses no culture-creating ability whatever, since he does not, and never did, have that quality without which man cannot truly develop toward a higher order: idealism. Therefore, his intellect will never act as a constructive force.

. . . He is and remains the typical parasite, a sponger who, like a malign bacillus, spreads more and more as long as he will find some favorable feeding ground. And the consequences of his existence, too, resemble those of the parasite: where he appears, the host nation will sooner or later die. . . .

Questions

1. What are the main ideas expressed by Hitler in these passages from *Mein Kampf*?
2. Do you think that the majority of people who joined the Nazi party, assuming they were aware of these views, would have joined the party because of them or in spite of them?
3. For those to whom the ideas of Hitler did appeal, what might have formed the basis of that appeal?
4. Could these ideas have gained any traction in Germany without its defeat in the First World War and the impact of the Great Depression?

JOSEPH STALIN, TROTSKYISM OR LENINISM?, INTRODUCTION

Lenin had serious doubts about both Trotsky and Stalin as future leaders of the Communist Party, doubts which he expressed prior to his death. Here Stalin attempts to pose as the bearer of Lenin's ideological legacy, even though Trotsky's ideas were actually closer to those of the founder of the Bolshevik party. Posing the choice as one of "Trotskyism or Leninism" was a brilliant ploy on Stalin's part, even though his victory over Trotsky would not be complete for another four years, when Stalin sent his rival into exile. The following excerpt provides a glimpse into the mind of the man who would dominate the Soviet Union for the next thirty years at a critical moment in his rise to power.

Joseph Stalin, Trotskyism or Leninism?*

What are the characteristic features of the new Trotskyism?

1) *On the question of "permanent" revolution.* The new Trotskyism does not deem it necessary openly to uphold the theory of "permanent" revolution. It "simply" asserts that the October Revolution fully confirmed the idea of "permanent" revolution. From this it draws the following conclusion: the important and acceptable part of Leninism is the part that came after the war, in the period of the October Revolution; on the other hand, the part of Leninism that existed before the war, before the October Revolution, is wrong and unacceptable. Hence, the Trotskyites' theory of the division of Leninism into two parts: pre-war Leninism, the "old," "useless" Leninism with its idea of the dictatorship of the proletariat and peasantry, and the new, post-war, October Leninism, which they count on adapting to the requirements of Trotskyism. Trotskyism needs this theory of the division of Leninism as a first, more or less "acceptable" step that is necessary to facilitate further steps in its struggle against Leninism.

But Leninism is not an eclectic theory stuck together out of diverse elements and capable of being cut into parts. Leninism is an integral theory, which arose in 1903, has passed the test of three revolutions, and is now being carried forward as the battle-flag of the world proletariat.

"Bolshevism," Lenin said, "as a trend of political thought and as a political party, has existed since 1903. Only the history of Bolshevism during the *whole* period of its existence can satisfactorily explain why it was able to build up and to maintain under most difficult conditions the iron discipline needed for the victory of the proletariat." . . .

Bolshevism and Leninism are one. They are two names for one and the same thing. Hence, the theory of the division of Leninism into two parts is a theory intended to destroy Leninism, to substitute Trotskyism for Leninism.

Needless to say, the Party cannot reconcile itself to this grotesque theory.

---

*http://www.marxists.org/reference/archive/stalin/works/1924/11_19.htm

2) *On the question of the Party principle.* The old Trotskyism tried to undermine the Bolshevik Party principle by means of the theory (and practice) of unity with the Mensheviks. But that theory has suffered such disgrace that nobody now even wants to mention it. To undermine the Party principle, present-day Trotskyism has invented the new, less odious and almost "democratic" theory of contrasting the old cadres to the younger Party element. According to Trotskyism, our Party has not a single and integral history. Trotskyism divides the history of our Party into two parts of unequal importance: pre-October and post-October. The pre-October part of the history of our Party is, properly speaking, not history, but "pre-history," the unimportant or, at all events, not very important preparatory period of our Party. The post-October part of the history of our Party, however, is real, genuine history. In the former, there are the "old," "pre-historic," unimportant cadres of our Party. In the latter there is the new, real, "historic" Party. It scarcely needs proof that this singular scheme of the history of the Party is a scheme to disrupt the unity between the old and the new cadres of our Party, a scheme to destroy the Bolshevik Party principle.

Needless to say, the Party cannot reconcile itself to this grotesque scheme.

3) *On the question of the leaders of Bolshevism.* The old Trotskyism tried to discredit Lenin more or less openly, without fearing the consequences. The new Trotskyism is more cautious. It tries to achieve the purpose of the old Trotskyism by pretending to praise, to exalt Lenin. I think it is worth while quoting a few examples.

The Party knows that Lenin was a relentless revolutionary; but it knows also that he was cautious, that he disliked reckless people and often, with a firm hand, restrained those who were infatuated with terrorism, including Trotsky himself. Trotsky touches on this subject in his book *On Lenin*, but from his portrayal of Lenin one might think that all Lenin did was "at every opportunity to din into people's minds the idea that terrorism was inevitable." The impression is created that Lenin was the most bloodthirsty of all the bloodthirsty Bolsheviks.

For what purpose did Trotsky need this uncalled for and totally unjustified exaggeration?

The Party knows that Lenin was an exemplary Party man, who did not like to settle questions alone, without the leading collective body, on the spur of the moment, without careful investigation and verification. Trotsky touches upon this aspect, too, in his book. But the portrait he paints is not that of Lenin, but of a sort of Chinese mandarin, who settles important questions in the quiet of his study, by intuition. . . .

The Party knows that Lenin was the greatest Marxist of our times, a profound theoretician and a most experienced revolutionary, to whom any trace of Blanquism was alien. Trotsky touches upon this aspect, too, in his book. But the portrait he paints is not that of the giant Lenin, but of a dwarf-like

Blanquist who, in the October days, advises the Party "to take power by its own hand, independently of and behind the back of the Soviet." I have already said, however, that there is not a scrap of truth in this description.

Why did Trotsky need this flagrant . . . inaccuracy? Is this not an attempt to discredit Lenin "just a little"?

Such are the characteristic features of the new Trotskyism.

What is the danger of this new Trotskyism? It is that Trotskyism, owing to its entire inner content, stands every chance of becoming the centre and rallying point of the non-proletarian elements who are striving to weaken, to disintegrate the proletarian dictatorship.

You will ask: what is to be done now? What are the Party's immediate tasks in connection with Trotsky's new literary pronouncements?

Trotskyism is taking action now in order to discredit Bolshevism and to undermine its foundations. It is the duty of the Party *to bury Trotskyism as an ideological trend*.

There is talk about repressive measures against the opposition and about the possibility of a split. That is nonsense, comrades. Our Party is strong and mighty. It will not allow any splits. As regards repressive measures, I am emphatically opposed to them. What we need now is not repressive measures, but an extensive ideological struggle against renascent Trotskyism.

We did not want and did not strive for this literary discussion. Trotskyism is forcing it upon us by its anti-Leninist pronouncements. Well, we are ready, comrades.

Questions

1. How does Stalin attempt to set himself apart from Trotsky as Lenin's true heir here? Is he successful at doing so?
2. To whom does Stalin's criticism of Trotsky seem to be addressed?
3. How convincing are his arguments, in particular his distinction between "old Trotskyism" and "new Trotskyism"?
4. What is the main message that he is trying to get across here?

LANGSTON HUGHES, "ADVERTISEMENT FOR THE WALDORF ASTORIA," AND JOHN STEINBECK, *THE GRAPES OF WRATH*, INTRODUCTION

The literary output by American writers in the 1920s and 1930s reads like a who's who of the greatest names in American literature: F. Scott Fitzgerald, William

Faulkner, Ernest Hemingway, Gertrude Stein, Robert Frost, and T. S. Eliot, just to name a few. While any of these writers might legitimately be included in any anthology, Langston Hughes and John Steinbeck represent two of the most important aspects of American culture and history during the interwar period, whose themes relate well to the larger history of Western civilization. Langston Hughes (1902–67) became one of the leading figures in the cultural movement known as the Harlem Renaissance, after moving from Joplin, Missouri, to New York City to attend Columbia University. A versatile writer whose later works included novels, plays, and short stories, Hughes began publishing his poetry in the 1920s. The Harlem Renaissance was a vibrant cultural response on the part of African-Americans, many of whom had migrated from the south to northern cities such as New York since the turn of the century. It was as much a product of the success of those African-Americans who were literate, culturally sophisticated, upwardly mobile, and economically self-sufficient as it was the dissatisfaction of a younger generation with the barriers that still remained to their full participation in American life.

John Steinbeck (1902–68), an almost exact contemporary of Hughes, was born on the West Coast in Salinas, California. Whereas Hughes attended Columbia, Steinbeck enrolled at Stanford; however, both failed to graduate. Whereas Hughes is best remembered for his poetry, Steinbeck will always be associated with his most famous novel, The Grapes of Wrath *(1939), for which he won a Pulitzer Prize. The novel depicts a downtrodden family from Oklahoma forced to flee to California in search of work because of the so-called Dust Bowl, referring to the drought-afflicted infertile farmlands that rendered many farmers in the area penniless during the Depression. John Ford's 1940 film version of the novel, starring Henry Fonda as the main character,* Tom Joad, *had as much impact as the novel in calling attention to the need for agricultural reform.*

Langston Hughes, "Advertisement for the Waldorf Astoria"*

Fine living . . . a la carte?
Come to the Waldorf-Astoria!

LISTEN HUNGRY ONES!
Look! See what Vanity Fair says about the
new Waldorf-Astoria:

"All the luxuries of private home. . . ."
Now, won't that be charming when the last flop-house
has turned you down this winter?

---

*http://www.poemhunter.com/poem/advertisement-for-the-waldorf-astoria/

Furthermore:
"It is far beyond anything hitherto attempted in the hotel
    world. . . ." It cost twenty-eight million dollars.
    The famous Oscar Tschirky is in charge of banqueting.
    Alexandre Gastaud is chef. It will be a distinguished
    background for society.
So when you've no place else to go, homeless and hungry
    ones, choose the Waldorf as a background for your rags—
(Or do you still consider the subway after midnight good
    enough?)

ROOMERS
Take a room at the new Waldorf, you down-and-outers—
    sleepers in charity's flop-houses where God pulls a
    long face, and you have to pray to get a bed.
They serve swell board at the Waldorf-Astoria. Look at the menu, will
    you:

GUMBO CREOLE
CRABMEAT IN CASSOLETTE
BOILED BRISKET OF BEEF
SMALL ONIONS IN CREAM
WATERCRESS SALAD
PEACH MELBA

Have luncheon there this afternoon, all you jobless.
Why not?
Dine with some of the men and women who got rich off of
your labor, who clip coupons with clean white fingers
because your hands dug coal, drilled stone, sewed gar-
ments, poured steel to let other people draw dividends
and live easy.
(Or haven't you had enough yet of the soup-lines and the
bitter bread of charity?)
Walk through Peacock Alley tonight before dinner, and get
warm, anyway. You've got nothing else to do.

John Steinbeck, *The Grapes of Wrath**

Once California belonged to Mexico and its land to Mexicans; and a horde
of tattered feverish Americans poured in. And such was their hunger for land

---

*John Steinbeck (1941, ©1939), *The Grapes of Wrath*, New York: The Modern Library, pp. 315–18.

that they took the land—stole Sutter's land, Guerrero's land, took the grants and broke them up and growled and quarreled over them, those frantic hungry men; and they guarded with guns the land they had stolen. They put up houses and barns; they turned the earth and planted crops. And these things were possession, and possession was ownership.

The Mexicans were weak and fled. They could not resist, because they wanted nothing in the world as frantically as the Americans wanted land.

Then, with time, the squatters were no longer squatters, but owners; and their children grew up and had children on the land. And the hunger was gone from them, the feral hunger, the gnawing, tearing hunger for land, for water and earth and the good sky over it, for the green thrusting grass, for the swelling roots. They had these things so completely that they did not know about them any more. They had no more the stomach-tearing lust for a rich acre and a shining blade to plow it, for seed and a windmill beating its wings in the air. They arose in the dark no more to hear the sleepy birds' first chittering, and the morning wind around the house while they waited for the first light to go out to the dear-acres. These things were lost, and crops were reckoned in dollars, and land was valued by principal plus interest, and crops were bought and sold before they were planted. Then crop failure, drought, and flood were no longer little deaths within life, but simple losses of money. And all their love was thinned with money, and all their fierceness dribbled away in interest until they were no longer farmers at all, but little shopkeepers of crops, little manufacturers who must sell before they can make. Then those farmers who were not good shopkeepers lost their land to good shopkeepers. No matter how clever, how loving a man might be with earth and growing things, he could not survive if he were not also a good shopkeeper. And as time went on, the business men had the farms, and the farms grew large, but there were fewer of them.

Now farming became industry, and the owners followed Rome, although they did not know it. They imported slaves, although they did not call them slaves: Chinese, Japanese, Mexicans, Filipinos. They live on rice and beans, the business men said. They don't need much. They wouldn't know what to do with good wages. Why, look how they live. Why, look what they eat. And if they get funny—deport them.

And all the time the farms grew larger and the owners fewer. And there were pitifully few farmers on the land any more. And the imported serfs were beaten and frightened and starved until some went home again, and some grew fierce and were killed or driven from the country. . . .

They were hungry, and they were fierce. And they had hoped to find a home, and they found only hatred. Okies—the owners hated them because the owners knew they were soft and the Okies strong, that they were fed and the Okies hungry; and perhaps the owners had heard from their grandfathers how easy it is to steal land from a soft man if you are fierce and hungry and armed. The owners hated them. And in the towns, the storekeepers hated them because they had no money to spend. There is no shorter path to a storekeeper's contempt, and all his admirations are exactly opposite. The town men, little bankers, hated Okies because there was nothing to gain from them. They had nothing. And the laboring people hated Okies because a hungry man must work, and if he must work, if he has to work, the wage payer automatically gives him less for his work; and then no one can get more.

Questions

1. Why does Langston Hughes advise his readers to go the Waldorf Astoria? To whom is the poem addressed? What literary techniques does he use to convey his message of social criticism? Are they effective?
2. What are some of the ways in which Steinbeck's use of language in these passages is meant to evoke images of the Depression?
3. What changes does he see as at the root of agricultural poverty in the American West?
4. What do these passages reveal about Steinbeck's political convictions?
5. Should literature covey a political message? Does it detract from great literature if it is overtly political?

Dorothea Lange (1895–1965) was a prominent photographer with a studio based in San Francisco who traveled the country during the 1930s creating a visual record of the men and women who suffered through the Depression, especially in rural areas. Although her photographs were sometimes posed and not the candid portraits they appeared to be, they nonetheless have become a huge part of American culture and of the historical record of the Depression era.

Questions

1. In what ways do these images supplement the reading in the chapter by Hughes and Steinbeck?
2. Are pictures worth a thousand words? Can these pictures tell a story just as effectively as writers such as Steinbeck or create poetic images just as effectively as Hughes?
3. Are photographers distorting truth and history by creating poses for their subjects? Or is this an act comparable to a novelist using fictional characters to convey important truths about an actual historical situation? Or perhaps somewhere in between?

FIGURE 11: Dorothea Lange, *Entering the California Desert*. Courtesy of Getty Images.

FIGURE 12: Dorothea Lange, *Poor Man Waiting in White Angel Breadline,
San Francisco*. Courtesy of Getty Images.

FIGURE 13: Florence Thompson, a 32-year-old pea picker with children in California. Photograph by Dorothea Lange. Courtesy of Getty Images.

LU XUN, *THE TRUE STORY OF AH Q*, INTRODUCTION

Many oppressed peoples throughout history have turned to literature to express their dissatisfaction with the status quo and to propose possible future solutions to the causes of oppression. The Chinese were no exception and one of their leading writers was Lu Xun, China's Dostoevsky, speaking out for the common man and voicing concerns about the human condition that transcended his time and place. Inspired by the Bolshevik Revolution in Russia, Lu Xun believed that China also needed to overthrow its landlord class and free its people from the ancient bonds of hierarchy and privilege. Like many Chinese intellectuals, Lu Xun had studied in Japan and become convinced of the need for Westernization in China. His most famous story, The True Story of Ah Q, *longer than a short story but shorter than a novel, deals with the disillusionment that sets in when the humble and somewhat obtuse Ah Q realizes that, even in revolutionary times, the more things change the more they stay the same.*

Lu Xun, *The True Story of Ah Q**

Chapter 7 The Revolution

On the fourteenth day of the ninth moon of the third year in the reign of the Emperor Hsuan Tung—the day on which Ah Q sold his purse to Chao Pai-yen—at midnight, after the fourth stroke of the third watch, a large boat with a big black awning came to the Chao family's landing place. This boat floated up in the darkness while the villagers were sound asleep, so that they knew nothing about it; but it left again about dawn, when quite a number of people saw it. Investigation revealed that this boat actually belonged to the successful provincial candidate!

The incident caused great uneasiness in Weichuang, and before midday the hearts of all the villagers were beating faster. The Chao family kept very quiet about the errand of the boat, but according to the gossip in the tea-house and wine shop, the revolutionaries were going to enter the town and the successful provincial candidate had come to the country to take refuge. Mrs. Tsou alone thought otherwise, maintaining that the successful provincial candidate merely wanted to deposit a few battered cases in Weichuang, but that Mr. Chao had sent them back. Actually the successful provincial candidate and the successful county candidate in the Chao family were not on good terms, so that it was scarcely logical to expect them to prove friends in adversity; moreover, since Mrs. Tsou was a neighbor of the Chao family and had a better idea of what was going on, she ought to have known. . . .

Ah Q had long since known of revolutionaries, and this year with his own eyes had seen revolutionaries being decapitated. But since it had occurred to him that the revolutionaries were rebels and that a rebellion would make things difficult for him, he had always detested and kept away from them. Who could have guessed they could so frighten a successful provincial candidate renowned for thirty miles around? In consequence, Ah Q could not help feeling rather "entranced," the terror of all the villagers only adding to his delight.

"Revolution is not a bad thing," thought Ah Q. "Finish off the whole lot of them . . . curse them! . . . I would like to go over to the revolutionaries myself."

Ah Q had been hard up recently, and was probably rather dissatisfied: added to this, he had drunk two bowls of wine at noon on an empty stomach. Consequently, he became drunk very quickly; and as he walked along thinking to himself, he felt again as if he were treading on air. Suddenly, in some curious way, he felt as if the revolutionaries were himself, and all the people in Weichuang were his captives. Unable to contain himself for joy, he could not help shouting loudly:

*Lu Xun (2003), *Selected Stories*, translated by Yang Hsien-yi and Gladys Yang, New York: W.W. Norton and Company, pp. 95–100.

"Rebellion! Rebellion!"

"Revolt? It would be fun. . . . A group of revolutionaries would come, all wearing white helmets and white armor, carrying swords, steel maces, bombs, foreign guns, double-edged knives with sharp points and spears with hooks. They would come to the Tutelary God's Temple and call out, 'Ah Q! Come with us, come with us!' And then I would go with them. . . ."

"Then all those villagers would be in a laughable plight, kneeling down and pleading, 'Ah Q, spare our lives.' But who would listen to them! The first to die would be Young D and Mr. Chao, then the successful county candidate and the Imitation Foreign Devil . . . but perhaps I would spare a few. I would once have spared Whiskers Wang, but now I don't even want him. . . ."

The next morning he got up very late, and when he went out in the street everything was the same as usual. He was still hungry, but though he racked his brains he did not seem able to think of anything. Suddenly an idea came to him, and he walked slowly off, until either by design or accident he reached the Convent of Quiet Self-Improvement.

. . . When he looked in all he could see was the old nun.

"What are you here for again?," she asked, giving a start.

"There is a revolution . . . don't you know?" said Ah Q vaguely.

"Revolution, revolution . . . there has already been one," said the old nun, her eyes red from crying. "What do you think will become of us with all your revolutions?"

"What?" asked Ah Q in astonishment.

"Didn't you know? The revolutionaries have already been here!"

"Who?" asked Ah Q in even greater astonishment.

"The successful county candidate and the Imitation Foreign Devil."

It had happened that morning. The successful county candidate in the Chao family learned the news quickly, and as soon as he heard that the revolutionaries had entered the town that night, he immediately wound his pigtail up on his head and went out first thing to call on the Imitation Foreign Devil in the Chen family, with whom he had never been on good terms before. Because this was a time for all to work, for reforms, they had a very pleasant talk and on the spot became comrades who saw eye to eye and pledged themselves to become revolutionaries.

After racking their brains for some time, they remembered that in the Convent of Quiet Self-Improvement there was an imperial tablet inscribed "Long Live the Emperor" which ought to be done away with at once. Thereupon they lost no time in going to the convent to carry out their revolutionary activities. Because the old nun tried to stop them, and put in a few words, they considered her as the Ching government and knocked her on the head many times with a stick and with their knuckles. The nun, pulling herself together after they had gone, made an inspection. Naturally the imperial tablet had been smashed into fragments on the ground, and the valuable Hsuan [bronze] censer before the shrine of Kuanyin, the goddess of mercy, had also disappeared.

Ah Q only learned this later. He deeply regretted having been asleep at the time, and resented the fact that they had not come to call him. Then he said to himself, "Maybe they still don't know I have joined the revolutionaries."

Questions
1. Ah Q seems to be confused about whether the revolution has actually happened or not. What is the source of his confusion?
2. What sense do you get from this passage about why Ah Q was originally opposed to the revolutionaries? Why does he change his mind and decide to join them?
3. What is the significance of the name "Imitation Foreign Devil"?
4. What is the overall message conveyed by Lu Xun in the course of this chapter (which is largely representative of the work as a whole)? Hint: Is he sympathetic to Ah Q? Why or why not?

NEW YORK TIMES, ACCOUNT OF THE NANJING MASSACRE, 1937, INTRODUCTION

Newspaper accounts of important historical events are sometimes too close to the action to give a full and adequate picture of everything that is happening at the time. However, they sometimes capture, in their very uncertainty, the chaotic and uncertain nature of a present that only later becomes subject to the analysis and interpretation of historians. Such is the case with the report below on the Nanjing (or Nanking, as it was referred to at the time) massacre, which invading Japanese troops inflicted upon the civilian population of the capital of the Guomindang beginning in December 1937. Perhaps as many as 300,000 (the somewhat official Chinese figure) residents of the city fell dead at the hands of the Japanese in the months that followed, while tens of thousands more were raped or wounded. Already remembered as one of the worst atrocities in human history, it would stand out even more had mass killings of civilians not become so common in the decade that followed in the course of the Second World War. To this day, the event is a sore spot in relations between the Chinese and the Japanese, who have apologized for the actions of their countrymen, but not to an extent acceptable to most Chinese.

New York Times, account of the Nanjing Massacre, 1937*

Further collaborative details of the almost complete collapse of the discipline of Japanese soldiers after their occupation of Nanking, resulting in wholesale massacres of civilians, executions of disarmed Chinese soldiers, the violation and murder of Chinese women and the systematic destruction and looting of property, including that owned by foreigners, were contained in letters received in Shanghai today from American missionaries who remained in China's abandoned capital.

Several of the letters giving an account of the reign of terror that has seized Nanking were written guardedly in carefully chosen words and phrases, indicating that the American writers feared interception of their accounts and possible Japanese reprisals. Others, however, abandoned caution and stated unequivocally that "the Japanese Army has thrown away a remarkable opportunity to gain the respect in Nanking of Chinese and foreign opinion." One prominent American missionary states:

"The disgraceful collapse of Chinese authority in this region has left vast numbers of persons ready to respond to the order and organization of which Japan boasts. The whole outlook has been ruined by frequent murders, wholesale looting and uncontrolled disturbance of private homes, including revolting offenses against the security of women."

The writer added that great numbers of dead civilians were victims of shooting and bayoneting, many of the cases being plainly witnessed by foreigners and . . . Chinese. Squads of Chinese who had discarded their arms and uniforms were tied together and executed, one report adds.

"Thus far there is no trace of Chinese prisoners in Japanese bands other than squads actually or apparently on the way to be executed," a letter said.

Many Chinese impressed into service as carriers of loot taken away by Japanese were said later to have been shot. An American missionary continued:

"Great amounts of food were first taken, but everything else useful or valuable later had its turn. Tens of thousands of private homes, large and small, Chinese and foreign, have been impartially plundered and scores of refugee camps entered and money and valuables as well as slight possessions removed during the mass searches.

"Members of the staff of the University of Nanking Hospital were stripped of their cash and watches while nurses in the dormitory were subjected to the plundering hordes."

New York Times, December 24, 1937.

The same American writes that motor cars and other property owned by foreigners were widely seized after the tearing down of national flags. It was indicated that abduction of girls and women by Japanese officers and soldiers was prevalent. The report ends with the comment:

"Under these conditions the terror is indescribable, and lectures by suave Japanese officers that their 'sole purpose is to make war against an oppressive Chinese government for the sake of the Chinese people' leave an impression that nauseates. . . ."

Questions

1. What is the general tone of this article? Is it what you would expect from a publication of the nature of the *New York Times*?
2. How valuable is this article as a historical source? What are its strengths and limitations as a source?
3. What does the article suggest will be the outcome of the massacre?
4. Should the world at the time have paid more attention to the Nanjing massacre than it did?

Chapter Questions

1. Compare the sources written by Mussolini, Hitler, and Stalin. Do they betray any similarities in the thinking of these three dictators?
2. Which of the sources by Mussolini, Hitler, and Stalin is most rhetorically successful? In other words, which was likely to be most convincing to the work's intended audience?
3. Are there similarities in the social message conveyed by Lu Xun, Langston Hughes, and John Steinbeck in the excerpts included here? Do these works speak to universal truths or are they mainly concerned with the unique historical circumstances that influenced and inspired their writing?
4. Do you see any connections between the sources in Chapter 7 dealing with the Boxer Rebellion and the two sources dealing with China here? Collectively, what do they suggest about the nature of modern Chinese history?

CHAPTER ELEVEN

Second World War

Introduction

1. Victor Klemperer, *I Will Bear Witness: A Diary of the Nazi Years, 1942–1945*
2. Anne Frank, May 22, 1944, *Diary of a Young Girl*
3. Elie Wiesel, *Night* and Rolf Hochhuth, *The Deputy*
4. Winston Churchill, *Closing the Ring: The Second World War*, Volume V
5. Harry Truman, *Memoirs*
6. Ki-Sheok Chong, *Black Flower in the Sky: Poems of a Korean Bridegroom in Hiroshima*

Chapter Questions

INTRODUCTION

The Second World War did not end as it had begun. The two most aggressive and expansionist military powers at the beginning of the war, Germany and Japan, ended the war in defeat and ruin, on the verge of total collapse. Without a doubt, the two most decisive turning points between the beginning and end of the war were Germany's invasion of the Soviet Union in June 1941 and the Japanese attack on the US naval base at Pearl Harbor, Hawaii, in December of that year. The war lasted almost another four years and involved a tremendous struggle on the part of the United States against the Japanese and the Soviets to resist and then repel the German invasion, but the entry of those two superpowers into the war clearly made a huge difference in the eventual defeat of the Axis powers.

Countless works are available on the military side of this global conflict and memoirs by generals and soldiers abound. However, this chapter will focus more on the dimensions of the period that made the Second World War more than just another war for land, power, or even global dominance. The German treatment of the Jews and the systematic attempt by Hitler to exterminate an entire race holds meaning and significance for the history of humanity and Western civilization quite apart from the military tactics, strategies, and battles, as important as they were. So will the decision of President Harry Truman of the United States to authorize the dropping of two atomic bombs on the Japanese cities of Hiroshima and Nagasaki in August 1945. Therefore, this chapter will focus on sources that will center on those two specific aspects of the war as these are the two legacies from that period most likely to be remembered and that still call forth an effort to comprehend exactly what they meant.

Once he had taken power in 1933, Adolf Hitler proceeded to ignore the provisions of the Treaty of Versailles by rearming Germany and then annexing territory, beginning with the Rhineland in 1936. The world stood by and watched as Hitler unified Germany and Austria in 1938, applauded when British Prime Minister Neville Chamberlain secured a promise from Hitler not to invade Czechoslovakia in exchange for the Sudetenland in September 1938, then grew concerned when Hitler broke that promise in March 1939, before launching an all-out attack on Poland the following September. Domestically, Hitler placed severe restrictions upon German Jews, depriving them of many of their rights as German citizens in the Nuremberg Laws of 1935 and sanctioning violence and destruction of Jewish property, culminating in Kristallnacht, "the night of broken glass," in November 1938. When the war began, conditions worsened for those Jews who had not yet left Germany in fear of their lives or been sent to concentration camps. As the Germans expanded their control over other countries in eastern and western Europe, many non-German Jews suffered the similar fates, as did Poles, Slavs, Russians, and the people known as the Roma, referred to at the time as Gypsies.

Several sources below provide different perspectives on the Holocaust and represent a tiny fraction of the human voices who speak in some ways for the millions who were deprived of that right. Victor Klemperer was a Jewish convert to Christianity who avoided arrest because of his marriage to a German "Aryan" woman. Not that he escaped the conflict without suffering. Deprived of his position as a university professor of Roman languages, forced to wear a yellow star on his clothing, treated with indignity and allowed barely enough rations to survive, living in constant fear that he would be deported to a death camp in the east, he has left a record of what life was like for him during the Hitler years. The excerpt in this chapter is from the war year of 1942, when the war still had three long years left to go.

The next source may be a more familiar one for many people; another diary, this one kept by a young teenage Jewish girl forced with her family into hiding during the Nazi occupation of the Netherlands. Anne Frank, like Victor Klemperer, found herself deprived of the normal freedoms and human rights that were being challenged by modern authoritarian states such as Germany and the Soviet Union. Unlike Klemperer, Anne Frank would not survive the war, one of six million victims of the Holocaust and one of tens of millions of civilians of various nationalities who died during the Second World War. Her father managed to survive the war and preserve her diary, which he had published in 1947. The next two sources are literary sources that deal with the Holocaust: an excerpt from Elie Wiesel's novel, *Night*, and a scene from Rolf Hochhuth's play, *The Deputy*, which deals in part with the failure of the papacy and the Roman Catholic Church to take a stronger stand against Hitler's regime and his persecution of the Jews.

This chapter also includes two excerpts from the memoirs of world leaders: the British Prime Minister, Winston Churchill, and the US President Harry Truman. Churchill, who led the British government and coordinated the war effort from May 1940 until the end of the war, wrote his six-volume memoir of the Second World War in the immediate aftermath of the war after the British electorate voted his Conservative Party out of office in 1945. In *Volume III: Closing the Ring*, Churchill deals with the later years of the war in which victory was not yet assured but when the tide was beginning to turn in the Allies' favor. In the passage below, Churchill reflects on the mistakes and miscalculations of Benito Mussolini in a way that reveals much about his own views on leadership, politics, and war. Harry Truman was a US Senator since 1934 who had played an important role in the passage of important legislation on aeronautics and transportation and served as chairman of a Senate Special Committee to Investigate the National Defense Program in 1940 before he became Franklin Roosevelt's vice president in 1945. He had only occupied that office a few months before he became president because of the death of Franklin Roosevelt in April 1945. That same month, US forces set foot on Japanese territory for the first time in the war, landing on the Japanese island of Okinawa. Truman, unlike Churchill, was still in office in the years immediately following the war. In this chapter he offers a frank assessment of the pressures of the presidency and details some of his efforts to keep atomic energy under civilian control following his controversial decision to allow the military to use the first atom bombs in the war with Japan.

Those reflections are thrown into relief by the haunting and powerful images of two poems by Ki-Sheok Chung, a Korean poet writing about the victims of the bombing of Hiroshima. No chapter or comparable number of sources can do justice to the fifty million people who died in the Second World War, approximately 35 million of whom are estimated to have been civilians. Against that number, the six million Jews, or the 75,000 souls who perished in a single flash of light in Hiroshima on August 6, 1945, may seem a relatively small proportion of the total, but we understand history through people, not through numbers, so here, as throughout this text, I have tried to allow some of those voices of the past to speak to us today.

VICTOR KLEMPERER, *I WILL BEAR WITNESS: A DIARY OF THE NAZI YEARS, 1942–1945,* INTRODUCTION

Whereas many Jews who were not imprisoned in concentration camps left Germany prior to the war, others had chosen to stay. After the war began, most of them had no way out. Klemperer did not suffer the same horrific fate as the millions of Jews who were shot to death, worked or starved to death, or sent to the gas chambers, but his diaries provide an invaluable account of life under the Nazi regime from the perspective of a Jewish convert to Christianity married to a German woman. He sometimes reflects on larger philosophical issues, but much of his diary is about everyday life. It also provides important historical evidence about what ordinary Germans knew about the Holocaust and when they knew it. Hitler and the Nazis tried to keep the "Final Solution" of exterminating the Jews, a policy they began to implement in 1942, a complete secret, but rumors and knowledge about the death camps in the east were fairly widespread, if Klemperer's diary is to be believed—and there is no reason to doubt it. The brief entries below reveal the diversity of the contents of the diary, as well as providing glimpses into the daily life and concerns of the writer.

Victor Klemperer, *I Will Bear Witness: A Diary of the Nazi Years, 1942–1945**

April 29, [1942], Wednesday morning

Another house search, another suicide. A physician, Dr. Korn, Catholic-Jew, wife Aryan. Pillnitzer Strasse. The Aryan wife was beaten; the husband was supposed to report to the Gestapo next morning. Suicide during the night. The usual. Kätchen brings the news home from the factory. In addition the squad's pronouncement: "We'll make sure that none of you gets out alive." In the newspaper, summing up the Reichstag session, it was stated once again, that the Fuhrer henceforth has the right, approved by the Reichstag and therefore by the people, not to adhere to articles of law and prescribed procedures, [and the right to] intervene directly in everything. From that and from the Jewish aria a path leads straight to the methods of the Gestapo.

May 3, Sunday afternoon

. . . I am never free of fear of a house search. I am never free of extreme tiredness—I fall asleep as I am reading and writing, walking gives me pains in my heart. I confidently preach to others that it is "11:59," but I am far from believing it myself.

May 8, Friday midday

"Jew sow, you only have young so you can bring them up to be rabble-rousers!" Gestapo pronouncement to seventy-year-old Frau Kronheim, who had been "summoned," as her daughter told us yesterday. (To be "summoned"—to be sent off on hour-long walks, to report for repeated abuse and blows, that is the usual torture following a house search.)

But yesterday also this. On Wasaplatz two gray-haired ladies, teachers of about sixty years of age, such as often came to my lectures and talks. They stop, one comes toward me, holding out her hand, I think: a former auditor, and raise my hat. But I do not know her after all, nor does she introduce herself. She only smiles and shakes my hand, says "You know why!" and goes off before I can say a word. Such demonstrations (dangerous for both parties!) are said to happen frequently. The opposite of the recent: "Why are you still alive, you rogue?!" And both of these in Germany, and in the middle of the twentieth century. . . .

What kind of wishes go through my head? Not to be afraid every time the doorbell rings! A typewriter. To have my manuscripts and diaries by me in the house. Use of a library. Food! Cinema. Car.—

The last war was such a decent business.

---

*Victor Klemperer (1999), *I Will Bear Witness: A Diary of the Nazi Years, 1942–1945*, translated by Martin Chalmers, New York: Random House, pp. 46–51.

May 11, Monday

On May 10 there was a commemorative article in the newspaper: The offensive in the West began on May 10, 1940. For me the time is divided up like this. In spring 1940, we were just moving into the Jews' House. I was very depressed: driven out of our house and Hitler seemingly the ultimate victor. Then the summer turned out a tiny bit better than I had feared: England held out, and Eva's [his wife] foot improved. Summer 1940 is the time of our beautiful long walks. There was also plenty to eat, bread was easy to get without coupons, fish was available in abundance.—The summer of 1941 saw the end of our beautiful long walks. If one was not in a restaurant by six, the acceptable dishes were sold out. But after dinner we took the bus to the Toll House, drank our apple juice, walked home, and had plenty of tea and bread there. At home we also feasted on fish. Now here are the first fine days of spring, the prelude to the summer of 1942. Since September 19, 1941, I am no longer allowed to go into a restaurant, I go out in the street only if it is absolutely necessary, and as it is getting warm now, I shall restrict going out even further—because I do not want to have the loathsome star sewn on my jacket, where I would constantly have to look at it, and so I am forced to wear a coat. And eating: sheer hunger. In the last few days the quality of the bread has grown worse and become more like that in the last war: It has a bitter taste, a gray color, is said to contain turnip (the turnip is nowhere on sale). Perhaps there is some comfort in all of that: the prospect of an end before the next winter. But perhaps it is only a false prospect after all? Here and there one hears people say now that the Americans will probably attack by way of Murmansk.

The tyranny grows worse with every day—probably also a comfort, as the deteriorating bread is. House search in the Güntzstrasse old people's home. Women between 70 and 85 years of age spat on, placed face to the wall, cold water poured over them from behind, their food, which they had bought on coupons as their weekly ration, taken from them, the filthiest words of abuse. . . .

I am fighting the hardest battle for my Germanness now. I must hold on to this: I am German, the others are un-German. I must hold on to this: The spirit is decisive, not blood. I must hold on to this: On my part Zionism would be a comedy—my baptism was *not* a comedy.

Questions

1. What does Klemperer mean when he writes that he tells people that it is "11:59"? Why does he say this if, as he admits, he does not himself believe it?
2. Is he being serious when he says that "the last war [the First World War] was such a decent business"? Is he being ironic? What, exactly, do you think he means by that statement?

3. How have his living conditions changed in the course of the war? Why?
4. What do these passages reveal about Klemperer as a person? What valuable insights do they provide into the war and Nazi Germany that are unique to this kind of source?

ANNE FRANK, MAY 22, 1944, *DIARY OF A YOUNG GIRL*, INTRODUCTION

On May 10, 1940, German forces rumbled into the Netherlands, as well as Belgium and Luxembourg, adding those previously independent countries to the vast portions of Europe then under Nazi control. The Dutch officially surrendered four days later. Anne Frank (1929–45), whose family had moved from Germany in 1933 after Hitler came to power, was eleven years old at the time. Like others of her generation, she would come into her teenage years in a time of heightened danger and uncertainty, her fate, like that of the rest of Europe, hanging in the balance. In 1944, some Dutch neighbors revealed the hiding place of the Franks to the Germans, leading to their capture and deportation. What set Anne Frank apart was not her extraordinariness, but her ordinariness, at least her attempt to live as normal an existence as possible under the most uncertain of circumstances. One must remember that when she wrote her diary she did not know what the future held, when Germany might go down in defeat, and certainly not that she would die of illness in the German concentration camp of Bergen-Belsen shortly before the end of the war. We all live with uncertainty about the future and most of us cope in much the same way that Anne did: by attempting to construct a meaningful life and finding value in the daily business of living, relationships, and reflection. Yet when her diary was made available to the reading public in 1947, they did know her fate, making her ability to relate her feelings a testament to the human spirit as well as to the times in which she lived. As the following excerpt shows, she was not oblivious to what was happening in the outside world, but she refused to let that deprive her of hope.

Anne Frank, May 22, 1944, from *Diary of a Young Girl**

Monday, 22 May, 1944

The suspense is rising to a climax. By no means everyone we had regarded as "good" Dutch have stuck to their faith in the English, by no means everyone

---

*Anne Frank (1993), *The Diary of a Young Girl*, translated by B. M. Mooyaart, New York: Bantam, pp. 237–39.

thinks the English bluff a masterly piece of strategy, oh no, the people want to see deeds at last, great, heroic deeds. Nobody sees beyond his own nose, no one thinks that the English are fighting for their land and their own people, everyone thinks that it's their duty to save Holland, as quickly and as well as they can.

What obligations have the English towards us? How have the Dutch earned the generous help that they seem so explicitly to expect? Oh no, the Dutch will have made a big mistake, the English, in spite of all their bluff, are certainly no more to blame than all the other countries, great and small, which are not under occupation. The English really won't offer us their apologies, for even if we do reproach them for being asleep during the years when Germany was rearming, we cannot deny that all the other countries, especially those bordering Germany, also slept. We shan't get anywhere by following an ostrich policy. England and the whole world have seen that only too well now, and that is why, one by one, England, no less than the rest, will have to make heavy sacrifices.

No country is going to sacrifice its men for nothing and certainly not in the interests of another. England is not going to do that either. The invasion, with liberation and freedom, will come sometime, but England and America will appoint the day, not all the occupied countries put together.

To our great horror and regret we hear that the attitude of a great many people towards us Jews has changed. We hear that there is anti-Semitism now in circles that never thought of it before. This news has affected us all very, very deeply. The cause of this hatred of the Jews is understandable, even human sometimes, but not good. The Christians blame the Jews for giving secrets away to the Germans, for betraying their helpers and for the fact that, through the Jews, a great many Christians have gone the way of so many others before them, and suffered terrible punishments and a dreadful fate.

This is all true, but one must always look at these things from both sides. Would Christians behave differently in our place? The Germans have a means of making people talk. Can a person, entirely at their mercy, whether Jew or Christian, always remain silent? Everyone knows that is practically impossible. Why, then, should people demand the impossible of the Jews?

It's being murmured in underground circles that the German Jews who emigrated to Holland and who are now in Poland may not be allowed to return here, they once had the right of asylum in Holland, but when Hitler has gone they will have to go back to Germany again.

When one hears this one naturally wonders why we are carrying on with this long and difficult war. We always hear that we're all fighting together for freedom, truth, and right! Is discord going to show itself while we are still fighting, is the Jew once again worth less than another? Oh, it is sad, very sad, that once more, for the umpteenth time, the old truth is confirmed. "What *one* Christian does is his own responsibility, what *one* Jew does is thrown back at all *Jews*."

Quite honestly, I can't understand the Dutch, who are such a good, honest, upright people, should judge us like this, we, the most oppressed, the unhappiest, perhaps the most pitiful peoples of the whole world.

I hope *one* thing only, and that is that this hatred of the Jews will be a passing thing, that the Dutch will show what they are after all, and that they will never totter and lose their sense of right. For anti-Semitism is unjust!

And if this terrible threat should actually come true, then the pitiful little collection of Jews that remain will have to leave Holland. We, too, shall have to move on again with our little bundles, and leave this beautiful country, which offered us such a warm welcome and which now turns its back on us.

I love Holland. I who, having no native country, had hoped that it might become my fatherland, and I still hope it will!

Questions

1. How much understanding does Anne convey about the reasons why she was living in hiding?
2. What is her attitude toward the English? Toward the Dutch?
3. Does she remain optimistic about the future? If so, what is the source of her optimism?
4. By 1960, Anne Frank's diary had already sold over 700,000 copies. It has now sold over 30 million copies and been translated into 65 languages, becoming one of the best-selling books in history. What do you think has accounted for the enormous popularity of this work?

ELIE WIESEL, *NIGHT*, AND ROLF HOCHHUTH, *THE DEPUTY*, INTRODUCTION

These two sources deal with the same subject from radically different perspectives. Elie Wiesel was born in 1928, making him just a year older than Anne Frank. Wiesel was a concentration camp survivor whose family perished in the Holocaust. The Nazis separated his father and him from his mother and sisters. Wiesel spent time in three different concentration camps, including the infamous camps at Auschwitz and Buchenwald. A renowned author of dozens of books, his novel, Night, *excerpted below, was based on personal experience. Rolf Hochhuth (b. 1931) was among those young Germans who felt ashamed of what many Germans of his parents' generation had perpetrated on the Jews and the world. In 1963, he wrote his play,* The Deputy, *which largely centers on the inaction of Pope Pius XII and the Catholic Church during the Holocaust. His play became highly controversial for that reason, leading to accusations of historical inaccuracy. But the play also raises questions about the motives behind the Nazi doctors and camp commanders who interpreted, carried out, and frequently justified the orders of their superiors to annihilate the Jews. Whatever the historical value of the play, it is an important document of postwar reaction to the Nazi past, especially because it raised issues that many Germans preferred to leave in the past. Though written from different perspectives, when taken together these literary sources provide an opportunity to reflect on the nature of and reasons for the Holocaust. They were both written with the intention of reminding the world not to forget what happened to the Jews of Europe under the Nazi regime. As with many sources included in this anthology, the author hopes that exposure to passages from works such as these will inspire readers to read the entire works at some point.*

Elie Wiesel, *Night**

He told me what had happened to him and his companions. The train with the deportees had crossed the Hungarian border and, once in Polish territory, had been taken over by the Gestapo. The train had stopped. The Jews were ordered to get off and onto waiting trucks. The trucks headed toward a forest. There everybody was ordered to get out. They were forced to dig huge trenches. When they had finished their work, the men from the Gestapo began theirs. Without passion or haste, they shot their prisoners, who were forced to approach the trench one by one and offer their necks. Infants were tossed into the air and used as targets for the machine guns. This took place in the Galician forest, near Kolomay. How had he, Moishe the Beadle, been able to escape? By a miracle. He was wounded in the leg and left for dead. . . .

Day after day, night after night, he went from one Jewish house to the next, telling his story and that of Malka, the young girl who lay dying for three days, and that of Tobie, the tailor who begged to die before his sons were killed.

Moishe was not the same. The joy in his eyes was gone. He no longer sang. He no longer mentioned either God or Kabbalah. He spoke only of what he had seen. But people not only refused to believe his tales, they refused to listen.

---

*Elie Wiesel (2006), *Night*, translated by Marion Wiesel, New York: Hill and Wang, pp. 6–7.

Some even insinuated that he only wanted their pity, that he was imagining things. Others flatly said that he had gone mad.

As for Moishe, he wept and pleaded:

"Jews, listen to me! That's all I ask of you. No money. No pity. Just listen to me!" he kept shouting in synagogue, between the prayer at dusk and the evening prayer. Even I did not believe him. I often sat with him, after services, and listened to his tales, trying to understand his grief. But all I felt was pity.

"They think I'm mad," he whispered, and tears, like drops of wax, flowed from his eyes.

Once, I asked him the question: "Why do you want people to believe you so much? In your place I would not care whether they believed me or not. . . ."

He closed his eyes, as if to escape time.

"You don't understand," he said in despair. "You cannot understand. I was saved miraculously. I succeeded in coming back. Where did I get my strength? I wanted to return to Sighet to describe to you my death so that you might ready yourselves while there is still time. Life? I no longer care to live. I am alone. But I wanted to come back to warn you. Only no one is listening to me. . . ."

This was toward the end of 1942.

Rolf Hochhuth, *The Deputy**

DOCTOR: Then do you find it more acceptable
that God in person is turning the human race on the spit of history?
History! The final vindication
of God's ways to man? Really?
(He laughs like a torturer.)
History: dust and altars, misery and rape,
and all glory a mockery of its victims.
The truth is, Auschwitz refutes
creator, creation, and the creature.
Life as an idea is dead.
This may well be the beginning
of a great new era,
a redemption from suffering.
From this point of view only one crime

---

*Rolf Hochhuth (1964), *The Deputy*, translated by Richard and Clara Winston, New York: Grove Press, pp. 248–50.

remains: cursed be he who creates life.
I cremate life. That is modern
humanitarianism—the sole salvation from the future.
I mean that seriously, even on the personal level.
Out of pity, I have always buried
my own children right away—in condoms.
RICCARDO (attempts mockery, but shouts in order to keep himself from
    weeping):
Redemption from suffering! A lecture
on humanism from a homicidal maniac!
Save someone—save just a single child!
DOCTOR (calmly): What gives priests the right to look down on the SS?
We are the Dominicans of the technological age.
It is no accident that so many of my kind,
the leaders, come from good Catholic homes.
Heydrich was a Jew—all right.
Eichmann and Göring are Protestants.
But Hitler, Goebbels, Bormann, Kaltenbrunner . . .?
Höss, our commandant, studied for the priesthood.
And Himmler's uncle, who stood godfather to him,
is nothing less than Suffragen Bishop in Bamberg!
(He laughs.) The Allies have solemnly sworn
to hang us all if they should catch us.
So after the war, it's only logical,
the SS tunic will become
a shroud for gallows birds.
The Church, however, after centuries
of killing heretics throughout the West
now sets itself up as the exclusive
moral authority of the Continent.
Absurd! Saint Thomas Aquinas, a mystic,
a god-crazed visionary like Heinrich Himmler,
who also babbles well-meant nonsense,
Thomas condemned the innocent for heresy
just as these morons here condemn the Jews . . .
But you do not cast him out of your temple!
The readers that they use in German schools
in centuries to come may well reprint
the speeches of Himmler made in honor of
the mothers of large families—why not?
(He is royally amused.)
A civilization that commits

its children's souls into the safeguard
of a Church responsible for the Inquisition
comes to an end that it deserves
when for its funeral pyre it plucks
the brands from our furnaces for human bodies.
Do you admit that? Of course not.
(Spits and pours a glass of brandy for himself.)
One of us is honest—the other credulous.
(Malignantly)
Your Church was the first to show
that you can burn men just like coke.
In Spain alone, without the benefit of crematoria,
you turned to ashes three hundred and fifty thousand
human beings, most of them alive, mind you.
Such an achievement surely needs the help of Christ.
RICCARDO *(furious, loudly)*:
I know as well as you—or I wouldn't be here—
how many times the Church has been guilty,
as it is again today. I have nothing more to say
if you make God responsible
for the crimes of His Church.
God does not stand *above* history.
He shares the fate of the natural order.
In Him all man's anguish is contained.
DOCTOR *(interrupting)*: Oh yes, I also learned that drivel once.
His suffering in the world fetters the evil principle.
Prove it. Where—when have I ever been so fettered?
Luther did not fool himself so badly.
Not man, he said, but God
hangs, tortures, strangles, wars . . .
Laughing, he slaps RICCARDO *on the back.* RICCARDO *shrinks from him.*
Your anger amuses me—you'll make a good partner.
I saw that right off. You'll help in the laboratory,
and at night we'll wrangle
about the product of neurosis
which for the present you call God
or about some other philosophical rot.
RICCARDO: I don't intend to act your court jester,
to cheer the hours when you are
face to face with your own self.
I have never seen a man so wretched,
for you know what you do . . .

Questions

1. What impact do you think these authors meant their works to have in the years after the war? In what ways were they keeping the lessons of the war alive?
2. Wiesel suggests in this passage that some Jews at the time refused to believe the horror stories told by eyewitnesses to Nazi atrocities. What might have accounted for their reluctance? Could this be related to the existence of Holocaust deniers after the world war, despite the overwhelming amount of evidence confirming the Holocaust?
3. In the exchange between the Doctor and Riccardo, is the Doctor at all justified in comparing the Nazi Party with the Catholic Church in its treatment of the Jews? How does Riccardo respond to this comparison?

WINSTON CHURCHILL, *CLOSING THE RING: THE SECOND WORLD WAR*, VOLUME V, INTRODUCTION

Winston Churchill succeeded Neville Chamberlain as prime minister of Britain on May 9, 1940. A month later, the Italian dictator, Benito Mussolini decided to bring Italy into the war on the side of Hitler, declaring war on both France and Great Britain on June 10. Historians have long assumed a kind of inevitability about this decision because Italy and Germany were both ruled by fascist dictators who had formed an alliance in 1936, the so-called Rome-Berlin axis. Furthermore, it looked like a smart decision at the time. France surrendered on June 22 and the British evacuated the Continent in a humiliating retreat at Dunkirk, even though they performed something of a miraculous salvage operation of military materiel. However, in the passage below Churchill suggests that there was no historical inevitability about Mussolini's decision. He even suggests that the Allies would have welcomed him with open arms and that, in fact, this would have been a wise decision on Mussolini's part. Churchill could be accused of exercising hindsight, writing secure in the knowledge that Britain had been on the winning side. After all, now that the war was over, he had no reason to convince Italy to join the Allies at that point—or did he?

Winston Churchill, *Closing the Ring: The Second World War*, Volume V*

Mussolini now had to bear the brunt of the military disasters into which he had, after so many years of rule, led his country. He had exercised almost absolute control and could not cast the burden on the Monarchy, Parliamentary institutions, the Fascist Party, or the General Staff. All fell on him. Now that the feeling that the war was lost spread throughout well-informed circles in Italy the blame fell upon the man who had so imperiously thrust the nation on to the wrong and the losing side. These convictions formed and spread widely during the early months of 1943. The lonely dictator sat at the summit of power, while military defeat and Italian slaughter in Russia, Tunis, and Sicily were the evident prelude to direct invasion.

In vain he made changes among the politicians and generals. In February General Ambrosio had succeeded Cavallero as Chief of the Italian General Staff. Ambrosio, together with the Duke of Acquatone, the Minister of Court, were personal advisers of the King and had the confidence of the Royal circle. For months they had been hoping to overthrow the Duce and put an end to the Fascist regime. But Mussolini still dwelt in the European scene as if he were a principal factor. He was affronted when his new military chief proposed the immediate withdrawal of the Italian divisions from the Balkans. He regarded these forces as the counterpoise to German predominance in Europe. He did not realize that defeats abroad and internal demoralization had robbed him of his status as Hitler's ally. He cherished the illusion of power and consequence when the reality had gone. Thus he resisted Ambrosio's formidable request. So durable however was the impression of his authority and the fear of his personal action in extremity that there was prolonged hesitation throughout all the forces of Italian society about how to oust him. Who would "bell the cat"? Thus the spring had passed with invasion by a mighty foe, possessing superior power by land, sea, and air, drawing ever nearer.

Thus ended Mussolini's twenty-one years' dictatorship in Italy, during which he had raised the Italian people from the Bolshevism into which they might have sunk in 1919 to a position in Europe such as Italy had never held before. A new impulse had been given to the national life. The Italian Empire in North Africa was built. Many important public works in Italy were completed. In 1935 the Duce had by his will-power overcome the League of Nations—"Fifty nations led by one"—and was able to complete his conquest of Abyssinia. His regime was far too costly for the Italian people to bear, but there is no doubt that it

---

*Winston Churchill (1951), *The Second World War: Volume V: Closing the Ring*, New York: Houghton Mifflin, pp. 40–41, 48–49.

appealed during its period of success to very great numbers of Italians. He was, as I had addressed him at the time of the fall of France, "the Italian lawgiver." The alternative to his rule might well have been a Communist Italy, which would have brought perils and misfortunes of a different character both upon the Italian people and Europe. His fatal mistake was the declaration of war on France and Great Britain following Hitler's victories in June 1940. Had he not done this he could well have maintained Italy in a balancing position, courted and rewarded by both sides and deriving an unusual wealth and prosperity from the struggles of other countries. Even when the issue of the war became certain Mussolini would have been welcomed by the Allies. He had much to give to shorten its course. He could have timed his moment to declare war on Hitler with art and care. Instead he took the wrong turning. He never understood the strength of Britain, nor the long-enduring qualities of Island resistance and sea-power. Thus he marched to ruin. His great roads will remain a monument to his personal power and long reign.

At this time Hitler made a crowning error in strategy and war direction. The defection of Italy, the victorious advance of Russia, and the evident preparations for a cross-Channel attack by Britain and the United States should have led him to concentrate and develop the most powerful German army as a central reserve. In this way only could he use the high qualities of the German command and fighting troops, and at the same time take full advantage of the central position which he occupied, with its interior lines and remarkable communications. As General von Thoma said while a prisoner of war in our charge, "Our only chance is to create a situation where we can use the Army." Hitler, as I have pointed out in an earlier volume, had in fact made a spider's web and forgotten the spider. He tried to hold everything he had won. Enormous forces were squandered in the Balkans and in Italy which could play no part in the main decisions. A central reserve of thirty or forty divisions of the highest quality and mobility would have enabled him to strike at any one of his opponents advancing upon him and fight a major battle with good prospects of success. He could, for instance, have met the British and Americans at the fortieth or fiftieth day after their landing at Normandy a year later with fresh and greatly superior forces. There was no need to consume his strength in Italy and the Balkans, and the fact that we was induced to do so must be taken as the waste of his last opportunity.

Questions

1. What is Churchill's overall attitude toward Mussolini? How would his attitude have been different if Mussolini had not declared war on Britain?
2. Does Churchill have an ulterior motive for his treatment of Mussolini here? Was he trying to convey a message to Italians in the postwar period?

3. What does he describe as Hitler's major blunder? Is he suggesting that the war would have turned out differently if Hitler had not made it?
4. What is the tone of Churchill's memoirs, as represented in these passages? How does the tone relate to the contents that he is describing? How might this have affected how people viewed the war in retrospect? Is this what Churchill intended?

HARRY TRUMAN, *MEMOIRS*, INTRODUCTION

Harry S. Truman was the first to admit that nothing could have prepared him for the job of being president when he took the oath of office on April 12, 1945, just following the death of Franklin Roosevelt and only months before the end of the Second World War. He inherited the Manhattan Project, a top secret effort on the part of several of the world's leading scientists to develop an atomic bomb that might be used to end the war. When that superweapon became available, Truman seems not to have hesitated for long before authorizing its use, not once but twice, on Japanese cities on August 6 and 9, 1945. On August 14 the Japanese surrendered, with the sole condition being that Emperor Hirohito be allowed to remain on the Japanese throne. As the opening passages from Volume II of his Memoirs *indicate, however, he did think seriously about the future of atomic energy after the war. On the one hand, Truman had hoped to use US possession of nuclear weapons to intimidate the Soviets during negotiations of a postwar settlement between the two wartime allies. On the other hand, Truman worried about these weapons being deployed without civilian oversight, something that he believed should extend to nuclear energy in general, as he outlines below.*

Harry Truman, *Memoirs**

Within the first few months I discovered that being President is like riding a tiger. A man has to keep riding or be swallowed. The fantastically crowded nine months of 1945 taught me that a President is either constantly on top of events or, if he hesitates, events will soon be on top of him. I never felt that I could let up for a single moment.

---

*Harry S. Truman (1956), *Memoirs: Volume II: Years of Trial and Hope*, New York: Doubleday, pp. 1–3. Available online at http://archive.org/stream/memoirsbyharryst012833mbp#page/n7/mode/2up.

No one who has not had the responsibility can really understand what it is like to be President, not even his closest aides or members of his immediate family. There is no end to the chain of responsibility that binds him, and he is never allowed to forget that he is President. What kept me going in 1945 was my belief that there is far more good than evil in men and that it is the business of government to make the good prevail.

By nature not given to making snap judgments or easy decisions, I required all available facts and information before coming to a decision. But once a decision was made, I did not worry about it afterward. I had trained myself to look back into history for precedents, because instinctively I sought perspective in the span of history for the decisions I had to make. That is why I read and re-read history. Most of the problems a President has to face have their roots in the past.

Two cruel wars were behind us in which we had seen totalitarian aggressors beaten into unconditional surrender. We had sponsored and helped establish the United Nations Organization, hoping to prevent again the too often recurring plague of humanity—war. I had met with Churchill and Atlee and Stalin at Potsdam, trying to achieve closer cooperation between the three leading powers.

But in spite of these efforts relations with Russia had become strained. Victory had turned a difficult ally in war into an even more troublesome peacetime partner. Russia seemed bent upon taking advantage of war-shattered neighbors for imperialistic ends. The whole balance of power in the Far East had shifted. Most of the countries of Europe were bankrupt, millions of people were homeless and starving, and we were the only nation that could come to their help. We had already taken emergency relief measures, and we were preparing to do everything we could to avert a great human disaster.

The economic and financial burdens confronting us were staggering. But the adjustments from war to peace were being accomplished in a vigilant and orderly manner, and our economy kept going in high gear with full peacetime employment at a time when we were demobilizing millions of men. We are witnessing the transformation of the United States into a nation of unprecedented power and growing capacity.

But one event occurred in 1945 of such magnitude that it was to revolutionize our relations with the world and usher in a new era for humanity, the fruits and goals and problems of which we cannot even now fully grasp. It was the atomic bomb. With it came the secret of how to harness nuclear energy. I now had a responsibility without precedent in history. The decisions I had to make and the policies I would recommend to Congress on the use and control of atomic energy could well influence the future course of civilization. This was to be the beginning of the period of hope and many trials.

A bill for the control of atomic energy was before the Congress. This bill was the May-Johnson bill, which had been drawn up in the early days after V-J [Victory in Japan] day, and its approach was military. Its aim was to set up a kind of permanent "Manhattan District" under military control.

In the message I had sent to Congress on October 3 I strongly emphasized the peacetime uses of atomic energy, and for that reason I felt that it should not be controlled by the military. During the fall months of 1945 legislative action had been delayed by a wrangle among Senate committees as to which should properly handle bills affecting atomic power. Behind this dispute was the basic disagreement on whether the new force was primarily a military weapon or a potential source for peaceful civilian development.

The legislative dispute was finally resolved when the Senate set up a Special Committee on Atomic Energy. The chairman of this committee was Senator Brian McMahon of Connecticut, a devoted and talented public servant who deserves a great deal of credit for his legislative leadership in his shaping of the atomic program.

On November 30 I sent a memorandum to certain officials on the handling of the atomic program, stating that I thought the May-Johnson bill should be amended to provide for civilian supremacy, and at the same time raised with Senator McMahon the necessity for establishing civilian control. The senator agreed to seek amendment of the bill. Within a few days, however, he requested an appointment, suggesting that the Secretaries of War and of the Navy also be present. The military services felt strongly that the control of atomic development should be under their auspices, if not under their immediate jurisdiction, and they were making strong representations to that effect to Congress.

The meeting took place in my office on December 4. . . .

I asked each member of the group to state his position. Then I stated mine, that the entire program and operation should be under civilian control and that the government should have a monopoly of materials, facilities, and processes.

Questions

1. Why does Truman begin this volume of his memoirs by discussing the importance of historical precedent prior to dealing with a situation that he describes as unprecedented?
2. How might his discussion of nuclear power in this excerpt relate to his earlier decision to drop two atomic bombs on Japanese cities?
3. What reasons might he have had for insisting that nuclear energy be placed under civilian control?

KI-SHEOK CHONG, *BLACK FLOWER IN THE SKY: POEMS OF A KOREAN BRIDEGROOM IN HIROSHIMA*, INTRODUCTION

Many nonfiction books, novels, and articles have been written about the August 1945 explosion of the atomic bombs on the Japanese cities of Hiroshima and Nagasaki. Because of the devastating and unprecedented effects of these new superweapons, as well as the fears that the bombs raised about the future annihilation of the human race, concerns were raised that went beyond those relating to the enormous destruction and loss of life caused by so-called "conventional weapons" during the two world wars and other conflicts of the twentieth century. Warfare has called forth the efforts of poets to recall the tragedy of war since Homer's Iliad. Here the renowned Korean poet Ki-Sheok Chong attempts to find poetic images to convey something of the human dimensions of the attack on Hiroshima. Words may never convey the totality of the horrors of the war, the Holocaust, or the use of nuclear weapons on human targets, but, like the other sources in this chapter, Chong uses the language at his disposal in the attempt to say something meaningful about what happened at Hiroshima—as if he recognized that the alternative of remaining silent was a far worse alternative. Chong, a high school principal, wrote an additional dozen books of poetry and one novel; he wrote these poems reproduced here as part of a book hoping to attract an audience for his work outside of his native country, particularly to expand his readership in the United States.

Ki-Sheok Chong, "A Gull of Hiroshima" and "A Hospital Ward for Victims of the Atomic Bomb"*

A Gull of Hiroshima

It rains.
From somewhere far away, with a gentle stroke, and a whisper,
soft as down, it rains.
On the days when the gulls cry, it rains,
letting my tired body rest, clearing the pain that's settled into my joints.
The sound of the rain wets down my burning heart—
with a scent of emotion, a scent of sadness, a scent of tears
the rain wets me.
The sound of the waves of the Seto Inland Sea drains the blood from

---

*Ki-Sheok Chong (2006), *Black Flower in the Sky: Poems of a Korean Bridegroom in Hiroshima*, Honolulu: Katydid Books, pp. 7–8, 51–52.

living things
while the waves call to the gulls, "pain, pain, pain, pain."

The sound of the blast bubbles up like an old dream!
And onto the Hiroshima that has been trampled on by a million
    bulldozers,
black raindrops fall.
Beads of oil drip from an atomic cloud rich with radioactivity
as the soul without sin whispers to the gulls, "not again, not again, not
    again."

The light that day! The wind that day! The rain that fell that day
has turned to sediment and stayed.
Humans turned to stone beat the ground and hide their twisted faces.
These are humans whose humanity was stolen.
Sheets of rain fall on the sea, on the earth, on the wilderness of the
    mind.
People walk forward through the rain, sinking into the bog, as darkness
    comes on.

The tyrant destroyed what was human. The tyrant destroyed me.
This land is set far apart from the world,
it is where I left myself behind.

My heart aches, The rain keeps company with all my friends who fell
    like wildflowers in the atomic bombing.
You are visited only by rain, rain, rain, rain—
My whole life is the cry of a seagull wet with rain

A Hospital Ward for Victims of the Atomic Bomb

A temporary building in the ruins of Hiroshima
From behind the broken hospital ward,
the moon with her hair disheveled,
moves her hand in circles over pale cheeks,

murmurs
and moans
like a fledgling actress,
recounting her forgotten lines.

Like acrobats
hanging from a long rope,

ghosts dangle, swaying back and forth
holding onto the lifeline.

As powerfully as a ball thrown with all the pitcher's might,
as solemnly as a sprinter holding his breath at the starting line,
just before the final breath, a catastrophic flash reaches the place.

Crushing pitiful lives,
erasing death again and again,
the messengers of Death come along afterward,
breathing noisily.
Will they leave their last will and testament,

becoming the guideposts of enlightenment,
becoming salt that will not go stale?

One dim lantern is lit
in the ward where death alone is cultivated.
Pain grows stronger
as the lights of life flicker.
Souls jostle about
in the rising sobs.

Tens of millions of sighs
will not erase this enmity,
Tens of millions of wails
will not put an end to the anger.
Vocal cords worn out from shouting tremble and rasp.

If that deep greed is set aside
can human beings be bound with love?
If the atomic bomb is set aside
can all human beings become kindhearted?

Questions

1. American defenders of the use of the atomic bombs during the Second World
   War justify their position on the basis of the need to save American lives by
   bringing a quick and decisive end to the war. How effective is the poetry of
   Ki-Sheok Chong at providing a rebuttal to that position? Is that the intent
   of these poems?
2. Does it make a difference that the author of these poems is Korean and not
   Japanese? Does the author's Korean background at all lessen or intensify the
   impact of the poems?

3. What is the value of these poems as a historical source?
4. In his postscript to *Black Flower in the Sky*, Chong wrote of his belief that
   "poetry is one of our best hopes for saving human beings from the destruc-
   tiveness of war." Do you agree? Why or why not?

FIGURE 14: Pearl Harbor, December 7, 1941. Courtesy of Getty Images.

FIGURE 15: Nijmegen, Holland, September 28, 1944. Courtesy of Getty Images.

FIGURE 16: Dresden, 1945. Courtesy of Getty Images.

FIGURE 17: Hiroshima, 1945. Courtesy of Getty Images.

Questions

1. The novelist Tatjani Soli has written that "every good war picture is an anti-war picture." Do you agree? Does this statement apply to these photographs?
2. What is the relationship among these four photographs? Could one write a history of the war around photographs such as these? Write one paragraph to outline what such a history might say.
3. The similarities in these photographs may be obvious. Are there differences as well? Do the similarities outweigh any differences that might exist?
4. What do these photographs reveal about the nature of the Second World War compared to the First World War or any previous wars?

Chapter Questions

1. Are there any important similarities between the diaries of Victor Klemperer and Anne Frank, despite the differences in their age and circumstances? In what ways were their circumstances the same? What are the key differences between their perspectives on the war? What can be learned from a comparison of these two sources?
2. Can the story of the Holocaust be told from just one perspective? Or do we need different accounts such as those by Anne Frank, Elie Wiesel, or Rolf Hochhuth in order for us to confront the enormity of the event on a human scale that does not merely deal in numbers or statistics?
3. What is the value of historical memoirs such as those by Churchill and Truman? What are their limitations?

CHAPTER TWELVE

The Cold War and the Postwar Period

INTRODUCTION

The period that followed the end of the Second World War is one of enormous complexity, but it is often reduced to the single theme of the Cold War. This is perhaps because of the very real danger that nuclear weapons posed to the existence of humanity that was heightened by the rivalry between the United States and the Soviet Union. The sources in this chapter have been selected to strike a balance between the prominence of the Cold War and the fears it engendered and the other complicated historical changes that accompanied this period. In addition, the sources here reflect the effects that the Cold War had on different parts of the world, as well as the hopes for a better world that certain individuals began to express in the aftermath of the devastation wrought by the Second World War.

In both the Soviet Union and the West, for example, women had reason to hope that the progress they had made toward equal rights with men since the end of the nineteenth century would continue in the postwar world. It is true that women gained the right to vote in France, one of the last holdouts against women's suffrage, in 1945, but by and large the right to vote did not translate to equal rights in the workplace or equal representation in politics—in France or anywhere else in the Western world. The French philosopher Simone de Beauvoir examined women's situation from the perspectives of history, philosophy, psychology, and biology in her landmark book, *The Second Sex*, first published in 1949. Just by calling attention to the historical fact that women in most places and at most times were considered inferior to men—that women were "the second sex"—she raised the question of why, in fact, this should be the case. Even if there were historical or cultural explanations for this fact, de Beauvoir showed that women would continue to question its relevance in the modern world.

If anything, women in the Soviet Union had more reason to hope for equal status given the egalitarian principles of the Communist Party and the strides that women had made in that direction under communism. However, in many ways, the Soviet Union, always dominated politically by men, remained a traditional patriarchal society, even with more women participating in the work force and holding jobs that in the West would have been associated with male-dominated careers such as medicine or engineering. To some degree, however, the prominence of women in the Soviet workplace after the Second World War occurred by necessity rather than choice. Millions of Russian men were killed in the Great Patriotic War, as the Second World War was known in the Soviet Union, leaving millions of women without the opportunity to marry or be supported by a husband. The Russian novelist Alexander Solzhenitsyn uses his 1968 novel *Cancer Ward*, which is set in the 1950s, to explore the underlying realities of the lives of Soviet women in the postwar period.

Following the Second World War, a number of countries outside of Europe, many of which were former colonies of European nations, sought to assert themselves in different ways. Egyptian nationalism received a boost from the *coup d'etat* sponsored by Gamal Abdel Nasser (1918–70) in 1952. Nasser not only wanted to secure Egyptian independence from European influence but also sought to avoid taking sides in the Cold War in order to preserve Egyptian autonomy. His government survived a major test during the Suez Crisis of 1956 that followed his nationalization of the Suez Canal and a failed attempt by Britain, France, and Israel to militarily intervene to prevent it. Nasser's success at fostering Egyptian independence inspired other nations in the nonaligned or "Third World" nations in the Middle East, Africa, and Asia, but leaders of many European colonies already had ideas of their own in that direction. In the former British African colony of the Gold Coast, for example, the Western-educated advocate of independence Kwame Nkrumah led a movement that resulted in the renamed country of Ghana in 1957. Algerians had already begun a rebellion against French rule in 1954, the same year that the French surrendered their control over their colony of Indochina, or Vietnam, in Southeast Asia. Nonalignment did not seem an option in that part of the world; Korea, for example, had just been divided following the Korean War into a Communist North and a NATO-backed South. When the nationalist rebellion led by the Communist Ho Chi Minh ousted the French in North Vietnam, the United States responded by backing an anti-Communist government led by Ngo Dinh Diem in the South. To this the Communists responded with the formation of the National Liberation Front (NLF) in South Vietnam, whose goals are outlined in the document that appears below.

Meanwhile, Israel, which had become an independent nation in 1948, was still recovering from the Suez fiasco and fighting for its survival in a largely hostile Arab world in the 1960s, culminating in the Arab-Israeli war of 1967. In 1958, Golda Meir, then serving as Israeli foreign minister, reasserted some of the principles of Israeli independence. Even though hers would be a minority voice in the decision to go to war in 1967, her principles and courageous leadership played an important role in defining the new nation at a critical stage in its history.

Still, the Cold War cast a large shadow over this entire period, never more so than during the Cuban Missile Crisis of 1962. This chapter includes excerpts from three important documents that illuminate both the nature of that crisis and the manner in which President John F. Kennedy handled it in an effort to bring the United States and the Soviet Union back from the brink of nuclear war. The first source is a nationally televised address in which he spoke directly to the American people (and the world), followed by excerpts of two letters that he sent to the Soviet leader Nikita Khrushchev. The last source of the chapter is an excerpt from a novel that is representative of several that reflected the anxieties of the Cold War by imagining what the aftereffects of nuclear war might be like. Nevil Shute's *On the Beach* appeared in 1957; read in conjunction with the documents of the Cuban Missile Crisis it provides a better context for understanding reactions to the crisis and serves as one example of the literary and cultural response to the Cold War and the fears associated with it.

SIMONE DE BEAUVOIR, *THE SECOND SEX*, AND ALEXANDER SOLZHENITSYN, *CANCER WARD*, INTRODUCTION

The French existentialist philosopher Simone de Beauvoir (1908–86) produced a truly remarkable and comprehensive book on women that should be read by anyone truly interested in the feminist movement of the twentieth century. The contents are too diverse and comprehensive to be adequately reflected in an anthology such as this one, but it is too important to be neglected altogether (even though her name does not even appear in many recent surveys of twentieth-century European history). Although only a brief passage appears here, it captures something of the overall philosophy that supports the work and provides insight into de Beauvoir's thinking on the subject of gender.

Cancer Ward may not be Alexander Solzhenitsyn's most famous or most critically acclaimed novel; those distinctions probably belong to his first novel, One Day in the Life of Ivan Denisovich *(1962), which humanized the plight of the victims of Stalin's labor camps following the Second World War, which included Solzhenitsyn himself. Among the many merits of* Cancer Ward, *however, was Solzhenitsyn's ability to humanize the plight of women in postwar Soviet society, as indicated in the passages below.*

Simone de Beauvoir, *The Second Sex**

... men profit in many ... subtle ways from the otherness, the alterity of women. Here is miraculous balm for those afflicted with an inferiority complex, and indeed no one is more arrogant toward women, more aggressive or scornful, than the man who is anxious about his virility. Those who are not fear-ridden in the presence of their fellow men are much more disposed to recognize a fellow creature in woman; but even to these the myth of Woman, the Other, is precious for many reasons. They cannot be blamed for not cheerfully relinquishing all the benefits they derive from the myth, for they realize what they would lose

---

*Simone de Beauvoir (1953), *The Second Sex*, New York: Alfred A. Knopf, pp. xxv–xxvii, xxix.

in relinquishing woman as they fancy her to be, while they fail to realize what they have to gain from the woman of tomorrow. . . .

We should consider the arguments of the feminists with no less suspicion, however, for very often their controversial aim deprives them of all real value. If the "woman question" seems trivial, it is because masculine arrogance has made of it a "quarrel"; and when quarreling one no longer reasons well. People have tirelessly sought to prove that woman is superior, inferior, or equal to man. Some say that, having been created after Adam, she is evidently a secondary being; others say on the contrary that Adam was only a rough draft and that God succeeded in producing the human being in perfection when He created Eve.

Alexander Solzhenitsyn, *Cancer Ward**

Many of the women in the trolley, like Ludmila Afanasyevna, were carrying not handbags but big bags like small suitcases that could hold a live piglet or four large loaves of bread. At every stop and with every shop that flashed by the window, Ludmila Afanasyevna's thoughts turned more and more to her housework and her home. Home was her responsibility and hers alone, because what can you expect from men? Her husband and son, whenever she went to Moscow for a conference, would leave the dishes unwashed for a whole week. It wasn't that they wanted to keep them for her to do, they just saw no sense in the repetitive, endlessly self-renewing work.

Ludmila Afanasyevna also had a daughter, already married and with a little one on her hands, but now on the point of being unmarried because divorce was in the air. This was the first time today she had remembered her daughter, and the thought did not cheer her.

Today was Friday. On Sunday she absolutely must get through a lot of washing that had piled up. This meant that dinner for the first half of the week had to be got ready and cooked, come what may, on Saturday evening (she prepared it twice a week). As for putting the washing to soak, that had to be done today, whatever time it meant getting to bed. Even though it was getting late, now was the only time left to go to the main market. The stalls there were not packed up until later in the evening.

She got out to change trolleys, but, looking through the plate-glass window of a nearby grocery store, decided to go in. The meat department was empty and the assistant had already gone. In the fish department there was nothing worth taking—herring, salt plaice, tinned fish. She walked past the picturesque

---

*Alexander Solzhenitsyn (1969), *Cancer Ward*, translated by Nicholas Bethell and David Burg, New York: Bantam Books; © Farrar, Strauss, and Giroux, pp. 91–92, 345.

pyramids of wine bottles and the brown cylindrical rods of cheese that looked just like sausages, on her way to the grocery department. She wanted to get two bottles of sunflower-seed oil (before there had only been cottonseed-oil), and some barley concentrate. From the grocery counter she cut across the quiet shop, paid at the cash desk and went back to collect them.

She was standing in line behind two men when suddenly there was hubbub in the shop. People were pouring in from the street, forming lines at the delicatessen counter and at the cashier. Ludmila Afanasyevna started, and without waiting to collect her goods in the grocery department hurried across to line up at the delicatessen counter and at the cashier. So far there was nothing to be seen behind the curved glass cover of the counter, but the jostling women were absolutely confident. Minced-ham sausage was going to be sold, one kilo for each buyer.

What a stroke of luck! It was worth going to the back of the line a bit later for a second kilo.

It was simply that we grow dull with passing years. We grow tired. We lose all true talent for grief and faithfulness. We surrender to time. Yet every day we swallow food and lick our fingers—in this respect we are unyielding. If we're not fed for two days we go out of our minds, we start climbing up the wall.

Fine progress we've made, we human beings.

Vega had not changed, but she was crushed. Her mother had died too; she used to live with her mother, just the two of them. Her mother died because she too was crushed. Her son, Vera's older brother, had been an engineer. In 1940, he'd been arrested. For a few years he still wrote. For a few years they sent him parcels somewhere out in Buryat-Mongolia. Then one day they received a strange notification from the Post Office, and they gave Mother her parcel back. It was ink-stamped all over and the writing was crossed out. She carried the parcel home like a coffin. . . .

So Vera stayed all alone.

Not exactly alone, of course, she wasn't the only one. She was alone among millions. There were so many lonely women in the country, it made one want to count up those who knew—who were there more of, those on their own or those who were married? These lonely women were all about her age, all born in the same decade, the same age as the men who were killed in war.

The war was merciful to men, it took them away. The women it left to suffer to the end of their days.

The bachelors who managed to drag themselves back from the ruins of war did not choose wives of their own age, but younger girls. As for those who were a few years younger still, they were a whole generation younger, like children. War hadn't crawled over them like a tank.

So there they were, those millions of women. No one ever formed them into an army. They had come into the world to accomplish nothing. They were a fallow patch left behind by history.

Questions

1. What does de Beauvoir suggest as the root cause of male hostility to women? Do you agree?
2. What is her main reservation about the feminist movement?
3. Do these brief passages suggest a solution to the relationship between the sexes and the problem of women's inequality?
4. In what ways do the above passages from Solzhenitsyn's novel support the assertions of de Beauvoir regarding the inequality of the sexes?
5. What do they reveal about the peculiar situation of women in the Soviet Union in the 1950s? What do they reveal about life in general in the Soviet Union at that time?

SPEECH DELIVERED BY ANWAR EL SADAT AT THE FIRST AFRO-ASIAN PEOPLE'S SOLIDARITY CONFERENCE, DECEMBER 26, 1957, AND KWAME NKRUMAH, "I SPEAK OF FREEDOM," 1961, INTRODUCTION

Anwar al-Sadat (1918–81) would later gain fame as Nasser's successor as president of Egypt from 1970 until his assassination by Muslim fundamentalist terrorists in 1981. Sadat had been a disciple of Nasser and had worked closely with him in the 1950s and 1960s. As president, he would dismiss Soviet military aid and negotiate a peace agreement with Menachem Begin of Israel mediated by President Jimmy Carter of the United States. His 1957 speech on nonalignment, a year following the Suez Crisis, provides some clues to his future policy but is more important as a document reflecting the aspirations of the decolonized African and Asian nations emerging at the time of the Cold War.

That same year Kwame Nkrumah (1909–72) became prime minister of a newly independent Ghana. Like many aspiring African leaders, Nkrumah had spent the interwar years receiving an education in the United States, in his case at Lincoln University in Pennsylvania. He represented the Gold Coast at the Fifth Pan-African Congress held in Manchester, England, in 1945, and returned committed to the cause of independence. He became secretary of the United Gold Coast Convention in 1947, which soon became known as the Convention Peoples Party, making him an obvious choice for prime minister when Ghana became an independent nation. In 1951, the British, who had imprisoned Nkrumah for sedition, released him from prison so that he could assume office after an election of that year resulted in a landslide victory for his party. After making Ghana a republic in 1960, Nkrumah would eventually be overthrown in a military coup after proclaiming himself president for life in 1964. Like many revolutionaries, he came to believe that his leadership was necessary to sustaining the gains that he hoped to make for his country. His 1961 speech on freedom needs to be read and understood against the same backdrop of decolonization, the Cold War, and the nonalignment movement that influenced Sadat's speech that here precedes it.

Speech Delivered by Anwar el Sadat at the First Afro-Asian People's Solidarity Conference, December 26, 1957*

More than two years ago twenty nine governments of independent states convened together at the Bandung Conference to declare to the world at large that the tide of history has changed its course, and that Asia and Africa, which hitherto have been common play ground, where trespassers went by unheeded or a forest in which foreign beasts of prey roamed at leisure, have now become free world powers, majestic and serene, with a decisive role in shaping the future of the whole family of Nations. The Conference of Bandung was likewise convened to stress to the peoples of Africa and Asia the great importance of solidarity and the great weight they would have on the trend of world affairs when united. Today this people's Conference of ours meets, partly in honour of the spirit of Bandung and as a reminder of the principles and ideals it stands for, and partly to push it a step forward. Because our Conference is a Conference of peoples, it has been able to muster, not only the countries recognized by International Law as independent units, but also those peoples whose status is a foregone conclusion, a historical fact, and a reality endorsed by the whole of mankind, in addition to peoples who are still trodden under the heel of imperialism in one form or another. But our Conference takes the interest of these very peoples to heart. They are the diseased organs in the body of Asia and Africa: consequently they stand in dire need of the greatest of care and

---

*The First Afro-Asian People's Solidarity Conference, 26 December 1957 to January 1, 1958 (1958), 2nd edn, Cairo: The Permanent Secretariat of the Organization for Afro-Asian People's Solidarity, pp. 7–12. Available online at http://www.fordham.edu/halsall/mod/1957sadat-afroasian1.html.

attention. A body cannot continue to exist with half of its structure safe and sound while the other half is diseased and decayed. . . .

The idea of Afro-Asian Solidarity did not emanate out of naught, so as to be born and see daylight at Bandung all of a sudden. But before materializing as an historical event, it was an impression and an innate volition instinctively developing in the mind of the colonized and the exploited-the human being whom imperialism had reduced to a typefied specimen of a subjugated specie and bondsman recognisable in every colonized country. Indeed the idea of solidarity was deeply rooted in the hearts of those subjected peoples, continually aspiring through diverse national movements to smash the fetters of bondage and redeem their salvation. In the course of time these national movements were destined to meet, to consolidate and to react with one another, purposefully in some instances, but unconsciously and spontaneously in the majority of cases.

It is evident therefore, that the Bandung Conference was not a haphazard event, but rather a natural psychological factor which led to the awakening of the peoples of Africa and Asia and roused them from their slumber to solve the problem of their very existence and survival, and to resume the struggle for the recovery of their liberty and freedom. This awakening would have been devoid of any historical significance had it not marked a point of departure towards a new progressive future, the fundamental broad lines of which have been laid down by the Bandung Conference. It is up to the Peoples' Cairo Conference to reap from it, to the fullest extent, the benefits of the positive results which have blossomed in the political, economic, social and cultural fields alike. It is here that we shall necessarily be confronted by a number of difficult problems, but to find adequate solutions to these problems is not an impossible task, if we succeed in overcoming the first difficulty from the outset. It is a problem which comes within our own selves. It is the problem of sound and unbiased judgment. . . .

No doubt each country has its own particular problems for which she is more competent than anyone else to gauge the nature of the difficulties they represent; but at the same time, there is not a shadow of a doubt also that it is within the power of each of us to extend a helping band [sic] to his brother in time of need, in an endeavour to assist in solving his problems, be it only in the form of a genuine, friendly counsel or an expert advice. Thus it becomes evident that it is the duty of each of us to foster a double interest-an interest in his own problems, and an interest in the problems of others.

In addition, there are problems which present a common interest to us all. They react on us, and reflect on all of us one and the same homogeneous picture. Consequently, our particular national problems, and the problems common to us all, must of necessity go along, side by side. . . .

These are not the only responsibilities we have to shoulder in our Conference; for in addition to the host of responsibilities we have towards our diverse specific countries, there are others we have towards our two Continents, Africa and Asia. Besides, we have definite responsibilities towards the whole of mankind as an entire, indivisible unit.

We cannot live peacefully in a world threatened by the shadow of war. We can no longer enjoy the products of our hands and the fruits of our labour in a world where plunder prevails and flourishes. We can no longer build and reconstruct in a world which manufactures weapons for destruction and devastation. We can no longer raise the standard of living of our peoples and stamp out diseases and epidemics in a world where nations vie with each other for the production of lethal weapons of massacre and annihilation. Gone for ever is the era where the future of war and peace was decided upon in a few European capitals, because today we happen to be strong enough to make the decision ourselves in that respect.

Our weight in the international balance has now become preponderant. Only think of the colossal number of our people, our natural resources, the vastness of the area covered by our respective countries, and our strategic positions. You will surely come to the conclusion that the outbreak of war is impossible so long as we insist on peace, especially if we do not content ourselves with a mere negative attitude, but assume one of positiveness in favor of Peace. This transition from the negative to the positive is a fundamental basis worthy of our adoption.

Here in Egypt we, for instance, believe in the principle of neutrality and non-alignment. Many of our friends in Asia and Africa share this belief. We are confident that by adopting this attitude, we eliminate the shadow of war and limit the area of conflict between the two belligerent blocks, thus creating a vast region for Peace, imposing its existence and its atmosphere day after day, until it prevails over the whole world. But this neutrality in which we believe, though it defines the principle of abstaining from entering into international blocks, yet it also means that we shall spare no positive effort in reconciling these belligerent blocks. . . . It is the very principle which has been stressed by the President Gamal Abdul Nasser in his speech at Port Said on the anniversary of its liberation, when he said:

Today in Port Said we turn to the whole world demanding the corroboration of the fundamental principles of justice, which is the right to self-determination. We look from Port Said towards the whole world and demand that every colonized State should be granted its independence, and the right to govern itself. . . .

In the name of Egypt, I address a message to the world at large, for the preservation of Peace, and the abolition of war; for the removal of world tension, and the cessation of the cold war of nerves. We have seen war at Port Said. We have been hit by it, and faced its ravages and woes. But a World War, once it breaks out with its nuclear weapons and hydrogen bombs, will unquestionably annihilate mankind and destroy for ever our existing civilization. As a section of humanity, which has been treacherously attacked by imperialistic States, we demand that atomic experiments should be abolished, and that manufacture and use of nuclear weapons should be prohibited. We further press for disarmament in the interests of World Peace.

The People of Egypt who are sparing no effort for the establishment of universal justice, equity, liberty and peace, welcome you as messengers of justice, equity, liberty and peace.

Kwame Nkrumah, "I Speak of Freedom," 1961*

For centuries, Europeans dominated the African continent. The white man arrogated to himself the right to rule and to be obeyed by the non-white; his mission, he claimed, was to "civilise" Africa. Under this cloak, the Europeans robbed the continent of vast riches and inflicted unimaginable suffering on the African people.

All this makes a sad story, but now we must be prepared to bury the past with its unpleasant memories and look to the future. All we ask of the former colonial powers is their goodwill and co-operation to remedy past mistakes and injustices and to grant independence to the colonies in Africa.

It is clear that we must find an African solution to our problems, and that this can only be found in African unity. Divided we are weak; united, Africa could become one of the greatest forces for good in the world.

Although most Africans are poor, our continent is potentially extremely rich. Our mineral resources, which are being exploited with foreign capital only to enrich foreign investors, range from gold and diamonds to uranium and petroleum. Our forests contain some of the finest woods to be grown anywhere. Our cash crops include cocoa, coffee, rubber, tobacco and cotton. As for power, which is an important factor in any economic development, Africa contains over 40% of the potential water power of the world, as compared with about 10% in Europe and 13% in North America. Yet so far, less than 1% has been developed. This is one of the reasons why we have in Africa the paradox of poverty in the midst of plenty, and scarcity in the midst of abundance.

Never before have a people had within their grasp so great an opportunity for developing a continent endowed with so much wealth. Individually, the independent states of Africa, some of them potentially rich, others poor, can do little for their people. Together, by mutual help, they can achieve much. But the economic development of the continent must be planned and pursued

---

*Kwame Nkrumah (1961), *I Speak of Freedom: A Statement of African Ideology*, London: William Heinemann Ltd., pp. xi–xiv. Available online at http://www.fordham.edu/halsall/mod/1961nkrumah.html.

as a whole. A loose confederation designed only for economic co-operation would not provide the necessary unity of purpose. Only a strong political union can bring about full and effective development of our natural resources for the benefit of our people.

The political situation in Africa today is heartening and at the same time disturbing. It is heartening to see so many new flags hoisted in place of the old; it is disturbing to see so many countries of varying sizes and at different levels of development, weak and, in some cases, almost helpless. If this terrible state of fragmentation is allowed to continue it may well be disastrous for us all.

There are at present some 28 states in Africa, excluding the Union of South Africa, and those countries not yet free. No less than nine of these states have a population of less than three million. Can we seriously believe that the colonial powers meant these countries to be independent, viable states? The example of South America, which has as much wealth, if not more than North America, and yet remains weak and dependent on outside interests, is one which every African would do well to study.

Critics of African unity often refer to the wide differences in culture, language and ideas in various parts of Africa. This is true, but the essential fact remains that we are all Africans, and have a common interest in the independence of Africa. The difficulties presented by questions of language, culture and different political systems are not insuperable. If the need for political union is agreed by us all, then the will to create it is born; and where there's a will there's a way.

The present leaders of Africa have already shown a remarkable willingness to consult and seek advice among themselves. Africans have, indeed, begun to think continentally. They realise that they have much in common, both in their past history, in their present problems and in their future hopes. To suggest that the time is not yet ripe for considering a political union of Africa is to evade the facts and ignore realities in Africa today.

The greatest contribution that Africa can make to the peace of the world is to avoid all the dangers inherent in disunity, by creating a political union which will also by its success, stand as an example to a divided world. A Union of African states will project more effectively the African personality. It will command respect from a world that has regard only for size and influence. The scant attention paid to African opposition to the French atomic tests in the Sahara, and the ignominious spectacle of the U.N. in the Congo quibbling about constitutional niceties while the Republic was tottering into anarchy, are evidence of the callous disregard of African Independence by the Great Powers.

We have to prove that greatness is not to be measured in stockpiles of atom bombs. I believe strongly and sincerely that with the deep-rooted wisdom and dignity, the innate respect for human lives, the intense humanity that is our heritage, the African race, united under one federal government, will emerge not as just another world bloc to flaunt its wealth and strength, but as a Great

Power whose greatness is indestructible because it is built not on fear, envy and suspicion, nor won at the expense of others, but founded on hope, trust, friendship and directed to the good of all mankind.

The emergence of such a mighty stabilising force in this strife-worn world should be regarded not as the shadowy dream of a visionary, but as a practical proposition, which the peoples of Africa can, and should, translate into reality. There is a tide in the affairs of every people when the moment strikes for political action. Such was the moment in the history of the United States of America when the Founding Fathers saw beyond the petty wranglings of the separate states and created a Union. This is our chance. We must act now. Tomorrow may be too late and the opportunity will have passed, and with it the hope of free Africa's survival.

Questions

1. What is the central point or argument of Sadat's speech?
2. What is the central point or argument of Nkrumah's speech?
3. On what points do the two speeches agree? Are there any points on which they diverge or disagree?
4. What do they each see as the contribution that Africa has to make to the world during the critical transition period in which they spoke?

PROGRAM OF THE NATIONAL LIBERATION FRONT OF SOUTH VIETNAM, DECEMBER 20, 1960, INTRODUCTION

When the French announced their decision to abandon Vietnam at the Geneva Convention of 1954, the other members represented there, including the communist powers, the Soviet Union and the People's Republic of China, as well as the United States and the United Kingdom, decided to divide Vietnam at the 17th parallel, with a communist-backed government in the north and a Western-supported regime in the south. No one was really satisfied with this compromise as a permanent solution, least of all the North Vietnamese communists, who saw themselves as the nationalist leaders of the entire Vietnamese people. In fact, the United States forced postponement of national elections scheduled for 1955 for fear that Vietnam would be united under a communist regime. The Korean War had ended in a stalemate, but the Eisenhower administration in the United States remained committed to the Truman Doctrine, the policy of containing the spread of communism throughout the world. Meanwhile, Ngo Dinh Diem assumed control of the government in South Vietnam and began to suppress his opponents who supported the government centered on Hanoi in the north. These efforts directly led to the formation of the National Liberation Front in 1960, making this one of the key developments—and the following one of the central documents—in the history of the escalating Vietnam War, since the United States responded to this development by sending military advisers and weapons to South Vietnam. The NLF eventually became known as the Vietcong, which was short for Vietnamese Communists. As Stanley Karnow pointed out in his classic history of the Vietnam War, the formation of this southern "front" allowed the North Vietnamese to claim that they had not invaded the south in violation of the 1954 Geneva accord.

Program of the National Liberation Front of South Vietnam, December 20, 1960*

I. Overthrow the camouflaged colonial regime of the American imperialists and the dictatorial power of Ngo Dinh Diem, servant of the Americans, and institute a government of national democratic union.

The present South Vietnamese regime is a camouflaged colonial regime dominated by the Yankees, and the South Vietnamese government is a servile government, implementing faithfully all the policies of the American imperialists. Therefore, this regime must be overthrown and a government of national and democratic union put in its place composed of representatives of all social classes, of all nationalities, of various political parties, of all religions; patriotic, eminent citizens must take over for the people the control of economic, political, social, and cultural interests and thus bring about independence, democracy, well- being, peace, neutrality, and efforts toward the peaceful unification of the country.

II. Institute a largely liberal and democratic regime.

1. Abolish the present constitution of the dictatorial powers of Ngo Dinh Diem, servant of the Americans. Elect a new National Assembly through universal suffrage.

2. Implement essential democratic liberties: freedom of opinion, of press, of movement, of trade-unionism; freedom of religion without any discrimination; and the right of all patriotic organizations of whatever political tendency to carry on normal activities.

---

*http://openrevolt.info/2011/12/20/program-of-the-nlf/

3. Proclaim a general amnesty for all political prisoners and the dissolution of concentration camps of all sorts; abolish fascist law 19/59 and all the other antidemocratic laws; authorize the return to the country of all persons persecuted by the American-Diem regime who are now refugees abroad.

4. Interdict all illegal arrests and detentions; prohibit torture; and punish all the Diem bullies who have not repented and who have committed crimes against the people.

III. Establish an independent and sovereign economy, and improve the living conditions of the people.

1. Supress [*sic*] the monopolies imposed by the American imperialists and their servants; establish an independent and sovereign economy and finances in accordance with the national interest; confiscate to the profit of the nation the properties of the American imperialists and their servants.

2. Support the national bourgeoisie in the reconstruction and development of crafts and industry; provide active protection for national products through the suppression of production taxes and the limitation or prohibition of imports that the national economy is capable of producing; reduce custom fees on raw materials and machines.

3. Revitalize agriculture; modernize production, fishing, and cattle raising; help the farmers in putting to the plow unused land and in developing production; protect the crops and guarantee their disposal.

4. Encourage and reinforce economic relations between the city and country, the plain and the mountain regions; develop commercial exchanges with foreign countries, regardless of their political regime, on the basis of equality and mutual interests.

5. Institute a just and rational system of taxation; eliminate harassing penalties.

6. Implement the labor code: prohibition of discharges, of penalties, of ill-treatment of wage earners; improvement of the living conditions of workers and civil servants; imposition of wage scales and protective measures for young apprentices.

7. Organize social welfare: find work for jobless persons; assume the support and protection of orphans, old people, invalids; come to the help of the victims of the Americans and Diemists; organize help for areas hit by bad crops, fires, or natural calamities.

8. Come to the help of displaced persons desiring to return to their native areas and to those who wish to remain permanently in the South; improve their working and living conditions.

9. Prohibit expulsions, spoliation, and compulsory concentration of the population; guarantee job security for the urban and rural working populations.

IV. Reduce land rent; implement agrarian reform with the aim of providing land to the tillers.

1. Reduce land rent; guarantee to the farmers the right to till the soil; guarantee the property right of accession to fallow lands to those who have cultivated them; guarantee property rights to those farmers who have already received land.

2. Dissolve "prosperity zones" and put an end to recruitment for the camps that are called "agricultural development centers." Allow those compatriots who already have been forced into "prosperity zones," and "agricultural development centers" to return freely to their own lands.

3. Confiscate the land owned by American imperialists and their servants, and distribute it to poor peasants without any land or with insufficient land; redistribute the communal lands on a just and rational basis.

4. By negotiation and on the basis of fair prices, repurchase for distribution to landless peasant or peasants with insufficient land those surplus lands that the owners of large estates will be made to relinquish if their domain exceeds a certain limit, to be determined in accordance with regional particularities. The farmers who benefit from such land and distribution will both be compelled to make any payment or to submit to any other conditions.

V. Develop a national and democratic culture and education.

1. Combat all forms of culture and education enslaved to Yankee fashions; develop a culture and education that is national, progressive, and at the service of the Fatherland and people.

2. Liquidate illiteracy; increase the number of schools in the fields of general education as well as in those of technical and professional education, in advanced study as well as in other fields; adopt Vietnamese as the vernacular language; reduce the expenses of education and exempt from payment students who are without means; resume the examination system.

3. Promote science and technology and the national letters and arts; encourage and support the intellectuals and artists so as to permit them to develop their talents in the service of national reconstruction.

4. Watch over public health; develop sports and physical education.

VI. Create a national army devoted to the defense of the Fatherland and the people.

1. Establish a national army devoted to the defense of the Fatherland and the people; abolish the system of American military advisers.

2. Abolish the draft system, improve the living conditions of the simple soldiers and guarantee their political rights; put an end to ill- treatment of the military; pay particular attention to the dependents of soldiers without means.

3. Reward officers and soldiers having participated in the struggle against the domination by the Americans and their servants; adopt a policy of clemency toward the former collaborators of the Americans and Diemists guilty of crimes against the people but who have finally repented and are ready to serve the people.

4. Abolish all foreign military bases established on the territory of Viet-Nam.

VII. Guarantee equality between the various minorities and between the two sexes; protect the legitimate interest of foreign citizens established in Viet-Nam and of Vietnamese citizens residing abroad.

1. Implement the right to autonomy of the national minorities: Found autonomous zones in the areas with a minority population, those zones to be an integral part of the Vietnamese nation. Guarantee equality between the various nationalities: each nationality has the right to use and develop its language and writing system, to maintain or to modify freely its mores and customs; abolish the policy of the Americans and Diemists of racial discrimination and forced assimilation. Create conditions permitting the national minorities to reach the general level of progress of the population: development of their economy and culture; formation of cadres of minority nationalities.

2. Establish equality between the two sexes; women shall have equal rights with men from all viewpoints (political, economic, cultural, social, etc.).

3. Protect the legitimate interest of foreign citizens established in Viet-Nam.

4. Defend and take care of the interest of Vietnamese citizens residing abroad.

VIII. Promote a foreign policy of peace and neutrality.

1. Cancel all unequal treaties that infringe upon the sovereignty of the people and that were concluded with other countries by the servants of the Americans.

2. Establish diplomatic relations with all countries, regardless of their political regime, in accordance with the principles of peaceful coexistence adopted at the Bandung Conference.

3. Develop close solidarity with peace-loving nations and neutral countries; develop free relations with the nations of Southeast Asia, in particular with Cambodia and Laos.

4. Stay out of any military bloc; refuse any military alliance with another country.

5. Accept economic aid from any country willing to help us without attaching any conditions to such help.

IX. Re-establish normal relations between the two zones, and prepare for the peaceful reunification of the country.

The peaceful reunification of the country constitutes the dearest desire of all our compatriots throughout the country. The National Liberation Front of South Viet-Nam advocates the peaceful reunification by stages on the basis of negotiations and through the seeking of ways and means in conformity with the interest of the Vietnamese nation.

While awaiting this reunification, the governments of the two zones will, on the basis of negotiations, promise to banish all separatist and warmongering propaganda and not to use force to settle differences between the zones. Commercial and cultural exchanges between the two zones will be implemented; the inhabitants of the two zones will be free to move about throughout the country as their family and business interests indicate. The freedom of postal exchanges will be guaranteed.

X. Struggle against all aggressive war; actively defend universal peace.

1. Struggle against all aggressive war and against all forms of imperialist domination; support the national emancipation movements of the various peoples.

2. Banish all warmongering propaganda; demand general disarmament and the prohibition of nuclear weapons; and advocate the utilization of atomic energy for peaceful purposes.

3. Support all movements of struggle for peace, democracy, and social progress throughout the world; contribute actively to the defense of peace in Southeast Asia and in the world.

Questions

1. What are the main objections of the NLF to the rule of Diem in South Vietnam?
2. What are the ultimate objectives of the NLF? Are they limited to Vietnam?
3. Why do you think the United States reacted so hostilely to this document? Were they justified in doing so?
4. Did the document leave any room for negotiation or is it a truly revolutionary document?

GOLDA MEIR, "ISRAEL'S FOREIGN RELATIONS ON THE TENTH ANNIVERSARY OF THE STATE," INTRODUCTION

The existence of the state of Israel since 1948 became a central issue in the politics of Arab nationalism and the relationship among the Arab states, the United States, and the Soviet Union. The life of Golda Meir (1898–1978) was inextricably intertwined with the history of the state of Israel. Born in Kiev, she moved to Milwaukee with her family at the age of eight, where she discovered and committed herself to the cause of Zionism. As Golda Myerson, she moved to Palestine with her husband, Morris Myerson, in 1921 where the couple lived on a kibbutz, one of the collective farms springing up in the area for Jews wishing to start a new life in what they regarded as their original homeland. She became politically active and ended up on the Provisional Council of State and signing Israel's Declaration of Independence in 1948. Before becoming foreign minister in 1956, she had served as Israel's ambassador to the Soviet Union, chairman of its United Nations delegation, and then as minister of labour and social insurance. She favored friendly relations with and technical assistance to African nations. She eventually became prime minister of Israel, resigning in 1973 after her peace efforts had failed to prevent another Arab-Israeli war. In 1958, two years after her own participation in the debacle of the Suez Crisis, she reflected on the significance of Israel's tenth anniversary as a nation from her perspective as foreign minister.

Golda Meir, "Israel's Foreign Relations on the Tenth Anniversary of the State"*

In what way does our political activity differ specifically from that of other countries? I do not know of another state in the world that is surrounded by enemies on all sides except for the sea, and that has to struggle constantly even for free passage of the sea itself. We were forced to carry on a military and political fight for free passage through the Straits of Tiran and we are still struggling with our rights in the Suez Canal. The enmity of our neighbors is reflected not only along our frontiers, but also in continuous, widely ramifying activity by the Arabs throughout the world to sap our position and blacken our good name. It follows that in many of the world's capitals, the Israeli diplomatic mission is pitted alone against numerous Arab missions fighting Israel by every means in their power. A striking example of this is the position in the U.N., where all the Arab states are represented. One speech by our U.N. representative is usually met by all the Arab League representatives attacking us like one man. Another example is the economic warfare the Arabs wage against us, and which also demands counteractivity on our part. All our relations with other countries reflect this very real and material enmity of the Arabs. Any state that is called on to decide one question or another concerning its relations with Israel will weigh its decision not only having regard to the point at issue but also in light of possible Arab reactions.

This great enmity that we are subject to and that we struggle against in our daily lives and in the international arena spurs us on to make extraordinary efforts to clear new paths for ourselves and to break through the ring of our besiegers. We have a faithful and fraternal ally in the Jews of the Diaspora. Our alliance is consecrated by the experience of Jewish history throughout the generations; it is an alliance consecrated entirely to the upbuilding and development of the State of Israel. I do not think there is another state in the world borne along on waves of love and affection as Israel is privileged to be. It is therefore a matter of course that one of the central and most essential tasks facing the Israeli foreign service is—with constant hard work and boundless devotion—to foster the ties linking Israel and the Jews in the dispersion. There have been not a few instances where we have been able to stand by the side of Jewish communities, just as Jewish communities have stood by our side in the hour of need. It is natural that the possibility of contact with a given Jewish community also decides in no small measure the relationship between us and

*Golda Meir (1962), *This is Our Strength: Selected Papers*, edited by Henry M. Christman, New York: Macmillan, pp. 108–09.

the state where this particular Jewish community lives. Possibility of contact with Jewish communities means their freedom of choice to come to us as immigrants or even just as visitors.

Questions

1. According to Meir, what is unique about Israel's situation as a nation?
2. How does this affect her foreign policy objectives?
3. What does she see as the relationship between Israel and Jews living in other countries?

JOHN F. KENNEDY, TELEVISED ADDRESS, OCTOBER 22, 1962, AND LETTERS TO NIKITA KHRUSHCHEV, OCTOBER 27, 1962; OCTOBER 29, 1962, INTRODUCTION

In October 1962, the United States conducted surveillance in Cuba that revealed that the Soviet Union had stationed missiles there capable of delivering nuclear warheads to the United States. Influenced by fears of a first strike such as the Japanese had administered at Pearl Harbor, an event within the living memory of the military and civilian advisers of the Kennedy administration, the United States responded with a threat of war unless the Soviets agreed to remove the missiles. Kennedy himself was known as a "Cold Warrior" who had publicly supported the Truman Doctrine calling for the containment of communism in the 1950s. The first document represents exactly what Americans heard about the situation; the next two documents illuminate Kennedy's efforts to negotiate with Khrushchev to defuse the crisis while at the same time not appearing weak before the Soviet leader. On Saturday, October 27, the American joint chiefs of staff had recommended an airstrike against Cuba to commence sometime within the next two days in advance of a land invasion. This makes Kennedy's letters to Khrushchev of enormous historical significance. Sometimes critical turning points in history hinge on events that do not occur instead of those which actually take place. The decision not to declare war on the Soviet Union in October 1962 represents one of those important turning points.

John F. Kennedy, televised address, October 22, 1962*

Good evening, my fellow citizens. The Government, as promised, has maintained the closest surveillance of the Soviet military build-up on the island of Cuba. Within the past week unmistakable evidence has established the fact that a series of offensive missile sites is now in preparation on that imprisoned island. The purposes of these bases can be none other than to provide a nuclear strike capability against the Western Hemisphere.

Neither the United States of America nor the world community of nations can tolerate deliberate deception and offensive threats on the part of any nation, large or small. We no longer live in a world where only the actual firing of weapons represents a sufficient challenge to a nation's security to constitute maximum peril. Nuclear weapons are so destructive and ballistic missiles are so swift that any substantially increased possibility of their use or any sudden change in their deployment may well be regarded as a definite threat to peace.

For many years both the Soviet Union and the United States, recognizing this fact, have deployed strategic nuclear weapons with great care, never upsetting the precarious status quo which insured that these weapons would not be used in the absence of some vital challenge. Our own strategic missiles have never been transferred to the territory of any other nation under a cloak of secrecy and deception; and our history, unlike that of the Soviets since the end of World War II, demonstrates that we have no desire to dominate or conquer any other nation or impose our system upon its people.

But this secret, swift, and extraordinary build-up of Communist missiles—in an area well known to have a special and historical relationship to the United States and the nations of the Western Hemisphere, in violation of Soviet assurances, and in defiance of American and hemispheric policy—this sudden, clandestine decision to station strategic weapons for the first time outside of Soviet soil—is a deliberately provocative and unjustified change in the status quo which cannot be accepted by this country if our courage and our commitment are ever to be trusted again by either friend or foe.

The 1930's taught us a clear lesson: Aggressive conduct, if allowed to grow unchecked and unchallenged, ultimately leads to war. This nation is opposed to war. We are also true to our word. Our unswerving objective, therefore, must be to prevent the use of these missiles against this or any other country and to secure their withdrawal or elimination from the Western Hemisphere.

---

*Ernest R. May and Philip D. Zelikov, eds (1997), *The Kennedy Tapes: Inside the White House During the Cuban Missile Crisis*, Cambridge, MA and London: The Belknap Press of Harvard University Press, pp. 270–80. From: *Public Papers of John F. Kennedy, 1962* (1964), Washington, DC: Government Printing Office, pp. 806–9.

Our policy has been one of patience and restraint, as befits a peaceful and powerful nation, which leads a worldwide alliance. We have been determined not to be diverted from our central concerns by mere irritants and fanatics. But now further action is required—and it is underway; and these actions may only be the beginning. We will not prematurely or unnecessarily risk the costs of worldwide nuclear war in which even the fruits of victory would be ashes in our mouth—but neither will we shrink from that risk at any time it must be faced.

But it is difficult to settle or even discuss these problems in an atmosphere of intimidation. That is why the latest Soviet threat—or any other threat which is made either independently or in response to our actions this week—must and will be met with determination. Any hostile move anywhere in the world against the safety and freedom of peoples to whom we are committed—including in particular the brave people of West Berlin will be met by whatever action is needed. . . .

John F. Kennedy, letter to Nikita Khrushchev, October 27, 1962*

Dear Mr. Chairman:

I have read your letter of October 26 with great care and welcomed the statement of your desire to seek a prompt solution to the problem. The first thing that needs to be done, however, is for work to cease on offensive missile bases in Cuba and for all weapons systems in Cuba capable of offensive use to be rendered inoperable, under effective United Nations arrangements.

Assuming this is done promptly, I have given my representatives in New York instructions that will permit them to work out this weekend—in cooperation with the Acting Secretary General and your representative—an arrangement for a permanent solution to the Cuban problem along the lines suggested in your letter of October 26. As I read your letter, the key elements of your proposals—which seem generally acceptable as I understand them—are as follows:

1. You would agree to remove these weapons systems from Cuba under appropriate United Nations observation and supervision; and undertake, with suitable safeguards, to halt the further introduction of such weapons systems into Cuba.

---

*Ernest R. May and Philip D. Zelikov, eds (1997), *The Kennedy Tapes: Inside the White House During the Cuban Missile Crisis*, Cambridge, MA and London: The Belknap Press of Harvard University Press, pp. 603–04.

2. We, on our part, would agree—upon the establishment of adequate arrangements through the United Nations to ensure the carrying out and continuation of these commitments—(a) to remove promptly the quarantine measures now in effect and (b) to give assurances against an invasion of Cuba. I am confident that other nations of the Western Hemisphere would be prepared to do likewise.

If you will give your representative similar instructions, there is no reason why we should not be able to complete these arrangements and announce them to the world within a couple of days. The effect of such a settlement on easing world tensions would enable us to work toward a more general arrangement regarding "other armaments," as proposed in your second letter which you made public. I would like to say that the United States is very much interested in reducing tensions and halting the arms race; and if your letter signifies that you are prepared to discuss a détente affecting NATO and the Warsaw Pact, we are quite prepared to consider with our allies any useful proposals.

But the first ingredient, let me emphasize, is the cessation of work on missile sites in Cuba and measures to render such weapons inoperable, under effective international guarantees. The continuation of this threat, or a prolonging of this discussion concerning Cuba by linking these problems to the broader questions of European and world security, would surely lead to an intensification of the Cuban crisis and a grave risk to the peace of the world. For this reason I hope we can quickly agree along the lines outlined in this letter and in your letter of October 26.

John F. Kennedy

Letter to Nikita Khrushchev, October 29, 1962*

Dear Mr. Chairman:

I am replying at once to your broadcast message of October 28 even though the official text has not yet reached me because of the great importance I attach to moving forward promptly to the settlement of the Cuban crisis. I think that you and I, with our heavy responsibilities for the maintenance of peace, were aware that developments were approaching a point where events could have become unmanageable. So I welcome this message and consider it an important contribution to peace.

---

*Ernest R. May and Philip D. Zelikov, eds (1997), *The Kennedy Tapes: Inside the White House During the Cuban Missile Crisis*, Cambridge, MA and London: The Belknap Press of Harvard University Press, pp. 636–37.

Mr. Chairman, both of our countries have great unfinished tasks and I know that your people as well as those of the United States can ask for nothing better than to pursue them free from fear of war. Modern science and technology have given us the possibility of making labor fruitful beyond anything that could have been dreamed of a few decades ago.

I agree with you that we must devote urgent attention to the problem of disarmament as it relates to the whole world and also to critical areas. Perhaps now, as we step back from danger, we can together make real progress in this vital field. I think we should give priority to questions relating to the proliferation of nuclear weapons, on earth and in outer space, and to the great effort for a nuclear test ban. But we should also work hard to see if wider measures of disarmament can be agreed and put into operation at an early date. The United States government will be prepared to discuss these questions urgently, and in a constructive spirit, at Geneva or elsewhere.

John F. Kennedy

Questions
1. How do you think Americans were likely to react to Kennedy's televised speech when they heard it at the time? How do you think you would have reacted to Kennedy's speech if you had heard it live?
2. What are the purposes of his speech? What is its value as a historical document? What are its limitations as a source?
3. What is the tone of Kennedy's two letters to Khrushchev? Is there a difference between the tone of the first letter and that of the second?
4. What specific proposals does Kennedy make to Khrushchev in his letters? What general proposals does he make? Why do you think that these letters were successful in helping to resolve the Cuban Missile Crisis?

NEVIL SHUTE, *ON THE BEACH*, INTRODUCTION

A British immigrant to Australia, Nevil Shute (1899–1960) was the author of twenty-three novels; his 1957 novel On the Beach *was one of his last. The novel is set in Melbourne in 1963 (presciently, the year following the Cuban Missile Crisis) and revolves around a group of people coping with the imminent effects from the radioactive fallout drifting toward them after a nuclear war. Shute concocted an elaborate scenario for the outbreak of the Third World*

War, which made the story more, not less, realistic, because it dealt with the use of nuclear weapons by smaller states that initiated mistrust and escalated into a larger conflict. In the novel, the detonation of nuclear weapons had already eliminated the entire human and animal populations of the Northern Hemisphere and sealed the fate of those living farther south. Shute's characters discuss the situation as each of them decides how to cope with their impending doom. The following passage gives some sense of the dilemma that they face and the discussion surrounding it. Twice made into films, most recently in 2000, Shute's novel is a reflection of the Cold War fears of the late 1950s, but it will remain relevant as long as nuclear weapons continue to exist.

Nevil Shute, *On the Beach**

Peter stirred uneasily. . . . "Is anybody writing any kind of history about these times?"

John Osborne said, "I haven't heard of one. I'll find out about that. After all, there doesn't seem to be much point in writing about stuff that nobody will read."

"There should be something written, all the same," said the American. "Even if it's only going to be read in the next few months." He paused. "I'd like to read a history of this last war," he said. "I was in it for a little while, but I don't know a thing about it. Hasn't anybody written anything?"

"Not as history," John Osborne said. "Not that I know of, anyway. The information that we've got is all available, of course, but not as a coherent story. I think there'd be too many gaps—the things we just don't know."

"I'd settle for the things we *do* know," the captain remarked.

"What sort of things, sir?"

"Well, as a start, how many bombs were dropped? Nuclear bombs, I mean."

"The seismic records show about four thousand seven hundred. Some of the records were pretty weak, so there were probably more than that."

"How many of those were big ones—fusion bombs, hydrogen bombs, or whatever you call them?"

"I couldn't tell you. Probably most of them. All the bombs dropped in the Russo-Chinese war were hydrogen bombs, I think—most of them with a cobalt element."

"Why did they do that? Use cobalt, I mean?" Peter asked.

The scientist shrugged his shoulders. "Radiological warfare. I can't tell you any more than that."

---

*Nevil Shute (1960; 1957), *On the Beach*, New York: W. Morrow, pp. 81–83.

"I think I can," said the American. "I attended a commanding officers' course at Yerba Buena, San Francisco, the month before the war. They told us what they thought might happen between Russia and China. Whether they told us what *did* happen six weeks later—well, your guess is as good as mine."

John Osborne asked quietly, "What did they tell you?"

The captain considered for a minute. Then he said, "It was all tied up with the warm water ports. Russia hasn't got a port that doesn't freeze up in winter except Odessa, and that's on the Black Sea. To get out of Odessa on to the high seas the traffic has to pass two narrow straits both commanded by N.A.T.O. in time of war—the Bosporus and Gibraltar. Murmansk and Vladivostok can be kept open by icebreakers in the winter, but they're a mighty long way from any place in Russia that makes things to export." He paused. "This guy from Intelligence said that what Russia really wanted was Shanghai."

The scientist asked, "Is that handy for their Siberian industries?"

The captain nodded. "That's exactly it. During the Second War they moved a great many industries way back along the Trans-Siberian railway east of the Urals, back as far as Lake Baikal. They built new towns and everything. Well, it's a long, long way from those places to a port like Odessa. It's only about half the distance to Shanghai."

He paused. "There was another thing he told us," he said thoughtfully. "China had three times the population of Russia, all desperately overcrowded in their country. Russia, next door to the north of them, had millions and millions of square miles of land she didn't use at all because she didn't have enough people to populate it. This guy said that as the Chinese industries increased over the last twenty years, Russia got to be afraid of an attack by China. She'd have been a great deal happier if there had been two hundred million fewer Chinese, and she wanted Shanghai. And that adds up to radiological warfare. . . ."

Peter said, "But using cobalt, she couldn't follow up and take Shanghai."

"That's true. But she could make North China uninhabitable for quite a number of years by spacing the bombs right. If they put them down in the right places the fall-out would cover China to the sea. Any left over would go round the world eastwards across the Pacific; if a little got to the United States I don't suppose the Russians would have wept salt tears. If they planned it right there would be very little left when it got round the world again to Europe and western Russia. Certainly she couldn't follow up and take Shanghai for quite a number of years, but she'd get it in the end."

Peter turned to the scientist. "How long would it be before people could work in Shanghai?"

"With cobalt fall-out? I wouldn't even guess. It depends on so many things. You'd have to send in exploratory teams. More than five years, I should think—that's the half-life. Less than twenty. But you just can't say."

Questions

1. In the above dialogue, Peter suggests that it would be worthwhile writing a history of the war, even if it would only be read for a few months. Do you agree? What would be the value of such an exercise?
2. Why does Shute include an analysis of Russia's geopolitical situation as part of this discussion? Is this merely an intellectual exercise?
3. Novels are generally meant to provide some insight into life, human nature, or history. Based on the above dialogue, what do you see as the value of Shute's novel? Would such a novel be likely to be popular today?

FIGURE 18: Soviet propaganda posters, Cold War Museum, Forest of Plokstine, Lithuania. Courtesy of Getty Images.

FIGURE 19: Checkpoint Charlie, Berlin. Courtesy of Getty Images.

FIGURE 20: Missile launch facility, Cooperstown, North Dakota. Courtesy of Getty Images.

Each of these three images carry important symbolic meaning related to the Cold War.

Questions
1. What do these three images collectively reveal about the Cold War?
2. Would it be possible to write a history of the Cold War based on these three images?
3. Optional: Write a brief synopsis of the Cold War on the basis of these three images.

Chapter Questions

1. Are there similarities between the speeches by Sadat and Nkrumah and the Program of the National Liberation Front of Vietnam? How do each of these documents reflect the larger concerns of the Cold War?
2. Are Shute's concerns about nuclear fallout reflected in the language and messages conveyed in the sources from John F. Kennedy during the Cuban Missile Crisis?
3. What additional insights into the Cold War period as a whole have you gained from the sources in this chapter?

CHAPTER THIRTEEN

Political and Cultural Revolutions, 1960–75

INTRODUCTION

The tensions of the first decade of the Cold War carried over into the 1960s amid raised hopes and bitter disappointments. The emergence of the nonaligned "Third World" and the success of decolonization in some parts of the world only intensified the frustrations of those former colonies yet to gain their independence. The United States stepped in to replace France as a Western power to prevent Vietnam from controlling its own destiny as part of its attempt to contain the spread of communism. Meanwhile, in 1960 the French had yet to grant independence to Algeria, where a nationalist rebellion had started to cause divisions within France as well as Algeria. African-Americans had seen some progress in the direction of Civil Rights by 1960, but still had years of bitter struggle ahead of them. China opened the decade in the midst of Mao Zedong's "Great Leap Forward," his attempt to catapult China quickly to the forefront as an industrial power. His program of rapid industrialization and radical transformation turned into one of the biggest human disasters ever. Finally, the youth culture that had emerged with the beginnings of American rock n' roll in the 1950s and the restless generation of beatniks seemed on the verge of dying out, having spent its energy with no clear direction for the future.

In retrospect, the early 1960s represents a critical turning point in history related to the transmutation of all of the developments mentioned. The first two sources deal with the subject of political revolution related to the delayed hopes of those people still in the throes of colonialism. First, in his memoirs, the French leader Charles de Gaulle explains the process behind his decision to grant Algeria its independence in 1962. The French war against the Algerian nationalists had caused much anxiety in France itself, presaging the angst of the protest movement in the United States against the Vietnam War later in the decade. For Westerners and non-Westerners alike, Frantz Fanon's polemical *Wretched of the Earth* provided a new alternative to Marxism for condemning Western imperialism.

Fanon's advocacy of violent revolution stands in contrast to the campaign of nonviolent civil disobedience led by Dr. Martin Luther King Jr. on behalf of African-Americans in the United States. Influenced by the ideas of Gandhi, King believed that he could achieve his goal of racial equality through the forces of morality and justice. King faced opposition from within the Civil Rights movement itself among those who believed, along with Fanon, that only violence could put an end to oppression supported by violence. In the 1960s the cause of African-Americans mirrored in the minds of many people the struggles against colonialism in other parts of the world. In his "Letter from the Birmingham Jail," King makes an impassioned plea for an end to racial discrimination that stands as one of the central documents, not only of the Civil Rights Movement, but also of the entire history of the twentieth century.

In China, the Communist Party led by Mao Zedong had successfully defeated the US-backed Guomindang and established the People's Republic of China in 1949. Mao had played a huge role in the communist revolution in China dating to the founding of the Chinese Communist Party (CCP) in 1919. Mao and the CCP aspired to nothing less than the total transformation of social relations within China at the same time as they wanted to modernize the country and increase Chinese power in the world at large. These tasks proved overwhelming, with setbacks accompanying success; decreasing the power of the old landlord class meant increasing the power and wealth of the party members in charge of running the country. The tragedy of the Great Leap Forward almost cost Mao his position of leadership within the party, despite his revolutionary credentials and the heroic status he gained during the Long March, the civil war with the Guomindang, and the war with the Japanese. The three poems by Mao in this chapter provide insights into his thinking during two troubled times in his life: the mid-1930s and the early 1960s.

Mao not only survived the attempts of his rivals to wrest control of the party, but he also reemerged stronger than ever during the Great Proletarian Cultural Revolution, which he launched in 1966. Primarily relying on the support of a younger generation that resented the privileges and compromises of the "Old Guard," Mao's youthful Red Guards denounced, attacked, and humiliated any of their elders who retained any elements of "bourgeois" values or lacked ideological purity. The Cultural Revolution turned China upside down and rivals the Great Leap Forward as the biggest disaster in Chinese history. In his memoir, Da Chen relates a story that illustrates how years later people in China still felt the effects of the Cultural Revolution.

In the United States and Britain, a different kind of "cultural revolution" occurred among a young generation deeply influenced by popular music, which led the way and belongs in any treatment of this period. This chapter includes the lyrics of several songs that reflect important aspects of the music that influenced that generation. John Lennon and Paul McCartney, the two lead songwriters of the Beatles, the most influential pop group of all time, showed their followers the potential of personal and creative growth through the evolution of their own music and lyrics throughout the decade. The Canadian singer-songwriter Joni Mitchell combined a folk sensibility with sensitivity to the cultural changes and issues of the late sixties and early seventies in songs like "Woodstock" and "Big Yellow Taxi," which her biographer Karen O'Brien described as "proto-environmental."

The relationship between humanity and technology continued to represent one of the main themes of modern history and its cultural expressions. The chapter concludes with excerpts from the popular philosophical manifesto from 1974, *Zen and the Art of Motorcycle Maintenance* by Robert M. Pirsig, which raises questions about human values at a time of profound technological change, and S. L. Lowry's painting, "Industrial Scene," from 1965.

CHARLES DE GAULLE, *MEMOIRS OF HOPE: RENEWAL AND ENDEAVOR*, INTRODUCTION

Charles de Gaulle became a national hero when he organized the Free French Army to continue to fight the Nazis after France had surrendered to Germany in June 1940. When the Allies liberated France from German control in 1944, de Gaulle marched into Paris at the head of a French army and assumed control of a provisional French government. After the war, the general temporarily retired from politics until the nation reached a new crisis point in the ongoing conflict with the revolutionaries fighting for Algerian independence. In the passage below, de Gaulle describes the state of the nation as he attempted to resolve the crisis. Algeria officially became an independent nation in 1962. De Gaulle retired from politics for good after an electoral defeat in 1969, which followed a year of turmoil marked by student protests and a general strike in 1968.

Charles de Gaulle, *Memoirs of Hope: Renewal and Endeavor**

. . . In Algiers, *pied-noir* activists were planning anti-de Gaulle demonstrations to take place on Armistice Day [11 November 1960]. Moreover, the bitterness which marked the budget discussions in France for the first time since 1958 was an indication of the impatience and anxiety of the French people. But in a broadcast to the nation on November 4 I deliberately appeared full of resolution and assurance. "Having resumed the leadership of France," I said, "I have decided in her name to pursue a course which will lead from government of Algeria by metropolitan France to an Algerian Algeria. That means an emancipated Algeria . . . an Algeria which, if the Algerians so wish—and I believe this to be the case—will have its own government, its own institutions, its own laws." I repeated that "the Algeria of tomorrow, as decided by self-determination, can be built either with France or against her," and that France "will abide by the result of the ballot, whatever it may be." I renewed my invitation to

---

*Charles de Gaulle (1971), *Memoirs of Hope: Renewal and Endeavor*, translated by Terence Kilmartin, New York: Simon and Schuster, pp. 90–91.

the leaders of the external organization of the rebellion "to take part, without restrictions, in discussions concerning the forthcoming referendum, then in the campaign itself, which will be conducted in complete freedom, and finally in the supervision of the ballot," the sole condition being that "we should come to an agreement to stop killing one another." But I categorically rejected their claims to assume power by virtue of the sub-machine gun alone, after France had withdrawn her troops and before the destiny of Algeria had been decided in advance by universal suffrage, on the ground that they were already to all intents and purposes "the government of the Algerian Republic." Such a Republic "will one day exist, but has never yet existed." Then I attacked those elements in our country who were bent on "fomenting trouble and whipping up public feeling. . . . Thus we see two rival packs, one on the side of sterile reaction, the other of ignoble abandonment, snarling and snapping in opposite directions, each of which would lead France and Algeria to catastrophe." Nor did I spare the outsiders who took up propagandist attitudes on the question: "While the Soviet empire, which is the most savagely imperialist and colonialist power ever known, strives to extend its domination, while Communist China prepares to follow its example, while enormous racial problems bedevil many parts of the world, America in particular, not only do we find threatening statements being hurled against France by the oppressors of the East but tendentious criticisms appearing in the free world. . . . In the face of these attempts at incitement both from within and from without . . . the State stands firm! . . . There is a government, which I appointed and which is fulfilling its task with exemplary ability and devotion. . . . There is a parliament, which debates, legislates and supervises. . . . The executive power and the legislative power are now completely separate, thus guaranteeing the government the necessary freedom of action. . . . There is a Head of State on whom the Constitution imposes a duty which is paramount." I ended: "The Republic is on its feet. The country's leaders are at their posts. The nation will be called upon to decide from the depths of its being. Frenchwomen, Frenchmen, I am counting on you. You can count on me!" I had spoken in the same vein on my visits to our provinces during the course of the year: Languedoc in February, Normandy in July, Brittany in September, and the Alps at the beginning of October. All of them had given me their fervent approbation.

Meanwhile, those to whom my warnings were addressed reacted according to their fashion. The leaders of the National Liberation Front issued a statement on the referendum: "Its purpose is clearly to impose a predetermined status on Algeria . . . with the object of preventing the Algerian people from declaring themselves for independence." They therefore called on Moslems to abstain. In France, the Communists declared: "To vote 'Yes' is to say 'No' to peace!" The activists made their opposition felt everywhere. . . .

Questions
1. Does de Gaulle take too much personal credit for Algerian independence?
2. One could argue that all memoirs are meant to be self-serving to some
   degree. Are de Gaulle's especially so? What purpose do you think he intends
   the above passage to serve?
3. Did de Gaulle find himself once again obliged to defend French honor, as he
   had during the Second World War?
4. Does the above passage achieve its intended purpose?

FRANTZ FANON, *WRETCHED OF THE EARTH*, INTRODUCTION

*Frantz Fanon's book made a profound impression on European intellectuals of
the 1960s, many of whom embraced it out of an apparent desire to repudiate their
own countries' past association with imperialism and oppression of colonized
peoples. The French existentialist philosopher Jean Paul-Sartre even wrote an
introduction to the French edition in which he praised Fanon's advocacy of
violence against Europeans by their colonists. Fanon concerned himself more
with the degrading effects of imperialism upon the individuals forced to live
under colonial regimes. In the passage below, he describes some of those effects
from a psychological and sociological perspective.*

Frantz Fanon, *Wretched of the Earth**

The colonized man will first manifest this aggressiveness which has been
deposited in his bones against his own people. This is the period when the
niggers beat each other up, and the police and magistrates do not know which
way to turn when faced with the astonishing waves of crime in North Africa. . . .
When the native is confronted with the colonial order of things, he finds he is
in a state of permanent tension. The settler's world is a hostile world, which
spurns the native, but at the same time it is a world of which he is envious.
We have seen that the native never ceases to dream of putting himself in the
place of the settler—not of becoming the settler but of substituting himself
for the settler. This hostile world, ponderous and aggressive, because it fends

*Frantz Fanon (1968; © 1963), *Wretched of the Earth*, translated by Constance Farrington, New
York: Grove Press, pp. 42–43.

off the colonized masses with all the harshness it is capable of, represents not merely a hell from which the swiftest flight possible is desirable, but also a paradise close at hand which is guarded by terrible watchdogs.

The native is always on the alert, for since he can only make out with difficulty the many symbols of the colonial world, he is never sure whether or not he has crossed the frontier. Confronted with a world ruled by the settler, the native is always presumed guilty. But the native's guilt is never a guilt which he accepts; it is rather a kind of curse, a sort of sword of Damocles, for in his innermost spirit, the native admits no accusation. He is overpowered but not tamed; he is treated as an inferior but he is not convinced of his inferiority. He is patiently waiting until the settler is off his guard to fly at him. The native's muscles are always tensed. You can't say that he is terrorized, or even apprehensive. He is in fact ready at a moment's notice to exchange the *role* of the quarry for that of the hunter. The native is an oppressed person whose permanent dream is to become the persecutor. The symbols of social order—the police, the bugle-call in the barracks, military parades and the waving flags—are at one and the same time inhibitory and stimulating: for they do not convey the message "Don't dare to budge"; rather, they cry out "Get ready to attack." And, in fact, if the native had any tendency to fall asleep and to forget, the settler's hauteur and the settler's anxiety to test the strength of the colonial system would remind him at every turn that the great show-down cannot be put off indefinitely. That impulse to take the settler's place implies a tonicity of muscles the whole time; and in fact we know that in certain emotional conditions the presence of an obstacle accentuates the tendency towards motion.

The settler-native relationship is a mass relationship. The settler pits brute force against the weight of numbers. He is an exhibitionist. His preoccupation with security makes him remind the native out loud that he alone is master. The settler keeps alive in the native an anger which he deprives of outlet; the native is trapped in the tight links of the chains of colonialism. But we have seen that inwardly the settler can only achieve a pseudo petrification. The native's muscular tension finds outlet regularly in bloodthirsty explosions—in tribal warfare, in feuds between sects, and in quarrels between individuals.

Questions

1. What does Fanon describe as the most important effects of colonialism in the above passages?
2. Why do internal divisions arise among the natives under colonialism, according to Fanon?
3. In what ways does Fanon imply that the master-servant relationship between colonizer and native is bad for the masters, too?

MARTIN LUTHER KING, "LETTER FROM BIRMINGHAM CITY JAIL," INTRODUCTION

Martin Luther King Jr. (1929–68) followed in his father's footsteps and became a Baptist preacher before emerging in the 1950s as a leader of the Civil Rights movement. King intervened in Montgomery, Alabama, in 1955 to organize a bus boycott to protest the policy of forced segregation on city buses brought to light when Rosa Parks refused to sit in the section reserved for "colored" people. In the late 1950s and 1960s, King traveled throughout the South to champion the cause of racial justice and equality. His "Letter from Birmingham City Jail" helped to publicize the plight of African-Americans and brought the issue down to the personal level of the effects of racial segregation on the individual. While he had that in common with Fanon, for the remainder of his life King remained committed to a path of nonviolent civil disobedience.

Martin Luther King, "Letter from Birmingham City Jail"*

. . . I am in Birmingham because injustice is here. Just as the eighth century prophets left their little villages and carried their "thus saith the Lord" far beyond the boundaries of their hometowns; and just as the Apostle Paul left his little village of Tarsus and carried the gospel of Jesus Christ to practically every hamlet and every city in the Graeco-Roman world, I too am compelled to carry the gospel of freedom beyond my particular hometown. Like Paul, I must constantly respond to the Macedonian call for aid.

Moreover, I am cognizant of the interrelatedness of all communities and states. I cannot sit idly by in Atlanta and not be concerned about what happens in Birmingham. Injustice anywhere is a threat to justice anywhere. We are caught in an inescapable network of mutuality, tied in a single garment of destiny. Whatever affects one directly affects all indirectly. Never again can we afford to live with the narrow, provincial "outside agitator" idea. Anyone who lives in the United States can never be considered an outsider anywhere in his country.

You deplore the demonstrations that are presently taking place in Birmingham. But I am sorry that your statement did not express a similar concern for the conditions that brought the demonstrations into being. I am sure that each of you would want to go beyond the superficial social analyst who looks merely at effects, and does not grapple with underlying causes. I would not hesitate to say that it is unfortunate that so-called demonstrations are taking place in

---

*Jaroslav Pelikan, ed. (1990), *The World Treasury of Modern Religious Thought*, Boston: Little, Brown and Company, pp. 607–11.

Birmingham at this time, but I would say in more emphatic terms that it is even more unfortunate that the white power structure of the city left the Negro community with no other alternative. . . .

Birmingham is probably the most thoroughly segregated city in the United States. Its ugly record of police brutality is known in every section of this country. Its injust [sic] treatment of Negroes in the courts is a notorious reality. There have been more unsolved bombings of Negro homes and churches in Birmingham than any city in this nation. These are the hard, brutal and unbelievable facts. On the basis of these conditions Negro leaders sought to negotiate with the city fathers. But the political leaders consistently refused to engage in good faith negotiation. . . .

We know through painful experience that freedom is never voluntarily given by the oppressor: it must be demanded by the oppressed. Frankly, I have never yet engaged in a direct action movement that was "well-timed," according to the timetable of those who have not suffered unduly from the disease of segregation. For years now I have heard the words [sic] "Wait!" It rings in the ear of every Negro with a piercing familiarity. This "Wait" has almost always meant "Never." It has been a tranquilizing thalidomide, relieving the emotional stress for a moment, only to give birth to an ill-formed infant of frustration. We must come to see with the distinguished jurist of yesterday that "justice too long delayed is justice denied." We have waited for more than 340 years for our constitutional and God-given rights. The nations of Asia and Africa are moving with jetlike speed toward the goal of political independence, and we still creep at horse and buggy pace toward the gaining of a cup of coffee at a lunch counter. I guess it is easy for those who have never felt the stinging darts of segregation to say, "Wait." But when you have seen vicious mobs lynch your mothers and fathers at will and drown your sisters and brothers at whim; when you have seen hate-filled policemen curse, kick, brutalize and even kill your black brothers and sisters with impunity, when you see the vast majority of your twenty million Negro brothers smothering in an airtight cage of poverty in the midst of an affluent society, when you suddenly find your tongue twisted and your speech stammering as you seek to explain to your six-year-old daughter why she can't go to the public amusement park that has just been advertised on television, and see tears welling up in her little eyes when she is told that Funtown is closed to colored children, and see the depressing clouds of inferiority begin to form in her little mental sky, and see her begin to distort her little personality by unconsciously developing a bitterness toward white people; when you have to concoct an answer for a five-year-old son asking in agonizing pathos: "Daddy, why do white people treat colored people so mean?"; when you take a cross-country drive and find it necessary to sleep night after night in the uncomfortable corners of your automobile because no motel will accept you; when you are humiliated day in and day out by nagging signs reading "white" and "colored"; when your first name becomes "nigger" and your middle name becomes "boy" (however old you are) and your last name becomes "John," and when your wife and mother are never given the respected title "Mrs."; when you are harried by day and haunted by night by the fact that you are a Negro, living constantly at tiptoe stance never quite knowing what to expect next, and plagued with inner fears and outer resentments; when you are forever fighting a degenerating sense of "nobleness"; then you will understand why we find it difficult to wait. There comes a time when the cup of endurance runs over, and men are no longer willing to be plunged into an abyss of injustice where they experience the blackness of corroding despair. I hope, sirs, you can understand our legitimate and unavoidable impatience.

Questions

1. In this letter, Martin Luther King uses biblical allusions and compares him-self to St. Paul. What effect did he intend for this to have on his readers? Is this an apt comparison?
2. How does he refute the argument that the South was not ready for segrega-tion?
3. Do his arguments bear any similarity to the points Fanon makes in *The Wretched of the Earth*? In what ways do the two sources differ?
4. Why has King singled out Birmingham for his indictment of racial oppres-sion and prejudice?

MAO ZEDONG, POEMS FROM "THOUSANDS OF SONGS DEDICATED TO THE HISTORY OF THE PARTY," AND DA CHEN, *SOUNDS OF THE RIVER: A MEMOIR*, INTRODUCTION

In late 1934, Mao Zedong and the Red Army of the Chinese Communist Party set out on a journey in which they would traverse 4,000 miles in flight from the Nationalist army of the Guomindang, a seminal event in Chinese history known as the Long March. Chingkangshan (Jinggangshan or Jinggang Mountain Range), which divides Hunan and Jiangxi Provinces in southern China, formed the base of the Communist rebels after the Guomandong had betrayed its former allies and attempted to eradicate the Communists in 1927. In Mao's first poem below, he reflects upon returning to the mountains from which the Long March had originated. This poem provides insight into Mao's thinking long before he would acquire the power that would allow him to launch such programs as the Great Leap Forward and the Great Proletarian Cultural Revolution.

The other two poems by Mao that appear here date from the years between the ignominious failure of the Great Leap Forward and the start of the Cultural Revolution. Mao's "Reply to Comrade Kuo Mo-Jo," in addition to representing a critique of a personal rival to some degree, reflects Mao's distrust of any intellectual who could rival or challenge his own authority. Kuo Mo-Jo (Guo Moruo, 1892–1978), an intellectual and high-ranking figure in the Communist Party, lost his positions at the beginning of the Cultural Revolution in 1966 and was forced to repudiate his own voluminous writings.

When Mao died in 1976, the People's Republic preserved his reputation as a Communist hero by blaming the crimes of the Cultural Revolution on a small cadre of Mao's advisers (including his widow, Jiang Qing) that became known as the "Gang of Four." The arrests and subsequent trial represented a virtual admission by Communist Party leaders that the Cultural Revolution had been a colossal mistake. However, they could not undo the damage overnight; those who had participated must have found it difficult to admit their error, while the victims of persecution must have found it difficult to put aside resentment toward their tormenters within the Party. In Da Chen's second memoir, Sounds of the River, *he writes of what it meant to come of age in modern China in the aftermath of the Cultural Revolution.*

Mao Zedong, Poems from "Thousands of Songs Dedicated to the History of the Party"

*"Reascending Chingkangshan," 1935**

I have long aspired to reach for the clouds
And I again ascend Chingkangshan.
Coming from afar to view our old haunt, I find new scenes replacing the old.
Everywhere orioles sing, swallows dart,
Streams babble
And the road mounts skyward.
Once Huangyangchieh is passed
No other perilous place calls for a glance.
Wind and thunder are stirring,
Flags and banners are flying
Wherever men live.
Thirty-eight years are fled

---

*http://www.marxists.org/reference/archive/mao/selected-works/poems/poems35.htm

With a mere snap of the fingers.
We can clasp the moon in the Ninth Heaven
And seize turtles deep down in the Five Seas:
We'll return amid triumphant song and laughter.
Nothing is hard in this world
If you dare to scale the heights.

"Winter Clouds," 1962*

Winter clouds snow-laden, cotton fluff flying,
None or few the unfallen flowers.
Chill waves sweep through steep skies,
Yet earth's gentle breath grows warm.
Only heroes can quell tigers and leopards
And wild bears never daunt the brave.
Plum blossoms welcome the whirling snow;
Small wonder flies freeze and perish.

"Reply to Comrade Kuo Mo-Jo," 1963**

On this tiny globe
A few flies dash themselves against the wall,
Humming without cease,
Sometimes shrilling,
Sometimes moaning.
Ants on the locust tree assume a great-nation swagger
And mayflies lightly plot to topple the giant tree.
The west wind scatters leaves over Changan,
And the arrows are flying, twanging.
So many deeds cry out to be done,
And always urgently;
The world rolls on,
Time presses.
Ten thousand years are too long,
Seize the day, seize the hour!
The Four Seas are rising, clouds and waters raging,
The Five Continents are rocking, wind and thunder roaring.
Our force is irresistible,
Away with all pests!

---

*http://www.marxists.org/reference/archive/mao/selected-works/poems/poems33.htm
**http://www.marxists.org/reference/archive/mao/selected-works/poems/poems34.htm

Da Chen, *Sounds of the River: A Memoir**

All seemed fine until one day our dean appeared in our classroom, demanding to see me in his office. This man held the key to my future. I wasn't ready to make matters worse. Nervously I followed him downstairs to his office, where he sat down without inviting me to sit in the empty chair. I waited for whatever he had to say. He looked at me with narrowed eyes. Nothing except coldness was emitted by this northern bearlike fellow. His Mao jacket was neatly buttoned to the last button, announcing his rigidity in following the dead man's fashion. It was a state of mind doggedly set on safeguarding Mao's tomb till his own death and beyond. "You have been skipping the political studies class in the afternoon." His voice was low and very serious.

"To study. Was in the lab," I explained.

"Study?" He ground his teeth, making his neat sideburns ripple and cheekbones rise.

"Yes, I have a lot to catch up with. Extra diligence is required on my part," I said, trying to convince this venerable dean of my conviction.

"Wrong attitude."

"How could I be wrong? Aren't I supposed to be devoting all my time to my studies so that our country doesn't waste a penny on me?"

"Wrong, wrong, wrong. And I am surprised how wrong you are in assessing your current task, especially considering your background."

"My background?"

"Yes." He opened a file in front of him. "I see that you are from a landlord's family in the south."

He knew the impact of that casually dropped line. He knew that anyone who had a connection with that damned word *landlord* would shrink at the tip of that cutting sword. It was a dirty secret, a skeleton, a disgrace, an incurable handicap, an ugly birthmark. I was quite shocked to hear him drop the bomb. The Cultural Revolution was long over but obviously not yet dead. And this was the office of the dean of the preeminent Foreign Language Department. Who was this monster? Did he hope that the specter of the Cultural Revolution would return? Did he keep a tracking diary of bad deeds others did to the dead revolution so that he could shout *revenge, revenge* as innocent people were hanged and shot in the head?

"But"—he flipped the file closed—"the times have changed. We are not talking landlord and no landlord anymore."

Times obviously haven't changed enough for you, you fossil, you intestinal buildup, you filthy philistine. I almost shouted the thought. Instead I said, "I did

---

*Da Chen (2002), *Sounds of the River: A Memoir*, New York: HarperCollins, pp. 43–44.

not choose to be the son of a landlord. I am my own body and mind. President Deng has wisely changed any discrimination against us. Why did you have to mention my background?"

"I mention it only when I find the usage of such information appropriate in assessing a situation. It wouldn't make a difference on your way up, but it does on your way down." He leaned back. "Where you are, there are many temptations. We have on our campus all the capitalistic, bourgeois-minded liberals with their corrupted lifestyles and very, very dangerous behavior. And the worst of them are the Americans. That's why we have three guards in the front entrance and another three at the back gate around the clock. No outsiders are allowed in here. Socialization between foreigners and Chinese is forbidden, and you bet we work hard on containing their contaminating influence, but still we find cheap girls smuggled into taxis into the foreign students' dorm to do their dirty thing. They call it love. I call it prostitution. We even caught a few girls climbing the walls to meet white and black students alike. They have the money, the hard currency, the cigarettes, perfume, and everything else. And here you are in the midst of everything, the most corrupted spot in China, coming in from the countryside. I, as dean, worry about your political growth here. But political meetings aren't the only things we have to keep control over you. We also have our model students, openly or secretly reporting to us directly about your daily conduct around here. Do you understand what I'm saying?"

"Yes sir."

Questions

1. "Reascending Chingkangshan" seems to reflect an ideal to which Mao sought to return in 1935? Does the poem parallel what Mao attempted to achieve in the 1960s as indicated in the two poems from the 1960s?

2. What connection exists between the Mao Zedong who authored the poems here and the Mao who launched the Cultural Revolution, the long-term effects of which Da Chen describes in his memoir? Is it possible to reconcile the two?

3. In what ways do Mao's "Winter Clouds" and "Reply to Comrade Kuo Mo-Jo" predict the fate of Kuo (Guo) (and so many others) a few years later when Mao launched his Cultural Revolution?

4. How does Da Chen's anecdote from his days as a student indicate that the divisions within Chinese society had not yet disappeared in post-Mao China? What inherent dangers exist in any society that insists on ideological purity?

JOHN LENNON AND PAUL MCCARTNEY, "A DAY IN THE LIFE"; JONI MITCHELL, "WOODSTOCK" AND "BIG YELLOW TAXI," INTRODUCTION

In 1963 and 1964 the Beatles seemed to produce one hit song after another as they achieved unprecedented success and popularity in Britain and the United States. In 1965, even as their commercial success continued, they showed signs of creative growth and disenchantment with the phenomenon of "Beatlemania." The albums Rubber Soul *(1965) and* Revolver *(1966) reflected the creative growth of the group as a new maturity appeared in the songwriting of Paul McCartney (b. 1942) and John Lennon (1940–80). "A Day in the Life" appeared a year later on the amazingly original album,* Sergeant Pepper's Lonely Hearts Club Band. *Lennon began composing the song, but it also represents a collaborative effort between the two Beatles. This song also infused images from modern life, some of which Lennon culled from items he read in the newspaper, into a highly innovative composition. The BBC banned the song from the radio before the Beatles even released the record because of McCartney's implied drug reference in the phrase "I'd love to turn you on."*

The Canadian-born Joni Mitchell (b. 1943) also achieved enormous fame and popularity as one of the more original and creative singer-songwriters of her generation. The two songs featured here served as anthems of sorts that have become an important and familiar part of the cultural legacy of this period. Mitchell composed "Woodstock" as an ode to the famed rock music festival held in New York State in August 1969. The song spoke to a generation still in search of itself and the meaning of life in the middle of a materialistic, consumer-oriented society and the ongoing Vietnam War. Ironically, Mitchell did not personally attend Woodstock herself, but the group Crosby, Stills, and Nash, which had a hit with a cover version of the song, did. "Big Yellow Taxi" sounds more lighthearted, but resonated just as strongly among those with emerging concerns about the environment and postindustrial society.

John Lennon and Paul McCartney, "A Day in the Life"*

I read the news today oh, boy
About a lucky man who made the grade
And though the news was rather sad

---

*© Sony/ATV Music Publishing LLC. Available online at http://www.lyricsfreak.com/b/beatles/a+day+in+the+life_10026556.html.

Well, I just had to laugh
I saw the photograph
He blew his mind out in a car
He didn't notice that the lights had changed
A crowd of people stood and stared
They'd seen his face before
Nobody was really sure if he was from the House of Lords

I saw a film today oh, boy
The English army had just won the war
A crowd of people turned away
But I just had to look
Having read the book
I'd love to turn you on.

Woke up, fell out of bed
Dragged a comb across my head
Found my way downstairs and drank a cup
And looking up, I noticed I was late
Found my coat and grabbed my hat
Made the bus in seconds flat
Found my way upstairs and had a smoke
And somebody spoke and I went into a dream
Ah

I read the news today oh, boy
Four thousand holes in Blackburn, Lancashire
And though the holes were rather small
They had to count them all
Now they know how many holes it takes to fill the Albert Hall
I'd love to turn you on.

Joni Mitchell, "Woodstock"*

I came upon a child of God
He was walking along the road
And I asked him where are you going
And this he told me
I'm going on down to Yasgur's farm
I'm going to join in a rock 'n' roll band

---

*Joni Mitchell (1970), *Ladies of the Canyon*, Warner Brothers, © 1969, Siquomb Publishing Co.

I'm going to camp out on the land
And try an' get my soul free
We are stardust
We are golden
And we've got to get ourselves
Back to the garden

Then can I walk beside you
I have come here to lose the smog
And I feel to be a cog in something turning
Well maybe it is just the time of year
Or maybe it's the time of man
I don't know who I am
But you know life is for learning

We are stardust
We are golden
And we've got to get ourselves
Back to the garden

By the time we got to Woodstock
We were half a million strong
And everywhere there was song and celebration
And I dreamed I saw the bombers
Riding shotgun in the sky
And they were turning into butterflies
Above our nation
We are stardust
Billion year old carbon
Caught in the devil's bargain
And we've got to get ourselves
Back to the garden.

"Big Yellow Taxi"*

They paved paradise
And put up a parking lot
With a pink hotel, a boutique
And a swinging hot spot
Don't it always seem to go

---

*Joni Mitchell (1970), *Ladies of the Canyon*, Warner Brothers, © 1969, Siquomb Publishing Co.

That you don't know what you've got
Till it's gone
They paved paradise
And put up a parking lot.
They took all the trees
And put them in a tree museum
And they charged all the people
A dollar and a half just to see 'em
Don't it always seem to go
That you don't know what you've got
Till it's gone
They paved paradise
And put up a parking lot.
Hey farmer farmer
Put away that D.D.T now
Give me spots on the apples
But leave me the birds and the bees
Please!
Don't it always seem to go
That you don't know what you've got
Till it's gone
They paved paradise
And put up a parking lot.
Late last night
I heard the screen door slam
And a big yellow taxi
Took away my old man
Don't it always seem to go
That you don't know what you've got
Till it's gone
They paved paradise
And put up a parking lot.

Questions

1. Poetry by definition expresses itself in images that prose cannot adequately convey, and thus offers more of an opportunity for individual interpretation. How would you interpret the lyrics of "A Day in the Life"? What identifies this song as a work of the mid-1960s, apart from its place in Beatles' history?

2. The main subject of Joni Mitchell's "Woodstock" is clear enough, but what else is the song about? What impact do you think the song had on listeners at the time? How does the message of "Woodstock" relate to that of "Big Yellow Taxi"?

3. John Lennon, Paul McCartney, and Joni Mitchell are all very close in age. Lennon and McCartney hailed from Liverpool, England, and Mitchell from Canada. What do these songs collectively say about the generation that came of age in the 1950s and 1960s? What significant similarities and differences exist among them?

ROBERT M. PIRSIG, *ZEN AND THE ART OF MOTORCYCLE MAINTENANCE: AN INQUIRY INTO VALUES*, INTRODUCTION

Robert Pirsig addressed the question of values and their relationship to technology and modern life in his 1974 reflective odyssey, Zen and the Art of Motorcycle Maintenance. *In the book, he interweaves mini-lectures on a variety of philosophical and scientific topics with his account of a motorcycle trip in the northwestern United States undertaken with his son and, for part of the journey, with his married friends, John and Sylvia. In the passage below, Pirsig contrasts John and Sylvia's aversion to technology with their utter and total dependence upon it. This provides the entry point to a brief discussion that relates to the central theme of the book. He then goes on to illustrate this central theme—the relationship between humans and technology—through his discussion of the language used to describe the parts of a motorcycle. His book became something of a popular manifesto for the 1970s.*

Robert M. Pirsig, *Zen and the Art of Motorcycle Maintenance: An Inquiry into Values**

It was cold all right, but not *that* cold. How do John and Sylvia ever get through the Minnesota winters? I wonder. There's kind of a glaring inconsistency here,

---

*Robert M. Pirsig (1974), *Zen and the Art of Motorcycle Maintenance: An Inquiry into Values*, New York: Morrow, pp. 51–52, 77–79.

that's almost too obvious to dwell on. If they can't stand physical discomfort and they can't stand technology, they've got a little compromising to do. They depend on technology and condemn it at the same time. I'm sure they know that and that just contributes to their dislike of the whole situation. They're not presenting a logical thesis, they're just reporting how it is. But three farmers are coming into town now, rounding the corner in that brand-new pickup truck. I'll bet with them it's just the other way around. They're going to show off that truck and their tractor and that new washing machine and they'll have the tools to fix them if they go wrong, and know how to use the tools. They *value* technology. And they're the ones who need it the *least*. If all technology stopped tomorrow, these people would know how to make out. It would be rough, but they'd survive. John and Sylvia and Chris and I would be dead in a week. This condemnation of technology is ingratitude, that's what it is.

A motorcycle may be divided into normal running functions and special operator-controlled functions.

Normal running functions may be divided into functions during the intake cycle, functions during the compression cycle, functions during the power cycle and functions during the exhaust cycle.

And so on. I could go on about which functions occur in their proper sequence during each of the four cycles, then go on to the operator-controlled functions and that would be a very summary description of the underlying form of a motorcycle. It would be extremely short and rudimentary, as descriptions of this sort go. Almost any one of the components mentioned can be expanded on indefinitely. I've read an entire engineering volume on contact points alone, which are just a small but vital part of the distributor. There are other types of engines than the single-cylinder Otto engine described here: two-cycle engines, multiple cylinder engines, diesel engines. Wankel engines—but this example is enough.

This description would cover the "what" of the motorcycle in terms of components, and the "how" of the engine in terms of function. It would badly need a "where" analysis in the form of an illustration, and also a "why" analysis in the form of engineering principles that led to this particular conformation of parts. But the purpose here isn't exhaustively to analyze the motorcycle. It's to provide a starting point, an example of a mode of understanding of things which will itself become an object of analysis.

There's certainly nothing strange about this description at first hearing. It sounds like something from a beginning textbook on the subject, or perhaps a first lesson in a vocational course. What is unusual about it is seen when it ceases to be a mode of discourse and becomes an object of discourse. Then certain things can be pointed to.

The first thing to be observed about this description is so obvious you have to hold it down or it will drown out every other observation. This is: It is just duller than dishwater. Yah-da, yah-da, yah-da, carburetor, gear ratio, compression, yah-da-yah, piston, plugs, intake, yah-da-yah, on and on and on. This is the romantic face of the classic mode. Dull, awkward and ugly. Few romantics get beyond that point.

But if you can hold down that most obvious observation, some other things can be noticed that do not first appear.

The first is that the motorcycle, so described, is almost impossible to understand unless you already know how one works. The immediate surface impressions that are essential for primary understanding are gone. Only the underlying form is left.

The second is that the observer is missing. The description doesn't say that to see the piston you must remove the cylinder head. "You" aren't anywhere in the picture. Even the "operator" is a kind of personalityless robot whose performance of a function on the machine is completely mechanical. There are no real subjects in this description. Only objects exist that are independent of any observer.

The third is that the words "good" and "bad" and all their synonyms are completely absent. No value judgments have been expressed anywhere, only facts.

The fourth is that there is a knife moving here. A very deadly one; an intellectual scalpel so swift and so sharp you sometimes don't see it moving. You get the illusion that all those parts are just there and are being named as they exist. But they can be named quite differently and organized quite differently depending on how the knife moves.

Questions

1. Pirsig criticizes John and Sylvia for their "ingratitude" for modern technology. What attitude does he take toward technology in these passages?
2. In particular, what larger points does he make in reference to the language used to describe a motorcycle and its parts?
3. What is the "knife" to which he refers in the last paragraph of the above passage? Why does he choose that terminology?
4. Is technology value-neutral? Does it mean whatever we want it to mean?

FIGURE 21: L. S. Lowry, *Industrial Landscape*, 1955. Courtesy of the Tate Gallery, London.

L. S. Lowry (1887–1976) hailed from the area near Manchester, one of the leading industrial cities in England. Friedrich Engels has based his 1845 treatise on *The Condition of the Working Class in England* on his experience there, calling attention to some of the worst abuses of the Industrial Revolution. Lowry painted a number of industrial scenes from the twentieth century and showed special interest in the relationship between technology and the human beings who worked in the factories of northern England.

Questions
1. Is this painting merely descriptive or does it make a statement about industrial technology and its relationship to humanity?
2. How would you describe the style of the painting?
3. What would you regard as the historical significance of this painting in the context of the 1960s compared to if it had been painted in the nineteenth, or even early twentieth, century?

Chapter Questions

1. How might Fanon have reacted to de Gaulle's discussion of the Algerian situation? How do you think de Gaulle might have reacted to Fanon's interpretation of colonialism?
2. Could Fanon's discussion of the settler-native relationship be applied to the relationship between the white majority and African-Americans in the southern United States as described by Martin Luther King? If so, why do you think that Fanon advocates violence, whereas King believes that only nonviolent civil disobedience will work?
3. Mao Zedong wrote poetry from a very different perspective and position than the Western songwriters featured in this chapter. How specifically would you compare and contrast his poems to the lyrics of Lennon and McCartney and Mitchell?
4. Do you see a relationship between the treatment of technology by Joni Mitchell, Robert Pirsig, and S. L. Lowry?

CHAPTER FOURTEEN

Religious Fundamentalism and Secularism in the Modern World

INTRODUCTION

Until about 1979, the topic of religious fundamentalism in the modern world would have seemed an unlikely choice to which to devote a chapter in a historical sourcebook. It is also highly unlikely that one would have thought to include a chapter on secularism, which most people would have regarded as the status quo and just part of the background to whatever other topics might be included. However, a number of historical developments since 1979 have made religious fundamentalism and its relationship with secularism an essential topic for understanding the modern, or postmodern, world. First, religious fundamentalism, by its very existence, has called attention to the extent to which modern culture has become increasingly secular. However, at the same time it has called attention to the growing importance of religion as a response to the secular nature of so much of modern life.

The dynamic power of religious fundamentalism and its potential for challenging the status quo first manifested itself during this period in Iran in 1979. Islam, like all religions, has experienced periodic reform movements and attempts to purify the religion from worldly influences, but there was something different about the Iranian revolution that overthrew the American-backed Shah Mohammed Reza Pahlavi (1919–80) in that year. The proponents of what one might call the "New Islam" (although they would undoubtedly call it a return to original Islam, much as the Protestant reformers of the sixteenth century viewed their Bible-based faith as original Christianity) shared with their historical predecessors a desire to see political leaders enforce the sharia, or Islamic law, as their religious duty. However, they also called for more than this. They called for an attack on Western influences and often on Westerners themselves, beginning with the seizure of fifty-two American hostages in Iran in November 1979 and culminating in devastating plane attacks on the World Trade Center in New York City and the Pentagon in Washington, DC, on September 11, 2001.

The terrorist attacks that struck the United States on 9/11 were actually part of a series of such attacks conducted by Islamic radicals under the banner of "jihad," or religious warfare. Pre-9/11 attacks included three bombings aimed at US targets in Aden, Yemen, in 1992, a previous explosion at the World Trade Center in New York in 1993, a series of attacks on US embassies in Africa in 1998, and the bombing of the *USS Cole* off the coast of Aden in October 2000.

The first selection in this chapter provides a definition of jihad by Abul A'la Mawdudi (1903–79), an important Islamic thinker who was among the first to see the politically radical potential in Islam and to call for the founding of an

Islamic state that could resist the challenge to the religion's foundations from modern secularism. Mawdudi was a systematic thinker who presented his ideas in a coherent and organized manner that attracted a following in Egypt and elsewhere in the Islamic world. He believed that Islam, rather than Marxism or any other secular ideology such as nationalism, held the key to the political freedom of Islamic peoples.

Developments in the Islamic world always had the potential to affect Israel, which has struggled to affirm its right to existence in Palestine in the face of Arab resistance since the founding of the Israeli state in 1948. However, the political reality of the state of Israel has always represented something of a conundrum for Jewish religious thinkers in and of itself. For example, this chapter includes a passage from the Jewish historian, Aviezer Ravitzky (b. 1945), dealing with the phenomenon of "Messianism," which represents an important concept in the sacred history of the Jews. In his book, *Messianism, Zionism, and Jewish Religious Radicalism*, Ravitzky explores the religious divisions within Judaism over the issue of Zionism, or the state as the fulfillment of Jewish aspirations and the key to Jewish identity. While some Zionist groups view the Israeli state as divinely inspired, others reject Zionism as a secular ideology that precludes the belief in a Messiah who will bring salvation from above.

A similar division exists among American Christians regarding the religious foundations of the United States. The appearance of Christian fundamentalism as a potent force in American politics largely coincided with the 1980 election to the presidency of Ronald Reagan, even though his predecessor, Jimmy Carter, was a Southern Baptist. Reagan seemed to represent a return to what many consider "traditional moral values" after the cultural turbulence and political dysfunction of the 1960s and 1970s associated with race riots, the counterculture, the Vietnam War, and Watergate scandal. Whereas Carter had been a Democrat, Christian fundamentalists such as Pat Robertson (b. 1930), a prominent and charismatic television evangelist from Virginia Beach, Virginia, aligned themselves with the Reagan Republicans and infused new energy into the party. Robertson and others attempted to rewrite American history and redefine the United States as a Christian nation. He and his supporters were as determined to have the US government rule according to Christian moral principles as Islamic fundamentalists were to see the sharia enforced. Robertson himself made an unsuccessful bid for the presidency in 1988, after which he continued to interpret contemporary history within a Christian framework. His perspective can be seen in the excerpt below from his book on *The New World Order*, which became a popular catchphrase after the end of the Cold War and its use by President George H. W. Bush in his 1991 State of the Union address.

Meanwhile, American Christians since 1979 have increasingly become divided themselves along religious lines over the difference between fundamentalist and moderate, or what the religious thinker Bruce Bawer (b. 1956) calls "liberal," Christianity, a term that he explains in the passage below. A major problem, however, is that much of the general public has remained unaware of this divide because of the tendency of the contemporary media to define all religion, including Christianity, in fundamentalist terms. Bawer points out in the introduction of his book *Stealing Jesus* that most people tend to avoid talking about religion to the same degree that conversations about sex were taboo in the Victorian era; therefore, he argues, the general public tends to get a skewed view of religion, based on what is presented in the media. Because some Muslims believe in a jihad supported by terror and these receive the bulk of the media attention, many people assume that all Muslims must believe this. Because the most vocal Christians in the political arena and the press are fundamentalist Christians, according to Bawer, fundamentalism has come to define Christianity for many people.

Bawer challenges this assumption for Christianity, but the same division between fundamentalists and moderates exists among Muslims and Jews as well. That, in fact, is the major premise of the important book, *The Battle for God*, by Karen Armstrong (b. 1944), a religious scholar and the author of a score of books on religious history. In this book, an excerpt from which appears below, she points out that the main "battle for God" in the modern world does not involve conflict between peoples of different faiths, but rather between fundamentalists and moderates within each of the monotheistic religions of Judaism, Christianity, and Islam.

Finally, the chapter ends with one dissenting voice, that of the cultural and literary critic, Harold Bloom (b. 1930), who turned to what he calls "religious criticism" in his 1992 book, *The American Religion*. Bloom sees an underlying thread connecting various religious denominations in the United States that holds together a common "American" religion. The reader of this chapter is invited to consider carefully the sources included in it and to make up her or his mind not only about the validity of the positions taken by each of these writers, but more importantly, about their historical significance as well.

ABUL A'LA MAWDUDI, INTRODUCTION

Abul A'la Mawdudi (1903–79) was born in India, where he founded a new Islamic party, the Jamaat-e-Islami, in 1941. He moved to Pakistan in 1947, as did many Muslims during a civil war that divided India and Pakistan.

In Pakistan, however, Mawdudi frequently ran afoul of the authorities, while at the same time continuing to develop his religious and political thought. Mawdudi crafted a political philosophy that was informed by the modern world but that reemphasized the obligation that political leaders of Islamic countries had to enforce the sharia and the responsibility that the people had to obey it. His other books include Islamic Way of Life *and* The Islamic Law and Constitution, *both of which develop his ideas on the relationship between Islam and the state. As he indicates below, he does not regard Islam as merely a religion, but as a powerful force for good in the world based on what it really means to follow God's will for humanity. The passage below, in addition to defining what he means by "jihad" (and he prefers this word to "war"), speaks to his conception of Islam as an ideology that transcends normal religious or political categorization. He compares Islam to other revolutionary ideologies at the same time that he rejects such a comparison.*

Abul A'la Mawdudi, *Jihad in Islam**

What Jihad Really is?

So if Islam be a "Religion" and the Muslims are a "Nation," "Jihad" (on account of which it has been accorded the dignity of "The Best of all Prayers" in Islam) becomes useless term. But the truth is that Islam is not the name of a "Religion," nor is "Muslim" the title of a "Nation." In reality Islam is a revolutionary ideology and programme which seeks to alter the social order of the whole world and rebuild it in conformity with its own tenets and ideals. "Muslim" is the title of that International Revolutionary Party organized by Islam to carry into effect its revolutionary programme. And "Jihād" refers to that revolutionary struggle and utmost exertion which the Islamic Party brings into play to achieve this objective.

Like all revolutionary ideologies, Islam shuns the use of current vocabulary and adopts a terminology of its own, so that its own revolutionary ideals may be distinguished from common ideals. The word "Jihad" belongs to this particular terminology of Islam. Islam purposely rejected the word "harb" and other Arabic words bearing the same meaning of "war" and used the word "Jihad" which is synonymous with "struggle," though more forceful and wider in connotation. The nearest correct meaning of the word "Jihād" in English can be expressed as under:

"To exert one's utmost endeavour in promoting a cause."

Source: Abul A'la Mawdudi (1939), *Jihad in Islam*, Lebanon: Holy Koran Publishing House, pp. 5–7. Available online at http://www.muhammadanism.org/Terrorism/jihah_in_islam/jihad_in_islam.pdf.

The question is why was the use of this new word preferred to the exclusion of all older synonyms? The answer to this question is none else than that the word "war" was and is still being used for struggles between Nations and States which are waged for the achievement of individual or national self-interest. The motive forces behind these conflicts are such individual or collective purposes as are completely devoid of any ideological bias or support for certain principles. Since Islamic War does not belong to this category, Islam shuns the use of the word "war" altogether. Islam has no vested interest in promoting the cause of this or that Nation. The hegemony of this or that State on the face of this earth is irrelevant to Islam. The sole interest of Islam is the welfare of mankind. Islam has its own particular ideological standpoint and practical programme to carry out reforms for the welfare of mankind. Islam wishes to destroy all states and governments anywhere on the face of the earth which are opposed to the ideology and programme of Islam regardless of the country or the Nation which rules it. The purpose of Islam is to set up a state on the basis of its own ideology and programme, regardless of which nation assumes the role of the standard-bearer of Islam or the rule of which nation is undermined in the process of the establishment of an ideological Islamic State. Islam requires the earth—not just a portion, but the whole planet—not because the sovereignty over the earth should be wrested from one nation or several nations and vested in one particular nation, but because the entire mankind should benefit from the ideology and welfare programme or what would be truer to say from "Islam" which is the programme of well-being for all humanity. Towards this end, Islam wishes to press into service all forces which can bring about a revolution and a composite term for the use of all these forces is "Jihad." To change the outlook of the people and initiate a mental revolution among them through speech or writing is a form of "Jihad." To alter the old tyrannical social system and establish a new just order of life by the power of sword is also "Jihad" and to expend goods and exert physically for this cause is "Jihad" too.

Questions

1. What is Mawdudi's definition of "jihad"?
2. Why does he insist on the use of this precise term instead of allowing for other synonyms to be used in its place?
3. Could Mawdudi's words be used as a justification for terrorism? Why or why not?

FIGURE 22: Woman walking past mural depicting heroes of the Islamic revolution, including Iman Khomeini, Hashan, Esfahan, Iran. Courtesy of Getty Images.

Questions

1. What is the mural that appears in this photograph meant to convey about the Iranian revolution of 1979?
2. What does this photo symbolically reveal about gender relations in Iran and Islamic fundamentalism?
3. What might the photographer have been trying to convey with the juxtaposition of these two images—the woman and the mural?

AVIEZER RAVITZKY, *MESSIANISM, ZIONISM, AND JEWISH RELIGIOUS RADICALISM*, INTRODUCTION

Aviezer Ravitzky is the author of many books and articles, most of which deal with the relationship between religion and politics in Israel since the founding of the Jewish state in 1948. In fact, for a time he codirected the "Religion and State" project at the Israel Democracy Institute in Jerusalem, a prominent think tank since its foundation in 1991. He is also an expert on Jewish religious thought and philosophy, with a special interest in religious radicalism. The passages below, taken from his most important book on that subject, refers to the philosophy of Rabbi Zvi Yehuda Kook, who believed that Jews had a sacred obligation to reclaim all of the land that had belonged to Israel in biblical times because that was a precondition to God's redemption of the Jewish people. Zionist groups such as those led by Rabbi Kook have put great pressure on the Israeli state not to yield land to the Palestinian Arabs as a precondition for peace. However, this has aligned them not only against the Arabs, but also against many in the West who have sought to restrict the territorial expansion of Israel in order to broker a peace agreement between Israel and the Palestinians. Israeli politicians have thus had to deal with religious fundamentalism as much as have the political leaders of the United States and those of many Muslim countries. In the following passages, Ravitzky explains the concept of Jewish Messianism and its connection to the founding of the state of Israel.

Aviezer Ravitzky, *Messianism, Zionism, and Jewish Religious Radicalism**

The nationalist ideology of Rabbi Kook and his followers views the history of Zionism as an inevitable and decidedly messianic process, leading to the realization of prophetic predictions: "the State of Israel as the fulfillment of the biblical vision of redemption." Messianism is no longer to be seen as the antithesis of concrete reality. It is no longer merely a critique of what is, nor is it addressed only to the future. Rather, messianic redemption springs from present events; it is embodied and realized in them. . . .

The establishment of the State of Israel and the reclaiming of the Land of Israel thus stand at the very heart of a decisively messianic process. This being

---

*Aviezer Ravitzky (1996), *Messianism, Zionism, and Jewish Religious Radicalism*, translated by Michael Swirsky and Jonathan Chipman, Chicago: University of Chicago Press, pp. 80, 82–84.

the case, the Jewish state can no longer be portrayed as a merely historical or social phenomenon; its very existence is fraught with religious meaning, and in the final analysis it appears to embody something quite metaphysical. "Zionism is a heavenly matter," Kook went so far as to say. "The State of Israel is a divine entity, our holy and exalted state!" In other words, the tidings of the redemption of Israel, the consciousness of present messianic realization, have not only toppled "the wall separating us from our land"; they have eliminated at one stroke the formidable barrier between the theological and the political, the heavenly and the earthly. . . .

Inevitably, the concrete actions of the Jewish state too become hallowed. "The holiness of the divine service [*avodah*, literally, work], the service of the Temple, is extended to the work of the state as a whole, both practical and spiritual, both public and private," wrote Zvi Yehudah Kook. By the same token, Israel's wars, too, come to be seen not merely in terms of national survival (in halakhic terms, "rescuing Israel from the enemy") or reclaiming the ancestral land. They are portrayed in ethical and theological terms, as a mighty struggle to uproot evil and achieve universal rectification.

"From the perspective of faith we see the divine hand spread over us, and especially over our wars. It leads us to recognize the righteousness of our actions and our wars and their indispensability, not only for us but for all the nations!" Thus writes Rabbi Zvi Tau, a leading light of this camp in the last two decades. "The wars of Israel are essentially wars against war, for whoever rises up against Israel rises up against the light of God in the world, which is the supernal peace!" A struggle that appears to be over particular national interests is in fact over universal human values. This conclusion is, in fact, a direct consequence of the peremptory identification of the political Israel and the theological one. From this point of view, the State of Israel's enemies are by definition enemies of the God of Israel, "the exaltation of Israel is the exaltation of heaven," military victory is tantamount to spiritual victory, and "the wars of Israel represent the steps of the Messiah, marching toward his own coronation."

Questions

1. What does Ravitzky mean when he says that "a struggle that appears to be over particular national interests is in fact over universal human values"?
2. Have Messianic Jews such as Rabbi Kook changed the meaning of Zionism, according to Ravitzky?
3. Why might be the appeal of Messianic Judaism? What might constitute some of the main objections of its opponents?

PAT ROBERTSON, INTRODUCTION

Pat Robertson was among a group of Christian fundamentalists that also included Jerry Falwell and Tim LaHaye who began to weigh in on politics and world events in the 1980s. Politically conservative, Christian fundamentalists provided a strong base of support for the Republican Ronald Reagan, who served two terms as president from 1981 to 1989. Reagan's tough anticommunist stance and his appeal to American patriotism, individualism, and traditional moral values all strongly appealed to the Christian right. However, when the Cold War ended in 1989 (see Chapter 16 of this volume), Christian fundamentalists had to come to terms with a new set of international realities, which they, however, continued to try to fit into their eschatological view of history. In the passage below, from his 1991 book, The New World Order, *Robertson attempts to do just that.*

Pat Robertson, "The Battle Ahead"*

How does the word of the Bible relate to the events of today? It is clear that the counterfeit world order will be waiting for the satanic dictator. It just doesn't happen spontaneously. Therefore, it must be prepared for him in advance by someone. The next conclusion is inescapable. Satan knows that a world government must soon be prepared for the man whom he is preparing to receive his particular empowerment and authority.

Such a world government can come together only after the Christian United States is out of the way. After all, the rest of the world can federate any time it wants to, but a vital, economically strong, Christian United States would have at its disposal the spiritual and material force to prohibit a worldwide satanic dictator from winning his battle. With America still free and large, Satan's schemes will at best be only partially successful. From these shores could come the television, radio, and printed matter to counter an otherwise all-out world news blackout. An independent America could point out Satan's lies. If America is free, people everywhere can hope for freedom. And if America goes down, all hope is lost to the rest of the world.

It is also clear that Satan's strategy will include a frontal assault on Israel. Rest assured that the next objective of the presently constituted new world order, under the present United Nations, will be to make Israel its target. The precedent has been set by all the action against Iraq.

A recalcitrant nation whose action does not accord with United Nations policy may be disciplined by military force. That is the newest law of world

---

*Pat Robertson (1991), *The New World Order*, Dallas: World Publishing, pp. 256–57.

order. The United Nations General Assembly has already voted to brand Zionism as racism. Surely we can expect, sooner or later, an unreasonable demand for Israel to vacate control of the West Bank and the half of her capital city in East Jerusalem.

Although Israel may be reluctantly conciliatory in regard to territory, it is absolutely adamant about not surrendering the city won by King David almost three thousand years ago, then won again by modern Israel in 1967. And if Israel refuses to vacate the Holy City, there will be war—under the world order as it is now constituted.

Beyond that, Satan will launch a war against the Christian people. The Book of Revelation speaks of a flood of water coming after Israel and its seed. I see that as false propaganda, ridicule, and demeaning comments—anything to ruin the influence of Christians and their ability to block Satan's plans. The Nazis used this technique against the Jews in Germany. First, they were ridiculed and blamed for the economic collapse of Germany. Then they were denied a few rights of citizenship. Then they were crowded into restricted ghettos. And finally their property and their lives were taken from them.

Above all, the propaganda was intended to make ordinary Germans uncomfortable and afraid to associate with the Jews, then suspicious of them, then hostile toward them, and then glad to be rid of them. This very technique is being used already against Christian people. It will intensify in years to come as the spiritual battle becomes more intense.

Questions

1. Does Robertson's view of history depend on what happens in the future? Does it allow him to rationalize anything that happens as consistent with his view of history?
2. How does his worldview differ from that of fundamentalists of other religions? What does it have in common?
3. Are there resonances of a Cold War mentality in Robertson's views of the "new world order"?

BRUCE BAWER, *STEALING JESUS,* INTRODUCTION

Bruce Bawer's 1997 book, Stealing Jesus: How Fundamentalism Betrays Christianity, *is part of a growing literature that points to a middle ground between faith and reason and rejects the extreme viewpoints of fundamentalist Christianity and radical atheism. This literature includes books as diverse as Deepak Chopra's* The Third Jesus *(Harmony Books, 2008) and Russell Shorto's* Descartes's Bones: A Skeletal History of the Conflict between Faith and Reason *(Vintage, 2009). Bawer puts a greater emphasis on Jesus' message of love and interprets his death more as a manifestation of his love for humanity than as a legalistic act of atonement for their sins. Bawer, who has also written in defense of gay rights and critiquing radical Islam, disavows any political label for himself and sees himself as an advocate for democracy and individual rights more than anything else. But in* Stealing Jesus, *he offers a powerful, if controversial challenge to religious fundamentalists for picking and choosing the teachings of Jesus that support their world view while ignoring some of the more spiritual, humanistic, and intellectual elements of the Christian faith and the teachings of Jesus.*

Bruce Bawer, *Stealing Jesus**

. . . Simply stated, conservative Christianity focuses primarily on law, doctrine, and authority; liberal Christianity focuses on love, spiritual experience, and what Baptists call the priesthood of the believer. If conservative Christians emphasize the Great Commission—the resurrected Christ's injunction, at the end of the Gospel according to Matthew to "go to all nations and make them my disciples"—liberal Christians place more emphasis on the Great Commandment, which in Luke's Gospel reads as follows: "Love the Lord your God with all your heart, and with all your soul, with all your strength, and with all your mind; and your neighbor as yourself."

Am I suggesting that conservative Christians are without love or that liberal Christians are lawless? No. I merely make this distinction: Conservative Christianity understands a Christian to be someone who subscribes to a specific set of theological propositions about God and the afterlife, and who professes to believe that by subscribing to those propositions, accepting Jesus Christ as savior, and (except in the case of the most extreme separatist fundamentalists) evangelizing, he or she evades God's wrath and wins salvation (for Roman Catholics, good works also count); liberal Christianity, meanwhile, tends to identify Christianity with the experience of God's abundant love and with the commandment to love God and one's neighbor. If, for conservative Christians, outreach generally means zealous proselytizing of the "unsaved," for liberal Christians it tends to mean social programs directed at those in need.

---

*Bruce Bawer (1997), *Stealing Jesus: How Fundamentalism Betrays Christianity*, New York: Crown Publishers, Inc., pp. 5, 300–01.

Over the course of the twentieth century, Americans—the vast majority of whom identify themselves as Christian—have grown used to a secular mainstream culture in which religion has little or no place. This marginalization of religion has greatly redounded to the benefit of the Church of Law—for a culture in which religion is not a regular subject of serious, free public meditation and discussion is one in which constructing, unreflective legalistic faith has a much more powerful sway over people's minds than it would otherwise have. When religion *does* enter into today's secular culture, moreover, it is almost invariably treated with kid gloves—and a culture in which questioning of irrational and morally offensive metaphysical proposition is discouraged is, again, one in which legalistic faith will enjoy a natural advantage.

Indeed, all of the elements of secular mainstream culture in America today—high and low, left and right—have come together to reinforce in the public mind the view that anything calling itself Christianity thereby places itself above criticism or at the very least establishes itself as something that must be handled with particular delicacy. As a result, religion has, in this century, rarely been examined in the public square in the kind of open, honest way that would almost certainly have made Americans more well-informed and contemplative than they are in matters of religion—and that would accordingly have kept millions of Americans from considering legalistic Christianity (to the extent that they consider it at all) as the serious, traditional, and moral entity that it represents itself as being.

Questions

1. Is Bawer attacking a straw man in his critique of fundamentalist Christianity? What arguments might be presented on both sides of this question?
2. What is the most important thing for which Bawer seems to be calling in the above excerpts?
3. What does Bawer see as the nature of the relationship between secularism and religion?

KAREN ARMSTRONG, INTRODUCTION

Karen Armstrong became a well-known and influential authority on the history of religion following the 1993 publication of A History of God: The 4,000 Year Quest of Judaism, Christianity, and Islam. *In* The Battle for God, *she continues her exploration of that subject by tracing the rise of religious fundamentalism in these three monotheistic and closely related faiths from the late fifteenth to the end of the twentieth century. Although she finds the historical roots of fundamentalism in the early modern period, she regards the increased popularity of the movement in all three religions during the twentieth century as a peculiarly modern phenomenon that could not exist without the secularism that it opposes and the threats—real or perceived—to religion in modern times. Furthermore, the twentieth century produced fascist and communist mass movements that caused many to lose confidence in humanity's ability to fulfill the dream of creating a better world based on the principles of the Enlightenment and the Scientific Revolution. The religious fundamentalists have attempted to bring society back to a faith-based ideology, but one completely informed by the modern world that they inhabit. In her "Afterword" to* The Battle for God, *Armstrong reflects on the unique characteristics of modern fundamentalism and its larger historical context.*

Karen Armstrong, *The Battle for God*, "Afterword"*

We cannot be religious in the same way as our ancestors in the premodern conservative world, when myths and rituals of faith helped people to accept limitations that were essential to agrarian civilization. We are now oriented to the future, and those of us who have been shaped by the rationalism of the modern world cannot easily understand the old forms of spirituality. We are not unlike Newton, one of the first people in the Western world to be wholly imbued by the scientific spirit, who found it impossible to understand mythology. However hard we try to embrace conventional religion, we have a natural tendency to see truth as factual, historical, and empirical. . . .

Hence, there is a void at the heart of modern culture, which Western people experienced at an early stage of their scientific revolution. Pascal recoiled in dread from the emptiness of the cosmos; Descartes saw the human being as the sole living denizen of an inert universe; Hobbes imagined God retreating from the world, and Nietzsche declared that God was dead: humanity had lost its orientation and was hurtling toward an infinite nothingness. But others have felt emancipated by the loss of faith, and liberated from the restrictions it had always imposed. . . . Others put their faith in the ideals of the Enlightenment, looking forward to a future in which human beings will become more rational and tolerant; they venerate the sacred liberty of the individual instead of a distant, imaginary God. . . .

---

*Karen Armstrong (2000), *The Battle for God*, New York: Ballantine Books, pp. 365–71.

Nevertheless, a large number of people still want to be religious and have tried to evolve new forms of faith. Fundamentalism is just one of these modern religious experiments, and, as we have seen, it has enjoyed a certain success in putting religion squarely on the international agenda, but it has often lost sight of the most sacred values of the confessional faiths. Fundamentalists have turned the *mythos* of their religion into *logos*, either by insisting that their dogmas are scientifically true, or by transforming their complex mythology into a streamlined ideology. . . . By insisting that the truths of Christianity are factual and scientifically demonstrable, American Protestant fundamentalists have created a caricature of both science and religion. Those Jews and Muslims who have presented their faith in a reasoned, systematic way to compete with other secular ideologies have also distorted their tradition, narrowing it down to a single point by a process of ruthless selection. As a result, all have neglected the more tolerant, inclusive, and compassionate teachings and have cultivated theologies of rage, resentment, and revenge. On occasion, this has even led a small minority to pervert religion by using it to sanction murder. Even the vast majority of fundamentalists, who are opposed to such acts of terror, tend to be exclusive and condemnatory of those who do not share their views.

But fundamentalist fury reminds us that our modern culture imposes extremely difficult demands on human beings. It has certainly empowered us, opened new worlds, broadened our horizons, and enabled many of us to live happier, healthier lives. Yet it has often dented our self-esteem. At the same time as our rational worldview has proclaimed that humans are the measure of all things, and liberated us from an unseemly dependence upon a supernatural God, it has also revealed our frailty, vulnerability, and lack of dignity. Copernicus unseated us from the center of the universe, and relegated us to a peripheral role. Kant declared that we could never be certain that our ideas corresponded to any reality outside our own heads. Darwin suggested that we were simply animals, and Freud showed that far from being wholly rational creatures, human beings were at the mercy of the powerful, irrational forces of the unconscious, which could be accessed only with great difficulty. This, indeed, was demonstrated by the modern experience. Despite the cult of rationality, modern history has been punctuated by witch-hunts and world wars which have been explosions of unreason. Without the ability to approach the deeper religions of the psyche, which the old myths, liturgies, and mystical practices of the best conservative faith once provided, it seemed that reason sometimes lost its mind in our brave new world. At the end of the twentieth century, the liberal myth that humanity is progressing to an ever more enlightened and tolerant state looks as fantastic as any of the other millennial myths we have considered in this book. Without the constraints of a "higher," mythical truth, reason can on occasion become demonic and commit crimes that are as great as, if not greater than, any of the atrocities perpetuated by the fundamentalists.

First, it is important to recognize that these theologies and ideologies are rooted in fear. The desire to define doctrines, erect barriers, establish borders, and segregate the faithful in a sacred enclave where the law is stringently observed springs from that terror of extinction which has made all fundamentalists, at one time or another, believe that the secularists were about to wipe them out. The modern world, which seems so exciting to a liberal, seems Godless, drained of meaning, and even satanic to a fundamentalist. . . .

Second, it is important to realize that these movements are not an archaic throwback to the past; they are modern, innovative, and modernizing. Protestant fundamentalists read the Bible in a literal, rational way that is quite different from the more mystical, allegorical approach of premodern spirituality. . . .

. . . If fundamentalists must evolve a more compassionate assessment of their enemies in order to be true to their religious traditions, secularists must also be more faithful to the benevolence, tolerance, and respect for humanity which characterizes modern culture at its best, and address themselves more empathetically to the fears, anxieties, and needs which so many of their fundamentalist neighbors experience but which no society can safely ignore.

Questions
1. What is Armstrong's main critique of religious fundamentalism?
2. At the same time that she criticizes some aspects of religious fundamentalism, how successful is she at explaining its rise and popularity in the modern world?
3. What is the appeal of secularism versus religious fundamentalism and vice versa? What are some of the problems identified by Armstrong associated with secularism?

HAROLD BLOOM, *THE AMERICAN RELIGION*, INTRODUCTION

Harold Bloom, who acknowledges himself as an agnostic Jew, has nonetheless written a compelling and controversial book about religion in the United States, in which he argues that a unique post-Christian form of Protestantism has become an integral part of American culture. Bloom's main field was literary criticism, on which he established himself as one of the leading authorities in numerous books and as a professor at prestigious institutions such as New York University and Yale. He absorbed some criticism for posing as a religious critic, and even for inventing the term "religious criticism" to serve his own interests when The American Religion *first appeared in 1992. Nevertheless, his provocative ideas represent an interesting complement to the other writings in this chapter, while still speaking to the importance of religious groups such as the Mormons and the Southern Baptists, for an understanding of modern religious history. In his own way, Bloom contributed to the identification of American Christianity with its more extreme denominations at the expense of the millions of Christians who continue to worship in those churches that might be considered more moderate or even liberal. Bloom was not optimistic about the religious divide in the United States and its potential for future conflict or even violence. Below he offers his own critique of modern religious fundamentalism.*

Harold Bloom, *The American Religion: The Emergence of the Post-Christian Nation**

What Fundamentalists cannot understand is that their attempted literalization of Scripture is itself a giant metaphor: a conversion of the Bible into a statue or an icon. It is in itself a restrictive interpretation, with not the slightest relation to the Bible's actual text. One of the great ironies of Protestant history is that the exaltation of Scripture, which in the seventeenth century endowed Baptists and other Protestants with freedom from institutional constraints and with spiritual autonomy, has become, as the twentieth century closes, the agency for depriving Baptists and other Protestants of their Christian Liberty, their soul competency to read and interpret the Bible, each person by her own Inner Light. In the Old Baptist Meeting House in Providence, Rhode Island, there stands a lectern as huge as an altar. There the Baptists of colonial America set their Bible as an emblem of spiritual freedom. Fundamentalism, in the America of the 1990s, is a frightening and degrading betrayal of the seventeenth-century Baptist dream of human dignity and freedom in fellowship with Jesus, the Word of God.

The overwhelming urgency (and viciousness) of Southern Baptist Fundamentalism surpasses all other American instances of that errancy, and

---

*Harold Bloom (1992), *The American Religion: The Emergence of the Post-Christian Nation*, New York: Simon and Schuster, pp. 243, 245, 293–94.

makes it shockingly similar to Iranian Shiite Fundamentalism or the worst excesses of the Neturei Karta in Israel. . . .

Christian Fundamentalism is essentially a North American phenomenon; except for the United States and Canada, it has an indigenous life only in Ulster. Its other worldwide manifestations tend to be exported from the United States. Yet I cannot regard it as anything but a parody of what I have called the American Religion. Its spiritual content, to the religious critic, is difficult to locate. This was not always so; there were some serious intellects involved in later nineteenth- through earlier twentieth-century Fundamentalism. Today, there are not, and yet Fundamentalism threatens to become almost a synonym for Evangelicalism in contemporary America. . . .

Humanly there is something quite cold about the religion of our climate. Our sacred frenzies are directed towards ourselves or towards the resurrected Jesus; the American Religion takes up the cross only as emblem of the risen God, not of the crucified man, if indeed it takes up the cross at all (the Mormons do not). Pentecostals and many other sectarians white and black experience a sacred violence as the Spirit hits them, but the violence assimilates very quickly to American secular violence, altogether as prevalent in the countryside as in the cities. The American Religion in itself is not violence, but confusion frequently attends both, and certainly our knowing is more often than not a violent knowing. A religion of the self is not likely to be a religion of peace, since the American self tends to define itself through its war against otherness. If your knowing ultimately tells you that you are beyond nature, having long preceded it, then your natural acts cannot sully you. No wonder, then, that salvation, once attained, cannot fall away from the American Religionist, no matter what he or she does. We export our culture abroad, low and high, and increasingly export the American Religion as well. If Woodrow Wilson proves correct, and we were intended to be a spirit among the nations of the world, then the twenty-first century will mark a full-scale return to the wars of religion.

Questions
1. How does Bloom say that Christian fundamentalists misuse the Bible?
2. Does Bloom make a convincing argument that Christian fundamentalism is part of a uniquely American religion since it is virtually unknown outside of North America?
3. What might account for the virtual absence of Christian fundamentalism in Europe?

Chapter Questions

1. Does Jewish Messianism, as described by Ravtizky, bear any similarity to the views expressed by Mawdudi with regard to Islam?
2. How does Robertson's defense of Christian history relate to that of St. Augustine in *The City of God* (see Volume I, Chapter 6)? Are there elements of Gnosticism in Robertson's worldview?
3. What criticisms of religious fundamentalism does Bloom offer here? How are they similar to or different from those of Bawer and Armstrong? What might account for the differences among these three authors in their approach to the topic?

CHAPTER FIFTEEN

Democracy and Dictatorship, 1970–89

INTRODUCTION

The two decades of the 1970s and 1980s saw the continuation of a number of political trends, some of which dated to the beginnings of the Cold War and some of which dated as far back as the French Revolution. In some ways the competing trends that had emerged in the previous two centuries met head-on in these decades. Classical nineteenth-century liberalism and individualism clashed with the socialist model of the welfare state brought about by the Great Depression and the Second World War. The "Third World" policy of nonalignment continued to compete with the attempt of the superpowers of the Cold War, the Soviet Union and the United States, to fight their battles by proxy around the world. In Latin America, right-wing military dictatorships, similar to those that had emerged in interwar Europe, struggled against socialist insurrection inspired by the ideas of Marx and Lenin. In South Africa, the civil rights movement continued the struggle against racist ideology that had begun in the southern United States. Finally, ideas of democracy competed with ideas of communist totalitarianism, as seen in the failed pro-democracy demonstrations in China in 1989. To illustrate the global nature of these trends, this chapter includes sources from outside of Europe, with one exception.

The starkest contrast between classical liberal economics (rebranded as "Conservatism") and the socialist model of the welfare state occurred in Britain more than in any other European state. Even in the countries of Western Europe, such as Sweden and Austria, where the government intervened most directly in the economy and provided cradle-to-the-grave benefits for its population, there existed a blend of capitalism and socialism, individualism and corporatism, free enterprise and government regulation. In Western Europe, governments generally proceeded by practical trial and error than by dogmatically imposing systematic economic theory as attempted by the Soviet Union and the communist governments of Eastern Europe. Despite their hostility to the Soviet Union and totalitarian style socialism, the experience of the Great Depression and the two world wars had convinced most people that the government had a responsibility to provide for its people. In the 1950s and 1960s, even the Conservative Party in Britain generally argued that it could run the welfare state better than the Labour Party, not that programs such as the National Health Service should be shut down. However, in those decades Western governments found it easier to fund these programs as a result of a growing economy and low unemployment rates. That became more difficult during the 1970s, when an oil embargo by the Organization of Petroleum Exporting Countries (OPEC) produced an energy crisis that contributed to inflation and a fairly severe economic downturn. Against this background, Margaret Thatcher rose to the head of the Conservative Party and became Prime Minister in 1979, promising an end to Britain's industrial decline, largely by relying on individual initiative and reducing the government's role in society and the economy.

A year after Margaret Thatcher became the first woman to serve as Prime Minister in Britain, its former colony, India, returned to power a female prime minister, Indira Gandhi (1917–84), who had previously served in that position from 1966 to 1977. The daughter of the former prime minister and leader of the Indian independence movement, Jawaharlal Nehru, Indira Gandhi had emerged in the late 1960s and early 1970s as a spokesperson for the developing nations of the world, giving her an importance that transcended Indian politics.

Unfortunately, many countries in the developing world still had their own internal conflicts to resolve. Even in India, religious divisions still plagued the country; Indira Gandhi provoked opposition from among the Sikhs in particular when she had a Sikh rebellion violently crushed in 1984, leaving a thousand people dead. A Sikh member of her bodyguard assassinated her later that year. Meanwhile, in the Central American countries of El Salvador and Nicaragua left-wing guerilla forces struggled against right-wing military dictatorships in conflicts that lasted decades but came to a head in both places in the late 1970s and 1980s. In El Salvador, the United States government during the presidency of Ronald Reagan attempted to intervene to support the military dictatorship to prevent another communist government similar to that of Cuba from emerging in the Western Hemisphere. US military aid helped the government of El Salvador in its struggle against the insurgents; in Nicaragua, a much more unified opposition under the Sandinistas managed to take control of the country in 1979. They retained power throughout the 1980s, despite the US government's ill-fated attempt to fund an overthrow of the newly-established regime through illegal arms sales to Iran.

In South Africa, Nelson Mandela, a lawyer in Johannesburg and one of the main leaders of the revolutionary front against the government-imposed system of racial segregation and discrimination known as apartheid, spent the entire period covered by this chapter in prison (1964–90). However, demands for his release and for an end to apartheid from inside and outside South Africa contributed to his freedom in 1990 and subsequent negotiations that led to an end to apartheid. Mandela told his own story of his role in ending apartheid and achieving reconciliation with his former enemies in his autobiography, *Long Walk to Freedom*, which serves as one of the sources for this chapter.

Finally, the 1970s and 1980s were revolutionary decades in China as well. Following the death of Mao Zedong and the end of the Cultural Revolution in 1976 (see Chapter 13), China embarked on a period of radical economic reform under Deng Xiaoping. Young people eager for a more democratic form of government in China assumed that Deng and the Chinese leadership would be receptive to political reform as well. When such changes had failed to materialize by the end of the 1980s, student leaders, including Shen Tong, excerpts from whose autobiography appear below, initiated a protest movement that, in Shen Tong's words, became "almost a revolution."

MARGARET THATCHER, *THE DOWNING STREET YEARS*, INTRODUCTION

Margaret Thatcher (1925–2013) began life as a grocer's daughter, but rose from her rather humble origins to become a lawyer and forge a successful career in politics, despite the disadvantages of being a woman in a male-dominated field. She served as minister for education in the Conservative government of Edward Heath in the early seventies, when the party introduced some of its first austerity measures, among them Thatcher's controversial decision to cut free milk with school lunches. This foreshadowed things to come during her term as prime minister from 1979 to 1990. Views of her leadership tend to fall into two contradictory camps. Some view her as the "Iron Lady," who restored British national pride and self-respect, successfully fought a war against Argentina over the Falkland Islands, made people more accountable and less dependent on government, and reversed trends of British economic decline and psychological defeatism. Others remember her as a hard-hearted conservative who lacked sympathy for the poor and underprivileged and under whom unemployment, homelessness, and racial tensions increased. However one views her politically, one cannot deny her historical impact or the historical forces that brought her to power in the first place. In the following excerpt from her memoirs, she discusses the causes and solutions for Britain's industrial decline.

Margaret Thatcher, *The Downing Street Years**

Britain's Industrial Problems
In the years since the war British politics had focused above all, on the debate about the proper role of the state in the operation of the economy. By 1979 and perhaps earlier, optimism about the beneficent effects of government intervention had largely disappeared. This change of attitude, for which I had long worked and argued, meant that many people who had not previously been Conservative supporters were now prepared to give our approach at least the benefit of the doubt. But I knew that this entirely justified lack of faith in the wisdom of the state must be matched by a renewed confidence in the creative capacity of everyone.

*Margaret Thatcher (1993), *The Downing Street Years*, New York: HarperCollins, pp. 92–93.

A sort of cynical disdain, often disguised as black humour, had come to characterize many people's attitude to industry and unions. We all enjoyed the film *I'm All Right, Jack*, but the problem was no laughing matter.

British goods will only be attractive if they can compete with the best on offer from other countries, in respect of quality, reliability and price, or some combination of the three, and the truth is that too often British industrial products were uncompetitive. This was not simply because the strong pound was making it difficult to sell abroad, but because our industrial reputation had steadily been eroded. In the end reputation reflects reality. Nothing less than changing that reality—fundamentally and for the better—would do.

In spite of what might seem the more immediate and pressing problems of strikes, price competitiveness and international recession, the root of Britain's industrial problem was low productivity. British living standards were lower than those of our principal competitors and the number of well-paid and reasonably secure jobs was smaller because we produced less per person than they did. Some twenty-five years earlier our productivity was the highest in western Europe; by 1979 it was among the lowest. The overmanning resulting from trade union restrictive practices was concealed unemployment; and beyond a certain point—certainly beyond the point we had reached in 1979—overmanning would bring down businesses and destroy existing jobs, and abort those which otherwise could have flourished. Outdated capacity and old jobs have to go to make the most of new opportunities. Yet the paradox which neither British trade unions nor the socialists were prepared to accept was that an increase in productivity is likely, initially, to reduce the number of jobs before creating the wealth that sustains new ones. Time and again we were asked when plants and companies closed, "where will the new jobs come from?" As the months went by, we could point to the expansion of self-employment and to industrial successes in aerospace, chemicals and North Sea oil. Increasingly we could also look to foreign investment, for example in electronics and cars. But the fact is that in a market economy government does not—and cannot—know where jobs will come from: if it did know, all those interventionist policies for "picking winners" and "backing success" would not have picked losers and compounded failure.

Questions
1. What does this passage say about Thatcher's personal economic and political philosophy?
2. On whom or what does she blame Britain's industrial decline and economic problems?
3. What does she propose as the solution to those problems?

INDIRA GANDHI, "ADDRESS AT THE THIRD CONFERENCE OF THE HEADS OF STATE OR GOVERNMENT OF NONALIGNED COUNTRIES," LUSAKA, SEPTEMBER 1970, INTRODUCTION

Indira Gandhi enjoyed a great deal of popularity in India during the early 1970s because of her concern for India's women, the poor, and the environment. She also nationalized India's banks, making her in some ways the opposite of Margaret Thatcher, at least in terms of her domestic policies. Unlike Thatcher, Gandhi's support came from those on the left of the political spectrum. Like Thatcher, however, Gandhi demonstrated strength and independence as a leader; in fact, her reputation suffered when she faced accusations of election fraud and declared a state of emergency to stay in power in 1975, jailing many of her political opponents without charges and without trial. Thus, like Thatcher, although for different reasons, she left a complex legacy, and guided India through a difficult transitional period of its history, but not without costs and a violation of democratic principles to remain in power. The source below, however, shows her in a different light—as one of the voices opposing the remnants of colonialism and asserting the independence of India and other nonaligned nations during the ongoing Cold War between the United States and the Soviet Union.

Indira Gandhi, "Address at the Third Conference of the Heads of State or Government of Nonaligned Countries," Lusaka, September 1970*

Here in Lusaka, we can feel the ebb and flow of the continuing battle against the remnants of colonialism in Angola and Mozambique. We can feel the vibrations of the struggle against the minority government in Zimbabwe, against the apartheid policies of the racist regime in the Union of South Africa, and of the stirrings of the national movements in Namibia and Guinea Bissau. These freedom fighters are engaged in the same battle as we were only recently. They are risking their lives for the same principles that we hold dear. All of us who are meeting here extend our support to these brave men and women.

As I said yesterday, the revolution of our times is unfinished, and the purpose of this conference is to formulate a clear program of action to carry it forward. This is the challenge that the decade of the seventies places before the nonaligned countries.

---

*Indira Gandhi (1975), *Indira Gandhi Speaks on Democracy, Socialism, and Third World Non-alignment*, edited by Henry A. Christman, New York: Taplinger Publishing Company, pp. 136, 138–39, 141–42.

Only a short while ago, the issues of war and peace, of the disposal of human beings and their destinies, were decided in a few capitals of the world. No longer is it so. Because millions of people in the resurgent continents of Asia, of Africa, of Latin America and the Caribbean have come into their own. Because we are determined that decisions involving us—whether concerning war or peace or the direction and pace of our social, economic and political development—could be made only by us, in our own way, and in our own countries. That is how nonalignment was born. It expressed our individual and collective sovereignty, our devotion to freedom and peace and our urgent need to give a better life to our people and the opportunity to live in freedom, in dignity and in peace. At no time was there any intention to set up a third world. . . .

Subjected to domination, exploitation and the humiliation of racial discrimination as we all had been, how could we compromise with racialism in any form? The pernicious theory that one man is superior to another merely on the ground of race or birth has been proved to be false, yet it continues to dominate the thinking of many.

We believe that today's world is a single entity. We are deeply convinced that by staying out of military pacts the nonaligned countries can use their collective wisdom and influence to tip the balance of power in favor of peace and international cooperation.

These have been the positive achievements of nonalignment. If today there is a weakening of the belief in the efficacy of military pacts, if historic animosities are giving way to essays in friendship and cooperation, if a breadth of realism is influencing international policies towards détente, the nations assembled here can claim some credit. However, this should not lull us into complacency, but encourage us to persevere.

The big powers have never accepted the validity of nonalignment. Neither colonialism nor racialism have vanished. The old comes back in new guise. There are subtle intrigues to undermine our self-confidence and to sow dissensions and mutual distrust among us. Powerful vested interests, domestic and foreign, are combining to erect new structures of neocolonialism. These dangers can be combated by our being united in our adherence to the basic tenets of nonalignment. . . .

The spirit of freedom goes hand in hand with the spirit of equality. Beyond the political problems of the unfinished revolution, there are complex and difficult economic tasks. However, a realistic appraisal of our natural resources, our capacities and our competence reveals the possibility for us to work together to reduce our dependence on those who do not respect our sovereignty so that economic leverage for thinly disguised political purposes cannot be used against us. Neocolonialism has no sympathy with our efforts to achieve self-reliance. It seeks to perpetuate our position of disadvantage. International markets are so manipulated in such a way that primary producing countries have a permanent handicap. The levers of technology are also operated against us through unequal collaboration and royalty agreements. . . .

The power to question is the basis of all human progress. We are free because we question the right of others to rule over us. But intellectual and cultural emancipation is just beginning. We are rediscovering ourselves and the fact that a country sees things in terms of its own geography and history. Those who dominated the world's political affairs and manned its economic controls also imposed a monopoly of ideas. For years we accepted their values, their image of the world and strangely enough even of ourselves. Whether we like it or not, we have been pushed into postures of imitation. We have now to break away from borrowed models of development and evolve models of the worthwhile life which are more relevant to our conditions—not necessarily as a group but as individual countries with their distinctive personalities.

The world today is united in peril, not merely the peril from nuclear destruction but from the more insidious daily pollution of our environment. It should be united in prosperity and in the blossoming of the spirit of man. The nonaligned countries must be in the vanguard of the movement to create the world of tomorrow and to enrich the content of human life.

The unfinished revolution can reach fulfillment if we have faith and confidence in ourselves and the assurance that however long and arduous the journey ahead we shall reach our destination.

Questions

1. What philosophical foundations does Indira Gandhi establish here for the principal of nonalignment?
2. How does she relate the cause of nonalignment to other contemporary movements, such as decolonization and civil rights?
3. What does she mean by "the unfinished revolution"? What does she regard as necessary for the fulfillment of the revolution?
4. Would you describe her goals as realistic or unrealistic?

MIGUEL CASTELLANOS, *THE COMANDANTE SPEAKS: MEMOIRS OF AN EL SALVADORAN GUERRILLA LEADER*, INTRODUCTION

El Salvador underwent a series of regime changes and a great deal of political turmoil accompanied by brutal violence from the 1960s to the 1990s. In the fall of 1972, in the midst of an economic recession, a military coup overthrew the presidential regime of José Napoleón Duarte, the leader of the Christian Democratic Party, and replaced him with Colonel Arturo Molina. In March 1980, a decade of political repression and state-sponsored violence against its opponents culminated with the assassination of Archbishop Oscar Romero, an outspoken critic of the government and advocate of reform. A month later opposition groups combined to form the Democratic Revolutionary Front (FDR), which advocated for political liberty, free elections, and social justice. In January 1981, guerilla armies coordinated their efforts to overthrow the US-backed regime through an organization called the Farabundo Martí National Liberation Front (FMLN). Civil war raged for the rest of the decade, with atrocities committed on both sides. The war seemed to reach a turning point in 1989, which, as we will see, was such a critical year for other revolutions around the world. The new US President George H. W. Bush showed greater reluctance to provide the El Salvadoran government with military support than had his predecessor, Ronald Reagan. Meanwhile, FMLN victories forced the government to the negotiating table with hopes of a resolution of the conflict. However, talks quickly broke down and the violence resumed. Four years earlier, in 1985 the guerilla leader Miguel Castellanos spoke about his reasons for abandoning the FMLN and his disillusionment with both sides in the conflict, neither one of which he believed desired true democracy. His former allies assassinated him for what they considered his betrayal in February 1989.

Miguel Castellanos, *The Comandante Speaks: Memoirs of an El Salvadoran Guerrilla Leader**

The lessons one learns the most are about Marxism-Leninism. I believe that Marxism-Leninism is not a science, and it is not exact. It's a theory, and in particular, a theory which has been surpassed. Now, I can say this with some degree of authority because I've had experience. That is a lesson I have learned; Marxism taught me a great deal about how to analyze society. It is a theory which has been passed by, and many of its philosophical, historical, and politicoeconomic aspects do not apply. Some things such as analytical methods do have certain validity, more than anything else the socioeconomic analysis. That, yes, but the solutions they provide, no! Who is going to deny that there are those who are rich and those who are poor, that there are those who are exploiting. That is inherent, but that is part of the analysis. Yet how are

---

*Miguel Castellanos (1991), *The Comandante Speaks: Memoirs of an El Salvadoran Guerrilla Leader*, edited by Courtney E. Prisk, Boulder, CO: Westview Press, pp. 114–15.

we going to solve that if it's something else? The Marxist solution is behind the times because it is dogmatic and fatalistic, inclusive historically.

I've learned how to analyze a society and the national reality based on a socioeconomic analysis as a method. Now, the others like Shafik, Villalobos, and Leonel continue believing that Marxism is an exact science. They still think that.

Another lesson I've learned, and I'm quite satisfied with, is that I now know what the best solution is for this country. Nobody is going to come to me and say, this is a dictatorship of the right, this is a dictatorship of the left, or a dictatorship of the proletariat, because I know what it is. They aren't going to fool me that easily, nor will a socialist. Now, I have my own criteria, I have my own concept, and I say that the solution is such and such.

That I have learned. Those who belong to the FMLN have learned the military line, and they follow a dogmatic military line exclusively—though not even Lenin dogmatized violence! During the state of revolution, Lenin claimed that violence is the midwife of history. However, that was at the historical level, not at the specific and tactical levels, because at this level, the conditions determine the method. That is why Lenin participated in the elections in Russia. After 1905–7, before the revolution, he was in a Parliament. He did not reject elections. Well, he was a genteel man within Marxism itself.

The FMLN leaders are dogmatists and they are even Trotskyites. They don't realize it, and they think they are right. Now, the mistake is that nobody makes them realize the truth of the matter. There is no ideological struggle in this country.

Questions

1. Why does Castellanos say that he has lost his faith in Marxist theory?
2. If Castellanos was right and the struggle in El Salvador did not involve ideology, what was it about?
3. Does he suggest a solution to El Salvador's problems and violence here?

DORIS MARÍA TIJERINO, FROM DENIS LYNN DALY HEYCK, *LIFE STORIES OF THE NICARAGUAN REVOLUTION*, INTRODUCTION

The following excerpt comes from one of a series of interviews that Denis Lynn Daly Heyck conducted with a variety of individuals from different walks of life in the aftermath of the successful Sandinista Revolution that ended in triumph in 1979. Doris María Tijerino had served as a comandante in the guerilla forces of the Sandinistas before they seized power and headed the national police force of the Sandinista government at the time of this interview. She explains why she joined the Sandinistas in the first place in opposition to the military dictatorship of the Somoza family, which had dominated Nicaragua since 1937. Inspired by the ideas of the revolutionary thinker Auguston César Sandino (1895–1934), a guerilla band calling itself the Sandinista National Liberation Front had formed in 1962. The group fought on behalf of the Nicaraguan peasantry for years before finally defeating Somoza's forces in 1979. Wealthy landowners who had their land confiscated and redistributed to the peasantry formed a counterrevolutionary army called the Contras in the 1980s; this was the group funded by the Reagan administration, leading to what was known as the Iran-Contra Scandal in the United States. Meanwhile, the Sandinista government made the transition from the temporary dictatorship of its leader, Daniel Ortega, to democracy when Ortega voluntarily gave up power after losing a general election to Violeta Chamorro in 1990.

Doris María Tijerino, from Denis Lynn Daly Heyck, *Life Stories of the Nicaraguan Revolution**

I come from a very wealthy family, whose background and possessions afforded me an extremely comfortable life. My family have been large landowners, proprietors of many businesses, and, a long time ago when I was very young, my father was also owner of various radio stations. I was born in the north, in Matagalpa; my mother was from Matagalpa, and was also born there, but my father is from the west, from León. My mother had strong personal values and principles, and she played the crucial role in the constitution and development of the family. Her centrality in family decision-making is probably what determined that we would leave León for Matagalpa and live there. I have fifteen brothers and sisters. Eleven are from my mother and father's marriage, and after my mother died he married again.

All my development took place within the framework of an extremely affluent life-style. I was educated in a very traditional nun's school; nevertheless, perhaps because of the way that family life develops in the countryside, there was evolving in me, spontaneously, as part of my own character, a deep interest in knowing the life of the poor, the marginalized classes. I wanted to become involved and try to solve some of their problems from a Christian

---

*Denis Lynn Daly Heyck (1990), *Life Stories of the Nicaraguan Revolution*, New York: Routledge, pp. 54–59.

perspective. Though I didn't realize it at the time, mine was a very bourgeois, individualistic approach to the problem. I was about nine or ten years old, and I had as my charge a poor family, for whom I obtained food, medicine, clothes, and whom I also visited regularly. All this made me feel good; it soothed my Christian conscience and my political conscience, not that I had developed any ideological position then, but I *was* aware that the phenomena of poverty and marginalization were political realities. Nevertheless, I never focused on the issue from an integrated perspective. I was unable to view the situation as a whole, to see it as a product of the system or of the repression of the dictatorship.

. . . However much I may criticize the motivation, I have to say that because of that experience I really got to know what misery is like, and I was shocked at the contradiction of people living in subhuman conditions in such a rich, fertile, coffee-producing zone, and of those who had nothing living alongside the great landholders who had an abundance of everything, and who even had their own banks. . . .

. . . [My mother] was very interested in progressive readings, which gave her a world view very different from that of other women of her class. She read all the classics of poetry and the novel; I remember she particularly enjoyed Gorki. And a very special thing for me, when she was only sixteen years old herself, my mother dedicated her books to her first daughter, who would receive them on her fifteenth birthday. But she gave them to me when I turned thirteen, because she understood that I would not be content in a traditional role, and since I already had more schooling than she ever did, I was in secondary school by then, she gave them to me.

. . . Without doubt, this experience helped me considerably to interpret the political phenomena which I heard talked about within the family, for example about the struggle of Sandino, and which, otherwise, I would not have been able to place in a framework. My mother gave me a framework, that of anti-imperialism, not anti-Americanism, which was more common, but anti-imperialism, because the root problem was the economic struggle.

To be anti-imperial was to be pro-Sandino, because many Nicaraguans realized that so much of our suffering, the history of our invasions from William Walker on, was the product of the bourgeois and the petit bourgeois ideology. Sandino represented for a large portion of the Nicaraguan people the national expression of our feelings, certainly for my mother, but not for my father.

You can see what the formative influences of my adolescence were and how I came of age in a country in which the dictatorship was so terrible that if one were a decent human being then one had to stand up and be counted. One couldn't remain apathetic, alienated, or isolated from the Somoza horror in this country. This is what gradually dawned on me as I was growing up, while I was still a child really.

After finishing my secondary studies, I decided to go on to university. I applied for a scholarship and studied Agronomy and Agricultural Administration for almost three years in the Soviet Union, from 1963 to the end of 1965. Already in '63 the Frente had had its first armed experience and I had begun to feel sympathy for the guerilla movement. In the first place, for merely emotional reasons, because I had a first cousin, Charlie Haslam, who had been head of a guerilla unit in '59. The guardia killed him and did away with Charlie's small group but I felt a natural identification with the armed struggle ever since that event. . . .

Questions

1. Given her background coming from a wealthy family of large landowners, how does Tijerino explain her decision to join the Sandinistas?
2. What role did nationalism play in her thinking, as described in this passage?
3. What might account for the differences in her perspective on the revolution in Nicaragua and that of Castellanos, who abandoned the revolution in El Salvador? Does the success of the Nicaraguan revolution disprove Castellanos's assumptions about revolutionary ideology?

NELSON MANDELA, *LONG WALK TO FREEDOM*, INTRODUCTION

Nelson Mandela (1918–2013) first joined the African National Congress in 1944, an organization committed to ending the segregationist system of apartheid in South Africa. Mandela spent the next twenty years in opposition to the government, the highlights of which were a "Defiance Campaign" in 1952 and a three-day national strike in 1961. In the meantime the government continued to pass legislation, such as the Population Registration Act of 1950 and the Bantu Education Act of 1953, which reinforced the legal boundaries between blacks and whites. Determined to crush the opposition, the government arrested Mandela on charges of political subversion in 1964 and sentenced him to life imprisonment. It took the reform government of F. W. de Klerk (b. 1936) to release Mandela in 1990. De Klerk's government also repealed the legislation that upheld apartheid and entered into negotiations with Mandela for a new constitution for South Africa that would make blacks and whites equal partners. However, despite these positive developments, racial violence continued, as well as violence between competing black parties that the white police force helped to cause. In these tense circumstances, Mandela and de Klerk met to debate the issues dividing them, with nothing less than the future of South Africa at stake. Mandela describes this confrontation, as well as a meeting that he initiated with the chief of police, in the following passages from his autobiography, Long Walk to Freedom.

Nelson Mandela, *Long Walk to Freedom: The Autobiography of Nelson Mandela**

Each day, each weekend, the newspapers were filled with fresh reports of new and bloody violence in our communities and townships. It was clear that violence was the number one issue in the country. In many communities in Natal and on the Reef around Johannesburg, a poisonous mixture of crime, political rivalries, police brutality, and shadowy death squads made life brutish and untenable. As long as the violence was not dealt with, the progress to a new dispensation would remain uneven and uncertain.

To try to arrest the violence, I contacted Chief Buthelezi to arrange a meeting. We met at Durban's Royal Hotel in January. Chief Buthelezi spoke first to assembled delegates and media and in the process opened old wounds rather than healing them. He catalogued the verbal attacks the ANC had made on him and criticized the ANC's negotiating demands. When it was my turn to speak, I chose not to respond to his remarks but to thank him for his efforts over many years to secure my release from prison. I cited our long relationship and underlined the many matters that united our two organizations rather than divided us.

Progress was made during our private talks, and Chief Buthelezi and I signed an agreement that contained a code of conduct covering the behavior of our two organizations. It was a fair accord, and I suspect that if it had been implemented it would indeed have helped to staunch the bloodletting. But as far as I could tell, Inkatha never made any effort to implement the accord, and there were violations as well on our own side.

The violence continued between our two organizations. Each month people were dying by the hundreds. In March, Inkatha members launched an attack in Alexandra Township north of Johannesburg in which forty-five people were killed over three days of fighting. Again, no one was arrested.

I could not sit idly by as the violence continued, and I sought another meeting with Chief Buthelezi. In April I went down to Durban and we again made strong statements and signed another agreement. But again, the ink was

---

*Nelson Mandela (1994), *Long Walk to Freedom: The Autobiography of Nelson Mandela*, Boston: Little, Brown and Company, pp. 514–15, 537–38.

no sooner dry than it was drenched in blood. I was more convinced than ever that the government was behind much of the violence and the violence was impeding the negotiations. Mr. de Klerk's failure to respond put our own relationship in jeopardy.

In April, at a two-day meeting of the National Executive Committee, I discussed my doubts about Mr. de Klerk. The NEC believed that the government was behind the violence and that the violence was upsetting the climate for negotiations. In an open letter to the government, we called for the dismissal of Magnus Malan, the minister of defense, and Adriaan Vlok, the minister of law and order; the banning of the carrying of traditional weapons in public; the phasing out of the migrant-worker hostels, where so many Inkatha members lived in the townships around Johannesburg; the dismantling of secret government counterinsurgency units; and the appointment of an independent commission to probe complaints of misconduct on the part of the security forces.

We gave the government until May to meet our demands. Mr. de Klerk responded by calling for a multiparty conference on violence to be held in May, but I replied that this was pointless since the government knew precisely what it had to do to end the violence. In May, we announced the suspension of talks with the government. . . .

Ten days before the vote, M.de Klerk and I held our single television debate. I had been a fair debater at Fort Hare, and in my early years in the organization I had engaged in many impassioned debates on the platform. On Robben Island, we had honed our debating skills while we chipped away at limestone. I was confident, but the day before, we held a mock debate in which the journalist Allister Sparks ably performed as Mr. de Klerk. Too ably, according to my campaign adviser, for they chided me for speaking too slowly and not aggressively enough.

When the time came for the actual debate, however, I attacked the National Party quite firmly. I accused the National Party of fanning race hatred between Coloureds and Africans in the Cape by distributing an inflammatory comic book that said the ANC's slogan was "Kill a Coloured, kill a farmer." "There is no organization in this country as divisive as the new National Party," I declared. When Mr. de Klerk criticized the ANC's plan to spend billions of dollars on housing and social programs, I scolded him, saying he was alarmed that we would have to devote so many of our resources to blacks.

But as the debate was nearing an end, I felt I had been too harsh with the man who would be my partner in a government of national unity. In summation, I said, "The exchanges between Mr. de Klerk and me should not obscure one important fact. I think we are a shining example to the entire world of people drawn from different racial groups who have a common loyalty, a common love, to their common country. . . . In spite of criticism of Mr. de Klerk," I said, and then looked over at him, "sir, you are one of those I rely upon. We are going to face the problem of this country together." At which point I reached over to take his hand and said, "I am proud to hold your hand for us to go forward." Mr. de Klerk seemed surprised, but pleased.

Questions

1. What insights do the above passages provide to an understanding of the difficulty of the situation facing Mandela and de Klerk as they attempted to move beyond South Africa's racial divisions?
2. How do you think that Mandela successfully managed to overcome a quarter-century in prison to play the role of peacemaker in the 1990s?
3. The student of history should—just as they would when he or she studies the other autobiographical sources included in this anthology—consider the motives and perspective of the author. How would you describe Mandela's perspective here? Does he betray any personal biases?

SHEN TONG, *ALMOST A REVOLUTION*, INTRODUCTION

As mentioned in the introduction, Deng Xiaoping had brought important changes to China in the 1980s, including some privatization of agriculture and the division of large collective farms into smaller units. Not all peasants embraced this change as some had enjoyed working with their neighbors, who suddenly had become competitors instead of allies. However, many young people, especially in the cities, embraced their new access to consumer goods and Western culture. They grew even more enthusiastic when Deng began to discuss introducing political reforms in 1986. Deng, who had fought in the revolution alongside Mao and devoted his life to the Communist Party, never intended to give up power or to make China a true democracy. He even backtracked on political reform when conservatives within the Party began to make noise about replacing him with someone less tolerant of dissent. On April 15, 1989, Hu Yaobang (1917–89), one of the reformists within the upper ranks of the party whom the hardliners had forced to step down in 1987, died. Students, who considered him a martyr to their cause of political reform, turned out in large numbers in Beijing to honor him, while their counterparts in Shanghai held demonstrations there. Within a week, 100,000 students had gathered in Tiananmen for a memorial service for Hu. At that point, they began to call for a meeting with government officials to hear their demands. Shen Tong, a student at Beijing University at the time, emerged as one of the leaders of the pro-democracy demonstrations that gripped Beijing for the next two months. The following excerpts from his account of those heady, but ultimately disappointing days, provide insight into the mind of a young man at the center of events that captivated the world, as well as an insider's perspective on a revolution that almost succeeded.

Shen Tong, *Almost a Revolution**

May 15, Monday

The television reporter read a moving letter that had been issued by the All-China Women's Federation, appealing to the hunger strikers to stop their fast: "Children, you have already given so much to the nation. We the citizens understand, sympathize with, and support you. You are patriots. But you have done enough." The rest of the letter tried to reason with the strikers, almost directly telling them that the government was not worth dying for. The reporter also said that numerous other national organizations, including the China Democratic League and the China Federation of Literary and Art Circles, as well as the presidents of eight universities, had asked the government to hold a dialogue with the students. All of these organizations operated as if they were independent groups for and by the people, but actually they were all controlled by the Communist Party and answered to the government. For the first time they were acting independently and openly disagreeing with the Party. The All-China Workers Union, China's only labor union, which was also under the Party's control, publicly gave the students in the square 100,000 yuan to help the hunger strikers, an amazing and exciting act, since the government had already labeled the strikers counterrevolutionaries.

Chai Ling was a very charismatic leader. She could move you to tears with her speeches, and without her the hunger strike would not have held together. Her leadership came directly from the heart. She was an idealist, but I thought her ideals were based very much on emotion and not on a real philosophy. I knew Zhang Boli from his work on the *News Herald*. We had met because he was a member of the Beida writers' seminar, not through any previous demonstrations. To my knowledge, he had never participated in any political activities before the hunger strike. I didn't know anything about Li Lu. I had heard that he was from Nanjing, which made him the only person from outside Beijing to assume a top leadership role. People were a little worried

*Shen Tong and Marianne Yen (1990), *Almost a Revolution*, Boston: Houghton Mifflin Company, pp. 274, 276, 291, 315.

about him because no one had ever seen his student identification card. When I heard about this leadership, I became concerned. Our movement was about democratic reform, but a lot of people in the square had lost their vision of what we were after, which was going to make it more difficult to accomplish our goal.

May 20, Saturday

The morning news broadcast showed Li Peng making a speech in which he called for an end to the turmoil and stressed the importance of stability. Just the sight of him made me angry. He had come to represent everything many of us disliked about the government. Some students called him a eunuch because of his high-pitched voice, baby-white skin, and pudgy face. Li Peng said that starting at 10 a.m., martial law was being imposed to restore order to the city. This made it illegal to hold demonstrations, class boycotts, work stoppages, or any mass gathering. It also gave the armed police, PLA soldiers, and other security officers license to do whatever was necessary to stop any violations. For Li Peng to say that martial law was necessary at this time was maddening, because Beijing had never been as orderly as it was during the student movement.

May 31, Wednesday

The federation leaders decided that the only thing we could do to keep the army from moving into the square was to ask the people of Beijing for their help. Many student leaders, including me, set out in vans equipped with public address speakers to give pep talks to the *laobaixing*. Wherever we went, people gave us food and drink and applauded us. It was a wonderful feeling to know that they were still behind what we were doing.

As we drove around the outskirts of the city, I saw truckloads of troops that had been stopped by citizens. Sometimes the people scolded the soldiers, but most Beijing residents were friendly to them, giving them food and drink too. There was a general feeling that the soldiers did not know why they had been brought into the city and that they didn't want to harm the students.

On one of our trips, I saw a crowd of people gathered around an army vehicle full of soldiers and weapons—machine guns, rifles with bayonets, cases of bullets. "Those bastards in the government!" a man in the street shouted at the army officer on the truck. "How can you use these things against the students?"

Later that day I heard that Guo Haifeng was now the director of the reorganization effort in the square, in charge of replacing the old tents with the new ones from Hong Kong. Apparently he was now working with Li Lu, making preparations to dig in for the long haul.

Questions

1. According to Shen Tong, what role did divisions among the students play in the failure of the pro-democracy movement in China?
2. What main developments occurred in China from the middle to the end of May as described here by Shen Tong? What role did each play in the outcome of the revolution?
3. How does Shen Tong's account of the course of events in the Chinese revolution of 1989 compare to the history of other revolutions that you have studied that have either succeeded or failed?

FIGURE 23: Student displays a banner reading "LIBERTY" in front of crowd of protesters, Tiananmen Square, Beijing, April 22, 1989. Courtesy of Getty Images.

FIGURE 24: Tanks depart Tiananmen Square, June 6, 1989. Courtesy of Getty Images.

Photographers produced some striking images of the events unfolding in Beijing in the spring of 1989. Nightly news programs broadcast live images as well around the world. These two photographs, one taken at the beginning of the demonstrations and one at the end, symbolize the hope and the despair experienced by those inside and outside of China who believed that the country had reached the verge of democracy and an end of the dictatorship of the Communist Party.

Questions

1. How do these two images accord with the events described by Shen Tong?
2. What role do photographs such as these play in the way in which we remember and interpret history?
3. How much and what can these photographs tell us about their subjects independent of written accounts of the same events?

Chapter Questions

1. What similarities do you see between Indira Gandhi's speech in Lusaka and Martin Luther King's "Letter from Birmingham City Jail" in Chapter 13?
2. What common themes run through the non-Western sources in this chapter?
3. After reading the sources in this chapter, do you get the impression that history was moving toward the resolution of some of the important issues facing society and political leaders at this stage or a sense that the same old problems had recurred and were likely to recur in the future?

CHAPTER SIXTEEN

The Post-Cold War Era

INTRODUCTION

Despite the failure of the Chinese revolution that occurred in Tiananmen Square in 1989, the wave of revolutions that swept across Eastern Europe in 1989 proved wildly successful at removing the authoritarian communist dictatorships that had dominated the region since the start of the Cold War. Poland led the way in many respects under the determined leadership of the Polish labor leader Lech Walesa, who had helped found the trade union, Solidarity, about a decade earlier. Although Walesa and Solidarity had met resistance and been outlawed in the early 1980s, by 1987 the Communist government was ready to negotiate. By 1989, Poland had a new constitution that permitted multiparty elections; the first free election in Poland since the start of the Cold War resulted in the elevation of Walesa to the presidency of the nation. In his 1992 autobiography, Walesa reflected on his life and the path that had led him from the shipyards of Gdansk to the presidency of a democratic Poland and set the stage for the fall of communism throughout Eastern Europe and the Soviet Union.

History does not stand still, however, and soon Europe was beset with a new set of problems and issues, some of which proved surprisingly easy to resolve and others that revived memories of the worst nightmares of the twentieth century. As the history of most previous revolutions had shown, the breakdown of an old order always carried with it the threat of disorder, which in turn frequently leads to even stronger rulers who emerge to restore order. Such had been the case in the English Revolution of the 1640s, which led from Charles I to Cromwell; the French Revolution of 1789 which ended up replacing Louis XVI with Napoleon; and the Russian Revolutions of 1917, after which first Lenin and then Stalin held power that rivaled or even exceeded that of the dethroned Romanov dynasty. Nothing could dim the euphoria across Europe and the West that accompanied the fall of communism in Europe and the end of the Cold War in 1989, but those with a historical consciousness might very well have asked what would emerge to replace the old order.

One of the optimists was Francis Fukuyama, a prominent political scientist at Harvard University, whose book *The End of History and the Last Man* (1992), viewed the revolutions as part of a general historical trend in the direction of the worldwide triumph of liberal democracy. The peaceful unification of Germany of that year, something that evoked memories of the efforts of previous German regimes to dominate the continent militarily, occurred with surprising ease and rapidity, as well as a commitment to democratic values that seemed to further validate Fukuyama's thesis. The collapse of the Soviet Union in 1991 and the promise of democracy in Russia raised hopes for a new world order that conformed to Fukuyama's thesis even higher.

Other signs were not so positive, however. By 1992, Solidarity was losing popularity in the face of continuing economic problems and the Communist Party soon reemerged as the largest party in democratic Poland. Developments in the collapsing state of Yugoslavia were even more troublesome, demonstrating that the transition to democracy would not be easy in all of the former communist states in the 1990s. Nationalism in places like Serbia, Croatia, Bosnia, and Kosovo, submerged under the strong-armed leadership of Tito and communism, revived in the 1990s in a particularly violent way. Slovenia and Croatia declared their independence in 1991, initiating a series of civil wars between Serbs and other ethnicities in Croatia, Bosnia, and Kosovo, as well as within the former Yugoslavia as a whole as Serbs attempted to hold the nation together. The bombardment of towns and cities, paramilitary forces driving people from their homes and villages, the systematic use of rape as a military strategy, and the revival of genocide under the euphemism of "ethnic cleansing" recalled the worst horrors of the Second World War and the previous calamities of the twentieth century. Slavenka Drakulic, a Croatian journalist, reflected on the causes and effects of these wars in her book, *The Balkan Express*. The British journalist Timothy Garton Ash, who chronicled the revolutions of 1989 and subsequent European developments in a series of books and articles, expressed his thoughts on the larger European context for developments in Bosnia and Croatia in the essay that appears in this chapter.

Meanwhile, despite an acceleration of the processes of European unity— or perhaps to some degree because of them—nationalist parties and fringe organizations reappeared in other parts of Europe as well. Far-right parties experienced surprising and, to some, alarming electoral success in Austria, Switzerland, and Italy, largely because of economic concerns about foreign immigrants taking jobs away from natives. In Switzerland, a feeling that Swiss responsibility for the Holocaust had been exaggerated contributed to a backlash against liberalism. The appeal of far-right parties had the effect of pushing even mainstream conservative parties further to the right to siphon off support from them. Perhaps even more disturbing was the reemergence of neo-Nazi groups and the resurgence of fascist ideology in a form known as neo-fascism. These developments hardly went unnoticed. One voice speaking out against them was the American folksinger Eric Andersen, who in 1998 penned the brilliant and evocative lyrics of his "Rain Falls Down in Amsterdam."

Another voice critical of the neo-fascists belonged to Petra Kelly, the founder and former leader of the German Green Party, at least before her premature murder in 1992. Kelly, however, is significant as well for calling attention to other great concerns of the period, including the protection of the environment and the dangers of nuclear power. In a talk, parts of which are reprinted below, Kelly explains the whole philosophy of the Green movement and its significance for her (and our?) times. Along the same lines, Kirkpatrick Sale drew inspiration from a group of nineteenth-century protesters against the technology that spawned the Industrial Revolution to warn about the dangers to humanity of a technologically-driven society in his 1994 book, *Rebels against the Future*, also excerpted below.

Finally, this chapter concludes with an excerpt from a 1995 book by the American political scientist, Samuel Huntington, called *The Clash of Civilizations and the Remaking of the World Order*. Writing only a few years after Fukuyama, Huntington responded to his book with a different take on what the future might hold in the post-Cold War world. Instead of a triumph of liberal democracy, Huntington forecast a shift away from the struggle of nations for international power in the direction of a cultural divide between peoples with fundamentally different world views. His controversial thesis gained almost as much attention as did Fukuyama's and serves as a useful conclusion to this chapter and transition to the final chapter of the book, which includes sources from the early twenty-first century and the world that changed after the al-Qaeda sponsored terrorist attacks on the World Trade Center in New York City in September 2001.

LECH WALESA, *THE STRUGGLE AND THE TRIUMPH: AN AUTOBIOGRAPHY*, INTRODUCTION

The rise of Lech Walesa from a worker in the shipyards of Gdansk to president of Poland in little more than a decade is one of the most remarkable stories of the late twentieth century. It is no more remarkable, however, than the fall of communism itself in Poland and the revolutions that it inspired throughout Eastern Europe. In the passage from his autobiography that follows, Walesa recalls his thinking and experience at the time when he took over the presidency. As you will see, he considered himself qualified for the job, not because he considered himself above the people that he represented, but rather because he considered himself one of them. He provides a powerful testimony to the optimistic spirit that accompanied the transition to democracy, tempered, however, by realism and the knowledge that political change alone would not be enough to achieve the goals of the people's revolution.

Lech Walesa, *The Struggle and the Triumph: An Autobiography**

On August 9 [1990], I issued a statement in which I declared, without pulling any punches, that the current political establishment no longer enjoyed popular support and that therefore it would be necessary to elect a new parliament and also a new president before the end of their terms of office:

> I think, and I have always thought, that Poland needs a strong president with a popular mandate, a president who, with the parliament, will get things moving, who can make decisions under political pressure, and who has the courage to wield power. . . . It's a matter not of finding people, but of finding programs that can bring Poland closer to democracy. Our struggle should be about programs, not name-calling.

I called for tolerance, political maturity, and an end to personal attacks during the election campaign that inevitably lay ahead, a campaign that would have to include electing a president to represent the whole nation—rather than allowing one to be chosen by a parliament that was only partially representative. . . .

Only work creates wealth. Consistent effort and work of good quality, when combined with competition, produce the best results. Individual success becomes the success of society as a whole. But before we can compete economically, we need to establish rules that we can all abide by. Thus wealth is inextricably linked with social justice, and that is why economic reform is so closely tied to political reform.

The election results surprised only those who had underestimated the effect of those years of frustration, or forgotten the contempt with which the totalitarian powers had treated society. As for me, I knew I was the right man for the job of being the first elected president of Poland's Third Republic. I couldn't hide my feelings. I knew that I would stand by my principles and maintain—as well as be inspired by—the loyalty and energy of my supporters, particularly the younger ones.

Above all, I knew that I would have to reconcile social forces and implement true reform—and do it quickly.

As the second round of elections approached, I grew confident and calm. I wanted to reach a position of power democratically, through elections. Once I became president, I would not perform miracles, but I would create the reforms our country needed so badly.

---

*Lech Walesa (1992), *The Struggle and the Triumph: An Autobiography*, translated by Franklin Philip in collaboration with Helen Mahut, New York: Arcade Publishing, pp. 279, 285–86, 293.

One struggle was ending; another was just beginning.

. . . I traveled to Nowa Huta, Cracow, Nowa Sacz, and Silesia. As an ordinary worker I experienced a triumphal trip through southern Poland, a land echoing with the patriotism of previous struggles for independence. In the course of my travels, on practically every square foot, I saw a statue, a monument commemorating the fall of some past national hero. I unwittingly was following in their footsteps. After years of Communist "class struggle" in which the individual had no place, the national thirst for a hero was so powerful that sometimes—even before the doors of my car could open all the way—I was swept into the embrace of some enthusiastic procession. Over and over I told the crowds that I wasn't a hero: "Look! I'm one of you! My hands are calloused by tools and blackened with machine oil. Pay no attention to my fancy speeches." They wouldn't listen to my protests.

Questions

1. What specific changes does Walesa call for here as essential to the success of his presidency and the revolution?
2. What seems to be the source of Walesa's confidence that he can be the leader that Poland needed at that point in its history?
3. Walesa speaks here of the "thirst for a national hero." To what extent was that a product of the revolution against communism? To what extent was that antithetical to what Walesa was trying to achieve? Why does he try to convince the people that he was not a hero?

FRANCIS FUKUYAMA, *THE END OF HISTORY AND THE LAST MAN*, INTRODUCTION

In 1992, Francis Fukuyama responded to the earliest concerns of people around the globe concerning the nature of the new world order emerging from the collapse of the Soviet Union and the communist regimes in Eastern Europe. His book created a firestorm as few books on political science ever have, perhaps gaining comparable attention to that lavished on Paul Kennedy's 1987 The Rise and Fall of the Great Powers, *which seemed to many to express concerns over the decline of the United States more than that of the Soviet Union. Historians scoffed at Fukuyama's title more than his actual thesis, resisting the notion of "an end of history," even though Fukuyama took his title from the German philosopher Friedrich Nietzsche who had prophesied a time when life would become too easy because of an absence of struggle. Fukuyama did not predict the end of historical events, but he did seem to suggest that history had entered its final phase since liberal democracy represented a pinnacle, which, once adopted around the world, would not likely be abandoned. The triumph of liberal democracy represented a defeat for fascism, communism, and other authoritarian systems whose palpable failures in the twentieth century no society would want to repeat. Only liberal democracy could provide the requisite combination of political freedom and material comfort that would truly satisfy the people of the modern world.*

Francis Fukuyama, *The End of History and the Last Man**

Looking around the world, there remains a very strong overall correlation between advancing socio-economic modernization and the emergence of new democracies. Traditionally the most economically advanced regions, Western Europe and North America, have also hosted the world's oldest and most stable liberal democracies. Southern Europe has followed closely behind, and achieved stable democracy in the 1970s. Within Southern Europe, Portugal had the rockiest transition to democracy in the mid-1970s because it started from a lower socio-economic base; a great deal of social mobilization had to occur after rather than before the passing of the old regime. Right behind Europe economically is Asia, whose nations have democratized (or are in the process of doing so) in strict proportion to their degree of development. Of the formerly communist states in Eastern Europe, the most economically advanced among them—East Germany, Hungary, and Czechoslovakia, followed by Poland—also made the most rapid transitions to democracy, while less developed Bulgaria, Romania, Serbia, and Albania all elected reform communists in 1990–1. The Soviet Union is at a roughly comparable level of development to the larger states of Latin America like Argentina, Brazil, Chile, and Mexico, and like them has failed to achieve a fully stable democratic order. Africa, the least developed region of the world, possesses only a handful of recent democracies, of uncertain stability.

An example of the way in which democracy could arguably be said to be more functional for developed countries is with respect to a central issue of our time, the environment. Among the most notable products of advanced industrialization are significant levels of pollution and environmental damage. . . . Despite various theories blaming ecological damage either on capitalism or socialism, experience has shown that neither economic system is particularly good for the environment.

---

*Francis Fukuyama (1992), *The End of History and the Last Man*, New York: Avon Books, pp. 112, 114–15.

Both private corporations as well as socialist enterprises and ministries will focus on growth or output and will seek to avoid paying for externalities wherever they can. But since people want not only economic growth but a safe environment for themselves and their children, it becomes a function of the state to find a fair trade-off between the two, and to spread the costs of ecological protection around so that no one sector will bear them unduly.

And in this respect, the communist world's truly abysmal environmental record suggests that what is most effective in protecting the environment is neither capitalism nor socialism, but democracy. As a whole, democratic political systems reacted much more quickly to the growth of ecological consciousness in the 1960s and 1970s than did the world's dictatorships. For without a political system that permits local communities to protest the sitting of a highly toxic chemical plant in the middle of their communities, without freedom for watchdog organizations to monitor the behavior of companies and enterprises, without a national political leadership sufficiently sensitized that it is willing to devote substantial resources to protect the environment, a nation ends up with disasters like Chernobyl, or the desiccation of the Aral Sea, or an infant mortality rate in Krakow that is four times the already high Polish national average, or a 70 percent rate of miscarriages in Western Bohemia. Democracies permit participation and therefore feedback, and without feedback, governments will always tend to favor the large enterprise that adds significantly to national wealth, over the long-term interests of dispersed groups of private citizens.

Questions
1. What historical conditions does Fukuyama suggest need to be present in order for democracy to flourish?
2. Is democracy a precondition for economic growth or is economic growth a precondition for democracy?
3. Does Fukuyama put too much faith in democracy when it comes to protecting the environment?

SLAVENKA DRAKULIC, *THE BALKAN EXPRESS*, AND TIMOTHY GARTON ASH, "CLEANSED CROATIA," INTRODUCTION

In 1991, the Croatian journalist Slavenka Drakulic provided a retrospective on communism in Eastern Europe in a book called How We Survived Communism and Even Laughed. *In that book, she looked back at the drawbacks of life under a communist regime but also spoke about the positive ideas that had inspired the people to believe in communism as an ideal for as long as they did. The book contains such perception, insight, and, yes, humor, that it made life in communism accessible to Western readers, in many ways for the first time. In* The Balkan Express, *Drakulic also included vignettes of life under communism in the former Yugoslavia, but this time in contrast to the chaos and destruction that ravaged the region during the mid-1990s. She focuses on how the civil wars affected her and the ordinary people who became the victims of the machinations of political and military leaders and the hate-filled brand of nationalism that they cultivated in their followers as a basis for their own support.*

The collapse of Yugoslavia revealed the extent to which the people of different nationalities and ethnic backgrounds had become integrated throughout its component parts. The Serbian-dominated Yugoslav government refused to sit idly by while Croatia, Bosnia, and Kosovo became independent nations with significant numbers of Serbs living in those regions. Croats, Bosnians, and Kosovars no longer wished to remain minorities in a Serbian-dominated Yugoslavia after Serbian nationalism had replaced communism as the prevailing ideology espoused by the Serbian leader Slobodan Milosevic. Perhaps more than any contemporary writer, Timothy Garton Ash, a professor of European Studies at Oxford University, has had his finger on the pulse of European politics during the post-Cold War era. He has travelled extensively in Europe, including southeastern Europe, giving him a firsthand perspective on events there at the same time that he was following and writing about topics such as the unification of Germany, the expansion of NATO and the European Community, and the move toward the common European currency known as the euro. He brings this unique perspective to his discussion of the Balkan wars in an essay entitled "Cleansed Croatia," which appears in a collection of his writings from the period called The History of the Present.

Slavenka Drakulic, *The Balkan Express**

. . . After forty-five years under communist rule, no matter how different or more lenient it was than in other Eastern bloc countries, one has no right to claim that people should have been aware of the consequences of nationalism— the tendency to form nation-states—would bring. They had simply no chance to become mature political beings, real citizens ready to participate, to build

---

*Slavenka Drakulic (1993), *The Balkan Express: Fragments from the Other Side of the War*, New York: HarperPerennial, pp. 13, 50–51.

a democratic society. When people in Croatia held the first free multiparty elections in 1990, as in most of the rest of Eastern Europe they voted primarily against the communists. Despite that, the new governments were all too ready to proclaim themselves the sole bearers of democracy, as if it were a fruit or a gift there for the taking. If there is any reason at all behind the historical animosities dividing the Yugoslav nations, it is that this society never had a proper chance to become a society not of oppressed peoples, but of citizens, of self-aware individuals with developed democratic institutions within which to work out differences, conflicts and changes and instead of by war. Continuing to live with the same kind of totalitarian governments, ideology and yet untransformed minds, it seems the people were unable to shoulder the responsibility for what was coming—or to stop it. War therefore came upon us like some sort of natural calamity, like a plague or a flood, inevitable, our destiny.

I have to admit that for me, as for many of my friends born after World War II, being Croat has no special meaning. Not only was I educated to believe that the whole territory of ex-Yugoslavia was my homeland, but because we could travel freely abroad (while people of the Eastern-bloc countries couldn't), I almost believed that borders, as well as nationalities, existed only in people's heads. Moreover, the youth culture of 1968 brought us even closer to the world through rock music, demonstrations, movies, books and the English language. We had so much in common with the West that in fact we mentally belonged there.

Some of my foreign friends from that time cannot understand that they and I have less and less in common now. I am living in a country that has had six bloody months of war, and it is hard for them to understand that being Croat has become my destiny. How can I explain to them that in this war I am defined by my nationality, and by it alone? There is another thing that is even harder to explain—the way the awareness of my nationality, because of my past, came to me in a negative way. I had fought against treating nationality as a main criterion by which to judge human beings; I tried to see the people behind the label; I kept open the possibility of dialogue with my friends and colleagues in Serbia even after all telephone lines and roads had been cut off, and one-third of Croatia had been occupied and bombed. I resisted coming to terms with the fact that in Croatia it is difficult to be the kind of person who says, "Yes, I am Croat, but. . . ."

In the end, none of that helped me. Along with millions of other Croats, I was pinned to the wall of nationhood—not only by outside pressure from Serbia and the Federal Army but by the national homogenization within Croatia itself. That is what the war is doing to us, reducing us to one dimension: the Nation. The trouble with this nationhood, however, is that whereas before, I was defined by my education, my job, my ideas, my character—and, yes, my nationality too—now I feel stripped of all that. I am nobody because I am not a person any more. I am one of 4.5 million Croats.

I can only regret that awareness of my nationhood came to me in the form of punishment of the nation I belong to, in the form of death, destruction, suffering and—worst—fear of dying. I feel as an orphan does, the war having robbed me of the only real possession I had acquired in my life, my individuality.

Timothy Garton Ash, "Cleansed Croatia"*

And so to Dayton, Ohio, where, once again, for the—what? third? fourth?—time this century, America is trying to resolve a European conflict which Europe has failed to resolve for itself.

I believe Europe should prepare to take over the leading role in providing the international roof under which the different communities in Bosnia might live side by side and then perhaps, gradually, over many years, grow together again. As a European, I shall do what I can to try to ensure that this becomes a priority for European leaders. But, alas, here, too, I simply don't believe that it will happen. On the flight to Zagreb, I read Helmut Kohl telling the *Süddeutsche Zeitung*, "We shall make the process of unifying Europe irreversible in the next two years or so." On the flight back, nearly three weeks later, I find the West European papers full of passionate debate about European monetary union.

There are quite other priorities here: no sense of urgency about what is happening just an hour's flying time away: no sense that there is any contradiction between the claim that Europe is peacefully, irreversibly uniting, and the fact that at the very same time a part of Europe is being brutally and, one fears, really irreversibly torn apart. The long tortuous process of polit-bureaucratic negotiation at the EU's next intergovernmental conference, scheduled to open in 1996, is supposed to produce improvements to the Union's so-called Common Foreign and Security Policy. But I'm afraid we can already guess what that will mean for Bosnia. More ice-cream men.

Before 1989, Europe was like Berlin: divided between east and west by a single wall. Now Europe is like a great American city, with prosperous and relatively peaceful neighborhoods, such as Georgetown or the Upper East Side of Manhattan, existing just a few blocks away from violent and miserable ghettos. There are no concrete walls across the streets. In theory, you can drive anywhere. But in practice the two are still worlds apart. This should shame us in Europe, just as it should shame America. But somehow we live with it. . . .

With the Polish experience in mind, Konstanty Gebert sarcastically puts the lesson thus: "If you want to 'return to Europe,' first do your ethnic cleansing, then wait a generation." One can turn it around another way and put it more

---

*Timothy Garton Ash (1999), *History of the Present: Essays, Sketches, and Dispatches from Europe in the 1990s*, New York: Random House, pp. 164–66.

mildly. Trying to describe the ethnic and cultural mélange of Sarajevo before the war, the painter Edo Numankadíc said to me, "We were Europe before Europe." Hyperbole perhaps, but with an element of truth. The democratization of Yugoslavia, and of Bosnia in particular, would, had it worked, have been a unique example of a part of Europe moving peacefully from a truly multiethnic society under an undemocratic framework. That it failed there does not mean it has to fail everywhere or that we should give up trying—let alone that we should accept ethnic cleansing as a necessary evil. But—alas, alas, for Europe!—it does seem to be the case that almost nobody has yet been able to avoid the painful path that has led through the formation of nation-states, to—if one is lucky—the securing of human and civil rights by a democratic nation-state, and thence,—if one is very lucky—to the peaceful cooperation and integration of those nation-states.

So this is not just a matter of confronting Europe's failure and Europe's continued responsibility in this part of Europe. Properly understood, Bosnia does, I believe, compel us to reexamine some of our most basic assumptions about the shape and direction of European history. . . .

Questions

1. What explanation does Slavenka Drakulic give for the historical animosities that divided the former states of Yugoslavia in the 1990s? How did these animosities come to affect her personally?

2. In general, is a nationality something that we choose or something that we have thrust upon us?

3. In his essay "Cleansed Croatia," Timothy Garton Ash attempts to put the Bosnian crisis in the broader context of European history. Why does he suggest that Europe did not do more to intervene to prevent "ethnic cleansing" in the Balkans? How was the crisis there related to broader developments in European history?

4. What do you think that Timothy Garton Ash means by the statement that Bosnia should lead to a reexamination "of our most basic assumptions about the shape and direction of European history"?

ERIC ANDERSEN, "RAIN FALLS DOWN IN AMSTERDAM," INTRODUCTION

The revival of the violent forces of extreme nationalism did not just manifest themselves in the Balkans during the 1990s, but also flourished in other parts of Europe from Belgium to Russia. Throughout Europe organized political parties on the far right gained in electoral strength, while informal groups of neo-Nazis, skinheads, and antiforeign gangs grew up on the fringes of society. In 1997, Martin Lee published the first edition of his book, The Beast Reawakens, *to explain the resurgence of neo-Nazism and far-right extremism in contemporary Europe, all part of a broader movement known as "neo-fascism," whose adherents were not restricted to the European continent. The American folksinger Eric Andersen (b. 1943) captured some of the disquieting concerns associated with these developments in the haunting lyrics of his song, "Rain Falls Down in Amsterdam." Andersen began his career in the 1960s when his early work drew favorable comparisons with Bob Dylan. Though not nearly as well known, like Dylan, he has continued to write, grow creatively, and perform throughout his life. From a historical perspective, his ability to evoke a particular moment in history in songs such as the one that follows and "Beat Avenue" (2003), which is about experiencing the news of John F. Kennedy's assassination from his vantage point in San Francisco in 1963, have the ability to command our attention because they raise issues that evoke the importance of the past, the past's relevance to the present, and concerns that are likely to remain important to future generations.*

Eric Andersen, "Rain Falls Down in Amsterdam"*

The rain falls down in Amsterdam the streets are wet and black midnight's like November by the glow of a cigarette the girls on hash in station square looking stupid from the drugs when Marlene heard the boots march there were reasons to be dumb shiny helmets in the shadows those trains that left the night those hiding in the cellars those eyes afraid of light something 'neath the border's potted poison in the well the creature has uncoiled and its crawling up from hell here comes nineteen-fourteen, nineteen thirty-two those cattle cars and yellow stars it's right back to the roots it's movin in the open with a snarl and a growl the cages have been broken and the beast is on the prowl

Fire-bomb those houses burn those refugees be the crowd and do your work applauding silently round up all the gypsies go sell them on the trains can't you smell the smoke now drifting through the rain Jews better draw your curtains

---

*Eric Andersen, *Memory of the Future* (CD), ©1999 Appleseed Recordings. The lyrics to this song appear as they did with the album and the format has been retained to remain consistent with their format there.

you better lock your doors up tight they're snarling up in Rostock in the beer hall-belly nights the Fourth Reich's coming, baby, they're writing out the page in Rome, Berlin, and Stockholm the beast has left the cage here comes nineteen thirty-two here comes déjà vu those cattle cars and yellow stars was there someone that you knew it's right there in the open something's smelling bad the cages have been broken and the beast is a-running mad

Those canals and cozy houses those reflections in the lights you can almost feel it moving the monster in the night it's looking with its yellow eyes it's out to settle scores in the dim medieval distance feel it breathing down your pores in Salt Lake and in Rio the beast can smell the flames it's faxing hate out in Marseille typing out your name you can hear the windows shatter as the time is drawing near Kristall Nacht is back in town welcome back to the house of mirrors

The fire and the armbands and the iron-arm salutes pointing to the scapegoat was it me or was it you? It's right there in the open don't just stand there hoping the leashes have been broken and the dogs are loose

Now I have been here thinking how lucky I have been I never touched the barb-wire never saw the money grin no rifle ever smashed my face no bare electric shock but I'll confess up all I know who I am and who I'm not to see retired killers is to see the lion yawn the skinheads do their dirty work for the cloak and dagger pawns the dark eyes will be waiting there when the borders they are crossed so keep your filthy swastika and shove your iron cross here comes nineteen-fourteen, nineteen thirty-two those cattle cars and yellow stars it's right back to the roots it's there in the open it's crawling on the move the cages have been broken and the beast is on the loose can't you smell the blood now can't you smell the truth.

Questions

1. What is the significance of the song's title, since it is not specifically about Amsterdam?
2. Martin Lee called his book about the same subject *The Beast Reawakens*. In the song Andersen refers as well to "the beast". What is "the beast"? Why is it referred to as such?
3. What is the emotional impact of the lyrics? Are they more important as a reflection of what was happening in 1990s Europe or as a warning about what might happen in the twenty-first century?
4. In what ways is this song a reflection not merely of the 1990s but of the twentieth century as a whole? How does it relate to the excerpt from Rolf Hochhuth's play *The Deputy* that appeared in Chapter 11?

PETRA KELLY, *THINKING GREEN!*, AND KIRKPATRICK SALE, *REBELS AGAINST THE FUTURE: THE LUDDITES AND THEIR WAR ON THE INDUSTRIAL REVOLUTION: LESSONS FOR THE MACHINE AGE*, INTRODUCTION

Whereas Eric Andersen saw a threat from the rise of neo-fascism in the post-Cold War era, others saw threats from the impact of technology and its potential harm to the environment. Of course, this was not a new concern—environmentalism dated to the 1960s. A commitment to environmental issues such as acid rain and the potential dangers of nuclear power plants led Petra Kelly (1947–92) to help found the Green Party in Germany in 1979. Kelly spent her teenage years in the United States and attended American University in Washington, DC, where she gained a reputation as a student leader and activist. In the 1970s she returned to her native country, where she became an influential and outspoken political organizer committed to feminism and the peace movement, in addition to her environmentalism. Her election to the German parliament, the Bundestag, provided validation for her party and her own status as one of the most important women in Europe. Kelly's essay, "Thinking Green!" was part of a collection of her talks that her friends and publisher released posthumously in 1994 under the same title following Kelly's murder in 1992. Some believe that she had been murdered by neo-fascists, although the police ruled her death part of murder-suicide committed by her longtime partner, Gert Bastion, a former general in the German army who had resigned in order to dedicate his life to Kelly and her causes.

In Rebels Against the Future (1995), Kirkpatrick Sale (b. 1937), who is mentioned in the preface to Kelly's book as a contributor to that project, produced a book that was at once a historical study of the Luddites, early nineteenth-century opponents to some of the new technology of the Industrial Revolution, and a warning to the present about the harm that industry and technology was still capable of inflicting on the best interests of humanity. He has written widely on environmental, technological, and political issues in books and articles in a variety of publications ranging from the leftist journal New Leader to The New York Times Magazine. In the "Author's Note" at the beginning of his book, he admitted to sharing "some affinity for the ideas and passions that motivated the subjects of this book, particularly their abiding sense that a world dominated by the technologies of industrial society is fundamentally more detrimental than beneficial to human happiness and survival." In an interview following the publication of Rebels against the Future, he defined a "modern Luddite" as one who is "trying to hold to certain elements of the past to resurrect the community" and who "would say that, of the array of technology around, we should choose what we want and what we don't . . . in a democratic basis within *this community and within this bioregion on the basis of the economic, social and environmental cost."* The passage below is from his conclusion, "Lessons from the Luddites."*

Petra Kelly, *Thinking Green!***

First and foremost, Green politics is grassroots politics. Politics from the top is almost always corrupt and compromised. To bring about change from below is to challenge the moral authority of those who make decisions on our behalf. Through grassroots organization, education, and empowerment, we work to reverse the state-orientation of politics and instead open up a civil space in which we are active subjects, not passive objects of those in power. Substantive change in politics at the top will come only when there is enough pressure from below. The essence of Green politics is to live our values. We in the West German Green Party hurt ourselves over and over again by failing to maintain tenderness with each other as we gained power. We need to rededicate ourselves to our values, respect each other, be tolerant of differences, and stop trying to coerce and control one another.

Nonviolence, ecology, social justice, and feminism are the key principles of Green politics, and they are inseparably linked. We know, for example, that the wasteful patterns of production and consumption in the industrial North deplete and ravage the environment and furnish the motive and means for the violent appropriation of materials from the weaker nations in the South and for the wasteful process of militarization throughout the world. In both capitalist and state socialist countries, human beings are reduced to economic entities, with little or no regard for the human or ecological costs. Politics from the top, the pattern of hierarchical domination, is the characteristic of patriarchy. It is not a coincidence that power rests in the hands of men, benefits accrue first and foremost to men, and that women are exploited at all levels of society.

The Green approach to politics is a kind of celebration. We recognize that each of us is part of the world's problems, and we are also part of the solution. The dangers and potentials for healing are not just outside us. We begin to work exactly where we are. There is no need to wait until conditions become ideal. We can simplify our lives and live in ways that affirm ecological and humane values. Better conditions will come because we have begun.

We have found so many ways to think each other to death—neutron warheads, nuclear reactors, Star Wars defense systems, and many other methods of mass destruction. We are killing each other with our euphemisms and abstractions. In warfare, we accept the deaths of thousands and millions of people we call

---

*http://www.culturechange.org/issue9/kirkpatricksale.html
**Petra Kelly (1994), *Thinking Green!: Essays on Environmentalism, Feminism, and Nonviolence*, Berkeley: Parallax Press, pp. 38–40.

our "enemy." When we dehumanize people, devalue nature, and exalt narrowly defined self-interests, destruction is sure to follow. The healing of our planet requires a new way of thinking about politics and about life. At the heart of this is the understanding that all things are intimately interconnected in the complex web of life. It can therefore be said that the primary goal of Green politics is an inner revolution. Joanna Macy calls this "the greening of the self."

Politics needs spirituality. The profound political changes we need in order to heal our planet will not come about through fragmented problem solving or intellectual analyses that overlook the deepest yearnings and intuitions of the heart. Some of my fellow Greens have maintained their dogmatic leftist perspectives and remain suspicious of spirituality, confusing it with organized religion. I share many of their criticisms of religious institutions, but I firmly disagree with their dismissing spiritual concerns and wisdom. The long work of bringing harmony to the Earth requires a holistic vision based on mature values and deep intuitions.

Kirkpatrick Sale, *Rebels Against The Future: The Luddites and Their War on the Industrial Revolution: Lessons for the Machine Age**

It may be that even those who do remember the past are condemned to repeat it, such is the regularity of the human condition, but at least those who learn from it may fashion the weapons with which to triumph the second time around. Armed with an understanding of the past, perhaps that can allow them to be rebels against the future.

Much there is to be learned from the experience of the Luddites, as distant and as different as their times are from ours. Just as the Second Industrial Revolution itself has its roots quite specifically in the first—the machine changes, but the machine*ness* does not—so those today who are inspired in some measure to resist or even reverse the tide of industrialism might best find their analogs, if not their models, in those original Luddites.

As I see it, these are the sorts of lessons one might, with the focused lenses of history, take from the Luddite past.

1. *Technologies are never neutral, and some are hurtful.*

It was not all machinery that the Luddites opposed, but "all Machinery hurtful to Commonality," as that March 1812 letter stated it, machinery to which their commonality did not give approval, over which it had no control, and the use of which was detrimental to its interests, considered either as a body of workers or a body of families and neighbors and citizens. It was machinery, in other words, that was produced with only economic consequences in mind, and those

*Kirkpatrick Sale (1995), *Rebels Against The Future: The Luddites and Their War on the Industrial Revolution: Lessons for the Machine Age*, Reading, MA: Addison-Wesley, pp. 261–63.

of benefit to only a few, while the myriad social and environmental and cultural ones were deemed irrelevant.

For the fact of the matter is that, contrary to the technophilic propaganda, technology is not neutral, composed of tools that can be used for good or evil depending on the user. . . . it comes with an inevitable logic, bearing the purposes and the values of the economic system that spawns it, and obeying an imperative that works that logic to its end, quite heedlessly. What was true of the technology of industrialism at the beginning, when the apologist Andrew Ure praised a new machine that replaced high-paid workmen—"This invention confirms the great doctrine already propounded, that when capital enlists science in her service, the refractory hand of labor will always be taught docility"—is as true today, when a reporter for *Automation* could praise a computer system as "significant" because it assures that "decision-making" is "removed from the operator [and] gives maximum control of the machine to management." These are not accidental, ancillary attributes of the machines that are chosen; they are intrinsic and ineluctable.

Tools come with a prior history built in, expressing the values of a particular culture. A conquering, violent culture—of which Western civilization is a prime example, with the United States at its extreme—is bound to produce conquering, violent tools. When U.S. industrialism turned to agriculture after World War II, for example, it went at it with all that it had just learned on the battlefield, using tractors modeled on wartime tanks to cut up vast fields, crop dusters modeled on wartime planes to spray poisons, and pesticides and herbicides developed from wartime chemical weapons and defoliants to destroy unwanted species. It was war on the land, sweeping and sophisticated as modern mechanization can be, capable of depleting topsoil at the rate of 3 billion tons a year and water at the rate of 10 billion gallons a year, as we have seen demonstrated ever since. It could be no other way: if a nation like this beats its swords into plowshares they will still be violent and deadly tools.

The business of cropping wool cloth with huge hand-held scissors was an arduous and tiring one, which the shearing frame could have done almost as well with much less effort and time, and the croppers might have welcomed such a disburdening tool if it had no history built in. But they knew, and became Luddites because they knew, what they would have to give up if they were to accept such a technology: the camaraderie of the cropping shop, with its loose hours and ale breaks and regular conversation and pride of workmanship, traded for the servility of the factory, with its discipline and hierarchy and control and skillessness, and beyond that the rule of laissez-faire, dog-eat-dog, buyer-beware, cash-on-the-line. The shearing frame was so obviously not neutral—it was machinery hurtful.

It does not seem hard in a modern context similarly to determine when machinery is hurtful or to define a commonality whose members might have something to say about a technology's introduction or use. Wendell Berry, the

Kentucky essayist, has produced a list of criteria that would serve well as a guide; a new tool, he says, should be cheaper, smaller, and better than the one it replaces, use less energy (and that energy renewable), be repairable, come from a small, local shop, and "should not replace or disrupt anything good that already exists, and this includes family and community relationships." To which need be added only two other crucial standards: that those "family and community relationships" embrace all the other species, plants and animals alike, and the living ecosystems on which they depend, and that they be considered, as the Irokwa have expressed it, with the interests of the next seven generations in mind.

Questions

1. How does Petra Kelly define "Green" politics? Is there a consistent philosophy behind her politics or does she gather an eclectic assortment of causes under one name?
2. What are some of the ways in which technology is a product of culture? Do you agree with Kirkpatrick Sale that it is not "morally neutral"?
3. Is Sale's approach to technology realistic? Has technology become too pervasive in our lives to place restrictions on its development, no matter how humane the motives might be?
4. How do the visions of Kelly and Sale reflect larger historical changes occurring at the end of the twentieth century?

Nam June Paik (1932–2006) was a Korean-American artist known for his interest in video art and the relationship between art and technology, particularly modern forms of mass communication.

FIGURE 25: Nam June Paik, *Smiling Buddha*, 1992. Courtesy of Getty Images.

Questions

1. What statement do you think the artist is trying to make here about the relationship between spirituality and technology?
2. Is there a relationship between spirituality and technology? What do you think that Kelly or Sale would have to say about this image?
3. Does this image reflect the increasing call in the 1990s for a fusion of Western and Eastern values?
4. Is this artwork merely an individual vision or does it reveal something about artistic trends at the end of the twentieth century?

SAMUEL P. HUNTINGTON, *THE CLASH OF CIVILIZATIONS AND THE REMAKING OF THE WORLD ORDER*, INTRODUCTION

Samuel Huntington's theory of post-Cold War politics was centered on the notion that religious and cultural differences under the general rubric of "civilizations" would divide people and replace political ideology and economic rivalries among traditional nation states as causes of conflict. He first developed his thesis in an article published in the journal Foreign Affairs *written in direct response to Fukuyama's book,* The End of History and the Last Man. *As seen in Chapter 14, events such as the Iranian revolution of 1979 and the rise of religious fundamentalism demonstrate that Huntington's thesis had some foundation in the period that predated the end of the Cold War. Nonetheless, the book was widely hailed as a significant contribution to an understanding of the new world order emerging after 1989.*

Samuel P. Huntington, *The Clash of Civilizations and the Remaking of the World Order**

All civilizations go through similar processes of emergence, rise, and decline. The West differs from other civilizations not in the way it has developed but in the distinctive character of its values and institutions. These include most notably its Christianity, pluralism, individualism, and rule of law, which made it possible for the West to invent modernity, expand throughout the world,

---

*Samuel P. Huntington (1996), *The Clash of Civilizations and the Remaking of the World Order*, New York: Simon and Schuster, pp. 311–12.

and become the envy of other societies. In their ensemble these characteristics are peculiar to the West. Europe, as Arthur M. Schlesinger, Jr., has said, is "the source—the *unique* source" of the "ideas of individual liberty, political democracy, the rule of law, human rights, and cultural freedom . . . these are *European* ideas, not Asian, nor African, nor Middle Eastern ideas, except by adoption." They make Western civilization unique, and Western civilization is valuable not because it is universal but because it *is* unique. The principal responsibility of Western leaders, consequently, is not to attempt to reshape other civilizations in the image of the West, which is beyond their declining power, but to preserve, protect, and renew the unique qualities of Western civilization. Because it is the most powerful Western country, that responsibility falls overwhelmingly on the United States of America.

To preserve Western civilization in the face of declining Western power, it is in the interest of the United States and European countries:

- to achieve greater political, economic, and military integration and to coordinate their policies so as to preclude states from other civilizations exploiting differences among them;

- to incorporate into the European Union and NATO the Western states of Central Europe that is, the Visegrad countries, the Baltic republics, Slovenia, and Croatia;

- to encourage the "Westernization" of Latin America and, as far as possible, the close alignment of Latin American countries with the West;

- to restrain the development of the conventional and unconventional military power of Islamic and Sinic countries;

- to slow the drift of Japan away from the West and toward accommodation with China;

- to accept Russia as the core state of Orthodoxy and a major regional power with legitimate interests in the security of its southern borders;

- to maintain Western technological and military superiority over other civilizations;

and, most important, to recognize that Western intervention in the affairs of other civilizations is probably the single most dangerous source of instability and potential global conflict in a multicivilizational world.

In the aftermath of the Cold War the United States became consumed with massive debates over the proper course of American foreign policy. In this era, however, the United States can neither dominate nor escape the world. Neither internationalism nor isolationism, neither multilateralism nor unilateralism, will best serve its interests. Those will best be advanced by eschewing these opposing extremes and instead adopting an Atlanticist policy of close cooperation with its European partners to protect and advance the interests and values of the unique civilization they share.

Questions

1. What does Huntington say is unique about the values of Western civilization? Do you agree that these are uniquely Western values?
2. Are all values relative to a particular culture or are there such things as universal values?
3. What seem to be the overall objectives of his recommendations to the United States and the West in the post-Cold War period?

Chapter Questions

1. What are the key points of difference between Fukuyama's views on the post-Cold War world and those of Samuel Huntington? Are they mutually exclusive?
2. How do Huntington's prescriptions for the future policy of the United States relate to other developments discussed in the chapter, such as the end of communism, the rise of neo-fascism, and the Balkan wars of the 1990s?
3. On the whole, has history borne out more the predictions of Fukuyama or Huntington?
4. In a way, the sources in this chapter could be divided into two categories of being optimistic or pessimistic. Which sources belong in which category? Would you expect to find a balance between these two perspectives in any period of history or did the decade from 1989 to the end of the century lead in one of these two directions more than at other times?

CHAPTER SEVENTEEN

The Turn of the Twenty-First Century

INTRODUCTION

As the sources in Chapter 16 demonstrate, the "new world order" of the post-Cold War era did not mean an end to problems facing the leaders of the late twentieth and early twenty-first century. Vaclav Havel, one of the leaders of the "Velvet Revolution" that overthrew Communist rule in Czechoslovakia in 1989, became profoundly disappointed when he could not hold the country together. Slovakia voted for independence in 1992, in effect seceding from what became the Czech Republic. Havel had served as president of Czechoslovakia and returned to the post of president of the Czech Republic from 1993 to 2003. During this period, he remained an active intellectual, writing numerous books and articles on contemporary history and politics, with a special emphasis on the role of the individual in both.

The challenges of the twenty-first century suddenly seemed much more daunting when radical Islamic fundamentalists launched terrorist attacks on the World Trade Center in New York City and the Pentagon in Washington, DC, on September 11, 2001. This event led the administration of US President George W. Bush to pursue an aggressive foreign policy that included wars in Iraq and Afghanistan and to place a greater emphasis on "homeland security" in its domestic policy. This tragedy also called forth a creative response from the great songwriter and rock guitarist Bruce Springsteen, who shortly thereafter released his album, *The Rising*. Springsteen's musical response, which included an appearance at a telethon for the families of the victims, ten days after the attacks, brought hope and encouragement to his many followers. At the same time, however, the album included songs that acknowledged the sense of loss and despair that he witnessed from his native New Jersey, from whence many of the Trade Center victims had come. Springsteen also paid tribute to the heroic police and firefighters who risked and, in some cases, sacrificed their lives in the attempt to rescue others, the album a perfect blend of empathy and resilience.

While the West faced a new wave of terrorist threats, efforts were underway in Northern Ireland and the Middle East to resolve two of the longest-standing conflicts at the end of the twentieth century. The "Troubles" that had afflicted Northern Ireland since the late 1960s had proven intractable, as outbreaks of renewed violence by the Catholic Irish Republican Army and the loyalist Protestant paramilitary organizations such as the Ulster Defense Association undid the numerous ceasefires and efforts at peacemaking that spanned the last three decades of the twentieth century. When Tony Blair, who became leader of the Labour Party in Britain in 1994, became prime minister in 1997, he made resolution of the conflict in Northern Ireland one of his top priorities. Blair recognized the need to negotiate directly with the IRA instead of through its political wing, the party known as Sinn Féin ("Ourselves Alone").

He successfully brought the IRA into peace talks that led to the Good Friday Agreement of April 10, 1998. The 9/11 terrorist attacks in the United States had greatly raised the level of intolerance toward terrorism, but by 2002 the peace process once again started to unravel. Blair's speech on Northern Ireland of October 17, 2002, called attention to the problems that remained and set the stage for the St. Andrew's Agreement of 2006 that reinforced the power-sharing arrangement between Catholics and Protestants in Northern Ireland.

The conflict between the Israelis and the Palestinians has proven just as difficult to resolve, despite continuous efforts to negotiate a peace agreement between the two sides. After Israel won its war of independence in 1948, the United Nations stepped in to help establish boundaries in the region. The state of Israel now comprised about three-fourths of Palestine within its borders; Egypt gained one strip of land and the rest made up the new state of Jordan (formerly Transjordan). Jerusalem became a divided city administered by both Israel and Jordan. Many Arab states did not respect this agreement. They claimed to champion the cause of the Palestinian minority living within Israel, but provided little practical help. This chapter includes three perspectives on the conflict: one from the Israeli side, one from the Palestinian side, and a third representing a neutral party. Benjamin Netanyahu, the author of the Israeli source, became prime minister of Israel in 1996. The early 1990s had witnessed increasing violence and rising tension between Israelis and Palestinians despite the election of a more conciliatory Labour government headed by Yitzhak Rabin in 1992. Rabin replaced Yitzhak Shamir, the head of the conservative Likud Party, who had refused to trade land for peace or make further concessions to the Palestinians. In 1993, Netanyahu wrote *A Durable Peace*, outlining his views on the peace process and Israel's right to exist. A major step toward peace occurred when Yasser Arafat, the leader of the Palestinian Liberation Organization, negotiated an agreement in principle calling for a degree of autonomy for Palestinians living in areas occupied by Israel. However, Israeli conservatives opposed that conciliatory approach. A right-wing extremist opposed to Rabin's willingness to negotiate with the Palestinians assassinated him in 1995. Against that background, Netanyahu took over as the head of the Likud Party, which the Israeli electorate returned to power in 1996.

One of the major issues in the conflict involved the right of Palestinian refugees to return to their homeland. Naseer Aruri addresses this issue thoughtfully and succinctly in his contribution to a book he edited devoted to the subject that appeared in 2001, *Palestinian Refugees: The Right to Return*. Saliba Sarsar, a native of Israel and now an academic political scientist, administrator, and colleague of mine at Monmouth University in the United States, has studied the Palestinian-Israeli peace process for the past thirty years. In an article that he published in 2001, he takes a larger perspective and outlines his view of the necessary preconditions for peace in the Middle East. As Jackson Diehl explained in a column in the *Washington Post* on July 21, 2003, "The paradox of the latest Israeli-Palestinian peace process is that just about everyone charged with carrying it out is deeply skeptical it can succeed—yet somehow, week after week, it crawls slowly forward." At that time, hope sprung primarily from the emergence of Mahmoud Abbas, frequently referred to by his honorific name, Abu Mazen, whom many Israelis regarded as more trustworthy and more committed to peace. Meanwhile, the Likud Party had moderated its stance toward the possibility of a measure of autonomy for Palestinians in territories occupied by Israel. As in Northern Ireland, it also looked as if the majority of the population on both sides of the conflict had tired of violence and supported the peace process moving forward.

VACLAV HAVEL, "THE RESPONSIBILITY OF INTELLECTUALS," INTRODUCTION

Vaclav Havel (1936–2011) made his living as a playwright until the communist regime of his native Czechoslovakia deemed his works subversive and imprisoned him in 1979. Havel had alienated the government with a direct attack on its legitimacy in a 1978 essay, "The Power of the Powerless." Havel obtained his release from prison four years later, but resumed his critique of the state. He found himself in prison again in 1989 when the communist authorities made one last effort to crush dissent before they gave up their power. Havel had founded Civic Forum, an organization that played a major role in the Revolution of 1989. By the end of the year, the people of Czechoslovakia had elected him their president and he found himself in the presidential palace instead of prison. In an essay published in 1995, excerpts from which appear below, Havel reflects on the importance of intellectuals to society at large and the responsibility that they have in the face of the challenges that still lay ahead.

Vaclav Havel, "The Responsibility of Intellectuals"*

. . . it is true that society, the world, the universe—Being itself—is a deeply mysterious phenomenon, held together by billions of mysterious interconnections. Knowing all this and humbly accepting it is one thing; but the arrogant belief that

---

*Vaclav Havel (1995), "The Responsibility of Intellectuals," *The New York Review of Books*, June 22, pp. 36–7.

humanity, or the human spirit or reason, can grasp and describe the world in its entirety and derive from this description a vision of its improvement—that is something else altogether. It is one thing to be aware of the interconnection of all events; believing that we have fully understood this is something utterly different.

In other words, I believe, as [Karl] Popper does, that neither politicians nor scientists, nor entrepreneurs, nor anyone else should fall for the vain belief that they can grasp the world as a whole and change it as a whole by a single action. Seeking to improve it, people should proceed with the utmost caution and sensitivity, step by step, always paying attention to what each change actually brings about. At the same time, however, I believe—possibly differing from Popper's views to some extent—that as they do so, they should be aware of all the global interrelations that they can know, while bearing in mind that beyond their knowledge is an infinitely wider range of interrelations. My relatively brief sojourn in the realm of so-called high politics convinces me time and again of the need to take this approach. Most of the threats hanging over the world now, as well as many of the problems confronting it, could be dealt with much more effectively if we could see past the ends of our noses and heed, to some extent at least, the broader interconnections that go beyond the scope of our immediate or group interests. This awareness, of course, should never become an arrogant utopian conviction that we alone possess the whole truth about these interconnections. On the contrary, it should emanate from a deep and humble respect for them and for their mysterious order.

. . . To me, an intellectual is a person who has devoted his or her life to thinking in general terms about the affairs of this world and the broader context of things. Of course, intellectuals are not the only ones who do this. But they do it—if I may use the word—professionally. That is, their principal occupation is studying, reading, teaching, writing, publishing, addressing the public. Often—though certainly not always—this makes them more receptive to more general issues; often—though certainly not always—it leads them to embrace a broader sense of responsibility for the state of the world and its future.

If we accept this definition of an intellectual, then it will come as no surprise that many an intellectual has done a great deal of harm to the world. Taking an interest in the world as a whole and feeling an increased sense of responsibility for it, intellectuals often yield to the temptation to try to grasp the world as a whole, to explain it entirely and offer universal solutions to its problems. An impatience of mind and a variety of mental shortcuts are the usual reasons why intellectuals tend to devise holistic ideologies and succumb to the seductive power of holistic social engineering. For that matter—were not the forerunners of Nazi ideology, the founders of Marxism, the first Communist leaders intellectuals par excellence? Did not a number of dictators, and even some terrorists—from the leaders of the former German Red Brigades to Pol Pot—start off as intellectuals?

Not to mention the many intellectuals who, though they neither created nor introduced dictatorships, time and again failed to stand up to them because they were more than others prone to the delusion that there was a universal key to eliminating human woes. . . .

It would be nonsense to believe that all intellectuals have succumbed to utopianism or holistic engineering. A great number of intellectuals both past and present have done precisely what I think should be done; they have perceived the broader context, seen things in more global terms, recognized the mysterious nature of globality and humbly deferred to it. Their increased sense of responsibility for this world has not made such intellectuals identify with an ideology; it has made them identify with humanity, its dignity, and its prospects. These intellectuals build people-to-people solidarity. They foster tolerance, struggle against evil and violence, promote human rights, and argue for their indivisibility. In a word, they represent what has been called "the conscience of society." They are not indifferent when people in an unknown country on the other side of the planet are annihilated, or when children starve, nor are they unconcerned about global warming and the prospects of future generations leading an endurable life. They care about the fate of virgin forests in faraway places, about whether or not humankind will soon destroy all its nonrenewable resources, or whether a global dictatorship of advertising, consumerism, and blood-and-thunder stories on TV will ultimately lead the human race to a state of complete idiocy.

My opinion is simple: when meeting with utopian intellectuals, we should resist their siren calls. If they enter politics, we should believe them even less. The other type of intellectual—those who are mindful of the ties that link everything in this world together, who approach the world with humility, but also with an increased sense of responsibility, who wage a struggle for every good thing— such intellectuals should be listened to with the greatest attention, regardless of whether they work as independent critics, holding up a much-needed mirror to politics and power, or are directly involved in politics.

. . . After all, who is better equipped to decide about the fate of this globally interconnected civilization than people who are most keenly aware of these interconnections, who pay the greatest regard to them, who take the most responsible attitude toward the world as a whole?

Questions

1. On the basis of this article, where would you situate Havel on the political spectrum? Does he advocate a particular political viewpoint here?
2. How does he define "intellectuals"? What or who is an intellectual? Do you agree or disagree with his definition? Why or why not?

3. Given his past opposition to the communist regime in Czechoslovakia, it is easy to imagine that he has communists in mind when he asks his readers to resist the "siren calls" of "utopian intellectuals." Do you think he is referring only to communists here? Are there others that you would put into the category of "utopian intellectuals"?

BRUCE SPRINGSTEEN, SONGS FROM *THE RISING*, INTRODUCTION

Bruce Springsteen (b. 1949) had a long and diverse career prior to the release of The Rising, *beginning with the release of his first album on Columbia Records in 1973 after gaining experience playing in rock 'n' roll bands on the Jersey Shore. His music and lyrics combined the hard-driving rhythms of rock with a folk sensibility that placed him in the tradition of Woody Guthrie and Bob Dylan. His long, energetic, and enthusiastic concert performances also attracted a devoted following and helped to establish a close emotional bond between artist and audience. The lyrics of three songs that appeared on* The Rising *appear below. Of the three, "Empty Sky" and "The Rising" were written after the 9/11 terrorist attacks, while Springsteen originally wrote "My City of Ruins" about the deterioration of Asbury Park, New Jersey. However, realizing how apt the lyrics were as a response to 9/11, he not only included it on the album but chose that song to perform at the* America: A Tribute to Heroes *telethon held on September 21 in the aftermath of the attacks. "The Rising" deals more with the collapse of the twin towers of the World Trade Center, while "Empty Sky" is representative of the songs that humanized the tragedy and helped his listeners to cope with its aftermath. In his unofficial biography,* Bruce, *Peter Ames Carlin wrote of Springsteen that "just as he'd synthesized gospel, rock 'n' roll, rhythm and blues, folk, jazz, and carnival music into a sound that echoed the clamor of the nation, Bruce's particular magic came from his ability to trace the connections that hold the world together, even when it seems on the verge of flying apart."[*]*

Bruce Springsteen, "My City of Ruins"[**]

There is a blood red circle
On the cold dark ground

---

[*]Peter Ames Carlin (2012), *Bruce*, New York: Touchstone Books, pp. 411–12.
[**]© Universal Music Publishing Group. Available online at http://www.azlyrics.com/lyrics/brucespringsteen/mycitysinruins.html.

And the rain is falling down
The church door's thrown open
I can hear the organ's song
But the congregation's gone
My city of ruins
My city of ruins

Now the sweet bells of mercy
Drift through the evening trees
Young men on the corner
Like scattered leaves,
The boarded up windows,
The empty streets
While my brother's down on his knees
My city of ruins
My city of ruins

Come on, rise up! Come on, rise up!
Come on, rise up! Come on, rise up!
Come on, rise up! Come on, rise up!

Now's there's tears on the pillow
Darlin' where we slept
And you took my heart when you left
Without your sweet kiss
My soul is lost, my friend
Tell me how do I begin again?
My city's in ruins
My city's in ruins

Now with these hands,
With these hands,
With these hands,
I pray Lord
With these hands,
With these hands,
I pray for the strength, Lord
With these hands,
With these hands,
I pray for the faith, Lord
We pray for your love, Lord
We pray for the lost, Lord
We pray for this world, Lord

We pray for the strength, Lord
We pray for the strength, Lord

Come on
Come on
Come on, rise up
Come on, rise up
Come on, rise up
Come on, rise up
Come on, rise up
Come on, rise up
Come on, rise up
Come on, rise up
Come on, rise up

Bruce Springsteen, "The Rising"*

Can't see nothin' in front of me
Can't see nothin' coming up behind
I make my way through this darkness
I can't feel nothing but this chain that binds me
Lost track of how far I've gone
How far I've gone, how high I've climbed
On my back's a sixty pound stone
On my shoulder a half mile line

Come on up for the rising
Come on up, lay your hands in mine
Come on up for the rising
Come on up for the rising tonight

Left the house this morning
Bells ringing filled the air
Wearin' the cross of my calling
On wheels of fire I come rollin' down here

Come on up for the rising
Come on up, lay your hands in mine
Come on up for the rising
Come on up for the rising tonight

Li,li, li,li,li,li, li,li,li

Spirits above and behind me
Faces gone, black eyes burnin' bright
May their precious blood forever bind me
Lord as I stand before your fiery light

Li,li, li,li,li,li, li,li,li

I see you Mary in the garden
In the garden of a thousand sighs
There's holy pictures of our children
Dancin' in a sky filled with light
May I feel your arms around me
May I feel your blood mix with mine
A dream of life comes to me
Like a catfish dancin' on the end of the line

Sky of blackness and sorrow (a dream of life)
Sky of love, sky of tears (a dream of life)
Sky of glory and sadness (a dream of life)
Sky of mercy, sky of fear (a dream of life)
Sky of memory and shadow (a dream of life)
Your burnin' wind fills my arms tonight
Sky of longing and emptiness (a dream of life)
Sky of fullness, sky of blessed life (a dream of life)

Come on up for the rising
Come on up, lay your hands in mine
Come on up for the rising
Come on up for the rising tonight

Li,li, li,li,li,li, li,li,li

Bruce Springsteen, "Empty Sky"*

I woke up this morning
I could barely breathe
Just an empty impression
In the bed where you used to be

I want a kiss from your lips
I want an eye for an eye
I woke up this morning to an empty sky

Empty sky, empty sky
I woke up this morning to an empty sky
Empty sky, empty sky
I woke up this morning to an empty sky

Blood on the streets
Yeah blood flowin' down
I hear the blood of my blood
Cryin' from the ground

Empty sky, empty sky
I woke up this morning to an empty sky
Empty sky, empty sky
I woke up this morning to an empty sky

On the plains of Jordan
I cut my bow from the wood
Of this tree of evil
Of this tree of good
I want a kiss from your lips
I want an eye for an eye
I woke up this morning to an empty sky

Empty sky, empty sky
I woke up this morning to an empty sky
Empty sky, empty sky
I woke up this morning to an empty sky
Empty sky, empty sky
I woke up this morning to an empty sky.

Questions

1. How did the meaning of "My City of Ruins," which was written before 9/11, change after 9/11? Why did Springsteen decide to sing this song in his first public performance after 9/11?
2. How does Springsteen turn a moment of tragedy into a moment of triumph in "The Rising"? How can artists help us to make sense out of what might at times seem to be the random senselessness of history? Is their role similar to or different from that of the historian?

3. Why do you think that "Empty Sky" might have resonated with people after the terrorist attacks on the World Trade Center? Does Springsteen succeed at making the personal historical and the historical personal?
4. What will historians in the future conclude from these songs about the post-9/11 response in the United States?

PRIME MINISTER TONY BLAIR'S SPEECH ON NORTHERN IRELAND, OCTOBER 17, 2002, INTRODUCTION

In 1998, Tony Blair had brokered the Good Friday Agreement in Northern Ireland, partly because of the support he had from Bill Clinton in the United States and Bertie Ahern in the Republic of Ireland, partly because public opinion had turned against the use of violence as a political weapon, and partly because of his own willingness to involve former terrorists in the peace process. The Good Friday Agreement called for a power-sharing arrangement in which the government of Northern Ireland would feature a first minister and a deputy first minister, one Protestant and one Catholic based on majority vote. Northern Ireland also received greater autonomy within the United Kingdom. Some issues remained unresolved, however, including the process by which the IRA would give up its weapons and the future composition of the police force. Furthermore, extremists on both sides still refused to acknowledge the agreement, including a terrorist group calling itself the Real IRA, which renewed the violence with a bombing in Omagh on August 15, 1998, that killed twenty-nine people and wounded at least 200 others. In 2002, Blair looked back on what the Good Friday Agreement had achieved and what remained to be accomplished to further the peace process in Northern Ireland.

Prime Minister Tony Blair's Speech on Northern Ireland, October 17, 2002*

On 16 May 1997 I came to Belfast on my first official visit outside London as Prime Minister and made a speech here. I said then that it was no accident that I had chosen Northern Ireland for my first visit. I had come because I wanted to explain why I was committed to Northern Ireland and to the people here. I am told I have visited Northern Ireland more than any Prime Minister before

---

*http://www.staff.city.ac.uk/p.willetts/DOCS/TBNI1002.HTM

me in five years of office. I have given this part of the UK as much energy and commitment as any other, because I value it as part of the UK which it will remain so long as a majority of people here wish to be part of it.

It is now four and a half years since the Belfast Agreement. Let us re-cap for a moment on the scale of what we agreed to do in April 1998. After 30 years of troubles, thousands of deaths, Northern Ireland part of the UK but governed unlike any other part of the UK, its communities divided, its daily life scarred in innumerable ways by sectarian bitterness; after all this, we agreed to shape a new future. Enemies would become not just partners in progress but sit together in Government. People who used to advocate the murder of British Ministers and security services, would be working with them. The police, the criminal justice system, the entire apparatus of Government would be reformed beyond recognition. People would put all the intransigence and hatred of the past behind them and co-operate. Britain and Ireland would reach a new relationship. The North and South of the island of Ireland would have a new set of institutions to mark change and co-operation within a wider framework of relationships within these islands. Paramilitaries who used to murder each other as a matter of routine would talk to each other and learn to live with each other. One of the most abnormal parts of the continent of Europe, never mind the UK, would become normal.

Did anyone seriously believe it would be easy? Did we seriously entertain the notion that the Agreement would be signed on the April 10th, 1998 and on the 11th it would all be different?

It was a brave undertaking and a vast one. Even now I think that only in the first flush of a new Government could we have contemplated it. . . .

All the time, of course, the malignant whisperings of those opposed to the process, always pointing out its faults, never aiding its strengths; and the evil violence from dissidents, from so-called loyalists, designed to re-ignite sectarian hatred to convulse such progress as we have made. At every step, those working for peace, trying to make the Agreement function, were being undermined, often from within their own community. . . .

Northern Ireland is different today. Different and better.
But not as it should and can be.
The disappointment comes not from the modesty of our achievements, which are considerable; but from the enormity of our expectations. . . .

So: what do we have? We have a situation where, in truth, the overwhelming majority of people in Northern Ireland and their political leaders want to see the Agreement implemented; want the institutions up and running again; accept the basic deal of justice for peace; but don't have the requisite trust to continue unless all the remaining bits of the puzzle are clear and fitted together.

Another inch by inch negotiation won't work. Symbolic gestures, important in their time, no longer build trust.

It's time for acts of completion. We will do our best to carry on implementing the Agreement in any event. But, should real change occur, we can implement the rest of the Agreement, including on normalisation, in its entirety and not in stages but together. And we are prepared to do what is necessary to protect the institutions against arbitrary interruption and interference. But that means also commitment from others. Unionism to make the institutions secure and stable. Nationalists to act if violence returns. Republicans to make the commitment to exclusively peaceful means, real, total and permanent. For all of us: an end to tolerance of paramilitary activity in any form. A decision that from here on in, a criminal act is a criminal act. One law for all, applied equally to all. . . .

And, as ever, ordinary people who work by instinct and who change naturally in their views, are ahead of politics which too often works by reference to established tradition and hallowed positions that survive the passage of time and sentiment, and make change, even when obvious, hard to acknowledge. The time in which we live, has two characteristics amongst others that are common in the civilised world. Especially post 11 September, there is a complete hatred of terrorism. No democratic political process can yield to it. That's why, quite apart from anything else, the violence in Northern Ireland is pointless. It is just an obstruction to politics. And the second thing is a complete intolerance of injustice on the basis of race or sex or religion. That's not to say such injustice doesn't exist. It does. But it has no place in respectable politics. It's regarded as unacceptable. And that is in fact true today in Northern Ireland in a way it wasn't thirty years ago. People may worry about loss of cultural identity but they know the days of justifying discrimination are gone.

In the end, justice for peace is in tune with our age. That's why this process in Northern Ireland despite it all, can still work.

Four and a half years on, the way forward remains the same. The question is: do we have the courage as politicians to do what the people want us to do? Do we trust each other enough to make the acts of completion happen? I can only tell you as British Prime Minister that I have that trust in all the parties I have worked with.

Now is the moment of choice. The same standards must apply to all. And we must implement the Agreement in full, because it is the choice of the people; the people here, the people in the South and the people of the United Kingdom as a whole.

Questions

1. What purpose do you think that Tony Blair intended this speech to serve? Do you think that he accomplished that purpose here?
2. What reasons for hope and optimism does he provide?

3. What does he regard as the historical significance of the Good Friday Agreement? What does he regard as the historical significance of his own role in the peace process?
4. What does he imply about the limitations of the Good Friday Agreement or the obstacles to its fulfillment?

BENJAMIN NETANYAHU, *A DURABLE PEACE: ISRAEL AND ITS PLACE AMONG THE NATIONS,* INTRODUCTION

In August 1996, when the government of Prime Minister Benjamin Netanyahu approved the expansion of Israeli settlements on the West Bank, Palestinians in the area responded with a general strike that once again heightened tensions and threatened the peace process. Within a month Netanyahu met with the Palestinian leader Yasser Arafat to renew negotiations between the two sides. This meeting did not halt the violence, however, as riots erupted in both the West Bank and the Gaza Strip. In 1993, Netanyahu had written A Durable Peace *outlining his principles for a final resolution of the Israeli-Palestinian conflict. For Netanyahu, the central principle remained Israel's right to exist and it did not depend primarily on establishing firm territorial boundaries. Although he negotiated Israeli withdrawal from Hebron in 1997 as part of the peace process, his government collapsed in 1999, replaced by a center-left coalition headed by Ehud Barak.* A Durable Peace *provides insight into the position Netanyahu has carried into his positions of leadership. Not all Israelis share his position, but enough do to make it essential for an understanding of their side of the conflict. Netanyahu returned as Prime Minister in 2009 and was re-elected to a third consecutive term in 2015, the first such occurrence in Israel's history.*

Benjamin Netanyahu, *A Durable Peace: Israel and Its Place Among the Nations**

Fundamentally, the problem is not a matter of shifting this or that border by so many kilometers, but reaffirming the fact and right of Israel's existence. The territorial issue is the linchpin of the negotiations that Israel must conduct with the Palestinian Authority, Syria, and Lebanon. Yet a territorial peace is

---

*Benjamin Netanyahu (1993; 2000), *A Durable Peace: Israel and Its Place Among the Nations*, New York, Warner Books, pp. 322–23.

hampered by the continuing concern that once territories are handed over to the Arab side, they will be used for future assaults to destroy the Jewish state. Many in the Arab world have still not had an irreversible change of heart when it comes to Israel's existence, and if Israel becomes sufficiently weak the conditioned reflex of seeking our destruction would resurface. Ironically, the ceding of strategic territory to the Arabs might trigger this destructive process by convincing the Arab world that Israel *has* become vulnerable to attack.

That Israel's existence was a bigger issue than the location of its borders was brought home to me in the first peace negotiations that I attended as a delegate to the Madrid Peace Conference in October 1991. In Madrid, the head of the Palestinian delegation delivered a flowery speech calling for the cession of major Israeli population centers to a new Palestinian state and the swamping of the rest of Israel with Arab refugees, while the Syrian foreign minister questioned whether the Jews, not being a nation, had a right to a state of their own in the first place. (And this at a peace conference!) Grievances over disputed lands and disputed waters, on which the conference sponsors hoped the participants would eventually focus their attention, receded into insignificance in the face of such a primal hostility toward Israel's existence. This part of the conference served to underscore the words of Syria's defense minister, Mustafa Tlas, who with customary bluntness had summed up the issue one year earlier. "The conflict between the Arab nation and Zionism is over existence, not borders."

This remains the essential problem nearly a decade later. The fact that the Syrians place such immense obstacles before the resumption of peace talks with us, and the fact that the Palestinians resisted for more than a year my call to enter fast-track negotiations for a final settlement, underscores their reluctance to make a genuine and lasting peace with us. To receive territory is not to make peace. Peace requires that you also give something in return, namely arrangements not to use the land that is handed over to you as a future staging area for attacks against Israel. Equally, peace requires that our Arab partners educate their people to an era of mutual acceptance, something we have failed to see in many parts of the Arab world.

To begin resolving the Arab-Israeli conflict, one must begin here. The Arabs must be asked forthrightly and unconditionally to make their peace with Israel's existence. The Arab regimes must move not only to a state of nonbelligerency but to a complete renunciation of the desire to destroy the Jewish state—a renunciation that will gain credibility only when they establish a formal peace with Israel. This means ending the economic boycott and the explosive arms buildup, and signing peace treaties with Israel. The Arab states must resign themselves to something they have opposed for so long: not merely the fact but the right of Israel's permanent presence among them. This necessarily means that they will have to accept mutual coexistence as the operating principle in their relations with the Jewish state.

Questions

1. What reasons does Netanyahu give for not trusting the Arabs in peace negotiations up to the time at which he wrote this?
2. Does he successfully articulate a coherent position for the grounds of a "durable peace"? Does he indicate his willingness to compromise on issues important to the Palestinians?
3. What does he see as the main obstacle to peace? Is this a one-sided or justified perspective?
4. What insights does this source provide into the peace process in general and the difficulties of achieving a lasting peace in Palestine?

NASEER ARURI, "TOWARDS CONVENING A CONGRESS OF RETURN AND SELF-DETERMINATION" IN *PALESTINIAN REFUGEES: THE RIGHT TO RETURN*, INTRODUCTION

Naseer Aruri was born in Jerusalem in 1934 and immigrated to the United States in 1954, where he received his doctorate from the University of Massachusetts and pursued a distinguished career in academia. However, he has also served as a member of the Palestinian National Council, the parliament-in-exile of the Palestinian people, and on the central committee of the Palestinian Liberation Organization. From 1984 to 1990, he sat on the board of directors of Amnesty International. As an advocate for the Palestinian people and Palestinian refugees in particular, he represents an important counterview to that expressed by Netanyahu and the collected writings in Palestinian Refugees *made a major contribution to an understanding of the multidimensional nature of the issue. Below he explains the need for a Palestinian homeland and makes the case for why they need to have a say in their own future.*

Naseer Aruri, "Towards Convening a Congress of Return and Self-Determination" in *Palestinian Refugees: The Right to Return**

. . . What can the Palestinians do in order to escape the fate of other native people who have been subjected to genocide and were forced onto reservations

---

*Naseer Aruri (2001), "Towards Convening a Congress of Return and Self-Determination," in *Palestinian Refugees: The Right to Return*, edited by Naseer Aruri, London: Pluto Press, pp. 269–71.

or Bantustans and other forms of quarantined and marginalized areas? To avoid becoming perpetual captives in isolated Gaza, or to remain forever a disenfranchised community or left to wander in exile, living on the sufferance of hostile Arab governments, they may consider taking action along the following lines.

First and foremost, they must cling tenaciously to the legal framework, which has been surrendered on their behalf, but without their consultation or authorization. The state of legal limbo inflicted on them must be terminated and their internationally guaranteed rights must be reaffirmed. They should recall Wakim's reminder that no one must be allowed to dictate undesired terms. To that end, an assemblage of the representatives of the 5.5 million living in the diaspora and the two million in the West Bank and Gaza, would begin to undo the implied surrender, reclaim their national rights and render all acts denying them these rights—implicitly or explicitly—in transitional arrangements or final status talks, null and void.

The Congress of Self-Determination and Return, as it may be called, is the irreducible minimal step which the Palestinian people can take as they embark on rectifying the wrongs of Oslo. Whereas concluding the DOP [Declaration of Principles, agreed to at Oslo 1993] had involved less than half a dozen confidants of Arafat, meeting in secret with Israelis outside the parameters of the public scrutiny, the Conference of Return would be an open forum for all Palestinians from all walks of life, meeting within the rules of accountability. It would be a culmination of a grass-roots effort with decisions by local committees and regional groupings moving from the bottom up in a democratic process and in an egalitarian spirit. It would be a non-partisan, non-ideological, non-sectarian project, aiming to uphold the right of return and self-determination. These rights, enshrined in the Universal Declaration of Human Rights and UN Resolutions 194 and 3236, and long supported by an international consensus, must be placed high on the agenda of any peace talks taking place at any time and in any place.

The conference would serve as a constituent assembly to remedy the legal vacuum which plagues the Palestinian nation. For neither the PNC in its present form, nor the so-called Legislative Council, representing the West Bank and Gaza, is qualified to fulfill that function. The PNC was last re-formed in 1991 and repackaged in the spring of 1996 to suit specific requirements conflicting with Palestinian rights and injurious to Palestinian interests. The "Legislative Council," on the other hand, is a product of the DOP and its derivative Agreements, and is, therefore, part of the problem and not part of the solution.

The omission from the DOP of the right of return within the meaning of Resolution 194 is the single most serious impediment to genuine redress of the refugees' grievances. How can a council representing two million Palestinians in the so-called self-rule areas, leaving the bulk of the Palestinian populations out, most of whom are refugees, negotiate momentous issues with Israel, under Israeli occupation and according to inequitable conditions imposed by Israel itself.

The proposed Congress of Return would be inclusive, rather than exclusive, comprehensive rather than segmental, and people-oriented rather than elitist. Its legitimacy is derived from the entire Palestinian nation and from the relevant international declarations and UN resolutions, which the United States and Israel are feverishly trying to render ineffective and superfluous. The Congress would be able to undo the negations of Albright and voice an eloquent reply to her decree that the UN resolutions are "contentious and obsolete."

Representatives of the Palestinian people from all walks of life, from the refugee camps of Lebanon, Jordan, and Syria, from the West Bank and Gaza, from Israel proper, the United States, Australia and elsewhere, would reaffirm their rights under these resolutions. They would re-establish the right of a reconstituted PLO to resolve the refugees question with Israel. They would declare in unison that they and not the handful of operatives who met in Oslo, Cairo, Taba and other such places have the right to claim and relinquish rights. It would be an experience that would initiate the process of redress, the process of real confidence-building, democratization, and the process that can give a real voice to the voiceless.

Questions

1. In the above passage, what does Aruri identify as the main obstacles to a solution to the problem of the Palestinian refugees?
2. What steps does he outline as a solution to their dilemma?
3. How does he take issue with the role of Yasser Arafat and the Palestine Liberation Organization?
4. What position does he take toward the role of the United States in resolving the Palestinian conflict?

SALIBA SARSAR, "RECONCILING THE CHILDREN OF ABRAHAM," INTRODUCTION

Saliba Sarsar, like Dr. Aruri, grew up in Jerusalem before migrating to the United States to pursue a college education. Part of a Christian minority in Jerusalem, he brings a unique perspective to the understanding of a region

*that is dominated by Jewish or Arab viewpoints. A member of the American
Task Force on Palestine, Sarsar has had a distinguished career that has included
a number of awards, including the Humanitarian Award from the National
Conference for Community and Justice in 2001, the same year he published
the article excerpted below. Although a political scientist by training, he brings
a historical perspective to the Palestinian-Israeli conflict and calls for a mutual
understanding of a shared history as a necessary prerequisite for peace. Where
others have seen despair, he sees hope, but only if the people who share this
historically significant region learn to embrace each other's history as well as
their own.*

Saliba Sarsar, "Reconciling the Children of Abraham"*

The Arab Palestinian-Israeli Jewish conflict has affected the lives of many people
and the policies of most states for many decades. Although the contested area
of Palestine/Israel is comparatively small and the casualties have been fewer
than in other places, the conflict remains intense.

Countless national and international attempts have been made to resolve
the conflict peacefully, in both its Arab-Israeli and Palestinian-Israeli contexts.
A mixture of failure and success has characterized the process. Psychological
barriers, religious dogmas, ideological extremism, territorial imperatives,
national interests, security concerns, and myopic policies continue to block
opportunities for solutions acceptable to the majority in both national
communities. Every time a step forward is taken in peace, two backward steps
prolong the agony and tragedy. Similarly, while some encounters between
Arabs and Jews promote understanding and joint activities, they remain
limited. Differing images of reality, power asymmetries, and expectations
stand in the way. Some progress, however, has been achieved over the years,
although it hasn't been very noticeable or appreciated during episodes of
violence.

Most children are born in love but are nurtured in fear. Most have kindness
in them but do not readily share it. Most seek peace but very few can find it.
Growing up in the clutches of "a hundred-year war" has robbed children of
their innocence and placed them into a cage of history and inherited agendas.

Some unlucky children face their death; war, terrorism, and bloody
demonstrations dot the historical landscape. Innocent children pay the ultimate
price. Many Palestinians have lost their lives or been wounded during the first

---

*Saliba Sarsar (2002), "Reconciling the Children of Abraham," *Peace Review: A Journal of Social Justice*, 14, 3, pp. 319–21, 324.

Intifada—a sustained general uprising among the Palestinians against Israeli occupation between 1987 and 1993—or during the second *Intifada*, what Palestinians call the *Al Aksa Intifada*, which began in late September 2000 and continues today. In bus and human bomb explosions by Palestinian extremists, many Israeli Jews and others have lost their lives or been injured over the years. The tragedy continues on both sides of the divide, with bereaved parents and friends left in pain, defiance, or silence. . . .

Environments of aggression adversely affect children's mental health and behavior. The most common symptoms include anxiety, crying, fearfulness, headaches, nervousness, and social impairment and withdrawal. Losing a parent seriously affects a child's development and social adjustment. While family communication and positive social support lessen the severity of war traumas, the negative effects last for years. In response, people need treatment that pursues immediate and long-term strategies and considers cultural, developmental, and societal factors.

Parents who seek normalcy for their children in an abnormal environment face many challenges. It is one thing to view war at a distance and another to live with war. It is one thing to endure war for days or months and another to live with its ramifications for years or decades. . . .

Is there a solution? A humiliating military occupation, the confiscation of Palestinian land, the demolition of Palestinian homes, and the expansion of Jewish settlements keep Palestinian children and their parents trapped. Boycotts, suicide bombings, and other acts of aggression against Israel by Palestinians and other Arabs prolong the cycle of violence and the conflict. Both parties fail to see the benefits of compromise. They blame and dehumanize each other. They rationalize their violent acts—violence that has always been counterproductive.

The children of Abraham, especially the adults among them, have an obligation to their children and their grandchildren's grandchildren. Peace opportunities for building a common future must be developed and sustained. Moving the relationship toward peace could be promoted in various ways.

At the adult level, commitments to the vision of peace must endure. Both Israelis and Palestinians must never be held hostage to extreme political or violent acts of the day. Peace cannot be imposed by coercion. Successfully resolving the conflict requires justice in the peace process. Creative problem solving and compromise must be directed toward underlying needs. Those who buy into the peace process cannot expect peace to flourish unless they respond to offers of friendship and coexistence. Those who reject the peace process cannot have it both ways: independence and security on the one hand, and violence on the other. For what is won in negotiations can readily be lost in renewed conflict. . . .

Palestinians and Israelis must let go of the old practices. With unprecedented compassion and creativity they can embrace the required new non-violent practices. Let them meet one another anew, as equals, acknowledging their interdependence. Only then can they heal their relationship.

Questions
1. What reasons does Sarsar give for the failure of the peace process in Palestine up to that point?
2. What solutions does he offer in this article? Does he offer practical solutions or do they seem too idealistic?
3. Does Sarsar's approach successfully address the concerns of both Netanyahu and Aruri, or at least provide a framework for doing so?
4. Can you think of other historical examples of people or nations who have resolved longstanding differences? How might they apply to the Israeli-Palestinian conflict?

This volume ends with two contrasting images intended to provoke reflection on the past and its relation to the present and the future. The first image, a photograph taken by Marco Venturini-Autieri, an Italian engineer working in

FIGURE 26: *No Longer Just a Blank Wall*, photograph by Marco Rosario Venturini Autieri. Courtesy of Getty Images.

FIGURE 27: *Renaissance Men Preferred Red Head Gear*, collage by Gerry Charm, 2011. Courtesy of Getty Images.

England, represents a minimalist approach to meaning and creativity, while creating its own paradox. The second image, a collage by Gerry Charm, an American artist from New York City, places together some iconic images from Western Renaissance art, the period that some people may still regard as the apex of Western civilization, in a way that is distinctly postmodern. Charm says on his website that each of his collages "is a visual stream of consciousness, a string of associations brought together into a coherent whole."*

Questions

1. What is the paradox of the statement "No Longer Just a Blank Wall"? Does it have any additional meaning? Is history itself a blank slate until we write or interpret it?
2. In what ways does the collage "Renaissance Men Preferred Red Head Gear" represent "a coherent whole"?
3. What does the collage say about the relationship between the past and the present?
4. Is the goal of the historian the same as what Charm attempts to do in his collages, that is, to bring "a string of associations" into "a coherent whole"? To what extent do you think that the collection of sources in this anthology has succeeded at doing that?

---

*http://www.gerrycharm.com/Welcome.html

Chapter Questions

1. To what extent do you think that each of the remaining authors (including Bruce Springsteen) represented in this chapter have lived up to what Havel calls in the first source "the responsibility of intellectuals"? Do poets, songwriters, and artists share the same responsibility?
2. On the basis of Blair's speech and the sources on the Israeli-Palestinian conflict included in this chapter, what similarities and differences do you see between the situation in Northern Ireland and that in Israel/Palestine?
3. Compare the perspectives offered by Netanyahu, Aruri, and Sarsar. Do these sources suggest room for compromise and hope for a permanent peace in the Middle East? What are the most important points that you took away from each of these sources?

CREDITS

TEXT

Chapter 1 The Enlightenment

An Essay on Man, Alexander Pope
Aubrey Williams (ed.), *Poetry and Prose of Alexander Pope* (Boston: Hougton Mifflin Company, 1969), pp. 122–23 and 125–30. (Public domain)

Candide, Voltaire
Richard Aldington (trans.), Bed Ray Redman (ed.), *The Portable Voltaire* (New York: Viking, 1949), pp. 324–28. (Public domain)

The Persian Letters, Montesquieu
C. J. Betts (trans.), *The Persian Letters* (Harmondsworth: Penguin Books, 1975), pp. 72–73 and 151–52. (Public domain)

Pardon for the Greatest Sinners, Jonathan Edwards
http://www.ccel.org/ccel/edwards/sermons.pardon.html (Public domain)

What is Enlightenment?, Immanuel Kant
Lewis White Beck, Robert E. Anchor and Emil L. Fackenheim (trans.), Lewis White Beck (ed.), *On History* (Indianapolis: The Bobbs-Merrill Company, 1963), pp. 3–5 and 9. (Public domain)

The Author's Profession of Faith, Thomas Paine
The Age of Reason in Basic Writings of Thomas Paine (New York: Wiley Book Company, 1942), pp. 237–38. (Public domain)

Emile, Jean-Jacques Rousseau
Barbara Foxley (trans.), *Emile* (London: J.M. Dent and Sons, 1971), pp. 48–49. (Public domain)

Greater Learning for Women, Kaibara Ekken
Basil Hall Chamberlain (trans.) (1878). http://public.wsu.edu/~brians/world_civ/
    worldcivreader/world_civ_reader_2/kaibara.html (Public domain)

Account of arrival in West Indies, 1756, Olaudah Equiano
The Interesting Narrative of the Life of Olaudah Equiano or Gustavus Vassa the African
    (1789): 84–88. http://history.hanover.edu/texts/equiano/equiano_contents.html
    (Public domain)

Chapter 2 *The American and French Revolutions*

The Declaration of Independence
http://www.archives.gov/exhibits/charters/declaration_transcript.html (Public domain)

The Declaration of the Rights of Man and Citizen
http://avalon.law.yale.edu/18th_century/rightsof.asp (Public domain)

Vindication of the Rights of Women, Mary Wollstonecraft
Vindication of the Rights of Women (New York: Walter Scott, 1891), pp. 189–94.
    (Public domain)

The Diary of a Citizen of Paris During the Terror, Edmond Biré
John de Villiers (trans.), *The Diary of a Citizen of Paris During the Terror* (London:
    Chatto and Windus, 1898), pp. 127–28. (Public domain)

The Confidential Correspondence of Napoleon Bonaparte with his Brother Joseph,
    Napoleon Bonaparte
The Confidential Correspondence of Napoleon Bonaparte with his Brother Joseph
    (Volume 2) (New York: D. Appleton and Company, 1856), pp. 13, 18 and 28.
    (Public domain)

Memoirs of Simón Bolívar, Henri La Fayette Villaume Ducoudray Holstein
Henri La Fayette Villaume Ducoudray Holstein, *Memoirs of Simón Bolívar* (Boston:
    S.G. Goodrich and Company, 1829), pp. 335–36. (Public domain)

Democracy in America, Alexis de Tocqueville
http://xroads.virginia.edu/~Hyper/DETOC/1_ch14.htm (Public domain)

Chapter 3 *The Industrial Revolution: Reaction and Ideology*

The Book of the New Moral World, Robert Owen
*The Book of the New Moral World Containing the Rational System of Society, Founded
    on Demonstrable Facts, Developing the Constitution and Laws of Human Nature
    and Society* (Glasgow: H. Robinson and Co., 1840), pp. xiv–xv. (Public domain)

The Condition of the Working Class in England, Friedrich Engels
http://www.marxists.org/archive/marx/works/1845/condition-working-class/ch04.htm
    (Public domain)

The Communist Manifesto, Karl Marx and Friedrich Engels
Robert C. Tucker (ed.), *The Marx-Engels Reader* (New York: W. W. Norton and Co,
    1978), pp. 469–500. (Public domain)

Chapter 4 Cultural Interaction between Europe
and the World, 1815–75

Chapter 5 Europe and the West in an Age of Nationalism

The Life of General Garibaldi, Giuseppe Garibaldi
Theodore Dwight (trans.), *The Life of General Garibaldi,* Written By Himself With the
    Sketches of his Companions in Arms (London: Sapson Low, Sons, and Co, 1859),
    pp. 81, 88 and 114–15. (Public domain)

Bismarck: The Man and the Statesman, Otto Von Bismarck
Bismarck: The Man and the Statesman (Volumes 1 and 2) (New York: Harper and
    Brothers, 1899), pp. 99–101 and 313–24. (Public domain)

Official Account of the Reestablishment of the German Empire, January 18, 1871
James Harvey Robinson and Charles A. Beard (eds), *Readings in Modern European
    History* (Boston: Ginn and Co, 1909), pp. 63–65. (Public domain)

Speech at Limerick, August 31, 1879, and Speech at a Banquet in Wexford, October
    10, 1881, Charles Stewart Parnell
Words of the Dead Chief (Dublin: University Dublin College Press, 2009, First
    published in 1892), pp. 31 and 67. (Public domain)

American Ideals and Other Essays, Theodore Roosevelt
American Ideals and Other Essays (1903): 45–48 and 50–51. (Public domain)

The Meaning of "Renewing the People", Ling Qichao
Wm. Theodore de Bary and Richard Lufrano (eds), *Sources of Chinese Tradition*
    (New York: Columbia University Press, 2000), pp. 289–91.
© Columbia University Press. Reprinted with permission of Columbia University Press.

Chapter 6 Reform Movements of the Nineteenth Century

Narrative of the Life of Frederick Douglass, Frederick Douglass
Narrative of the Life of Frederick Douglass (Boston: The Antislavery Office, 1845),
    pp. 2–3 and 4–5. (Public domain)

"Letter to Joshua Speed, 24 August 1855," Abraham Lincoln
http://www.abrahamlincolnonline.org/lincoln/speeches/speed.htm (Public domain)

Gettysburg Address, Abraham Lincoln
http://avalon.law.yale.edu/19th_century/gettyb.asp (Public domain)

Second Inaugural Address, Abraham Lincoln
http://www.lbl.gov/IT/CIS/dp/samples/lincoln-2nd-inaug.pdf (Public domain)

A Planter's Account of the Ending of Slavery in Brazil, Paula Souza
Robert Edward Conrad (ed.), *Children of God's Fire: A Documentary History of Black
    Slavery in Brazil* (State College: Penn State University Press, 2000), pp. 476–79.
    (Public domain)

Letters from the Country, 1872–1887, Aleksandr Nikolaevich Engelgardt
Cathy A. Frierson (trans. and ed.), *Letters from the Country, 1872–1887* (New York:
    OUP, 1993), pp. 172 and 239–40.
© 1993 by Oxford University Press, Inc. Reprinted by permission of Oxford University
    Press, USA.

Letter, November 11, 1867, Benjamin Disraeli

Michael Pharand and Ellen Hawran (eds), *Benjamin Disraeli Letters* (Volume IX)
   (New York: OUP, 2013), p. 409. (Public domain)

Speech in St Andrew's Hall, Glasgow, December 5, 1879, William Gladstone
Midlothian Speeches 1879 (1971): 209–10. (Public domain)

Chapter 7 The New Imperialism

The White Man's Burden, Rudyard Kipling
http://www.kipling.org.uk/poems_burden.htm (Public domain)

Kim, Rudyard Kipling
Kim (New York: Bantam Books, 1983), pp. 214–15. (Public domain)

How I Found Livingstone, Henry M. Stanley
How I Found Livingstone (London: Marston Low, Samson, Low and Searle, 1872),
   pp. 6–7 and 9. (Public domain)

Exploration Diaries, Henry M. Stanley
Richard Stanley and Alan Nearne (eds), *The Exploration Diaries of H. M. Stanley*
   (New York: Vanguard Press, 1961), pp. 163–64. (Public domain)

On Imperialism in India, Karl Marx
Robert Tucker (ed.), *The Marx-Engels Reader* (New York: W. W. Norton and Co,
   1978), pp. 657–59 and 662–64. (Public domain)

Heart of Darkness, Joseph Conrad
http://www.gutenberg.org/catalog/world/readfile?fk_files=3273932&pageno=1
   (Public domain)

The Last Will and Testament of Cecil Rhodes, Cecil Rhodes
W. T. Stead (ed.), *The Last Will and Testament of Cecil Rhodes*, with Elucidatory Notes
   (London: Review of Reviews' Office, 1902), pp. 3–6. (Public domain)

The Boxer Rebellion, Fei Ch'i-hao
Luella Miner (ed.), *Two Heroes of Cathay* (New York: Fleming H Revell Co, 1903),
   pp. 63–65. (Public domain)

The Boxer Rebellion, Eva Jane Price
China Journal, 1998-1900: An American Missionary Family During the Boxer Rebellion
   (1989): 216 and 225–26. (Public domain)

Chapter 8 First World War

Memorandum to Theobald von Bethmann Hollweg, July 29, 1914, Helmuth von
   Moltke
Max Monteglas and Walther Shucking (eds), *Outbreak of the War* (New York: OUP,
   1924), p. 349. (Public domain)

The Serbia Crisis, Prince Lichnowsky
Heading for the Abyss: Reminiscences (New York: Payson and Clark, 1928), pp. 71–75
   (Public domain)

All Quiet on the Western Front, Erich Maria Remarque

A. W. Wheen (trans.), *All Quiet on the Western Front* (New York: Fawcett Crest, 1956), pp. 134–35, 179 and 263–64.
Reproduced by permission of the Estate of the Late Paulette Goddard Remarque c/o New York University Press.

Goodbye to All That, Robert Graves
Goodbye to All That (Garden City, NY: Doubleday and Company, 1929), pp. 59, 68, 114 and 132–33. Reprinted by permission of United Agents on behalf of The Trustees of the Robert Graves Copyright Trust.

The Soldier, Rupert Brooke
The Collected Poems of Rupert Brooke (1915). http://www.gutenberg.org/files/262/262-h/262-h.htm#link2H_4_0059 (Public domain)

Attack, Siegfried Sassoon
http://www.best-poems.net/siegfried_sassoon/poem-18323.html (Public domain)

Dulce et Decorum Est, Wilfred Owen
http://www.warpoetry.co.uk/owen1.html (Public domain)

Fire and Ice, Robert Frost
http://www.poetryfoundation.org/poem/173527 (Public domain)

Ten Days That Shook the World, John Reed
Ten Days That Shook the World (Harmondsworth: Penguin Book, 1919), pp. 100 and 116. (Public domain)

The Balfour Declaration, 1917
The London Times, November 9 (1917) (Public domain)

Chapter 9 Revolution and Cultural Change in the Early Twentieth Century

The Underdogs: A Novel of the Mexican Revolution, Mariano Azuela
E. Munguia, Jr. (trans.), *The Underdogs: A Novel of the Mexican Revolution* (New York: Penguin, 1963), pp. 55–56 and 72–73. (Public domain)

Civilisation and its Discontents, Sigmund Freud
James Strachey (trans.), *Civilisation and its Discontents* (New York: W.W. Norton and Co, 1961), pp. 333–34. (Public domain)

Three Guineas, Virginia Woolf
http://gutenberg.net.au/ebooks02/0200931h.html (Public domain)

Chapter 10 The Crisis of the Interwar Years

Fascism, Benito Mussolini
http://www.fordham.edu/halsall/mod/mussolini-fascism.asp (Public domain)

Advertisement for the Waldorf-Astoria, Langston Hughes
Arnold Rampersad with David Roessel (eds), *The Collected Poems of Langston Hughes.* http://www.poemhunter.com/poem/advertisement-for-the-waldorf-astoria/

Chapter 11 Second World War

The Deputy, Rolf Hochhuth
Richard and Clara Winston (trans.), *The Deputy* (New York: Grove Press, 1964),
   pp. 248–50.
Taken from: Rolf Hochhuth, *Der Stellvertreter*. Originally published under the title
   Der Stellvertreter.
Copyright © 1963 Rowohlt Verlag GmbH, Reinbek bei Hamburg. Reprinted with
   permission from Rowohlt Verlag GmbH and Oberon Books.

Memoirs, Harry Truman
Memoirs (Volume II: Years of Trial and Hope) (New York: Doubleday, 1956), pp. 1–3.
Reprinted with permission from D4EO Literary Agency on behalf of The Truman
   Estate.

Black Flower in the Sky: Poems of a Korean Bridegroom in Hiroshima, Ki-Sheok
   Chong
Naoshi Koriyama and Elizabeth Ogata (trans.), *Black Flower in the Sky: Poems of a
   Korean Bridegroom in Hiroshima* (2006): 7–8 and 51–52.
Published by Katydid Books. Reprinted with permission.

Chapter 12 The Cold War and the Postwar Period

Cancer Ward, Aleksandr Solzhenitsyn
Nicholas Bethell and David Burg (trans.), *Cancer Ward* (New York: Bantam, 1969),
   pp. 91–92 and 345.
Copyright © 1968, 1969 by The Bodley Head Ltd. Reprinted by permission of Farrar,
   Straus and Giroux, LLC.

The Second Sex, Simone de Beauvoir
The Second Sex (New York: Alfred A. Knopf, 1953), pp. xxv–xxvii and xxix.
Copyright © 1952, copyright renewed 1980 by Alfred A. Knopf, a division of Random
   House LLC; from *Second Sex* by Simone De Beauvoir, translated by H. M. Parshley.
   Used by permission of Alfred A. Knopf, an imprint of the Knopf Doubleday
   Publishing Group, a division of Random House LLC. All rights reserved.

Speech Delivered at the First Afro-Asian People's Solidarity Conference, Anwar el Sadat
The First Afro-Asian People's Solidarity Conference, December 26, 1957 to January
   1, 1958 (Cairo: The Permanent Sectretariat of the Organisation for Afro-Asian
   People's Solidarity, 1958), pp. 7–12. (Public domain)

I Speak of Freedom, Kwame Nkrumah
I Speak of Freedom: A Statement of African Ideology (London: William Heinemann
   Ltd, 1961), pp. xi–xiv.
Reprinted with permission from Earthlink Net on behalf of Panaf Books.

Israel's Foreign Relations on the Tenth Anniversary of the State, Golda Meir
Henry M. Christman (ed.), *This is our Strength: Selected Papers of Golda Meir*
   (New York: Macmillan, 1962), pp. 108–09.
Copyright © 1962 by The Macmillan Company, copyright renewed © 1990 by Henry
   M. Christman. All rights reserved. Reprinted with the permission of Scribner
   Publishing Group, a division of Simon & Schuster, Inc.

Program of the National Liberation Front of South Vietnam, December 20, 1960
http://openrevolt.info/2011/12/20/program-of-the-nlf/ (Public domain)

Televised address, October 22, 1962, John F. Kennedy
Public Papers of John F Kennedy, 1962 (1964): 806–9. (Public domain)

Letters to Nikita Khrushchev, October 27, 1962, John F. Kennedy
Ernest R. May and Philip D. Zelikov (eds), *The Kennedy Tapes: Inside the White House During the Cuban Missile Crisis* (Cambridge, MA and London: The Belknap Press of Harvard University Press, 1997), pp. 603–4 and 636–37.
Reprinted with permission from Philip Zelikow.

On the Beach, Nevil Shute
Nevil Shute, *On the Beach* (New York: W. Morrow, 1960), pp. 81–83.
Reprinted with permission from A P Watt at United Agents on behalf of The Trustees of the Estate of the late N S Norway.

Chapter 13 Political and Cultural Revolutions, 1960–75

Memoirs, Charles de Gaulle
Terence Kilmartin (trans.), *Memoirs of Hope: Renewal and Endeavour* (New York: Simon and Schuster, 1971), pp. 90–91.

A Day in the Life, John Lennon and Paul McCartney
Words and Music by John Lennon and Paul McCartney © 1967. Reproduced by permission of Sony/ATV Tunes Music Publishing, London W1F 9LD.

Woodstock, Joni Mitchell
Words and Music by Joni Mitchell.
© 1969 (Renewed) Crazy Crow Music. All Rights Administered by Sony/ATV Music Publishing, 8 Music Square West, Nashville, TN 37203. All Rights Reserved. Reprinted with permission from Alfred Publishing Co., Inc.

Big Yellow Taxi, Joni Mitchell
Words and Music by Joni Mitchell.
© 1970 (Renewed) Crazy Crow Music. All Rights Administered by Sony/ATV Music Publishing, 8 Music Square West, Nashville, TN 37203. All Rights Reserved. Reprinted with permission from Alfred Publishing Co., Inc.

Letter from Birmingham Jail, Martin Luther King
Jaroslay Pelikan (ed.), *The World Treasury of Modern Religious Thought* (Boston: Little, Brown, 1990), pp. 607–11.

The Wretched of the Earth, Frantz Fanon
Constance Raffington (trans.), *The Wretched of the Earth* (New York: Grove Press, 1963), pp. 42–43.
English translation copyright © 1963 by Présence Africaine. Used by permission of Grove/Atlantic, Inc. Any third party use of this material, outside of this publication, is prohibited.

Reascending Chingkangshan, Mao Zedong
http://www.marxists.org/reference/archive/mao/selected-works/poems/poems35.htm (Public domain)

Reply to Comrade Kuo Mo-Jo, Mao Zedong
http://www.marxists.org/reference/archive/mao/selected-works/poems/poems34.htm
  (Public domain)

Winter Clouds, Mao Zedong
http://www.marxists.org/reference/archive/mao/selected-works/poems/poems33.htm
  (Public domain)

Sounds of the River: A Memoir, Da Chen
Sounds of the River: A Memoir (New York: HarperCollins, 2002), pp. 43–44.
Copyright © 2002 by Da and Sunni Chen Family Enterprise. Reprinted by permission
  of HarperCollins Publishers.

Zen and the Art of Motorcycle Maintenance, Robert M. Pirsig
Zen and the Art of Motorcycle Maintenance: An Inquiry into Values (New York:
  Morrow, 1974), pp. 51–52 and 77–78.
Copyright © 1974 by Robert M. Pirsig. Published by Transworld. Reprinted by
  permission of The Random House Group Limited and HarperCollins Publishers.

Chapter 14 Religious Fundamentalism and Secularism in the Modern World

Jihad in Islam, Abdul A'la Mawdudi
Abdul A'la Mawdudi, *Jihad in Islam* (Lebanon: Holy Koran Publishing House, 1939),
  pp. 5–7. (Public domain)

Messianism, Zionism, and Jewish Religious Radicalism, Aviezer Ravitsy
Michael Swirsky and Jonathan Chipman (trans.), *Messianism, Zionism, and Jewish
  Religious Radicalism* (Chicago: University of Chicago Press, 1996), pp. 80 and 82–84.
Published by the University of Chicago. Reprinted with permission from University of
  Chicago Press.

The Battle Ahead, Pat Robertson
The New World Order (Dallas: World Publishing, 1991), pp. 256–57.
Reprinted with permission from HarperCollins Christian Publishing Inc.

Stealing Jesus: How Fundamentalism Betrays Christianity, Bruce Bawer
Stealing Jesus: How Fundamentalism Betrays Christianity (New York: Crown
  Publishers Inc, 1997), pp. 5 and 300–01.
Copyright © 1997 by Bruce Bawer. Used by permission of Crown Books, an imprint
  of the Crown Publishing Group, a division of Random House LLC. All rights
  reserved.

The Battle for God, Karen Armstrong
The Battle for God (New York: Ballatine Books, 2000), pp. 365–71.
Copyright © 2000 by Karen Armstrong. Used by permission of Alfred A. Knopf, an
  imprint of the Knopf Doubleday Publishing Group, a division of Random House
  LLC. All rights reserved.

The American Religion, Harold Bloom
The American Religion: The Emergence of the Post-Christian Nation Source (New York:
  Simon and Schuster, 1992), pp. 243, 245 and 293–94.

Chapter 15 Democracy and Dictatorship, 1970–89

Chapter 16 The Post-Cold War Era

The End of History and the Last Man, Francis Fukuyama
The End of History and the Last Man (New York: Avon Books, 1992), pp. 112 and
    114–15.
Copyright © 1992 by Francis Fukuyama/ All rights reserved. Reprinted with the
    permission of ICM (International Creative Management, Inc.) and Simon &
    Schuster Publishing Group, a division of Simon & Schuster, Inc, from the Free Press
    edition of *The End of History and the Last Man* by Francis Fukuyama.

Thinking Green!, Petra Kelly
Petra Kelly, *Thinking Green!: Essays on Environmentalism, Feminism and Nonviolence*
    (Berkeley: Parallax Press, 1994), pp. 38–40.
Published by Parallax Press. Reprinted with permission.

Rebels Against the Future, Kirkpatrick Sale
Kirkpatrick Sale, *Rebels Against the Future: The luddites and their War on the Industrial
    Revolution: Lessons for the Machine Age* (Reading, MA: Addison-Wesley, 1995),
    pp. 261–63.
Republished with permission of Perseus Books Group; permission conveyed through
    Copyright Clearance Center, Inc.

Rain Falls Down in Amsterdam, Eric Andersen
Memory of the Future (CD) (1999).
© Eric Andersen 1998. From Album *Memory of the Future*, Wind and Sand Music,
    Adm. BMG/Chrysalis. Reprinted with permission from Eric Andersen.

The Clash of Civilizations and the Remaking of the World Order, Samuel P.
    Huntington
The Clash of Civilizations and the Remaking of the World Order (New York: Simon and
    Schuster, 1996), pp. 311–12.
Copyright © 1996 by Samuel P. Huntington. All rights reserved. Reprinted with the
    permission of Simon & Schuster, Inc.

Chapter 17 The Turn of the Twenty-First Century

The Responsibility of Intellectuals, Vaclav Havel
The New York Review of Books, June 22 (1995) (Public domain)

Empty Sky, Bruce Springsteen
Copyright © 2002 Bruce Springsteen (ASCAP). International Copyright secured.
    All rights reserved. Reprinted by permission from Grubman Shire & Meiselas, P.C.
    on behalf of Bruce Springsteen.

The Rising, Bruce Springsteen
Copyright © 2002 Bruce Springsteen (ASCAP). International Copyright secured.
    All rights reserved. Reprinted by permission from Grubman Shire & Meiselas, P.C.
    on behalf of Bruce Springsteen.

My City of Ruins, Bruce Springsteen
Copyright © 2001 Bruce Springsteen (ASCAP). International Copyright secured.
    All rights reserved. Reprinted by permission from Grubman Shire & Meiselas, P.C.
    on behalf of Bruce Springsteen.

Speech on Northern Ireland, October 17, 2002, Tony Blair
"Finding a way through the crisis," Speech by Tony Blair, Prime Minister of the
    United Kingdom, at the Labour Party Conference, 2002. Belfast, Northern
    Ireland, Thursday October 17, 2002. http://www.staff.city.ac.uk/p.willetts/DOCS/
    TBNI1002.HTM (Public domain)

A Durable Peace, Benjamin Netanyahu
A Durable Peace: Israel and its Place among the Nations (New York: Warner Books,
    1993), pp. 322–23.
Copyright © 1993, 2000 by Benjamin Netanyahu. All rights reserved. Reprinted by
    permission of Grand Central Publishing.

Towards Convening a Congress of Return and Self-Determination, Naseer Aruri
Palestinian Refugees: The Right to Return (London: Pluto Press, 2001), pp. 269–71.
Published by Pluto Books Ltd. Reprinted with permission.

Reconciling the Children of Abraham, Saliba Sarsar
Peace Review: A Journal of Social Justice, 14(3) (2002): 319–24.
Reprinted by permission of Taylor & Francis Ltd, http://www.tandf.co.uk/journals
    via Copyright Clearance Center's RightsLink service.

IMAGES

1. Derby Museum

2. DEA/G. Dagli Orti/Getty

3. Peter Willi/Getty

4. DEA/G. Dagli Orti/Getty

5. Culture Club/Getty

6. Culture Club/Getty

7. DEA picture library/Getty

8. Universal History Archive/Getty

9. DEA/G. Dagli Orti/Getty

10. The Granger Collection, New York

11. Science Source/Photo Researchers

12. Science Source/Photo Researchers

13. Science Source/Photo Researchers

14. Library of Congress—edited version © Science Faction/Getty

15. Stocktrek Images/Getty

16. William Vandivert/Getty

17. PR Inc/Picture Researchers

18. Franz Aberham/Getty

19. Stuart Black/Getty

20. Ron Koeberer/Getty

21. Tate Images

22. Tim Baker/Getty
23. Catherine Henriette/Getty
24. Chip Hires/Getty
25. Horst Ossinger/Getty
26. Marco Rosario Venturini Autieri/Getty
27. Gerry Charm/Getty